To my Davey, a success story 2004 Dec.
that I hope you will enjoy.
I guess it is very good luck to
outgrow your hair.
I enjoy this book!
Love,
Jeanne

Leo: *a life*

Leo
a life

LEO KOLBER
WITH L. IAN MACDONALD

McGill-Queen's University Press
Montreal & Kingston · London · Ithaca

Legal deposit fourth quarter 2003
Bibliothèque nationale du Québec

Printed in Canada on acid-free paper.
Reprinted 2003

McGill-Queen's University Press acknowledges the support of the
Canada Council for the Arts for our publishing program. We also
acknowledge the financial support of the Government of Canada through
the Book Publishing Industry Development Program (BPIDP) for our publishing activities.

National Library of Canada Cataloguing in Publication

Kolber, Leo
    Leo: a life / Leo Kolber with L. Ian MacDonald.

    Includes bibliographical references and index.
    ISBN 0-7735-2634-X

    1. Kolber, Leo. 2. Canada. Parliament. Senate – Biography.
    3. Businessmen – Canada – Biography. I. MacDonald, L. Ian II. Title.

    FC636.K64A3 2003   328.71′092   C2003-903570-0

This book was typeset by Dynagram inc. in 10.5/13 Sabon.

For my children, Lynne and Jonathan,
for my grandchildren, Olivia, Benjamin, Daniella, and
Michael, and for the memory of my beloved Sandra

Contents

Leo: *a life*

Introduction

The prime minister was buying lunch.

It was pretty informal, standing up at a hot dog stand on a golf course at Grand-Mère, Quebec, a six-minute stop after the ninth hole. Jean Chrétien mentioned that if Tiger Woods came to the Canadian Open in a month's time, he would be invited to play with Woods in the pro-am the day before the 72-hole championship began at Royal Montreal.

I thought the chances of Tiger showing up were pretty good, since he was the defending champion and since Royal Montreal's famous Blue Course was the only place he had ever missed the cut, four years earlier, in 1997. I also thought that it would be a nice day for the prime minister, and then I forgot about it.

A few weeks later, I got a call from Bruce Hartley, the PM's executive assistant.

"The boss is going to play with Tiger Woods Wednesday at Royal Montreal," Bruce began.

The prime minister was looking for a place to sleep. Apparently, Tiger agrees to play in a pro-am only if he goes off in the first group at seven o'clock in the morning. For Chrétien, this would mean leaving Ottawa at 4:30 a.m. to make his starting time. Even if he slept in downtown Montreal, he would have to leave his hotel at the crack of dawn.

But Chrétien remembered being my guest a few years earlier at Elm Ridge, a Jewish club down the road from Royal Montreal on Île-Bizard, west of the city. I had got the PM a bedroom upstairs in the clubhouse so that he could have some privacy while he was changing. Now Chrétien was wondering if I could arrange for him to sleep over before his round with Tiger. Elm Ridge would also have to set up a few cots in the men's locker room for his RCMP detail.

When I called the club, the manager said they would be delighted to host the prime minister, and so it was arranged. The next morning, he would hit a few balls at Elm Ridge. He didn't want to be on Royal Montreal's practice tee with the pros in front of the public.

On the Wednesday morning, I got up at five o'clock and drove out to have breakfast with Chrétien at Elm Ridge.

"Goddamn it," Chrétien said, "I'm pretty nervous. I played with Fred Couples last year, but this is Tiger Woods, and it's pretty embarrassing when your first shot goes in the woods."

Then it was time for the PM to hit a few balls at the driving range. The club had set up his golf bag on an electric golf cart.

"You be my chauffeur, Leo," he said. "Take me over there."

A few members had got word that the prime minister was going to be there, and they came out to watch him on the practice tee. And about half a dozen RCMP formed a semi-circle around him to make sure he wasn't assassinated on the practice range in the middle of nowhere. As his practice balls disappeared into the pre-dawn darkness, I found the scene a bit surreal.

I drove over with the prime minister to Royal Montreal. Chrétien was understandably nervous, playing in front of Tiger's huge gallery, and he struggled with his game all day. At one point, on the fifteenth hole, he successively moved his ball, improved his lie, and walked across Tiger's putting line on the green. Visibly annoyed, Woods muttered to another of his playing partners, Jean-Pierre Ouellet, vice-chairman of RBC Dominion Securities, "Give him a 20 on his own ball." The kidding aimed at Chrétien from behind the ropes was much more good-natured, and he played the gallery like the masterful retail politician he was, at one point saying it was a great Liberal crowd.

I had to leave before they completed their round. My wife Sandra was in the last days of her final illness, and I went to the hospital to be with her. It was September 5, 2001, just six days before the terrible events of September 11 and one week before her death after living courageously for a decade with the disabling effects of a paralytic stroke.

But that morning back at Elm Ridge, I thought what a journey it has been in life, a tremendous ride. I had been an adviser to the Bronfman dynasty, a protégé of the founding father, Mr Sam, and a close friend of his sons, Edgar and Charles. I had helped them build a great commercial empire, and I'd lived to see its tragic dissolution. I had met prime ministers and presidents, and some of them, like Pierre Trudeau, Brian Mulroney, and Jean Chrétien, had become good friends. I had travelled across Russia with Trudeau on the Trans-Siberian Railway, sung Irish duets with Mulroney, and played golf with Chrétien. I'd been a director on the board of a Hollywood studio and had had nights out with the stars, from Danny Kaye to Frank Sinatra and Cary Grant. I had played a major role in building a great real estate company, Cadillac Fairview, and had worked with the renowned architect Mies van der Rohe on the Toronto-Dominion Centre, which changed the skyline of Toronto and announced its arrival as one of the great cities of the world. I'd had a great family life, a good marriage for forty-four years, two accomplished children, Lynne and Jonathan. I'd even been a minor character, and not a very attractive one, in *Solomon Gursky Was Here*, Mordecai Richler's thinly disguised novel on the Bronfmans. Harvey Schwartz, the guy with the argyle socks, that was me.

I've been a man of some influence and have enjoyed every moment of it. And on this day I was hosting the prime minister of Canada, for whom I had raised millions of dollars as a Liberal party bagman. And we would be walking around inside the ropes with Tiger Woods.

Standing in the darkness and mist of that September morning, I thought it was a long way from Villeneuve Street, all those years ago.

I

Neither Rags, nor Riches

I was born on the eve of the Depression in 1929. My first childhood recollection is of being woken up by my parents on Hanukkah and finding presents hanging on my little bed in the back room of our house in Montreal.

We lived at 262 Villeneuve Street, a Jewish neighbourhood near Park Avenue in the north end of the city. My father, Moses Kolber, was a dentist, and his office and waiting room were at the front of the house. When I started going to school, I would tiptoe in so as not to disturb anyone. It wasn't a normal house where you could be rambunctious or raise your voice; it was always, "Daddy is working. Be quiet."

My mother, Luba Kahan Kolber, kept the books for my father's business. When I was a teenager, she would show them to me, and in those days, the 1940s, he was billing about $200 a week. Dentistry then was nothing like it is today, with its emphasis on preventive treatment and orthodontics that makes it a high-paying profession. But my father did well enough for his time, and eventually we moved to a larger house at 201 Villeneuve, a block away. It was a duplex, and so he had his office downstairs, with a dining room, den, and kitchen in the back, and our bedrooms upstairs. Compared with what we had before, we lived in a much grander style. It wasn't rags, but it wasn't riches.

My first school was Bancroft Elementary, a block away on St Urbain Street, the heart of the Jewish neighbourhood celebrated by Mordecai Richler in *St. Urbain's Horseman* and other novels. When they started to teach reading in grade one, I was ahead of the class because I had learned to read at age four while spending months confined to bed after being diagnosed with a heart murmur. I was turned into an invalid – they even carried me to the bathroom. Although I wasn't sick, I appar-

ently wasn't getting better either, until they called in Dr Alton Goldbloom, a pediatrician renowned for his on-the-spot diagnoses. Dr
Goldbloom stuck his fingers down my throat, grabbed my adenoids and
squeezed them. "There is nothing wrong with this child," he said, "except infected tonsils and adenoids." So the next day, they took my tonsils out.

As a result of this confinement, I became a lifelong hypochondriac.
And because my reading was advanced, I immediately skipped a grade,
which was not a good thing, as I was by far the youngest kid in the
class, as well as the smallest.

It was at Bancroft that I did my first entrepreneurial thing. It was during the Quebec provincial election of October 1939. There was a voting
station at our school, and as a ten-year-old on election day, I became a
runner for poll workers, going next door to Beauty's Restaurant to get
them sandwiches, coffee, and soft drinks. I made two or three dollars,
and Adélard Godbout's Liberals won the election, defeating Premier
Maurice Duplessis and the Union Nationale.

I also made nickels and dimes, literally, by selling the *Montreal Star*. I
didn't have a paper route, but during the summer, when we lived with
our grandparents at their cottage in Préfontaine in the Laurentians,
there was a vendor who sold the *Star* on the nightly train from Montreal. We would meet the train, and I would buy his papers for a nickel
each and then sell them for six cents. So in that way I used to make ten
or twelve cents a night. Occasionally, I'd return to the cottage with two
Stars that I couldn't sell, but my grandmother Kahan would take pity
on me and give me ten cents to cover the loss.

In May 1939 King George VI and Queen Elizabeth, later the Queen
Mother, came to Montreal on their royal tour of Canada. Their motorcade came right down Villeneuve Street on its way downtown from
the Park Avenue station, where the royal train had arrived from Quebec. We went to a neighbour's house to watch them pass by, and
waved Union Jacks from an upstairs window. "All over the city,
householders lucky enough to be on the royal route were selling seats
in their windows," William Weintraub would write in *City Unique*,
his wonderful 1996 book on life in Montreal in those days. "If you
had a really wide window, you might take in enough money that afternoon to pay an entire month's rent." We watched it for free, and I remember that my father later went out and bought purple ice cream, in
the shape of a crown, made in honour of the visit. The entire city
turned out to cheer the royal couple, and afterwards, Montreal's legendary mayor Camillien Houde, who had been riding in the second

car with Prime Minister Mackenzie King, turned to King George and famously said, "Your Majesty, some of those cheers were also for you."

The royal visit was intended to bolster Canada's support of Britain in the event of war with Germany. The war wasn't long in coming, but it seemed to me that it was something far away that didn't affect our lives. I certainly had no sense, none whatsoever, of the Holocaust that was unfolding in Europe.

But I do remember distinctly, in 1939, 1940, and 1941, my parents and grandparents listening to Hitler's speeches on the short-wave radio. I knew that Hitler was some sort of bad guy somewhere, but nothing beyond that. Yet I remember the grown-ups talking in worried tones about the possibility of Germany invading Canada, something that seemed impossible to me, even though German U-boats were spotted in the Gulf of St Lawrence. And I remember being glued to the radio for the speeches of Hitler, Neville Chamberlain, and then Winston Churchill after he became British prime minister in May 1940, as well as for the wartime radio talks of Mackenzie King and Franklin Roosevelt. For all of those events, the family would gather around one of those big Philco radios with all the buttons and the glowing radio dial.

My father was too old for military service, but he volunteered for Civil Defence as an air raid warden. Twice a week, with a helmet, binoculars, a water canteen, and a whistle, he would go out and scan the skies until midnight. Now the chances of Montreal being hit with an air raid were somewhere between slim and none, but that was his volunteer role, and he was quite proud of it. And because he was a dentist, we got gas-rationing coupons, and he was able to keep driving the family car. As a high school senior at the end of the war in the spring of 1945, I joined the Air Cadets, and they taught us how to hold a rifle and march in formation. They issued us with blue cadet uniforms but they did not supply shoes, and if you didn't own a pair of black shoes, you couldn't go on parade. I finally found a pair of black shoes at home and joined my fellow cadets in a parade through the McGill campus. It was a stifling hot day, and in those thick woollen uniforms, some of the cadets fainted. I somehow made it through. That was the extent of my contribution to the war effort.

My father was born in Montreal near the turn of the century in 1899. My grandparents on that side, Samuel and Naomi Kolber, came to

Canada from Austria in the late nineteenth century, and they had nine children, four boys and five girls. It was a huge family, and I can remember going to Passover Seders there. They would start quite late at night because my grandfather kept the store open well into the evening so as not to lose any business. He was very close with a buck and insisted my grandmother buy only day-old bread because it was sold at half price.

Samuel Kolber was a merchant and moneylender. He owned a three-storey building on the Main, St Lawrence Boulevard, and on the ground floor he had a men's and boys' clothing store, which was quite successful. He also owned other commercial property on St Hubert Street and held mortgages on homes in Westmount. He was very successful in his terms and active in the community. When the campaign to build the Jewish General Hospital was launched in the 1930s, my grandfather was one of the initial donors. Years later, when I became president of the Jewish hospital, I noticed his name on the donations board for giving more than $500, a generous gift for a man of his means in the middle of the Depression. And when he died a few years later, he left an estate of about half a million dollars, a lot of money in those days.

But my grandfather was determined that none of his sons would go into his business and that all of them would have professions. He was not concerned about his daughters' education, only that they married well – that's how it was then. And all four of the sons did become professionals. One of them was an eye specialist, a pioneer in the field of ophthalmology. Another was an MD, a general practitioner with a family practice. Another brother was a notary. And there was my father, the dentist.

In 1943 my father had a heart attack, and then was sick, on and off, for the remaining two years of his life. In those days, if you had a heart attack, the doctors put you to bed, closed the drapes, and ordered complete rest for six weeks. Which was precisely the wrong road to recovery, as it turned out, but the doctors didn't know that then. There was no such thing as heart bypass surgery, and no heart drugs. Now, when you have a heart attack, one of the first things they do is encourage you to walk around slowly so the blood doesn't clot.

He had some disability insurance that paid him $200 a week, but when that ran out, he would have no income, not one cent, coming in. The question of how he would support his family completely preoccupied him, and it also had a profound effect on me.

I decided then that I would never, in any way, rely on my own two hands to make a living. I kept repeating to myself that someday, somehow, somewhere, I would be in a position where people, or money, or both, would work for me. I became a very driven person, and if you asked me why, I would say it was because I saw my father dying, worried about how he was going to feed his family.

In September 1945, at the age of sixteen, I entered McGill as an undergraduate. I mistakenly chose the faculty of science instead of arts. The science students were shipped out to what was then called Dawson College in St Jean d'Iberville, some twenty-five miles southeast of Montreal, where we all lived in dormitories. Not only was I at least a year younger than the other freshmen, but the class was full of men in their midtwenties, returning veterans of the war. With the war's end, the student population doubled. Early one morning in November, a friend of the family named Joe Venis came into the dormitory and took me aside. "Your father died last night," he said. I went into a state of shock. I didn't cry. I didn't say anything. I was just shocked. After his funeral, I went to see William Hatcher, the assistant dean of arts and science at McGill, and asked if I could transfer to arts because my father had just died and I needed to be close to my mother in the city. And the university very graciously allowed me to do that.

When my grandfather Kolber had died a few years earlier, his estate was distributed piecemeal to his children rather than sold for cash. Part of my father's inheritance was a little house in Notre-Dame-de-Grace, then a WASP enclave in the west end of the city. From an all-Jewish neighbourhood, we moved in the early 1940s to one that was all *goyim*. In the sheltered Jewish world of my boyhood, I had had no idea that anti-Semitism even existed. It wasn't long before I got my first taste of it in our new neighbourhood along NDG Avenue, where I soon got used to being chased home after school and being called a "dirty Jew." I wasn't sorry to leave the neighbourhood when my mother sold the house after my father's death.

We then moved in with my maternal grandfather, Evzar Kahan, with whom we lived for one year. There was nothing fancy about his home – my bedroom was in the basement, next to the furnace room.

Grandfather Kahan had been a grain trader in Russia, buying future crops from wealthy Russians and reselling them on the open market. He apparently did well enough that in 1916, just before the Russian Revolution and in the middle of the First World War, his family of two sons and three daughters, one of whom was my mother, was able to set sail to Canada first class rather than in steerage.

My father had left an estate of perhaps $40,000 in insurance and the like, and my grandfather got my mother to buy a small apartment building for $25,000 at the corner of Van Horne and Dollard, a street where he had built and owned most of the housing. And I used to go and collect rent on behalf of my mother. They didn't send in cheques; it was all cash. There were fourteen small apartments in this building and three stores on the ground floor. And I thought to myself, this is a really interesting business. You finance a building, you build it, you rent it, and from then on it is cash flow. There is really not much else to do.

My father's death had a deeper impact on my brother Sam than on me. Eight years younger, he was terribly affected, had a hard time as an adolescent, ran away from home at one point, and did all kinds of rebellious things. And then in his twenties, to get out from under the shadow that I was beginning to cast as the guy running the Bronfman investments in Montreal, he moved to Toronto. He inherited our grandfather's flair for construction and real estate and got a good job at the Cadillac Corporation. In 1974 our Fairview real estate division merged with Cadillac, and I became chairman of Cadillac Fairview. So my brother, who had escaped me, ended up working for me.

He has been lucky in love and lucky in life. His wife, Jacquie, a serious dancer and a founding member of the Alberta Ballet company, was brought to Toronto as line captain for the Canadian National Exhibition show Canadettes, a Canadian version of the Rockettes. They have three fine children, Daniel, Andrea and Tamara. Jacquie was an active fundraiser in the Jewish community and involved with the Women's Auxiliary of Mount Sinai Hospital. Following a bout with breast cancer in 1983 and a recurrence in 1991, she has been an involved participant in the Run for the Cure and the Canadian Breast Cancer Foundation. She is also a charter member of Dragons Abreast, a group of breast cancer survivors offering support for one another through dragonboat paddling, both competitively and for camaraderie.

My brother and I weren't close as children, but we've become very close since. Sam is one of the funniest men I've ever known. He has this *shtick* where he calls every New Year's Eve – and again on my birthday – and does Charles Laughton as Quasimodo in *The Hunchback of Notre Dame*. "I'm deaf you know," he says. "The bells have made me deaf." He even built a bell tower at his country house. He's also a serious photographer. Photography has been a lifelong passion since he had "a darkroom" as a kid under the stairs of our grandfather's basement. His work has been published in Hallmark calendars and is represented in a number of private and corporate photo collections.

In my mother's declining years, when I was travelling constantly on business, Sam took a heavy weight of filial duty off my shoulders by frequently going down to visit her in Fort Lauderdale, where she lived until her death at ninety-three.

We were both close to our mother. When widowed, she worked in the dental lab our father had been involved with, eventually opening a ladies hat store at the corner of Peel and what was then Burnside, now de Maisonneuve Boulevard. She was driven to get ahead, aggressively upwardly mobile, both socially and financially, and at some level I inherited that from her. She invented the "overdraft," as we were never without and she was never in funds. Luba Hats became one of the leading shops of its kind in the city. For the Jewish High Holidays, it was not unusual for her to ring up sales of $1,000. These were $20 and $40 hats in the 1940s. She got to know the upper-crust clientele, especially the Jewish ladies, quite well.

She remarried at the end of the 1950s and moved to New York, where her second husband, Phil Lassar, owned a very good company that made gift boxes for Tiffany's and the like. When he died in 1995, he left a $7-million trust fund from which she drew the income. To the end of her life, my mother was always insecure about money. To allay her fears in her later years, I would send her a big cheque as a present for the holidays at the end of the year. And I would say, "Mum, if there are a few extra things you need that you can't afford, please use this. If you want more, I'll send you more."

She never touched a nickel of it, of course, and when she died in 1999, she left an estate of over a million dollars. She was quite a lady, a beauty in her time, and very successful in business on her own terms in an era when it was difficult for entrepreneurial women. As my brother has said, "Centre stage was defined by where she stood."

Getting an undergraduate arts degree was neither intellectually demanding nor very time-consuming. We had five hours of class, three days a week. I hung around the student union on Sherbrooke Street and played a lot of competitive pool, once making the university semi-finals. Things were looking up in Canada after the war. There was a lot of optimism.

The peacetime economy was buoyant. Life at university was good. We didn't have to work too hard, and we partied around a lot.

It was at McGill that I met Charles Bronfman, who would become my best friend for life. He had season tickets for the Canadiens, third row in the reds, right behind the Canadiens' bench, and often he would invite me to the Forum on Saturday night. We both have very good memories of the great Maurice "Rocket" Richard breaking in on goal. There was a saying, don't get between the Rocket and the net, and when he scored, the roar in the Forum was unlike anything else I've ever heard in my life.

On Friday nights Charles would often say, "Let's get dates and go to the Normandy Room." The Normandy Room was a rooftop restaurant at the Mount Royal Hotel, a very fancy and expensive dining and dancing place. "Charles, I can't afford it," I said once. "I'll pay for it," he said. "I'm not going to go if you're paying for it," I said. "But you go." Well, we didn't go. I didn't want him to think I was taking advantage of him because of his money. I was sensitive to his being sensitive. And maybe that is what led to our friendship.

It was only in law school at McGill, beginning in 1949, that I began to get serious about my work, and I graduated in the top third of my class in 1952. It wasn't a very outstanding law faculty in those days, but there were some professors who stood out from a pretty mediocre group. F.R. Scott, the poet and constitutional expert, had a superior mind. He was arrogant, he was miserable, but he was a great constitutional lawyer. Maxwell Cohen was an excellent professor of jurisprudence. And there was one great lecturer, Phil Vineberg, the lawyer who wrote all the Bronfman family trusts. Phil was an advocate for all seasons. He was both a great constitutional and a great commercial lawyer, with an elephantine memory. He would tell you which line to look for on what page of a judgment. He taught summer courses in law school and, then as later, proved to be in a class by himself.

The system was pretty arbitrary: 110 applicants were accepted in first-year law, and 55 of them were automatically flunked at the end of the year. By third year, we graduated 23 and only 12 ever practised. So from 110 in first year, they got 12 practising lawyers.

And then I did my articling year at a firm called Mendolsohn, Rosentzveig and Schacter. It later became a mid-sized law firm of about fifty lawyers, but when I was there, it consisted basically of the three guys with their name on the door of their office in the financial district of Old Montreal. Articling students were paid ten dollars a week in those days, and most days I brought my own lunch. Occasionally, I would go to Delmo's seafood restaurant on Notre-Dame in Old Montreal, sit at the bar, and eat a piece of fish and drink a glass of ginger beer for ninety-five cents.

I worked Saturdays, and one weekend a guy came in off the street, an American who'd been in a car accident and wanted to know about damages. I told him he'd have to get an estimate, and he asked, "What about whiplash?" It was the first time I'd ever heard the expression. And then it struck me that while the guys I was working for were making money, this was no way to make a living. It also struck me that the really successful lawyers never quit, they just worked harder as they got older. I had seen what happened to my father, a dentist unable to work, unable to support his family, and I thought, what a lousy way to go through life, working for others like this.

So when I passed the bar exams at the end of my articling year in 1953, I opened a little office of my own. And I do mean little. You could not, as they used to say, swing a cat in there. But it was mine, and it was in the same building as Mendolsohn, the Transportation Building on St James Street, as Saint-Jacques was then known. And I was already starting to do my first real estate deals.

I had a friend named Stanley Shenkman, an architect who had studied at Syracuse University in New York and was a disciple of Frank Lloyd Wright – he later built a lot of the split-level homes in upper Westmount in that stark modernist style. Stanley had an option on five lots in the new part of the Town of Mount Royal (TMR), a suburb just north of Outremont that had first been designed in the 1930s as a model city, with churches, schools, and municipal services clustered on a roundabout in the centre of the town. If I could finance the homes, Stanley would design them. I spoke to Charles and Edgar, and said, "I have this option, and of course I can't pay for it, but I would like to build some homes there." So they sent their uncle, Moe Levine, the guy who made the Seagram Crown Royal bags, to negotiate with me, since they thought that, as friends, they should deal with me at arm's-length. "It wouldn't be fair of me to negotiate with you," Charles said. "I will send my Uncle Moe."

I knew nothing about negotiating, but I also knew that Moe's offer would leave me with virtually no profit of my own. So I told Charles and Edgar that I would have to look somewhere else. In our family apartment on Van Horne Avenue, we had a neighbour named Manny Hershman. He owned a label business that was making him very decent money for those days. I talked to him about it – I can still hear his thick German accent – and he said, "I will finance you." He agreed to put up $50,000, the best part of his life savings, and we built five homes on Athlone Avenue in TMR. It was the summer of 1953, and I would go to the construction site every morning at six o'clock to make sure the crews showed up and the work got done. The main thing that goes into a home is the carpentry. Nowadays, such work is entirely subcontracted, but back then the builder did it. So I had to be there all day to make sure no one was sleeping on the job, since we were paying our workers by the hour. We built the homes, we sold them, and we made some money, though not as much as I had thought. Manny and I split about $15,000 and we went home. It was my first real estate deal.

Then I heard about some vacant land that had become available at the top of Westmount, behind St Joseph's Oratory. It hadn't been developed because at that time it was very difficult to get to in winter. There was 60,000 square feet for sale at 60 cents a square foot. You do the math – 60,000 square feet at 60 cents is $36,000 and I didn't even have 36,000 cents.

Charles had been embarrassed as a friend that we couldn't do the first deal together. But it turned out to be a good thing in that it demonstrated I wasn't depending on his friendship or, more to the point, his money. So I showed Charles and Edgar the new deal, and this time they put up all the money, with my end being 20 percent of the profit. As someone who had grown up at the top of the hill, Charles understood the potential of this land at the summit of Mount Royal.

Six months later, some developer came along and offered us $1.20 a square foot, which was twice our investment. We doubled our money, and my cut was $7,200. There was no capital gains tax in those days, and at the age of twenty-five, I felt truly rich. And to show you what a genius I was, that land at 60 cents a square foot became $100 a square foot within the next twenty-five years.

If not the first investment Charles and Edgar made on their own, it was certainly their first real estate deal. Very quickly after that, we did another four or five residential real estate deals around Montreal, and everything we touched made money. And it got to the point where they were paying me a retainer of $500 a month just to bring them deals. It was a nice gesture on their part, they didn't have to do that, and that $6,000 a year was enough for me to live on. I was living at home with my mother in those days, and I wasn't even spending $125 a week. So that modest retainer alone paid all my living expenses.

By 1956, I was making $25,000 a year doing real estate deals, partly with other developers and partly with Charles and Edgar. And it was at this point that they started talking to me about coming into Cemp Investments, the trust set up by their father, and running the family business.

There was considerable opposition to the idea from the trustees, particularly Phil Vineberg, who with his partner Laz Phillips was the family's trusted legal counsel. He thought I was totally unschooled in these matters, and he wasn't wrong about that. I was only twenty-eight years old when I was named managing director of Cemp. I knew nothing about running a trust. I knew nothing about running anyone's investments other than my own. But Sam Bronfman liked the idea. He liked it that I did not come from the sheltered and privileged world of his sons. He liked it that I was burning with ambition, as I was. "He knows how to squeeze a quarter," Sam Bronfman said of me, whereas his sons didn't. And so in 1957 I joined Cemp at a salary of $250 a week, plus 10 percent of the profit of every deal I brought in. When I married Sandra later that year, they raised my weekly salary to $300, but in 1959 Edgar slashed my profit sharing to 5 percent. I didn't think that was right, but Sandra was pregnant at the time with our daughter, Lynne, and I didn't have the guts to quit over it. But I did tell Edgar: "I'm not just going to give up 5 percent. You have got to buy me out." So for giving up 5 percent of the profits, they paid me a quarter of a million dollars cash, tax free, plus a $50,000-a-year payout over five years, half a million dollars in all.

With the quarter million up front, I bought a small building in Toronto that was fully leased. And so I was getting an income of $25,000 a year on my own, which was more than I was making with the Bronfmans. From then on, and for as long as I worked for them, which was more than thirty years, I was in the fortunate position of having an inside and outside stream of income. I had my own investments, unrelated to the Bronfmans, so that if one of them decided to fire me one day, I could say, "It's been nice knowing you, goodbye." I had very conservative rules of personal finance – no mortgages and no bank loans. When we bought our lovely home on Lexington Avenue in upper Westmount, I paid cash with an interest-free loan from Cemp. When I bought a car, I paid cash. When we sent the kids to private school, we paid cash up front. And I always kept more cash on hand than we needed. By the early 1970s, I had $2 million in the bank. In those days my living expenses were $60,000 a year, so I figured I could go for about twenty-five years. That's how insecure and driven I was at the time.

My mother had drummed into my head that I should never work for anyone, and she was very much opposed to my becoming an employee of the Bronfmans. She had taught me a saying in Yiddish, which translated means: "It is better to earn 50 cents on your own than a dollar for somebody else." And when I went to work for the Bronfmans, she said she was going to sit *shiva*. That's how upset she was. She got over it, and I got on with a very productive and prosperous life.

2

"Mr Sam"

Everyone else called him "Mr Sam." I just couldn't bring myself to do that. I called him "Mr Bronfman." Always did. He was my father figure, my mentor, and I was extremely fond of him. But he could be pretty tough. And when he let loose with a string of epithets, I never heard such profanity in my entire life.

I was eighteen, in third-year university, when I first met him in 1947. He told me that when he was my age, starting out in Brandon and Winnipeg, he had a vision that someday he would create a brand of whisky that people from all over the world would want to buy. He and his brothers owned hotels in Manitoba, but when they realized they were making more money in the bar than in the rooms, they decided that was the business to be in. Or at least Sam Bronfman did.

"You can run flophouses or piddle about in land deals if you want," Mr Bronfman told his brother Harry, as recounted by Michael Marrus in his authoritative biography, *Mr Sam*. "I'm going east to get in the liquor business."

And so he did. Ironically, Bronfman was Yiddish for "Whisky Man," and that is exactly what he became, a whisky baron. He was not only an industrial titan and a financial tycoon, he was the founder of a family dynasty that author Peter C. Newman once styled "the Rothschilds of the New World." Newman wasn't wrong about that. The Bronfmans were to liquor what the Rothschilds were to banking.

Mr Sam's story was one of those heroic immigrant tales of striving and success, striving for social acceptance while achieving unrivalled success in business. But he found that money – new money, Jewish money, whisky money – could not buy the social eminence he craved. And rejection just drove him harder to achieve acceptance.

For many years, McGill University would not name Mr Bronfman to its board of governors or accept his money, but near the end of his life, it finally did both and also announced a new building with his name on it, right out front on Sherbrooke Street. And for a long time, even though Seagram and Cemp were major clients of the Bank of Montreal, the bank refused to invite Mr Bronfman on its board, until it was afraid of losing our business to the Toronto-Dominion Bank. Over three decades, from the 1940s to the 1960s, Mr Sam actively sought an appointment to the Senate, seeing it as the crowning achievement of his career, only to have salt rubbed into the wound when Prime Minister Pearson named Mr Bronfman's own lawyer, Laz Phillips, instead.

By then, in 1968, Sam Bronfman had passed the Senate's retirement age of seventy-five, but Laz's appointment just reminded him that he had endured a quarter century of disappointment. After all, he had financed Laz's unsuccessful run for Parliament in a 1943 by-election in the hope that Phillips would be named to cabinet, where he would lead the campaign for Sam's appointment as the first Jewish member of the Senate. That scenario went out the window when Laz was defeated by another Jewish candidate, the noted Communist Fred Rose. Sam nurtured his dream of becoming the first Jewish member of the Senate for another decade, only to have his hopes dashed by the appointment of David Croll in 1955.

The bank directorship that eluded him for so long, the Senate appointment that he was denied, both came rather easily to me, precisely because I worked for him and was the representative of his family. There is no greater irony in my life, and no one to whom I owe more than Sam Bronfman.

Through his sons, Edgar and Charles, I met Sam Bronfman a hundred times. He took a liking to me, and he would talk to me a lot, about business, about the Jewish community, and about anti-Semitism, which was very much on his mind. He was concerned that his children had been sheltered from it, but he knew from bitter experience that it was out there, as I had already discovered. Years later he told his wife, Saidye, that one of the reasons he had hired me at Cemp was that I had felt the sting of anti-Semitism and knew what it was like in the real world. "It's a good idea," Mr Bronfman apparently told her at the time, referring to me as "a little Jewish boy on the make. That's the best kind to have handle our money." It may not have been a very flattering description, but it was essentially accurate.

The Bronfmans lived in this incredible mansion at 15 Belvedere Road in Westmount, an eagle's nest near the summit of Mount Royal, overlooking all of Montreal. Their children's world was not only sheltered, but completely enclosed, a private compound that included the home of their cousins, Edward and Peter, the sons of Allan Bronfman, Mr Sam's brother. Sam's sons had their own skating rink, and we played hockey there. They had a swimming pool that had its own clubhouse, with a pool table and changing rooms.

It was another world, particularly for me, coming from our small family apartment on Van Horne Avenue near Côte-des-Neiges Road. I used to go up there most Saturdays for brunch with the boys. We were served by a butler in a morning suit whose name was Jensen. He was a veteran of the Danish Royal Guard, very formal and distant in bearing and quite intimidating. Once when he was serving a tomato soup, I asked whether it was Campbell's or homemade, he drew himself up to his full six feet and in a very offended tone replied, "At 15 Belvedere Road we do not serve canned soup."

Mr Bronfman was often late for lunch or dinner, and his wife would berate him for his tardy arrival at the table. "She doesn't understand," he would say, "that I have to make a living."

Sam and Saidye Bronfman had a marvellous relationship. They were very affectionate, always holding hands. He told me that she was the only woman he had ever been to bed with. She was a lovely woman, but I think she was a bit suspicious of me in the beginning, as any mother in her position would have been. She undoubtedly wondered what my motives were, whether I really liked Charles or was hanging around him for his money.

In time, she warmed to me. A few months after Mr Sam's death in 1971, she invited me for tea.

"My children won't tell me the truth," she said. "I know you will."

"Yes, Ma'am," I replied. "What would you like to know?"

"What can I afford?" she asked.

"You can afford everything."

"But my darling," she said of Mr Sam, "my darling taught me to be very careful with money."

"Mrs Bronfman," I assured her, "if you want to be careful, be careful. If you don't want to be so careful, you don't have to be."

⌒⌒

Sam Bronfman first dated Saidye Rosner, as his biographer Michael Marrus wrote, at a B'nai Brith dance in Winnipeg in November 1921. They became engaged on Valentine's Day in 1922 and married in June of that year. His parents, Yechiel and Minnie Bronfman, were described by historian Michael Bliss as "poor Jewish refugees from Russian anti-Semitism who came to Canada in 1889." They brought with them a daughter, Laura, and three sons, Harry, Abe, and the infant Samuel, born in southern Russia in 1889, evidently just before the Bronfman family emigrated to Canada. The date and place of his birth were two secrets that Sam Bronfman kept to the end of his life. He always maintained that he had been born in Brandon, Manitoba, in 1891, but after his death, his son Edgar found a Canadian passport stating that he had been born two years earlier in Bessarabia, Russia. Edgar speculated that his father's motive was not to lie about his age, but to "establish that he had been born in Canada" rather than in the "lustily hated" Soviet Union. Whatever his motives, Sam Bronfman successfully maintained the fiction of his age and place of birth. When he celebrated his eightieth and last birthday in 1971, he was really eighty-two years old. Mordecai Richler couldn't have made it all up in *Solomon Gursky Was Here*.

In Montreal, where Sam had already been in the liquor fulfilment business since 1916, Sam and Saidye had four children, Minda in 1925, Phyllis in 1927, Edgar in 1929, and Charles in 1931. The first letters of their names became the acronym CEMP, the investment trust I was eventually hired to run in 1957. By then, Mr Bronfman was not only a fabulously wealthy man, but a uniquely influential figure within the Jewish community in Montreal and Canada. He became a man of means first and a man of influence second.

In the beginning, Sam Bronfman was in the business of shipping whisky, but by the mid-1920s, he got into the business of making it. In 1924 he paid $11,000 for eleven acres of land next to the Lachine Rapids in suburban Ville LaSalle, and he named the company he founded there Distillers Corporation Limited. More than three-quarters of a century later, the sunken expressway running by the distillery is known as the whisky ditch. As Michael Marrus recalled in his biography, when a friend asked what he knew about making whisky, Mr Bronfman replied with characteristic candour, "I don't know the first goddamn thing about making whisky, but I'll be goddamned if I'm not going to learn."

But he did know how to grow the business. With his brother Allan, he travelled to Britain and eventually persuaded the Distillers Company Limited, whose corporate brand he had deliberately evoked in naming his own, to put up half of $2.5 million for an expanded DCL in Canada. In 1927, for $1.5 million, he acquired the Joseph E. Seagram distillery in Waterloo, Ontario, and created a new holding, the Distillers Corporation–Seagrams Limited. To this day, despite the company's having been broken up in the ill-fated sale to Vivendi at the end of 2000, the names of Distillers Corporation Limited and Joseph E. Seagram and Sons Limited are still raised letters on brass plates on either side of the entrance to the company's former headquarters, "the castle," as it was known, built on Peel Street in Montreal in 1928 and eventually donated to McGill University in 2002.

The donation was an appropriate gesture, since the building was designed in 1928 by David Jerome Spence, architect of McGill's Strathcona Hall, also known as Royal Victoria College. As biographer Michael Marrus recounted, Mr Bronfman "told the architect I wanted a baronial castle." That's certainly what he got, and while Seagram's operations eventually moved south to New York, especially after the completion of the Seagram Building on Park Avenue in 1957, the castle was Mr Bronfman's home office until his death in 1971. As he wrote at the end of his life in *From Little Acorns,* a personal and corporate summing up first published as a supplement to the 1970 Seagram annual report only months before his death: "I have never lost my affection for this unique, baronial castle-like building." Indeed, the castle remained Seagram's titular head office until the company was sold nearly thirty years after its founder's passing.

As with the renovations to the mansion at 15 Belvedere Road, also underway at the end of the 1920s, Mr Sam's instructions were simple: "Buy the best." At the Belvedere house, which was apparently in a state of disrepair when he bought it, also in 1928, he brought in the original architect, Robert Findley, well known for designing the Westmount Municipal Library and Westmount City Hall. More than five decades after I first visited the house in the 1940s, I returned for a charity event, where leading Montreal designers each did over one room. The house looked a lot brighter, and a lot smaller, than I remembered it. But it remains in the family. Charles's son, Stephen, has bought it and intends to live there some day.

Mr Sam acquired more than the name of Seagram from the Waterloo distillery. He also acquired 1.4 million gallons of aging whisky in barrels that could be exported to the United States, where it would be warmly received by millions of customers parched by Prohibition. And he acquired two important brand names in Canadian rye whisky, Seagram's 83 and V.O. Charles Bronfman would make "83" the number on the uniform he sported as the owner of the Montreal Expos at spring training. Eventually, his "number" was retired and hung in right field at Montreal's Olympic Stadium.

V.O. would become Seagram's flagship brand and the best-selling Canadian whisky in the world. Sam Bronfman was a marketing genius who missed no opportunity to promote his products. Owning the Seagram name, which would be synonymous with his own until the breakup of the company, he made the most of the Seagram stable's success in thoroughbred racing – twenty Queen's Plate winners – by putting a ribbon in the Seagram racing colours around the neck of the bottle. This added up to quite a lot of ribbon, 10,000 miles by 1970.

When Seagram listed on the Montreal, Toronto, and New York stock exchanges, its symbol on the stock ticker was VO. This was Mr Bronfman's own idea. As he once observed, "Marketing is the problem in all business. If you don't sell, you don't have anything to make."

It was from Mr Bronfman that I learned the importance of brand names. Nowadays everyone talks about branding, brand equity, and trademark value. But this guy was one of the founders of brand value. It was no accident that we were able to build Fairview, and then Cadillac Fairview, as a top brand in the real estate industry. Tenants all over Canada flocked to our malls, because we built better than anyone else, we managed better than anyone else, and we had better locations than anyone else. There was a period of about twenty years where nearly every major shopping centre deal in Canada was offered to us first.

In the liquor business, you get a premium on price because of brand value. In the vodka segment, Seagram had a brand called Bolshoi, and we made next to nothing with it because in the United States there are two brands of domestic vodka, Smirnoff's and the others. By law in the U.S., all domestic vodkas are made by the same formula, but Smirnoff's owns the market and they make an extra dollar a bottle because they have established brand preference. The vodka segment alone in the U.S. is about 13 million cases a year – larger than the entire Canadian market in distilled spirits. So that gives you some idea of the worth of brand value.

Sam Bronfman also had a notion that associating with royalty would take his brands upmarket. One of the first blended brands produced by Distillers Corp. in the 1920s was called Prince of Wales. In 1939, in honour of the royal tour of Canada by King George VI and Queen Elizabeth, he brought out a premium rye called Crown Royal and even succeeded in having a few cases taken aboard the royal train that crossed Canada. Crown Royal came in a bottle that looked like a decanter, in a purple silk sack with tassels. There was also a certificate in the bag attesting that the whisky had been aged at least ten years. The bags were made by his brother-in-law, Moe Levine, who was married to Saidye's sister, Freda. Dowager ladies stored their sterling silver in the purple bags. Three generations of kids in Canada and the United States inherited the bags and used them to hold their marbles, becoming aware even as children of the Crown Royal brand. Observant Jews used them to carry their phylacteries, the ribbons they wore on their sleeves for morning prayers. "In the pantheon of packaging, the Crown bag is undeniably Zeus," Kevin Brooker would write more than sixty years later in *En Route* magazine, observing that Sam Bronfman's "true genius lay in bestowing the glass coronet's lordly sleeve – that purple velvet wampum bag of our lives."

Sam Bronfman was equally brilliant at representational advertising and promotions that built good will and, ultimately, trademark value. It was Mr Sam's own idea to launch the "Drink moderately" advertising campaign. "We received over 150,000 complimentary letters," he later wrote. "Hundreds of editorials approved. There were even sermons from pulpits praising our message." For a whisky baron, demonized as a bootlegger, it was the ultimate endorsement and vindication.

As a Canadian concerned that the war effort was flagging in 1942, Sam Bronfman felt, as he wrote near the end of his life, "that it would be a useful contribution if we were to publish a book which ... would help renew the confidence of Canadians." Seagram commissioned the noted Canadian writer and humorist Stephen Leacock, and the resulting book, *Canada: The Foundations of Its Future,* became a wartime morale builder. "Since then," Mr Bronfman wrote, "we have printed and distributed over 165,000 copies and each one has been sent out in response to an individual request." To this day, it remains one of the most widely read books in the history of Canadian publishing. Leacock biographer David M. Legate later recorded that when Distillers Corp.'s legal department in New York wrote Leacock that they had in mind a fee of between $3,000 and $5,000, Canada's favourite humorist dryly replied that the figure *he* had in mind was $5,000. But neither Leacock nor his estate ever received anything remotely approaching the royalties he would have otherwise earned on the book.

Sam Bronfman himself wrote the introduction, or at least it appeared under his signature in the handsomely bound book, illustrated by noted Canadian artists, that came complete with twin ribbons as bookmarks. "The House of Seagram, it is true, is not a publishing house," he wrote. "That under its imprimatur is issued Professor Leacock's inspiring history of our country is the result, both of an appreciation of the extreme timeliness of the subject and of a consciousness of the wider civic interests of industry." The subject was war, as we "strive to preserve our way of life against the onslaught of a ruthless foe," but with the book's publication, Sam Bronfman was also building good will for the company name, and his own.

In the early 1950s, Sam Bronfman marketed a scotch whisky called Chivas Regal, which became the biggest-selling premium scotch in the world, all because of brand value. Intrigued by its success, even among blue-collar customers, Mr Bronfman and Edgar once checked out a bar near a construction site where Chivas was a big seller. "A construction worker comes in here and he wants a drink," the bartender told them, as Edgar recalled in his excellent 1998 memoir, *Good Spirits*. "For ten cents more you can ask for Chivas Regal and be a big shot." Exactly. Later on, it was Edgar who shrewdly acquired The Glenlivet, a Scottish distillery that made several brands of premium single malt whisky, to which many discerning consumers would move up from Chivas. From 100,000 cases in 1952, sales of Chivas grew by the mid-1990s to almost 4 million cases, or nearly 48 million bottles, a year, all of it bottled at a single distillery that Mr Bronfman built in the Scottish Highlands. The brand equity, and the premium markups, were extraordinarily positive for Seagram's operating margins.

Sam Bronfman definitely had a thing about royalty. Not only was the royal association a way of moving to the upscale segment of the market; it also lent a veneer of respectability, an aura of class. This was important to him as a whisky man who was extremely sensitive to the public perception that he'd made his name, and his fortune, as a bootlegger during Prohibition in the United States.

"There is little foundation for stories of the Bronfmans selling rotgut whisky or having been bootleggers," Michael Bliss concluded in *Northern Enterprise,* his authoritative history of business in Canada. But there was no shortage of insinuation and innuendo about the mail-order activities of the Bronfman brothers in western Canada when liquor was outlawed in the U.S., particularly after the 1922 murder of Paul Matoff, a brother-in-law of the Bronfmans and an agent for the family firm. In Bienfait, a railway town in southern Saskatchewan near the American border, Matoff was gunned down as he collected a payment from an American bootlegger. "Two men entered the room," Michael Marrus wrote, "and took the cash, a sum of $6,000, together with Matoff's ring and diamond pin." The murder brought an air of the Wild West to the peaceful Canadian prairies. It was sensationalized in the press, one paper calling it "the most cold-blooded crime in the history of the provincial police."

For some reason, suspicions centred on Sam's older brother Harry Bronfman, though the American bootlegger was tried and acquitted of the crime. In 1930 Harry was charged with having attempted to bribe a federal customs official in 1920, and he faced a second trial on at-tempted witness tampering in a 1922 liquor charge against another Bronfman brother-in-law. He was acquitted on both counts. It took the jury only ten minutes to deliberate on the witness tampering charge. This was after a brilliant sting – proposed by Sam – of a federal witness. The witness accepted money to change his story, and a court reporter, concealed in the Regina hotel room, overheard the negotiations. Be-cause of the sensationalized murder and bribery rumours attached to the Bronfman name in the Prohibition era, however, an urban legend that he was a bootlegger dogged Sam Bronfman for decades. "Distillers in America were indicted, while in England, they were knighted," he once told Edgar.

Mr Sam wasn't a bootlegger. But there is no doubt that he sold liquor to a lot of people who were. During the Prohibition era in the U.S., boats would leave the East Coast Canadian ports of Halifax and St John, loaded with rum, nominally bound for Cuba and Jamaica, where all they made was rum. Talk about shipping coals to Newcastle! Of course, their real destinations were Boston, New York, Baltimore, and the major ports along the eastern seaboard of the United States. "Of course we knew where it went," he told *Fortune* magazine many years later, quickly adding that there was "no legal proof, and I never went to the other side of the border to count the empty Seagram bottles." And in those days, apparently, the Seagram books would not have led foren-sic accountants on a trail to bootleggers. Max Henderson, who would go on to become Canada's first auditor-general, was a young accoun-tant with Seagram in those days and noted in his memoirs that "ex-treme care was taken not to commit anything beyond the absolute minimum to paper." But it wasn't illegal to manufacture and sell liquor for export in Canada. Nor was the Canadian government in any hurry to prevent these activities by cooperating with American authorities and stopping legal exports at the border, where they became illegal imports. That would have deprived the Canadian government and the provinces of the lucrative revenues from excise taxes. As Michael Marrus noted in his biography, according to one report, "approximately one-eighth of all Dominion and all Provincial revenue was derived from the trade in alcoholic beverages," in 1928 reaching the then staggering sum of $72 million. The Department of External Affairs used all its skills and diplo-macy to fend off American entreaties that Canada enforce Prohibition from the Canadian side of the border. As Marrus wrote, young officials such as "Lester Pearson and Vincent Massey cut their diplomatic teeth on the issue of liquor smuggling, working out the means to defend their country against American pressures on the issue."

With the repeal of Prohibition after Franklin Roosevelt took office in 1933, the American market was open again, a development Sam Bronfman had long foreseen. And in a remarkable coup, he was able to buy out his Scottish partners, Distillers Company Limited, who, as he noted in *From Little Acorns,* "indicated that they preferred not to become American distillers," instead offering "to sell us their shares, and we accepted." When the pent-up demand was released south of the border, he was ready for it. Millions of gallons of whisky had been aging in casks for years. But he refused to be rushed into selling whisky that was, as they say, "hot off the still." In fact, he had a famous falling-out with Lew Rosenstiel, the head of Schenley, who was bottling his stuff straight from the still. There had been talk of their going into the U.S. market together, and they were touring a company distillery in Schenley, Pennsylvania, when Mr Bronfman noticed they were making hot whisky, and that was effectively the end of it. In his book, *Good Spirits,* Edgar recalled his father telling how he'd said, "Lew, we're both going to build great businesses. But you'll take the low road while I'll take the high road."

That was his motto, and I must have heard him say it a thousand times: "Always take the high road." Another of his favourite sayings was "Go first class." And he always did. He had real vision, real ideas. And since I'd lost my own father at an early age, it was nice to have an older man to talk to. I knew him over the last quarter century of his life, first as a friend of his sons and later as an employee of the family. We would sit out at the back of the Belvedere house, under the awnings on warm summer days, and he would spin out dissertations on how he would run other companies, such as General Motors or Procter & Gamble. In his mind, he knew how to run them better than their owners did, and in that sense his self-confidence was boundless.

But in other ways, he was quite insecure, especially about his Jewishness in the company of prominent Gentiles. He was always very impressed by socially prominent *goyim.* I remember when he finally became a member of the Century Golf Club in Westchester, near Tarrytown, New York, where he had a magnificent twenty-acre estate. When I played golf with him a couple of times at the Century in the 1960s, he was always letting people through, so as not to hold anyone up. It was as if he still wasn't quite sure that he belonged there.

I also remember when he and Saidye were flying to Charlottetown for the centennial of the Confederation Conference in 1964. It was a big deal. Queen Elizabeth was going to open the Confederation Centre of the Arts complex next to Province House, the cradle of Canadian Confederation. Edgar had recently bought the first company jet, and Mr Sam was all excited that he was able to invite Senator Hartland Molson and his wife to fly down with him. Now Mr Sam's net worth was probably ten times the senator's, but the senator was the patriarch of the Molson clan, and the Molsons had been in business in Montreal since 1786. It was an important moment for Sam Bronfman, a sign that he had socially arrived. A part of him always remained the insecure little Jewish guy from Winnipeg. We all have our insecurities, and he certainly had his.

Until the trip to Charlottetown, Mr Bronfman had been unaware that Seagram even had a plane. Senator Molson and he were talking about flying Air Canada when Edgar suggested, "Dad, you should use the company plane."

"What company plane?" Mr Sam asked.

"The one I just bought," Edgar replied.

"Hartland," Mr Sam said, "we'll go on the company plane." After that, he hardly ever flew commercial again.

But Sam Bronfman was in no way insecure about his leadership role in the Jewish community. Nor was there ever any doubt in the community about that role. It was here that his wealth and his influence converged. "You were somebody if you had money, and if you had a lot of money you were more of a somebody," Michael Marrus quoted him as telling Edgar. In the Jewish community of Montreal and Canada, he was more of a somebody long before he became known for his philanthropy to the larger communities of the city and the country.

Because he had become so successful by the end of the 1920s, he was looked up to by the Jewish community. Because he had become so wealthy, he was counted upon. And he never, ever let them down, whether the Jewish cause was local or national or had to do with Israel. As early as 1931, he was co-chair of the Jewish Immigrant Aid Society. By 1934 he was president of the Jewish Philanthropies of Montreal, the forerunner of United Jewish Appeal and, later, Combined Jewish Appeal.

From my own conversations with Mr Bronfman, I can attest to the accuracy of Marrus's assessment that his diligence and devotion when it came to Jewish causes were based on three principles: first, a very Jewish sense of responsibility, that sense of philanthropy towards fellow Jews as a Jewish duty; second, a sense of Jewish unity in the community; and third, what Marrus described as dignified Jewish standing in the non-Jewish universe, particularly Canada.

As Sam Bronfman put it in his inaugural address as Canadian Jewish Congress (CJC) president in 1939: "In Montreal, we have a good feeling within the Jewish community and with the other sections of the community at large. This feeling has been built up over a period of years and, to a large extent, by the citizens of the (Jewish) community in Montreal going out of their way to make themselves friendly with the other sections of the community."

Sunday was the day Mr Bronfman devoted to what he called "Jewish business." There was no Canadian more prominent in the affairs of the community, and no one in North America more devoted to the cause of Israel. For nearly a quarter century, from 1939 to 1962, he served as president of the Canadian Jewish Congress. Even before his first visit to Israel in the mid-1950s, he was a powerful advocate of Israel in Ottawa and a tireless fundraiser on its behalf. Nobody said no to Mr Sam. Everyone was terrified of him.

At the time of Sam Bronfman's arrival in Montreal, the city had the most populous and most influential Jewish community in Canada. With 56,000 Jews as measured by the 1921 census, the community comprised the third-largest group in the city after the French and English, "the third solitude," as Marrus noted. Mr Sam's biographer wrote: "In Montreal, the most important city of Canadian Jews, nothing happened without Sam Bronfman's blessing."

As the most prominent Jewish industrialist in Canada, as the long-time president of the Canadian Jewish Congress, and as a generous donor to the Liberal party, to the point where critics accused him of trying to buy his way into the Senate, Sam Bronfman was in a unique position to advance the Israeli cause in Ottawa. And advance it he did.

Shimon Peres, who became my closest friend in Israel, still tells the story of the first time he came to Canada. It was 1950, and his mission was to procure artillery for the Israeli armed forces. When the sale was finally approved for $2 million, Peres set off to Ottawa by car with Mr Sam and his friend Sol Kanee. It was a cold winter's day, and the three of them kept warm with blankets and, at Mr Bronfman's insistence, a nip of V.O. Sam Bronfman had managed to get Peres an appointment with C.D. Howe, the powerful minister of industry and commerce, and had even succeeded in getting the price for the artillery knocked down to $1 million. Shimon then had the arms, but no money to pay for it. The very next evening, Sam Bronfman hosted a dinner to raise the cash.

Canada was among the first members of the United Nations to recognize Israel at the end of 1948, but it wasn't until 1953 that the first Israeli ambassador to Canada, Michael Comay, arrived to take up residence in Ottawa. Except, as Sam Bronfman discovered after accompanying him to the capital from Montreal, he had no residence. Mr Sam loaned the Israeli diplomat the money to buy a gracious residence in Rockcliffe, decided on the spot that a Jewish community campaign would pay for it, and donated the first $25,000 himself.

After his first visit to Israel in 1956, where he was received by David Ben-Gurion, the founding father of the modern Israeli state, Sam Bronfman's devotion to Israel was complete. When war broke out that October over the Suez Crisis and the Israelis occupied the Sinai Peninsula, Mr Sam immediately pledged $250,000 of his own money to the war effort and spearheaded a $20-million Israel Bonds campaign in Canada. By the time of the Six Day War in 1967, Sam Bronfman occupied a unique position within the Jewish community. As Marrus observed in his biography, "In the Jewish world, Sam was revered and honoured as no other leader in Canadian history."

By then, I had worked for Sam Bronfman for a decade and had the opportunity, in the context of the Six Day War, to observe his power in the community. Summoning Jewish leaders from across the country to a lunch at the Montefiore Club in Montreal, he summed up the situation. After breaking up into caucuses, the Montreal group in one room, the Toronto group in another, the western group in a third, the leaders of Canada's Jewish communities decided, at Mr Bronfman's suggestion, that everyone would triple his normal gift to Israel, cash up front. As I recall, he was in for $1 million himself, and raised $13 million in that afternoon alone. But he wasn't satisfied with Sam Steinberg's donation and there was a terrible shouting match between them. Not only was Sam Steinberg, after Sam Bronfman, the most important member of the Montreal Jewish community, he was also the most generous. Furthermore, Fairview was in business with Steinberg's. The grocery chain was in many of our malls, and we partnered with their Ivanhoe real estate division in several shopping centres, so the relationship was important to us.

It was up to me to go and make the peace. So I called the other "Mr Sam" and went to see him at his house. "He shouldn't have insulted me like that," Steinberg said, but agreed to have lunch at the Montefiore Club. I brought Mr Bronfman to his table in the club's dining room, and the two of them patched it up. And it being the Montefiore Club, of course, the entire Jewish community knew the story before sunset.

There is no doubt that Sam Bronfman had a harsh tongue and a terrible habit of berating people, including his own brothers, Harry, Abe, and, particularly, Allan. There is no doubt, either, that over time he cut them all out of the business. As Michael Marrus wrote in *Mr Sam,* the first family trust established in Winnipeg in 1922 saw Sam and Harry each with a 30 percent share, Abe with 19 percent, Allan with 14 percent, and brother-in-law Barney Aaron with 7 percent. In a revised agreement in 1939, Sam was to receive 40 percent, Harry 20 percent, Allan 19 percent, Abe 14 percent, and Barney 5 percent. When Sam assembled the family to disperse the capital in 1951, he got them to agree that he would get $8 million, Allan $3 million, Abe and Harry $2 million each, and their four sisters $1 million each. As for the family's 53 percent ownership of Distillers Corporation–Seagrams Limited, Mr Sam took 37.5 percent for himself and divided the rest among his siblings. By then, only Allan Bronfman, as vice-president and director, was involved in the family business, but he should have been under no illusions about his role. "The business is mine," Sam told Allan, as Marrus recounted. "You must understand that the words 'we' and 'us' no longer apply."

Allan Bronfman was a lawyer and a highly cultivated man, as elegant as Sam was rough-cut. There is a story that Sam once threw an ashtray at Allan and later said that he should have ducked. Perhaps Sam Bronfman resented that his brother was an educated and erudite man, and that his own entrepreneurial gifts made possible the philanthropic activities, such as the Jewish General Hospital and Israel Bonds, that Allan directed. "Allan was well-spoken, and Sam felt undereducated," Edgar would write in *The Making of a Jew.* "Worst of all, Allan told his wife and children that he was an equal partner, and that galled Sam to no end."

But it was always set up, in the nature of the Seco Investments holding, that Sam Bronfman would retain control of Seagram and pass it on to his children, while Allan's would be cut out. It was simple mathematics: Sam controlled two-thirds of Seco through Cemp Investments; Allan one-third through Edper Investments, named for his sons Edward and Peter. In the early 1960s, Sam forced his brother out by buying Edper's one-third share of Seco for $16 million. I had the unpleasant task of accompanying Phil Vineberg to the meeting with Allan where we informed him Cemp was buying Edper out. Theirs was never an equal partnership, and Mr Sam was very unsparing, and often cruel, in his tirades against his brother.

I was on the receiving end once, and only once, and that was enough. Mr Bronfman called me at the usual time, seven o'clock on a Sunday morning, apologized for waking me, and invited me over for breakfast. When I got there, he had no agenda – he just wanted someone to talk to and mentioned that he had met someone in his office who, in my view, had no business being there, and I told him so. He blew his stack and called me a "no good cocksucker." That was his favourite swear word. Charles and Edgar had warned me and told me not to be too upset if he directed it at me, unless it went back four generations. "What does that mean?" I asked. "Well," Charles said, "if he says this person is a no good cocksucking son of a cocksucking cocksucker, then he's really mad. If he just says cocksucker, no problem, forget it."

In fact, he used to swear like that at the dinner table, until Saidye finally put him in his place. "Cocksucker," she said, "isn't that a charming word?" She said it again. "Cocksucker, I'm going to learn to use that word." Mr Sam slowly turned purple, and said, "I'll never use that word again." And he didn't – at the dinner table.

But he did that time with me, letting me have it with both barrels. When he finally stopped, I said, "You know, Mr Bronfman, I didn't come here to upset you, and if I did, I want to apologize right now. But on the other hand, if you are going to put me in a position where I can't be truthful to you, I won't be useful to you, because that is at least partly what you pay me for." I went on: "I like working with your family. Things are going well. But I am of no use to you if I have to guard every word."

And he looked at me with that slight smile of his and replied, "Young man, you are right. It will never happen again."

And it never did. I'm still amazed that I spoke up to him. I was taking my life, or at least my career, in my hands. He was a pretty fearsome guy. There was a time in the 1950s when the Major League Baseball winter meetings were held in Montreal at the Mount Royal Hotel, and reporters filed their stories from the Seagram Suite, which was stocked with all our brands. It was great free publicity, but one night a guy named Jack Clifford came over from the hotel to the Seagram castle across the street and informed Mr Sam that his brother, Abe Bronfman, had decided not to restock the bar because the reporters and baseball people were drinking too much. Mr Bronfman went ballistic. He picked up the phone, which was on a rubber extension, and threw it at Jack, but it boomeranged back and hit him in the face. He started to bleed but that didn't stop him from swearing. "You, you cocksucker, you're fired," he told Jack.

An hour or so later, Mr Bronfman was making his nightly rounds of turning off all the lights in the building – he actually thought it saved money – when he came upon Jack packing up his boxes in his office. "What the hell are you doing?" he yelled. "You fired me," Jack replied. "I didn't fire you," Mr Sam said, "I was just mad."

And Jack, who had been with Seagram since 1936, went on to become a vice-president of the House of Seagram in Canada.

∞

Mr Bronfman wholeheartedly approved of the idea of bringing me in as managing director of Cemp in 1957.

At the time, the trust was very conservatively invested in low-yield bonds and the like. Mr Bronfman was conservatively invested himself. I didn't run his personal portfolio, but I knew what was in it because it was part of my job to look at it. Once when he had me up to the house he said, "I think I should sell the whole thing and go into bonds." "Why would you do that?" I asked. "Well, you know," he said, "one of these days I'm going to retire from Seagram, and I'm going to need a bigger income."

As if he was ever going to retire. And as if he was ever going to be short of money.

At Cemp, my instructions were to grow the investments, but I could never put up Seagram shares to do it. In other words, I couldn't hawk the stock. Mr Sam was very clear about that. There were some shares in a company called Royalite in the Alberta oil patch and some stock in a Cuban sugar company called Atlantica del Golfo. Atlantica was later seized by Fidel Castro. After quite a spell, we finally negotiated a deal where the Cubans would pay us over fifty years in non-interest–bearing Cuban bonds. Some deal that was.

Edgar got us into Polaroid stock at the time it was becoming one of the "Nifty Fifty" in New York. And Minda's husband, the Baron Alain de Gunzberg, persuaded us to take a position in Club Med, the French-based resort and vacation company, and we actually did quite well in that, making about $20 million on our investment by the time we sold.

From the beginning, I wanted to do on a larger scale what I had done with Charles and Edgar on a small scale – real estate deals. In 1958 we did our first deal of any consequence, to build the Parkway Plaza Shopping Centre in Toronto. It was not enclosed, in those days they weren't, still it was a good-sized mall with a Grand Union supermarket as the anchor tenant. But Mr Bronfman refused to make a decision for the longest time. He was actually quite nervous about real estate – apparently he had lost money once in a building in Winnipeg – and it took many months to close.

It was because the Parkway Plaza project turned out well that Mr Bronfman gave me his approval to do our first big deal – a $7-million purchase of seventeen pieces of property in Toronto, some land, some shopping centres, and some partially developed properties that we bought from Principal Investments. Every one of the properties owed money to Loblaws, through first, second, or third mortgages, and I wrote the cheque, drawn on our account at the Bank of Montreal. In those days, $7 million was a lot of money, and I remember being pretty nervous when I signed the cheque. Many years later, someone found the cancelled cheque in our bank records, had it framed, and presented it to me on the fifteenth anniversary of my joining Cemp, in 1972. I still have it in my Montreal office.

Once Mr Bronfman gained confidence in me, he became quite respectful of what we were doing. I think he loved the idea that his sons were involved, that they were doing things that were so much different from what he had done and were getting the respect of the entire Canadian business community. We were highly respected at Cemp, and for him, it was a joy to behold.

In 1962, when we announced the plans for Toronto-Dominion Centre, the biggest office tower development in Canadian history, Mr Bronfman flew up with Charles and me to Toronto for a big cocktail party to mark the event. The premier of Ontario was there, the mayor of Toronto, and the entire WASP business establishment. It was a very impressive turnout, and he was quite proud.

In those days, we didn't have a corporate plane, and we flew back together on what was then called Trans-Canada Airlines, before it became Air Canada, in a turboprop airplane called a Viscount. Arnold Hart, the chairman of the Bank of Montreal, had been invited to our announcement because the BMO banked both Seagram and Cemp. He was on the flight back and got hold of me on the plane. "I hope this doesn't harm our banking relationship," he said. "Arnold, I can't guarantee that," I replied, "but if I were you, I would put Mr Bronfman on your board." The next morning, or very soon thereafter, Hart was in Mr Bronfman's office inviting him to go on the board. I don't think Mr Sam ever knew about my conversation with the BMO chairman. I certainly hope not. But he finally made it to a bank board.

We changed other business relationships as well. The Bronfmans had always dealt with Dominion Securities as their investment bankers, but I brought in Wood Gundy on a couple of major deals, initially to the chagrin of Laz Phillips, the family's lawyer. Laz tried to get Mr Bronfman to fire me on the grounds that I was going to sully their reputation. Several years later, I ran into him in the lobby of Place Ville Marie, where he had his office, and he was excitedly waving a prospectus, saying that for the first time Phillips and Vineberg were in a deal with

Wood Gundy. "How do you think that happened?" I asked sarcasti-
cally. I had introduced them through our dealings at Cemp. And to
think he tried to have me fired over it.

By the 1960s, we had moved Cemp's office from modest space on the
mezzanine of the Mount Royal Hotel to the top floor of what was then
CIL House, a few blocks away at the corner of Dorchester Boulevard
and University Street. We took the entire thirty-second floor and had
the space done over like a British merchant bank, with mahogany pan-
elling throughout and a private dining room with a fabulous view of
Montreal. Once again, we operated under two of Mr Bronfman's mot-
tos: "Buy the best" and "Go first class." Occasionally, when someone
offered us a major deal or when we had a distinguished visitor, Mr Sam
would come over to our office to meet with the important guest.

One day the representative of the Chase Manhattan Bank in Canada
came to see me and said that David Rockefeller, their chairman, would
be coming to Montreal. Mr Rockefeller would be having a dinner to
which Mr Bronfman and I would be invited, but he also wondered if he
could pay a courtesy call on me. The first thing I did was call Mr Bronfman. "David Rockefeller wants to pay a courtesy call on Cemp," I informed him. "How about if I ask him to go to your office and I will
meet him there with you?"

"No, no," he said. "He is coming to pay a call on you, and it should
be in your office, and I will come over there." That was typically generous of him, and I was very touched by it. It also demonstrated his highly
developed sense of occasion.

So Mr Bronfman came over to my office for the meeting and then
went away glowing. He was thrilled that his children's business had attracted a courtesy call from David Rockefeller, scion of the great American dynasty. The Bronfmans were at the same table as the Rockefellers.
It was an important moment for him and a thrilling one for me.

In an odd sense, Mr Bronfman had more success in winning acceptance
from the economic and political establishment in the United States than
in Canada. He was a great supporter of Dwight Eisenhower, who he had
heard drank Chivas Regal. In July 1953 President Eisenhower invited
him to the White House for a private lunch, accompanied by Ellis Slater,
head of Seagram's office in Frankfort, Kentucky, and a member of the Republican establishment. Mr Bronfman had a plan for world peace that involved economic alliances of powers such as the United States, Britain,
France, and Germany – not unlike the G7 that later emerged in the 1970s.

"He explained to Eisenhower that governments should be run much
like large industrial enterprises," biographer Michael Marrus wrote of

the meeting in *Mr Sam*. Far from regarding Mr Bronfman's idea as half-baked, Eisenhower apparently listened attentively. In fact, as Ike's biographer Stephen E. Ambrose observed in *Eisenhower: Soldier and President*, one of the reasons Eisenhower was such a strong supporter of NATO was that he thought that the military defence of Europe would eventually lead to economic and political unity in Europe. "It is difficult to foresee any effective method of preventing struggles among nations, with resulting waste and destruction, except through amalgamation of groups of those now existing," President Eisenhower later wrote to Slater, as Marrus recorded in his biography. "I enjoyed the luncheon, and the presence of the two of you was the exact opposite of an imposition."

Mr Sam had come a long way indeed, from running a hotel bar in Brandon to discussing world peace at the White House in a private luncheon with the president of the United States.

One of the things I remember best about Sam Bronfman was his love of food. When I would go to the Belvedere house on Sunday morning, he had this ritual where the butler would ask what he wanted for breakfast. Mr Bronfman would always reply, "Whaddya got?" The butler would run through everything they had in the kitchen – and they had everything – and Mr Bronfman would inevitably order a couple of eggs, fried so hard they could bounce off the floor. And he'd wash them down with a gin and tonic, saying he had to get rid of the greasy taste. He'd do the same thing at the office every morning, always asking his secretary, Miss Shanks, to bring him "the usual" because he'd had greasy eggs for breakfast.

He planned his day around where he was having lunch. From time to time, when the Cemp office was in the Mount Royal Hotel, across the street from the castle, he would call me at home at seven in the morning and say, "Now, when you get to work, call the chef in the hotel, and have him broil two chickens, and make a cucumber salad. And then let the chickens get cold and we'll have cold broiled chicken and salad in your office."

Lunch was such an important part of his day that he even planned his in-flight meals. Once when he was leaving from Vancouver on a commercial flight for Montreal, he called the chef in the hotel where he was staying and ordered a chicken basket for himself and a Seagram executive who was travelling with him and who would receive the order at the hotel. When they got on the plane, in first class of course, the flight attendant approached him and asked what he would like for lunch. And he said, "I've brought my own lunch." But it turned out that the Seagram guy had forgotten to bring it. The chef had delivered it to the suite, but he had left it there. Mr Bronfman went into one of his trademark rages, and said, "I'm surrounded by idiots, how can I survive?" He made the guy go and sit someplace else on the plane. The flight wasn't non-stop, and when they landed in Winnipeg, he went in and had a bowl of soup at a restaurant in the terminal, muttering under his breath the whole time. Food was very important to him.

He was also a very dapper man and a very natty dresser. When I would go to the Belvedere house for breakfast on Sunday mornings, he was always formally dressed in a dark or grey suit, usually double-breasted, with a pocket puff. I never saw him in sports clothes except occasionally at the summer house in Tarrytown. When Shimon Peres first went to Ottawa with him, in 1951, Mr Bronfman noticed on their return to Montreal that his companion was wearing white socks. He had his driver pull over to a men's store to buy him a more appropriate pair of dark socks. Shimon still tells the story.

In 1961, on the occasion of his "official" seventieth birthday, the family sort of commissioned me to find some way of honouring him, and we established the Bronfman Biblical Museum. David Ben-Gurion, the venerable Israeli prime minister, attended the museum's dedication in Jerusalem with him in 1962. And for his "eightieth" birthday in 1971, we arranged for the donation of a building in his name at McGill, which had finally invited him to join the university board of governors in 1966. And while he never did get to the Senate, he was named a Companion of the Order of Canada, the country's highest civilian honour, after it was established in 1967.

By the time of his eightieth birthday, actually his eighty-second, he was clearly in declining health, suffering from an extremely painful cancer of the prostate. His cancer had metastasized to the point where it had gone into the bone. But the worst of it for him was that he couldn't walk downstairs. Phyllis was designing a private elevator that would have gone on the outside of the house, but that was going to take six months, and he didn't have six months.

Saidye Bronfman called and asked if I could come up with a better solution. This was a Monday morning at nine o'clock. I called Syd Bregman, our lead consulting architect in Toronto – he had his own firm but he was on all our major projects – and explained the problem to him. He told me about a company in Omaha that made these seats that go up and down the sides of staircases. It was a sliding seat on a steel beam. Then he called me back ten minutes later. "You won't believe it," he said, "but they have a representative in Montreal, and here's his number." I called the guy and explained the problem, and he said he'd be right over. So by ten o'clock he was at the Bronfman house, looking over the winding staircase. No problem, he said, he could do it, in six months.

"What is the number in Omaha?" I asked. He gave it to me and I called the general manager at their head office. "I hear the delivery is six months," I said.

"Yes," he replied, "five to six months."

"Tell me," I said, "are you in business to make a profit?"

"Absolutely," he said.

"I will pay you double your price of $9,000," I said, "but I need it tonight."

"You got a deal," he said.

"There will be a Seagram plane on the tarmac at Omaha tonight at six o'clock," I told him and handed the phone back to his representative, who gave him the measurements of the staircase. The Seagram plane picked the chair-lift up, flew it to Montreal, where they assembled it Tuesday morning, and by Tuesday noon Mr Bronfman was using it. The contraption allowed him to get up and down the stairs, and thus out into the garden, during the last difficult months of his life.

The end came on a weekend in July 1971. On July 10, I was out for dinner with Edgar at Ruby Foo's when he was summoned to his father's side. I went with him to the Belvedere house and an hour or two later, Mr Sam was gone.

Charles and Edgar asked me to help with the arrangements, and so I ran the funeral. The next morning we had thirty people in my office, planning everything from numbering the limousines to the seating plan inside the Shaar Hashomayim (Hebrew for "Gates of Heaven") Synagogue. At Mrs Bronfman's request, he was laid out at the Samuel Bronfman House, the headquarters of the Canadian Jewish Congress that he had got me involved in building on Côte-des-Neiges Road.

Then there was the question of who should deliver eulogies. Saul Hayes, who ran the CJC for many years, was one obvious choice. And to Charles and Edgar, Laz Phillips was another. "Your father would kill you," I said. "He barely spoke to the guy." But they insisted, and so I tracked down Laz at Claridge's in London, where he was on a business trip.

"Mr Bronfman died," I said. "Are you coming home for the funeral?"

He had heard the news, but said it would be difficult to break off his busy schedule.

"The family wants you to do the eulogy," I said.

"Oh," he said, "I'll be on the next plane."

And he was. At his death, Mr Bronfman brought a closure to the gap that had separated them and interrupted their friendship for so many years.

It was a state funeral in all but name, with four federal and two provincial cabinet ministers in attendance, Senator Jacob Javits from New York, Mayor Jean Drapeau of Montreal, and all the captains of Canadian industry, from the chairman of the Royal Bank to the chairman of Canadian Pacific. It was quite a send-off, even though a downpour peeled all the numbers off the side doors of the limos, creating a scene of total chaos after the funeral. It was a complete mess, but impressive in its own way.

And for Sam Bronfman, perhaps it was a kind of revenge for all the snubs he had endured from many of these same establishment figures. In death, he left them all in a confused crowd on the sidewalk, standing in the pouring rain.

3

Charles

My relationship with Sam Bronfman, and his sons, Edgar and Charles, has sometimes been compared to that of Robert Duvall as Tom Hagen, the *consigliere* to the Corleone family in *The Godfather,* in the sense that I was a surrogate son as well as an adviser to the father, and a friend as well as a counsellor to the sons. There's a certain amount of truth to that, in that I was brought into the family as an outsider and became privy to its innermost secrets.

When I first met Charles, he was a skinny kid with big ears. As I later learned, he had a difficult childhood in that he had many illnesses, including double pneumonia, which accounted for his underfed appearance. And I guess he was a bit sensitive about being a Bronfman. The name immediately stood out in the small Jewish contingent at McGill, where I met Charles in 1947 during my junior, and his first, year of university. Somehow, we became friendly, I can't even remember how. But we became best friends and have remained so for all the years since, and there's a lot I remember about that.

We became close colleagues at work, especially at Fairview Corporation, where Charles played an active role in our phenomenal growth in real estate. He was so involved that he personally chose the Fairview name and designed the company logo, which became the most recognizable brand in Canadian real estate. I used to call him my design chief, and we still laugh about that. And we became so involved as friends that we were godfathers to one another's sons, Charles to Jonathan Kolber and me to Stephen Bronfman. Charles and Jonathan later become so close that in the 1990s they went into business together in Israel.

Charles and I worked together in various parts of his family's business for nearly thirty-five years. From Cemp to Cadillac Fairview, from Seagram to DuPont, I served not only as a family retainer, and an exec-

utive and corporate director, but equally as a friend and colleague. But
then in the late 1980s and early 1990s, as the Bronfmans wound up
Cemp and sold off Cadillac Fairview, our business contacts became increasingly infrequent, especially after Seagram's 25 percent stake in
DuPont was sold so that Edgar Bronfman Jr could acquire MCA Studios in 1995.

But while our working relationship ended, our friendship endured. It
has even deepened since the Bronfman family's humbling reversal of
fortune after selling their controlling interest in Seagram, which consis-
tently produced profits and dividends, for a minority stake in Vivendi, a
French water utility and broadcaster that nearly drowned in debt after
the convergence bubble burst.

After the Bronfmans finally moved to take control of Vivendi, ousting
president Jean-Marie Messier in a messy boardroom putsch in the summer of 2002, Charles came to Montreal in early September for one of
his periodic visits. We went out for a Chinese meal at the Piment Rouge,
and he was generous enough to remind me that I had questioned both
the MCA/Universal acquisition and the DuPont sale in 1995 as well as
the sale of Seagram itself to Vivendi in 2000, six months after I'd gone
off the board in late 1999. And then the discussion turned to staff cuts
he would have to make at Claridge Inc., the Montreal holding that
managed both his investments and his charitable activities through the
CRB Foundation, the Sam and Saidye Bronfman Foundation, and other
family philanthropic activities that were bound to shrink.

At one point, he said, "I can't afford this anymore." In my entire life,
I had never heard Charles, or any member of the Bronfman family, say
anything like that. But I am getting ahead of the story.

When I first met Charles, I was living with my mother and my brother
Sam in our top-floor apartment on Van Horne Avenue near Côte-des-
Neiges Road. Charles would often visit us there. For reasons I've never
quite fathomed, he loved coming to our little place. Perhaps he liked it
precisely because it was so small, so different from the grandeur of his
own surroundings. In the house on Belvedere Road where he was
raised, he was literally waited on hand and foot. There was a staff of
nine live-in servants, including the butler, Albert Christianson, known
as Jenson, who answered the door in striped pants and a morning coat.
Charles was sixteen when I met him, and he was getting his shirts
custom-made. I thought that was the height of luxury. When he needed
to change into a fresh shirt, he would open a drawer full of shirts, all
beautifully pressed. I was taking my shirts to the laundry. I lived in a different world than he did, and his father liked the idea that I lived in a

different world. Charles and I took a real shine to each other, and there is no doubt that his name being Bronfman kind of intrigued me.

Charles had difficulty in school, or rather, difficulty with exams. I remember going to his house one day when he was studying for a first-year philosophy exam. He was having trouble with syllogisms, and I tried to explain them with the example of a grey cat: this is a cat, all cats are grey, therefore what colour is the cat? He was so psyched out that he couldn't answer. So I went to McGill and saw his philosophy professor and explained that one of his students, Charles Bronfman, was so worried about the exam it was making him sick. And the professor, Roderick MacClennan, said, "It's all right, I'll give him a passing grade." I went and told Charles that he didn't have to write the test, to his immense relief. And after that we developed a kind of symbiotic relationship.

But in his junior year, Charles dropped out of McGill, not because he didn't like school but because he was frustrated by the discrepancy between his efforts and his results. His father, understandably upset, asked the principal of McGill, Cyril James, to try to get Charles to change his mind. So Charles went to see Dr James, who attempted to persuade him to re-enrol at McGill, but the best reason he could put forward was that if Charles didn't graduate, he wouldn't be eligible to join the University Club. Nowadays, of course, anyone can belong to the University Club, but in those days you had to be a university graduate.

By then, I was beginning law school, but I never had a sense, then or later, that Charles ever regretted dropping out or that anything Principal James might have said would have made any difference. Charles just wasn't comfortable at McGill, but this is one of the ironies of his life, in view of what happened later. In the half century and more since Charles left McGill, the Bronfmans have been closely associated with the university, and it is Charles who has maintained and reinforced the link.

Charles was the driving force behind the family's 1971 donation to McGill for a new building named for Mr Sam, announced on the occasion of his official eightieth birthday (in truth, his eighty-second). It was my job to coordinate the donation, and in 1969 I went to see Rocke Robertson, the principal. We were sitting in his office discussing the donation when he took a call and suddenly excused himself.

"What's the problem?" I asked. "The students are occupying the Arts Building," he replied. "Why don't you call the police?" I suggested. "I couldn't do that," he said, explaining that there was the issue of dissent and academic freedom to consider. Which was my introduction, in those tumultuous days of student revolution, to the politics and governance of universities.

McGill, it turned out, had decided to demolish the Prince of Wales Terrace, a prestigious block of nine heritage row houses built in the 1860s, to make way for the Bronfman Building on Sherbrooke Street. That hadn't been the family's call, and it wasn't mine, but the furor was understandable. I suspect that if we had had the chance to do it over again, we would have found a way to keep the row houses, or at least their façade, and build over them. Subsequent to the outcry, this was the solution later adopted in building the Mercantile Place two blocks further east, opposite the Roddick Gates on the corner of McGill College and Sherbrooke.

When a building bears your name because you are the principal donor, there are always nagging concerns about its maintenance and upkeep, as we've seen with the Samuel Bronfman Building. Although it is home to McGill's prestigious faculty of management and is prominently situated on Sherbrooke Street, the Bronfman Building is now in a very rundown condition. This is because McGill, and every Canadian university, is seriously underfunded. Part of the problem is that Quebec has by far the lowest student tuition fees in North America. The undergraduate tuition fee for Quebec students at McGill in 2002 was $1,668, less than half the fee paid by Ontario students, $4,107, to attend the University of Toronto. Mr Bronfman would have been very disappointed to see the dilapidated state of the building that bears his name, and I suspect he would have done something about it. In 1994 the Charles and Andrea Bronfman Foundation established the McGill Institute for the Study of Canada with a $10-million endowment. Under the leadership of Desmond Morton, the eminent Canadian historian, the MISC within five years built an enviable reputation for excellence in conferences, symposia, and lectures.

In 1999 Charles was clearly delighted to attend a national conference on the teaching of history in Canada, called *Giving the Past a Future*. The conference drew nearly a thousand delegates and included screenings by students from two Montreal high schools, one French and one English, of their own Heritage Minutes, in the style of the history capsules produced by the Heritage Project of the CRB Foundation. Later in 1999, the MISC organized a major economic conference, *Free Trade @ 10*, on the first decade of North American free trade, initially between Canada and the United States and then, with NAFTA, including Mexico.

Major economic impact studies were presented, and keynote speakers included the first president George Bush and former prime minister Brian Mulroney. All of these programs and conferences were made possible by a McGill dropout, Charles Bronfman.

∽

When Charles left school and went to work for his father, we began to see even more of each other. We basically hung out together. We were in our early twenties, we were both single, and so we went on a number of trips together. One year in the month of July, we flew out west to the Calgary Stampede and then drove to Banff. For an easterner, there is nothing quite like the first sight of the Rockies rising out of the road to Banff. Then, in 1953, we flew down to Florida together, on one of those old DC-7s, to see his brother, Edgar, who had just married his first wife, Ann Loeb, and had a lovely rented home in Palm Beach.

Then we flew from Miami to Cuba – this was before Fidel Castro's time, during the reign of the previous dictator, Fulgencio Batista, who had just come to power. Havana was a wide-open city, with casinos in all the big hotels and hookers hanging out of windows. From the airport, our cab driver took us to one of the better hotels, where we dropped our bags, and from there drove us to a number of other places. We must have seen two or three hundred women, all of them gorgeous and all of them prostitutes. You hired them for the night. You went to the Copacabana with them, you had dinner with them, you danced with them, you had sex with them.

For Charles and me, the trip to Cuba was a rite of passage. I was quite taken with one of the girls I "dated" there, and when I got home, I showed my mother a picture of her. "Mum, I am engaged," I informed her. "Here is the girl." She freaked out. Here I was, apparently announcing my engagement to a "dancer" and, probably worse from my mother's standpoint, a *shikse*.

My mother got over it, and so did I. When I finally did marry Sandra at the Ritz-Carlton Hotel in 1957, both Charles and Edgar were ushers at our wedding. They had organized my bachelor supper at the Elm Ridge Golf Club and presented me with a silver cigarette box with their signatures engraved on it. I have it to this day, a treasured keepsake.

It was the era of dining and dancing in huge restaurants, and Charles and I went out a lot, providing he allowed me to pay my own way. We often went to Ruby Foo's on Decarie Boulevard, a huge Chinese restaurant seating over a thousand people and a big hangout for the Jewish community. Lawyers, landlords, and *shmatte* guys all went there to be seen and enjoy the copious servings of Ruby's excellent Cantonese cuisine. A lot of the wrong people hung out there as well. So Ruby's was where the action was, in more ways than one.

In his youth, Charles was an ardent advocate of Seagram products. In every restaurant and in every hotel, even at big weddings and bar mitzvahs, Charles and Edgar would always check the bar to make sure it was stocked with Seagram products. Even at Claridge Inc., in the 1990s, the staff of Charles's holding company had a list of the Seagram brands that were to be stocked at events, right down to Tropicana – they were even expected to carry the right orange juice. And with Charles, this went back to nights at Ruby Foo's in the 1950s, where he had this routine of ordering a V.O., and then after tasting it, telling the waiter, "This isn't V.O., this is Canadian Club." And they would have to bring the bottle to prove it was V.O.

Very soon after I joined Cemp in 1957, we founded Fairview. The company began with me and a secretary in an office on the mezzanine level of the Mount Royal Hotel, and eventually became Cadillac Fairview.

As Fairview grew, Charles withdrew to the point where he got off the board. As he said, "What's the point of going to meetings? Leo knows what he is doing." It got to the point where Charles, when approached with a business proposition, would reply, "Call Leo. He runs the family business."

Then Charles married Barbara Baerwald in 1961, and Sandra and I became exceptionally close to them as a couple. To this day, Barbara remains a close friend. Sandra and I managed not to choose sides when he left her in the early 1980s for Andrea Morrison, whom he later married after his divorce. I am very fond of Barbara – she was a great mum to Stephen and Ellen, and a great friend to us, especially after Sandra was stricken with her incapacitating illness in 1991.

Charles and Barbara's first place was a magnificent penthouse on top of the east wing of Le 4300 on de Maisonneuve Boulevard in Westmount. The canopied terrace had a panoramic view of downtown Montreal and beyond, across the St Lawrence River to the South Shore. It was breathtaking, especially in the evening when we would sit out for cocktails, all the lights of the city aglow. I was involved in their home's construction in that I brought in Fairview's top consulting architect, Syd

Bregman, from Toronto. He gutted and redesigned the place under my supervision, and Barbara turned it into a magnificent apartment.

Later on, they moved up near the top of Westmount to a custom-built, ultra-modern, low-slung place with an indoor swimming pool that opened onto a beautiful back lawn. You pressed a button by the pool and the back windows opened onto the garden – it was that kind of modern home. It wasn't particularly my taste, but you had to admire it.

By the mid-1950s, Charles was in charge of his own spirits sales company, Thomas Adams. As his father wrote in *From Little Acorns,* "In 1954, when we created the Thomas Adams Company, he took complete charge of its development. Charles paid careful attention to every detail, particularly blending, packaging, advertising and marketing. He selected, engaged and trained an entire work force ... Charles did an excellent job." At the time, Charles was not even twenty-five years old. In 1958 he was appointed president of the House of Seagram, responsible for Canada, the Caribbean, and Israel. He was also in charge of Seagram's sponsorship of the Canadian Open golf championship, where the winners of the Seagram Gold Cup included Arnold Palmer. In fact, Palmer won his first professional tournament in the Canadian Open at Toronto's Weston Golf Club in 1955. Some years later, Charles was hosting him in a pro-am event and asked me to walk around with them. I had recently birdied all four par threes at Elm Ridge, and Charles mentioned this to him as he introduced me. "I've done that dozens of times," Arnie said. So much for my golfing prowess.

For all of Charles's early success, it was sort of preordained that Edgar would be their father's successor. Charles would be the equal partner, but he wouldn't run the place. "Somehow," Edgar wrote in *Good Spirits,* "it was just understood that I would be in charge." And so it was, ever since Edgar moved to New York in 1955, with Charles destined to take charge of Seagram in Canada. Edgar was very fond of Charles, but I don't think he had a high enough regard for his business acumen.

Charles was very good on issues of corporate governance. He understood that Seagram's reputation and good name built the brand and were the ultimate guarantors of shareholder value. As chairman of the executive committee over a nearly twenty-five–year period, he recruited a first-rate board. As Edgar acknowledged in his memoir, "Charles has played the major role in selecting and securing members for what many consider the most talented and outstanding board in Canada, and perhaps in North America."

In 1999, the last year I sat on the Seagram board, it included only four members of the family and only one other inside director, CFO Bob Matschullat. There were thirteen outside directors, all of them outstanding and most of them recruited by Charles: Laurent Beaudoin, the chairman of Bombardier; Matt Barrett, the former chairman of the Bank of Montreal and by then CEO of Barclay's Bank in London; David Johnston, the former principal of McGill and president of the University of Waterloo, rated by *Maclean's* magazine in 2002 as the top university in Canada; Cornelius Boonstra, the chairman and president of Philips Electronics; Dick Brown, the chairman and CEO of Electronic Data Systems (EDS); John Weinberg, the managing director of Goldman Sachs, the most prestigious investment banking firm on Wall Street; Bill Davis, the former premier of Ontario; André Desmarais, the president of Power Corporation; Barry Diller, the Hollywood mogul and CEO of USA Networks, who was close to Edgar Jr; Marie-Josée Kravis of the Hudson Institute, who is married to Henry Kravis, the takeover artist; Michele Hooper, the president and CEO of Voyageur Expanded Learning; and Sam Minzberg, the president of Charles's holding company, Claridge Inc., who would later organize the ouster of Jean-Marie Messier at Vivendi.

Charles had very sound business sense and conservative investment instincts. These he reluctantly set aside in order to maintain a united family front when Junior sold off Seagram's position in DuPont and bought MCA and subsequently sold Seagram itself to Vivendi. Then in an interview with *Fortune*, in late 2002, Edgar Jr suggested that Charles was the author of his own reversal of fortune in the Vivendi fiasco.

While the Edgar side of the family sold a large block of Vivendi stock for $1 billion after the expiry of a ninety-day lockup period, *Fortune* reported that "the Canadian Bronfmans chose to sell only $100 million of their shares. Worse, they dumped 2.7 million shares last August, when the price was hovering around $12. 'For whatever reason they didn't [sell earlier],' Edgar Sr says, 'I think in hindsight my brother was very upset about that.'" To which Edgar Jr added, "One of the things that appears to be difficult for the Charles side of the family to do is accept responsibility for its own decisions. They should have sold all their positions for $65 or $70 a share."

And then Edgar Sr, master of understatement, observed, "It's very personal between my brother and myself. I think he holds a real grudge." It was a measure of how far the family fortunes had fallen, and in particular how desperate the Edgars were to salvage their shattered reputations, that both father and son broke Mr Sam's inviolate rule that the Bronfmans should settle all family differences in private and present a united front to the world. Charles, meanwhile, suffered in silence. It was not as if he hadn't been warned, specifically by me, as he himself graciously, if ruefully, acknowledged after it all went terribly wrong.

The seeds of misfortune were sown in a 1986 *Fortune* interview, where Edgar designated Junior his successor without even informing his brother, who was co-chairman of Seagram, not to mention the Seagram board. Edgar had no right to do that. He could nominate Junior but he couldn't appoint him, only the board could do that, and both Charles and the board were presented with a *fait accompli* in America's leading business magazine. Furious, I walked into Charles's office.

"Charles," I said, "he seems like a nice young man. But he is a high school dropout and has no college education for the very kind of complex world we now live in. To the best of my knowledge, he knows nothing about finance or money, and if you allow this to happen, you will look back someday and say it is the biggest single mistake you ever made in your life." And Charles has occasionally reminded me of that.

When Edgar and Charles walked into a room, they were Mr Seagram and Mr DuPont. No Jewish family since the Rothschilds has controlled such important assets as the biggest liquor company and the biggest chemical company in North America, both of them blue chips on the New York Stock Exchange, both of them huge profit centres that threw off hundreds of millions of dollars a year in dividends.

But Edgar Sr came to think that DuPont "was a very boring company," as he put it in *Fortune*, and Junior was also bored by it. He didn't want to be Mr DuPont or even Mr Seagram, as it turned out. He wanted to be Mr Hollywood. So he sold our 25 percent interest in DuPont, which in 2003 alone would have paid Seagram $350 million in dividends. As Yogi Berra has said, you get cash and it is almost as good as money.

In 1995 Seagram was the world's second-largest distiller, with 230 brands of spirits and 195 wine brands. Our own brands included Chivas Regal, the world's number one premium scotch, and Crown Royal, the number one premium Canadian whisky, as well the prestigious single malt brand The Glenlivet, Mumm's champagne, and Martell cognac.

DuPont was an industrial complex that had grown to more than 100,000 employees since its founding in 1802 by a French immigrant, E.I. du Pont. It was in chemicals; it was in fibres; it was in oil. It had discovered Nylon and still had proprietary rights to innovations such as Teflon, Orlon, and Dacron.

And what did we get for our one-quarter interest in one of the greatest industrial companies in the world? A second-rate movie studio, MCA, which was into a lot of things, but was not number one in any of them. Not in pictures, not in television, not in music, not in theme parks.

The buying of DuPont in 1981 had been a stroke of genius on Edgar's part. Seagram lost the battle for Conoco to DuPont, but ended up with 20.2 percent of DuPont instead, and Seagram kept buying stock on the open market until, by the time we sold, our share of DuPont had reached nearly 25 percent. Buying DuPont was the deal of the century. In retrospect, selling DuPont was the dumbest deal of the century. Charles reiterated DuPont's value to Seagram but didn't want to risk a family fight at the Seagram board. Yet as *Fortune* accurately noted in its November 2002 article, flagged on the cover as THE BRONFMANS: DYNASTY IN CRISIS, "Edgar Jr could take a proposal to the directors only if his father and uncle signed off on it first." Seagram could have bought MCA without selling DuPont.

"Look," I argued, "if we have to buy MCA, we don't have to sell DuPont to do it. We can finance it with DuPont dividends." It would have been a cinch. But it never happened. Junior wanted out of DuPont, not for any good business reason, but because he wanted to go Hollywood, as his father had before him when we bought a piece of MGM back in the late 1960s.

Seagram sold its stock back to DuPont for $8 billion in 1995, and they were more than happy to have it. In 1997 the stock split 2 for 1, and by 1998 the dividend had increased to $1.40 per share. With nearly 1 billion shares in the float, Seagram's former stake in the company was then nearly 250 million shares worth about $12.5 billion. That should have been, could have been, would have been our company – dammit, it was our company.

There was even worse to come, when Seagram itself was sold to Vivendi in 2000, which proved to be one of the first great corporate debacles of the new century. Again, it was Junior's doing. "By then," Charles later told me, "Junior had messed up our balance sheet." The Seagram name itself, synonymous with the house of Bronfman for three generations, would be swallowed up and sold off in the merger with Vivendi.

∞

It was at Edgar's invitation, with Charles's full support, that I joined the
Seagram board after their father's death in 1971, taking Mr Bronfman's
seat as a director. It was at Charles's suggestion that Allen Lambert
nominated me to the board of the Toronto-Dominion Bank in 1971,
making me one of the first Jewish directors of one of the Big Five Canadian banks. It was at Charles's and Edgar's invitation that I went on the
board of DuPont, where I was happy to serve for a decade until we sold
our interest in 1995. The Bronfman brothers had absolute confidence in
me as head of Cemp and Cadillac Fairview. And it was because of my
association with the Bronfmans that Pierre Trudeau named me to the
Senate in 1983. I might have made more money on my own as a real estate entrepreneur, but I wouldn't have been involved with projects on
the scale of the TD Centre and the Eaton Centre, I wouldn't have been
named to the boards I sat on, I wouldn't have met the people I've met
or been to the places I've been, if I hadn't represented the Bronfmans. I
said that publicly at my own fiftieth birthday party in Montreal and,
some twenty-two years later, at Charles's seventieth birthday, which
Andy organized on a yacht in the south of France in 2001. Previously,
on my seventieth birthday in 1999, Charles and Andy gave a memorable dinner for me.

As time went on, though, Charles and I saw much less of each other
on business occasions after we sold Cadillac Fairview and wound up
Cemp in the late 1980s, and after he and Andy began spending most
of their time in New York, Palm Beach, and Jerusalem in the early
1990s. His focus had shifted from business to philanthropy, from
Montreal's Jewish community to world Jewry, and from Canada to Israel. As Charles later explained it, one of the reasons he went to New
York was "that I wanted to devote much of my life to North Ameri-
can/Israel Jewish philanthropy, and New York was, and is, the place
to do so." Indeed, Andy threw herself with equal fervour into the philanthropic activities for which they were both named Honorary Citizens of Jerusalem, the first North American Jews and the first couple
to be so honoured. Andy has made a great wife and a terrific partner
for Charles.

In Montreal, he was the richest man in the city and the leading figure in
the Canadian Jewish community. In New York, he was in some sense just
another rich Jew, of which there were hundreds in Manhattan. But as he
told me, "Andy likes New York, I like New York," and so they went.

In the Seagram Building in New York, the company occupied about five floors, with all the bosses – Edgar, Junior, and a few others – on the fifth floor. Sheer magnificence – that's the only way to describe the executive suite in Mies van der Rohe's most famous building. But Edgar didn't want Charles on the fifth floor, even though he was co-chairman and co-equal in terms of equity. Edgar's argument was that Charles was not part of management. When Charles, who was quite miffed, related Edgar's rationale to me, I simply blew up: "What kind of statement is that for Edgar to make? You are co-chairman and you own the same amount of stock as him. You can't take second billing." And he didn't – he got the office next to Edgar, and they shared the same secretarial pool. My sense is that Edgar, because he had been in the Seagram Building since it opened in 1957 and had been outright boss since Mr Sam's death in 1971, got a bit territorial about sharing executive space with his younger brother, but in the end he did so quite agreeably and without further incident.

So Edgar and Charles had a very good thing going in New York. Though the Seagram Building had been sold to a teachers' pension fund in 1980, company headquarters remained at the prestigious Park Avenue address and the Seagram name remained on the building. It was a monument to their father's vision and their sister Phyllis's impeccable taste in hiring Mies. Architects and architectural critics recognized the Seagram Building as one of the greatest American buildings of the twentieth century. At lunchtime, Edgar and Charles had their own reserved tables, the best in the house, downstairs at the Four Seasons, the most renowned restaurant in America, in which Seagram had a half interest.

Edgar did great work as president of the World Jewish Congress, and Charles became co-founder of Birthright Israel, with the goal of providing a free trip to Israel for the world's Jewish youth, and later in the 1990s he became chairman of United Jewish Communities, which as the *Jewish Times* reported in a cover piece on him, "raised an enormous $840 million in its 1998 annual campaign in the United States and Canada plus at least as much in endowment and other funds."

What Charles and Edgar may not have fully understood or appreciated then was that there was a big difference between a rich and powerful business leader and a guy with just a lot of money. It was their power and wealth in business that leveraged their influence in the community, even the Jewish community. Without the power of Seagram and later DuPont, they were just another couple of rich Jewish guys in New York. And then it turned out that thanks to Junior, they weren't as rich as they used to be, either. In New York, power and wealth equal influence and fame. Wealth without power equals fame without influence. And when you're not as rich as you used to be, it turns out you're not so famous, either.

Over three decades, from the late 1950s to the late 1980s, we built one of the premier real estate companies in North America – Cadillac Fairview. Edgar, with Charles's unstinting support, expanded Seagram to the number one position in America and the world in premium Scotch whisky, rye whisky, cognac, and champagne. Thanks to Edgar, we had 25 percent of the most important chemical company in America – that was entirely his deal, and he deserves all the credit for it. And we had the most famous office building and the most famous restaurant in America.

Can someone please tell me what was wrong with any of that and with the huge cash flow that went with it? Nothing, by all the recognized rules of business, except that Edgar found it "boring." And then Junior, after doing the MCA deal, started piling up debt with foolish acquisitions, like paying $10.4 billion for Polygram NV records in 1998. He evidently hadn't changed since the days he was writing songs as a kid – he still wanted to be on Tin Pan Alley.

Finally, he got caught up in the convergence craze in 2000, when AOL, an Internet dial-up service, swallowed Time Warner in the biggest media merger in history. After the tech bubble burst, the story ended with the ouster of Time Warner CEO Gerald Levin in 2002 and ultimately of AOL founder Steve Case in 2003. But before the meltdown, the AOL–Time Warner merger drove convergence deals, none bigger than the Seagram sale to Vivendi.

Looking to unload debt and maximize shareholder value, Junior sold Seagram, including its heritage liquor assets, to Vivendi for $34 billion in an all-stock deal, from which the family was supposed to realize $6.5 billion. Vivendi stock, which traded at $83 when the deal was made, sank to $11 two years later, when Charles was still holding most of his. In the end, Junior traded 25 percent of DuPont and control of Seagram for about 8 percent of Vivendi, ending up with less than 5 percent after various Bronfman positions were sold off.

The Vivendi deal was not yet on the horizon when I, having reached the compulsory retirement age of seventy, attended my final board meeting as a Seagram director in December 1999. Seagram's fiscal 1999 numbers were very eloquent: U.S.$12.6 billion of revenues, but operating losses of $126 million in the music division and $206 million in film, offset slightly by a $45-million profit in theme parks and significantly by a healthy $552 million profit in spirits and wines, which as noted pointedly in the annual report continued to "bring us approximately $500 million in pre-tax cash flow annually." Booze, which had built a famous empire, was still the heart of our business, our core competence in terms of earnings and cash flow, but Junior was oblivious to it.

Sam Bronfman, in a 1966 interview with *Fortune,* the family's magazine of choice for making prophetic statements, famously said, "You've heard about shirtsleeves to shirtsleeves in three generations. I'm worried about the third generation. Empires have come and gone." In a *Report on Business Magazine* article in the *Globe and Mail*, Junior had been quoted as saying that he wasn't "going to be the one who pissed away the family fortune." Turns out that's exactly what he did. In a tale of biblical proportions, he sold his heritage for a mess of pottage. By the turn of the twenty-first century, the great empire Sam had built in the twentieth century had indeed come and gone, dismantled by the third generation.

It was Charles that I felt badly for, the good and dutiful son who had kept his own counsel for the sake of the family in the DuPont sale and the Vivendi deal, only to see the façade of unity finally shattered in the public recriminations that ensued after the Vivendi meltdown in 2002. Charles deserved much better, given all his contributions to family, community, and country.

∞

From the outset, he liked to be called Charles – never Charlie, much less Chuck. He was quite insistent about that, even with sportswriters covering the Expos. The only exception was Ted Blackman of the Montreal *Gazette,* and that was a one-shot deal. In the Expos' inaugural year of 1969, Charles agreed that Ted could call him Charlie if and when the club surpassed 1.6 million in attendance at Jarry Park, for an average attendance of 20,000 a game. The milestone was achieved on the final weekend of the season, and the next day's lead on Ted's column was "Call him Charlie."

The Expos were something that Charles kind of fell into in 1968, when Mayor Jean Drapeau was looking for investors in the new Major League Baseball franchise. Charles came forward to do his civic duty, but as other prospective investors dropped out, his share kept increasing until he became the majority owner. Montreal was in very real danger of losing the franchise even then, when it almost failed to meet an August 1968 deadline for making a $1-million down payment on the $10-million cost of the franchise. It was Charles who stepped up to the plate. "The money will be there before the deadline," he promised, and as always, he proved to be as good as his word. "Mayor Drapeau wanted it, and I didn't want to let him down," Charles said at the time. "I learned from my father that citizenship means more than paying taxes or writing cheques for charity."

I advised Charles against investing in the Expos, and it turned out I was wrong about that. Owning the Expos was his thing, one of the best things he ever did. It had nothing to do with his father; it was something he did entirely on his own. There is a story, perhaps apocryphal, that on the first Opening Day, in April 1969, a friend approached Sam Bronfman during a pre-game reception at the Windsor Hotel. "Mr Sam, this is terrible, Charles is going to lose a million dollars a year," the friend supposedly said. "Yes," the old man evidently replied, "and at that rate he'll be broke in one hundred and fifty years."

Mr Bronfman was immensely proud that Charles had created something of this importance to the community and to the sports world. Until the Toronto Blue Jays came along in 1976, the Expos were "Canada's Team." Charles ran the team on a businesslike basis for the twenty-two years he owned and operated it. He was kind enough to overlook my early opposition to the project and invited me onto the board, where I served happily until he sold the Expos in 1991. We often flew down to spring training together, and the team even had uniforms for us, number 83, as in Seagram's 83.

From an initial investment of $10 million in the Expos, Charles and his remaining minority partners sold for $100 million in 1991 to a consortium of Montreal interests led by Claude Brochu, the club's president and CEO, who had moved over from Seagram where he'd run one of our brands. Charles could have made much more by moving the Expos to the United States and then selling them, but he very much wanted the team to stay in Montreal. And when you look at it over a twenty-year period, he actually did quite well on his investment.

One of Charles's fondest dreams had been to hear "O Canada" at the World Series, and the Expos almost got there in 1981, only to lose the National League pennant to the Los Angeles Dodgers in the fifth and deciding game of the playoffs on a ninth-inning homer by

Rick Monday, a moment known thereafter in Montreal as Blue Monday. Apart from building a farm system that was the envy of the Majors, Charles was also prepared to spend to acquire talent in the free-agent market. In the mid-1970s, Reggie Jackson flew into Montreal with his agent on a Friday night for a weekend of negotiations. Things got off to a rocky start when immigration officials at Dorval Airport found a small quantity of hashish in his luggage, an incident we somehow persuaded them to overlook. Then Charles and Barbara threw a blow-out of a party for Reggie on the Saturday night, to which *le tout Montréal* turned out. On the Sunday, Reggie and his agent convened with Expos president John McHale at my house to see if we could agree on a contract. Reggie had a terrible hangover and needed a hair of the dog.

"Hey, kid," he said to my son, Jonathan, "make me a milkshake, but it has to have eggs in it."

His verdict was that there weren't enough eggs. The negotiations bogged down, and Reggie eventually signed with the New York Yankees and became Mr October. And Jonathan got to tell his schoolmates that he had made a milkshake for Reggie Jackson.

By the beginning of the 1990s, owning a baseball team no longer made sense as an investment, and the economics of baseball made no sense whatsoever. Indeed, the economics of baseball is an oxymoron. There are two problems with the game, the greed of the players and the stupidity of the owners. Until there is a salary cap and meaningful revenue sharing of local broadcast revenues, the small teams will never be competitive with the likes of the New York Yankees. The Expos were always challenged to be competitive with their much smaller payroll, and they faced a steep additional premium on the exchange rate from Canadian to U.S. dollars. And the most the Expos ever received from television revenues was $600,000, Canadian, while at the same time the Yankees were getting $60 million, a hundred times as much, plus the exchange rate, for local television rights. It's not by accident that the National Football League has achieved both competitive and financial parity between small-market and large-market franchises. It has both a salary cap and revenue sharing. How else would Green Bay, a small town in northern Wisconsin, be competitive in every sense with the New York Giants?

Charles also got involved in football as one of the owners of the Montreal Concordes, after the Alouettes franchise in the Canadian Football League folded in the mid-1980s. There were three problems with the Concordes, starting with the name. The owners couldn't get naming rights to the Alouettes without assuming the team's liabilities, but it was the only football name with brand equity in the Montreal market, as we've seen with their revival and remarkable renaissance in the late 1990s and into the new century, culminating in their Grey Cup victory in 2002, their first in a quarter century. Also, the Concordes weren't very good. And finally, they played in the vast and empty Olympic Stadium, hardly an ambience to attract spectators, something the Alouettes figured out when they moved to McGill's Molson Stadium in 1997, where they've been sold out ever since. The Concordes lost a lot of money before they folded in 1987.

Charles always had excellent relations with sports writers and broadcasters covering the Expos. I think he liked it that they weren't intimidated by him. For several years, we owned CFCF radio and television as well as the Expos, and there was an occasional conflict between baseball and Alouette football broadcasts, which we also carried on radio. Apparently, while at his summer home in Ste-Marguerite in the Laurentians, Charles had once been unable to pick up an Expos game because CFCF was carrying football. When he later ran into Ron Reusch of CFCF in the Expos' press box, he asked, "What's the matter with your radio station?" "No, Charles," Reusch replied, "it's *your* radio station." Charles, who has a great sense of humour about himself, appreciated the irony of it.

When we folded Cemp Investments in the late 1980s, the families of the four Bronfman siblings waved goodbye and went their own ways. Charles then established Claridge Inc. as the holding company for himself and his two children, Stephen and Ellen, and asked me to become chairman, which I was delighted to do.

Charles had another idea, which was to marry his investment company with his charitable giving at the CRB Foundation, as well as with his and the family's other philanthropic activities at the Charles and Andrea Bronfman Foundation and the Sam and Saidye Bronfman Foundation. He wanted to put the giving together with the getting in the same office.

"Why would you want to do that?" I asked.

"It will be a good intermix of the people who make and the people who give," he said, "and we will learn from each other."

"Boy, I sure don't see that," I replied.

Best friends and free spirits: Charles Bronfman and I kick up our heels at the Elm Ridge Golf Club in the 1950s.

Wedding toast: Charles and Edgar Bronfman joined my mother, Luba, and me for a drink before my wedding in Montreal, September 1957.

The happy couple: Sandra and I, the lucky guy, leave our wedding at the Ritz in September 1957. Her family paid for the reception, my mother paid for the orchestra, and Sandra paid for her own dress.

With Charles at the Montreal Expos spring training camp in Florida.

Quebec premier Jean-Jacques Bertrand throws out the first pitch at the Expos' inaugural Opening Day at Montreal's Jarry Park in 1969. (Left to right) Barbara Bronfman, Charles, Gabrielle Bertrand, Montreal Executive Committee chairman Lucien Saulnier, Sandra, Montreal mayor Jean Drapeau, and me.

With Charles and Maurice "Rocket" Richard,
the greatest hockey player I ever saw and one of
the nicest men I ever met. I was even more thrilled
when the Rocket autographed the picture.

Charles and I listening to his father, Sam Bronfman, speaking at an office Christmas party.

In the mid-1960s, Charles looks on with Simpsons executives Edgar Burton (second from left) and Allan Burton (right) and Anjou mayor Ernest Crépeault while I adjust a maquette of Les Galeries d'Anjou, our second big super-regional shopping centre in Montreal.

Charles, our lead architect Syd Bregman, and I, along with architect John Parkin and Toronto-Dominion Bank chairman Allen Lambert, at the unveiling of a scale model of Mies van der Rohe's Toronto-Dominion Centre in 1963. At fifty-four storeys, the Toronto-Dominion Tower would be the tallest building in Canada.

Princess Alexandra and the TD's Allen Lambert at the opening of the TD Tower in 1967. The princess's husband, Angus Ogilvy, is accompanied by Marion Lambert, while I bring up the rear with the naval attaché.

The TD Centre, viewed from across the street at the corner of King and Bay in 2003. Forty years after its conception by Mies van der Rohe, it remained a timeless statement. The TD Centre announced Toronto's arrival as a world-class city.

With Sam Bronfman (second from right) at the ground-level ceremony for the Toronto-Dominion Centre topping off. Charles is in the middle with TD chairman Allen Lambert on his left, while TD president Sam Paton (left) and former Ontario premier Leslie Frost look on. For Mr Sam, it was a moment of immense pride in what we had built.

Charles and I at the topping-off ceremony for the TD Centre. We were standing on plywood boards spanning steel girders, 730 feet above ground. And as you can tell from the Canadian flag, the wind was blowing. I was terrified.

Still best friends: With Charles in the 1990s.

Sandra with Danny Kaye and Premier René Lévesque backstage at Place des Arts following Danny's benefit concert with the Montreal Symphony Orchestra. Lévesque had a hard time believing Danny wasn't being paid.

My fiftieth birthday party at the Ritz in January 1979: Premier René Lévesque, Sandra, Harry Belafonte, and Corinne Côté-Lévesque. It was quite a night.

John Turner with Sandra and me at a political fundraiser we hosted when he was Liberal leader and I was the party's chief bagman in the mid-1980s. I later told Turner privately that the voters would hand him his head if he insisted on fighting free trade in the 1988 election.

Liberal Leader Jean Chrétien is introduced by Marc Lalonde, co-chair of the Laurier Club, and me at a fundraiser at our home in October 1993, just three weeks before his election as prime minister.

A word with the prime minister: On board Prime Minister Chrétien's plane, flying to Israel in the spring of 2000.

With Pierre Trudeau at the Expos' Opening Day, 1987. "You have to go to the ball game with me to get your picture in the paper," I told the former prime minister when this picture made the front pages the next day.

Paul Reichmann and I with Prime Minister Brian Mulroney and Jonathan Dietcher, who managed Mulroney's investments.

"When Irish Eyes Are Smiling": Mulroney entertains guests at a party in Charles Bronfman's backyard.

Prime Minister Trudeau arrives at our house for a Liberal party fundraiser in the early 1980s. He liked it that he didn't have to speak and that we served a full hot meal. I never met a man with such an appetite.

Montreal's legendary mayor, Jean Drapeau, in a quiet moment with Sandra and me. Drapeau was notorious for running late and would usually keep me an hour past our scheduled time together. I learned to schedule him last in the day.

Prime Minister Chrétien introduces me to Palestinian Authority chairman Yasser Arafat in Gaza. Senator Marcel Prud'homme, a longtime Palestinian sympathizer, looks on.

Israeli foreign minister Shimon Peres makes a point to Paul Desmarais, while Charles and I listen attentively. Shimon is my oldest and dearest friend in Israel and one of the most gifted men of a remarkable generation of Israelis.

Mugging with Israeli prime minister Ehud Barak in Jerusalem in 2000. As Israel's most decorated soldier, he had unique credentials for the peace that was lost when Arafat walked away from a good deal at Camp David a few months later.

With Shimon at an Israel Bonds dinner in Montreal during the 1980s.

With Sandra and Henry Kissinger at an
Israel Bonds dinner which I chaired in honour
of Charles Bronfman and where the former U.S.
secretary of state spoke of the prospects for
peace in the Middle East.

With Federal Reserve Chairman Alan Greenspan during the Senate Banking Committee's trip to Washington in 2003. Security was tight – it was half an hour before I was allowed into the meeting. Before he became head of the Fed, Greenspan had worked on a couple of deals for Seagram in New York. That's how we met.

With Royal Bank president Gordon Nixon at the Senate Banking Committee's hearings on large bank mergers and the public interest in November 2002. From the time the government punted this political football to us, we held hearings and wrote a well-regarded report within six weeks, recommending mergers be allowed in the interests of building a world-competitive financial services sector in Canada.

(Courtesy Royal Bank of Canada Financial Group)

Charles's idea meant that we wouldn't have enough space in the former Cemp headquarters on the top floor of what was then CIL House in Montreal, and I hated the prospect of giving up our mahogany-panelled offices there. But we had just built Place Montreal Trust, which basically had about twice as much space per floor, so I said to Charles, "Let's take the top floor there." We would have had enough space in this brand new office tower, built by us, on McGill College Avenue, the very best location in Montreal. But no, our offices had to be in Le Windsor, the retrofit of the old Windsor Hotel on Peel Street. I was pretty pissed off about the whole thing. It was a lousy idea.

"We have too much money," Charles said to me at one point. "We have to give it away."

"I understand, Charles," I replied. "But my job is to make money."

So we took the top three floors of Le Windsor initially, though we later scaled back to two floors in the 1990s, and when some of our staff lost their jobs after the Vivendi fiasco, we had quite a bit of surplus space on our hands by 2003. As for the idea of the money-makers and the money-givers learning from one another, the only place they ever met was in the executive dining room, which the staff jokingly called "the kitchen." You had foundation people giving away money in space that was costing $35 per square foot. Explain to me how that makes any sense. They should have been in a loft somewhere uptown. They didn't make money, they gave it away. And they didn't have to impress the people coming to see them – those people were coming as supplicants. But when you are a multi-billionaire, you can afford to indulge yourself and the cost of office space is not an issue. Later, after the Vivendi disaster, it became one.

When Saidye Bronfman died in July 1995, Edgar came immediatly from New York, but Charles, who was flying in from Europe, didn't arrive until the following day. By then, Edgar and I had gone to Paperman's to select a casket for her and had arranged for her service to be at Shaar Hashomayim Synagogue rather than at the funeral home. Funeral services at the synagogue were highly unusual, an honour accorded only to the most prominent members of the community. But then Charles arrived and reversed the whole plan. He said his mother would really have wanted the service to be held at the Saidye Bronfman Centre, which was certainly a lovely sentiment but it made it difficult to accommodate all the people we were expecting – the Shaar seats a thousand people, the Saidye about six hundred. So there was an issue about that. Then Charles called me and said, "Look, I'm not trying to cut you out." "No problem," I said. "No," he said, "we're having a big meeting about it, and I want you to be in it." So I was given the job of greeting Jean Chrétien when the prime minister came to the funeral. And that was the first time Charles had ever overtly cut me out.

By then, he was rarely in Montreal anymore except for meetings of the Seagram board or the CRB Foundation, which did a lot of good work in Canada and Israel. The foundation had two vocations. The first was to remind Canadians of the importance of their history, which it did very effectively through the Heritage Project's popular Heritage Minutes vignettes, as well as its history programs and products for schools. Here's a statistic that should give you some idea of how successful the Heritage Minutes were: a poll by the Dominion Institute in 1998 found that only 13 percent of Canadians were aware that the Constitution had been patriated from Westminster in 1982, but 41 percent were able to identify the Halifax Explosion of 1917, an event remote from the experience of most living Canadians but one featured in a Heritage Minute. But in 2000 the Heritage Project merged with other history stakeholders in Histori.ca, which was established in Toronto rather than Montreal. However, he maintained CRB's other vocation, of interesting young Canadians in Israel by helping them spend time there.

And one of the people he managed to attract to Israel was my own son, Jonathan, who had a background in Middle East studies and a grandfather on his mother's side who had been a leader of the Zionist movement at the time of Israel's birth. Charles always had the view that, short of living there, the best commitment Diaspora Jews could make to Israel was to invest in it. Charles may well have been influenced by the speech David Ben-Gurion made at the laying of the cornerstone of the Samuel Bronfman Museum in Jerusalem in 1962, in the presence of Mr Sam, as recorded later by his biographer Michael Marrus. "I want to tell Mr Bronfman," said the Israeli prime minister, "that with all his money – I don't know how much he has, but it's certainly more than I have – he cannot get a real personal share in Israel unless and until one of his children or grandchildren lives permanently in this country."

By the 1990s, Charles, one of Mr Sam's children, was living part time in that country. And my own son was living there full time as CEO of Charles's Israeli holding. From a start-up investment, Super-

Sol had gone on to become the biggest grocery chain in Israel. When Charles sold his share for U.S.$45 million, he and Jonathan invested in Teva Pharmaceutical as well as in a food company and other companies in Israel, holdings that grew to a value of $500 million. They then sold those positions and bought Koor Industries, one of Israel's largest industrial conglomerates. As the *Jerusalem Post* wrote approvingly in a 1999 profile, "Although his ownership of Koor makes him the largest single foreign investor in Israel, billionaire Charles Bronfman's biggest gamble is on the future of the Jewish people." The value of Charles's Israeli investments decreased sharply with the high-tech meltdown of 2000, and the Palestinian *intifada* also badly undercut the value of their portfolio. Like everyone else, the Israeli holding company took a hit, even more so because of the troubles in the region, but hopefully their investments will recover as confidence and stability gradually return.

Jonathan, who had worked on Wall Street after university, had been very happy to leave that rat race and come to work with us at Claridge Inc., and with his interest in Israel, it was a natural fit that he would run Charles's investments there. I wished Jonathan well, but a part of me also wished he had gone out on his own.

"I know this is a great opportunity for you," I told him when he moved to Israel in 1991. "But part of me is also disappointed for you, because I was always a Bronfman employee, and although you have a piece of equity, you are also working for the Bronfmans. There are worse things in life, but I really wish you had found something on your own."

It was true that I had achieved a lofty position, but I was still working for someone. I guess it went back to what my mother had told me all those years ago, when she threatened to sit *shiva* if I went to work for anyone, even the Bronfmans, about how it was better to make 50 cents on your own than a dollar working for someone else.

Yet in the fullness of time, I could only be pleased that Jonathan had an office next to his godfather, Charles Bronfman, in Israel, while I had an office next to my godson, Stephen Bronfman, in Montreal. Stephen is a terrific young man, remarkably unspoiled. He grew up in the Expos' locker room, so he was a natural to become part of a local consortium that tried to save the Expos in 2000, only to be undermined by the senior managing partner, Jeffrey Loria, a carpetbagger from New York. Stevie, as I call him, is also an environmental activist, and he's had his share of fun and profit bankrolling the Rolling Stones' last two tours.

His sister, Ellen, is married to a film producer named Andrew Hauptman, and they have two lovely children, Lila and Zack.

And I can say that Charles has been the best friend of my life. There isn't even a close second. I am a guy without a lot of friends, because in the same way the Bronfmans were wary about people getting close to them and taking advantage, I was a bit paranoid. I had nowhere near their money, but on their behalf, I had a lot of clout.

Besides, Charles is a wonderful guy. As Edgar wrote in *Good Spirits*, "There is a gentleness about him, humour in his eyes, and a sense of goodness when he speaks." Edgar was right about that.

4

Edgar, Minda, and Phyllis

Edgar Bronfman and I were born in the same year, 1929, in the same city, Montreal, though we grew up in rather different circumstances. I was the son of a middle-class dentist and a mother, widowed early, who opened a hat shop to pay the Kolber family bills. Edgar was the scion of the wealthiest and most powerful Jewish family in Montreal. My issue with my father, Moses Kolber, was that he had died so young. Edgar's issue with his father, as he would tell you to this day, was that Sam Bronfman never told him he loved him.

Which may explain Edgar's rebellious and even reckless behaviour in his youth. At some level, he may have been trying to get his father's attention. Sent away to Williams College in Massachusetts in 1946, Edgar at age eighteen casually proposed to a Bennington College girl and cabled his parents in Europe that he was getting married. They quickly put a stop to that. After promising his father he would never ride a motorcycle, he then got into a serious motorcycle accident. "I was out of control," he later wrote in *Good Spirits,* a memoir in which he was brutally honest about everyone in his life, beginning with himself. He re-enrolled as a junior at McGill and graduated with an honours arts degree in 1951.

But he would have missed his graduation ceremony if I hadn't got him there.

In those days they held the convocation ceremony outdoors on McGill's lower campus, except when it rained, and then they moved it to the Montreal Forum, as they did that year. The convocation was called for ten in the morning, and I went up to 15 Belvedere Road, where Mr and Mrs Bronfman were having coffee. But there was no sign of Edgar – he was still in bed, actually sleeping off a night of partying. If he was trying to get his father's attention in that way, he certainly succeeded – the old man was fuming. So I went up to Edgar's bedroom on the third floor and was able to get him up and dressed. He was seriously hungover, and we had to bundle him into the car. At the Forum, the convocation line snaked through the back corridors. I found his faculty, and his place, and stuck him in the line.

That was Edgar, then as always. In some ways he was brilliant, marked by destiny, and in others he was a self-absorbed young man in no apparent hurry to grow up.

Edgar was devastatingly handsome and completely charming. Even if he hadn't been the richest kid in town, the girls would have flocked to him. And did they ever. Edgar didn't have to spend forty dollars, let alone forty million, as his father suggested, to get laid.

Some nights out with Edgar were unforgettable adventures, but what I recall most is Saturday afternoons at the Belvedere house. I would be invited over for brunch with Edgar and Charles. Later, we would sit around the fireplace in the library, playing bridge when we could find a fourth.

It was during this time that I began to do small residential land deals with Edgar and Charles. Meanwhile, after graduating from college, Edgar had gone into the family business as an assistant blender at the Seagram distillery in the Montreal suburb of LaSalle. As Edgar later wrote, Seagram's chief blender, Roy Martin, agreeably undertook his education in the business, and Edgar remained at the LaSalle plant for three years, becoming an excellent taster and blender and learning other aspects of the business, from warehousing inventory in wooden kegs to getting it into bottles on the assembly line. He then took charge of Canadian production and did a one-year stint at head office in the Seagram castle before moving to New York at the end of 1955, by which time he had passed his twenty-sixth birthday and would no longer be eligible for the U.S. military draft. At head office, Edgar had figured out, as his father had before him, "that the real business was not in Montreal, but in New York."

By this time, Edgar had married Ann Loeb, the daughter of the German Jewish American investment banker John Loeb and a granddaughter of a Lehman, as in Lehman Brothers. It doesn't get more establishment in the Jewish world than the gentrified Jews of Wall Street, and Sam Bronfman was so delighted with the merger that he later invited John Loeb onto the Seagram board, where he served for many years. Mr Sam believed in breeding. He used to say, "People spend more time breeding horses than they do breeding people," and he was a huge believer in the breeding of people. The old man was thrilled that Edgar had married a Jewish blueblood, and the breeding began soon enough, with the arrival of Sam in 1953 and Edgar in 1955. In all, they would have five children.

It was always understood that Edgar would be the son to take over the family business. First of all, he was two years older than Charles. And he had a broader education in the business; for example, he'd moved to New York in his mid-twenties and worked there with his father for the last fifteen years of Mr Sam's life. Whereas Charles was always deferential to his father, Edgar did a pretty good job of standing up to him. Charles, in those days, was very happy to remain in Montreal as head of Canadian operations. And if he was unhappy with Edgar's emergence as the heir apparent, he never showed it. Later, when Charles was co-chairman of Seagram, it was always clear that no deals would be made without his approval, and none ever was.

Edgar always treated me very well. It was at his invitation, after his father's death, that I joined the Seagram board in 1971. He may have had particular reasons for asking me, primarily to thwart the wishes of his sister Minda, who thought her husband, Baron Alain de Gunzburg, should assume her father's seat on the board and take his place in the affairs of the Bronfman family. Edgar would have none of it, and he arranged my appointment to the board instead, at the first meeting following their father's death. So that was one more thing I owed to Mr Sam – his own seat on the Seagram board.

Edgar and I were also closely involved in the 1968 purchase of a controlling block of stock in MGM. He became non-executive chairman of the Hollywood studio, and I joined the board. Less than a year later, we lost control of MGM to Kirk Kerkorian, who simply accumulated a larger position than Cemp's 15 percent stake. It was all very friendly, and Kirk even asked Edgar to remain as chairman. Edgar declined with thanks, but I remained on the board for a decade, and we both held on to our MGM shares. They went south for a long time but eventually recovered, and we actually made a nice profit when we finally sold.

Edgar was very good about not interfering in the management of Cemp, Fairview, or, later, Cadillac Fairview. He had great confidence, as Charles did, in what we were doing. Sometimes, they weren't even aware of what we were doing.

By the early 1980s, we were running out of things to develop at Cadillac Fairview, but not running out of money. The revenues from our properties were huge, around $2 million a day or more than $700 million a year, and we were thinking of taking a run at a major conglomerate. So we started accumulating Canadian Pacific Limited, which under Ian Sinclair's leadership had diversified out of its railway origins to become a mammoth management holding with no less than twenty-two operating companies, in everything from ships to hotels, from an airline to trucks, from forestry to coal, not to mention rail. If you bought CP, you were buying the Canadian economy, and with the holding company discount, we were buying it cheap.

Then one day I got a call from Paul Desmarais, whose fondest dream was to control Canadian Pacific. "Leo," he said, "I know you are accumulating Canadian Pacific shares. Will you sell them to me?"

"At what price?" I asked, cutting straight to the chase.

He gave me a price, and I did the rough math in my head and realized that for three months' effort we could make somewhere between twenty and twenty-five million dollars. So I immediately agreed to sell. Not only was it a nice windfall profit, but Paul Desmarais was a nice man to do business with – as good as his word. He and his wife, Jackie, who was often the musical entertainment at her own parties, became good friends of mine. He later joined the Seagram board, and when he went off it, his son André took his seat. The Desmarais sons, Andy and Paul Jr, may be the exception to the rule that children shouldn't go into the family business.

"My son will be at your house tonight at seven o'clock with a written offer," Paul said on this occasion. I called our guys in Toronto and told them we were out of CP. Then I kind of forgot about it.

A few weeks later, I got a call from Edgar in New York. "I hear you had some shares in Canadian Pacific and sold and made a lot of money," he began. "How much did you make?"

"Frankly, Edgar," I replied, "I don't know the exact amount."

"What do you mean, you don't know?"

"It will show up in the next quarterly statement."

"Why didn't you tell me?"

"I didn't think you had any interest," I said. "It's somewhere between twenty and twenty-five million."

"Find out," he said.

So I got the numbers and called him back. "We made $25 million."

"That's fabulous," he said. "But you have to tell me something like that. I need to know."

"Sure," I said, "but why would you need to know?"

"Well, people have heard about it, and it's a windfall, a bit of a coup we pulled off, and I didn't even know about it."

"You know," I conceded. "I hadn't thought of it that way. You may have a point."

And he did. Not in terms of running the company, but when he met people socially, it had to appear that he knew what was going on inside his own family's business.

On the second weekend of August 1975, I was out for dinner with Sandra at Ruby Foo's, when I was informed by the maître d' that Edgar's eldest son, Sam, had been kidnapped. I immediately phoned Charles, who had also just learned of his nephew's abduction. He had already called Execaire, owned by Harry Bronfman's grandson Mitch, where the Seagram planes were maintained, and reserved a jet to take us to New York. We flew out that same night to be with Edgar at his apartment on Fifth Avenue, and we basically remained for the duration of the crisis.

Charles was understandably concerned for the safety of his own son, Stephen, who was away with my son, Jonathan, at summer camp in Vermont. It turned out that the FBI shared our concerns. They had posted agents to patrol the campgrounds and go on canoeing trips with our sons. Both boys were old enough by then to figure out that they were under police protection.

Sam, then twenty-two years old, was abducted on the evening of August 8, after parking his car in the garage of his mother's house in Purchase, New York. As his father later wrote: "He was accosted by an armed man wearing a ski mask, who blindfolded Sam and led him away at gunpoint to a car on the Hutchinson River Parkway, where his accomplice was waiting."

Ever since the kidnapping of Charles Lindbergh's son in the 1930s, wealthy and famous families such as the Bronfmans had lived with a certain dread for the safety of their children, and now it had happened to Edgar. Sam was allowed to phone his father to tell him that he had been kidnapped and that the abductors would be in touch regarding a ransom. The next day, Edgar received a letter from the kidnappers, informing him that his son was buried alive, with only so long to live. Edgar was instructed to go from one drop point to the next in the vicinity of Kennedy Airport and finally to leave a ransom of $2.3 million in the back of a car. Sam was released, badly shaken but otherwise unharmed, and his abductors were shortly captured and convicted of extortion, though not kidnapping. Because Sam's filthy clothes had been sent out to be cleaned, crucial evidence was lost.

Sam eventually married and moved to California, where he became head of Seagram's important wine division, including Sterling Wines and Monterey Vineyards. Later he joined the Seagram board. Like the rest of us, he read in *Fortune* magazine in 1986 that he had been passed over as heir apparent at Seagram in favour of his younger brother, Edgar Jr. As Edgar himself later acknowledged, his naming of Junior as the third generation dauphin in a magazine interview was "a huge mistake," in terms of both family unity and corporate governance.

The decade of the 1970s was not a happy time for Edgar. First, there was Sam Bronfman's death in 1971, leaving Edgar with all those unresolved issues with his father. There's no doubt that Edgar and Charles both suffered from an affection deficit from Mr Sam. Mr Bronfman was not very demonstrative in his love for his children, but I don't know how Edgar could have thought that his father had anything but confidence in his abilities and pride in his achievements. Sam Bronfman's pride in both his sons was apparent in the Seagram history *From Little Acorns*. "Well done, Edgar and Charles," the old man had written. In a way, I may have seen and heard more evidence of Mr Sam's paternal affection for them than they did.

Then Edgar's marriage to Ann Loeb ended later that year, and he married a British woman, Lady Carolyn Townshend, on the rebound, a marriage that quickly ended in a contested annulment that Edgar won. He then met Rita Webb, known as George, whom he married twice. Sam's kidnapping occurred in the middle of all this personal upheaval, which clearly affected Edgar's performance as CEO. In those years, he fell to drinking heavily, and if you wanted a decision from him, it was best to get it before lunch.

But the 1980s were a good decade for Edgar. He did the fabulous DuPont deal in 1981. He took a global leadership role as head of the World Jewish Congress. And two of his sons, Sam and Edgar Jr, were becoming increasingly involved in the family business.

Edgar deserves a lot of credit for masterminding the acquisition of Seagram's 20 percent stake in DuPont in 1981. There was no shortage of good advisers, but it was his deal all the way. He sensed the opportunity and he made it happen. Seagram started out to buy Conoco and ended up with 20 percent of DuPont.

In the Cemp portfolio, from the time I joined, we had some shares in a company called Royalite in the Canadian oil patch, one of the few businesses outside liquor in which Mr Sam was willing to consider an investment. As he said, "If it's good enough for the Rockefellers, it's good enough for me." That was the first Bronfman investment in the oil business, but it was held in the family trust in Canada rather than in an operating company in the United States, where it would have been eligible for the oil depletion allowance. In the mid-1950s, Edgar persuaded his father to establish Frankfort Oil, to be run out of Oklahoma City by a man named Ray Shaffer, who specialized in drilling dry holes. Eventually Edgar replaced Shaffer with Carroll Bennett, an economist who moved the company to Texas, where its growth was steady if unspectaular.

In 1957 Mr Bronfman said to me, "One of the first things I want you to do is go down to New York and have dinner with Mark Millard."

Good advice, for in 1963 Mark Millard brought the Bronfmans a company called Texas Pacific Oil and Coal, and after an initial investment of $65 million in the 1960s, Edgar sold it to Sun Oil Company for $2.3 billion at the top of the market in 1981.

Mark Millard was more than an investment banker and senior partner in John Loeb's Wall Street firm. He was a statesman of the financial services business, a close adviser to the Bronfmans, and a mentor to me. He was, as Edgar wrote, "a brilliant man, he had great vision and clarity of thought, as well as great integrity." An American of Hungarian Jewish origin, he spoke something like six languages, had been married at least three times, and had one of those beautiful New York apartments near Central Park, full of books and paintings. He took me for dinner to the Oak Room at the Plaza. In those days they had cigarette girls, and he called one over after the meal and asked for a pack of Marlboros. She said she didn't have any, but went out to buy him a pack. When she returned, he carefully took out a cigarette and put it in his mouth. I offered him a light. "I don't smoke," he said. He had given up smoking because of a heart attack, but still liked the aroma of the leaf, and it had to be Marlboros.

After Mark got Mr Bronfman and Edgar to buy Texas Pacific, Edgar became a genuine expert on oil and gas. Just as he had learned about

the liquor business, he learned all about the oil business, from acquiring
oil fields, to drilling costs, to the odds of success, from the importance
of proven reserves, to the costs of refining crude. Edgar knew, as he
later put it, that "the earnings of selling oil had to be greater than the
cost of finding it."

Oil is an incredibly capital-intensive business, and the Texas Pacific
guys would keep coming around every year saying they needed $300
million or $500 million for drilling, to the point where Edgar had heard
enough and decided to convene a seminar at his estate in Yorkton
Heights in the summer of 1980. This was after the second oil shock, following the Iranian Revolution of 1979, and in that summer of 1980 oil
prices peaked around $30 a barrel. There were lineups at gas stations
all over America, and that, coupled with the hostage crisis at the U.S.
Embassy in Teheran, created an impression of anguished indecision in
Jimmy Carter's White House, all of which effectively cost him the election to Ronald Reagan in November.

Texas Pacific, a relatively modest investment in the beginning, was
now worth a king's ransom. Edgar's instinct was to sell, and Charles
and I agreed, as did Phil Beekman, the president of Seagram, and
Harold Fieldsteel, the CFO, a man, as Edgar later wrote, of "remarkable
financial instincts." Edgar got me to call Mark Millard, by then an old
friend, and he brokered a fantastic deal with Sun Oil Company. As
Edgar himself graciously noted, "The credit for this coup goes entirely
to Mark Millard, who negotiated the whole deal."

We walked away in early 1981 with an incredible profit of more than
$2 billion, or nearly four times the value of Texas Pacific as it was then
carried on our books. Then the question became, how would we reinvest the proceeds of the sale? Edgar formed an acquisition committee,
and we began to look at potential investments.

The best thing that happened to us then was the deal we didn't
make, the acquisition of St Joseph Lead, which was rich in natural resources, such as gold, copper, and other important commodities. Seagram offered $48 a share for stock then trading in the low 30s, and
luckily for us, as Edgar later observed, we were outbid by the Flour
Corporation. As part of our bid preparation, we had calculated the
price of gold at $500 an ounce, a level it has never achieved in all the
years since.

Then, in the spring of 1981, Jack Gallagher of Dome Petroleum in
Calgary bid on a block of Conoco oil stock. He wanted to swap the
stock back for Conoco's Canadian operations, and he succeeded in this.

But his offering was greatly oversubscribed, which meant that Conoco was widely held and could be easily accumulated.

Once again, it was the brilliant Mark Millard who proposed that even though Seagram had just got out of the oil business, Conoco represented a compelling opportunity to get back in. Edgar was persuaded, and in May 1981 he went with Charles to Conoco's head office in Stamford, Connecticut, and presented a friendly offer to purchase a significant interest in the company, with a five-year standstill provision against accumulating further shares. Seagram would become significant owners but would not seek control. But then DuPont and Mobil got involved. In those days, Mobil was never going to get the U.S. regulator's approval to acquire another oil company, and their outlandish offer of $125 a share was the equivalent of a stink bid in bridge – you know, one heart, six no trump.

It was again Mark Millard, along with Harold Fieldsteel, who saw the opportunity of leveraging up from Conoco to DuPont. "We could trade it in for DuPont stock," Harold said, "and end up with a huge piece of DuPont at wholesale prices." Which was exactly what happened. DuPont offered $97 cash per share for 51 percent of Conoco and DuPont stock for the remaining 49 percent. So, cash or stock. Seagram's offer, for 50 percent of Conoco, was $90 per share, an all-cash deal. Our bet was that the arbitrageurs and others who were accumulating the stock would tender to Seagram for the cash. But Edgar thought we should sweeten the offer by two dollars and asked me to get Charles's agreement.

"Charles," I said to him, "trust me, this is the deal of the century. For us to end up with 20 percent of DuPont is unheard of. Your father would be dancing in the streets."

Charles was a bit doubtful – not that he didn't like the deal, but he didn't know quite enough about it. He called a special meeting of the Seagram board on July 22, 1981, and Edgar flew in to Montreal non-stop from Nice, France, aboard a Seagram G3 jet.

The buffet before the evening meeting included smoked meat sandwiches from Ben's, a deli around the corner from the Seagram castle. Edgar had been going there since he was a kid, and he always visited it whenever he was in Montreal. The Kravitz family, who owned Ben's, treated Edgar like visiting royalty, and smoked meat sandwiches from Ben's were always offered at Seagram board meetings.

Our lead investment bankers, Mark Millard and Felix Rohatyn, of Lazard Frères, took the board through the process of acquiring Conoco and swapping it for DuPont stock.

"Edgar," I said at one point, "why don't you put the question to a vote?"

"Because," he said, as recounted in *Good Spirits,* "I am not sure whether Charles has agreed to a figure."

At which point, again according to Edgar's account, Charles "put up two fingers," as in $92 a share.

We put up a "safety net" requiring that if 50 percent of Conoco stock weren't tendered to us, our offer would become non-binding. That worked against us with investors, and Edgar, acting on pure intuition, dropped the safety net.

Once we had Conoco, we accepted DuPont's offer of stock and ended up with 20 percent of DuPont. It was entirely due to Edgar's instincts – and leadership – that we did it.

Edgar also did marvellous work as president of the World Jewish Congress, and brought renown to an organization that had previously been rather ineffectual and somewhat obscure. Founded by Nahum Goldman in 1936, the WJC was a global federation of Jewish organizations. Goldman had succeeded in recruiting Sam Bronfman as a vice-president at the onset of the Second World War, and in 1971 he got Edgar involved as head of the North American section. Edgar acceded to the presidency in 1979 and asked me to replace him as North American chair. There wasn't really anything for me to do, and gradually I lost interest. But not Edgar, to his great credit. He was on a mission of retribution and restitution.

In the 1980s, he pursued Kurt Waldheim with the zeal of a war crimes prosecutor, engineering the public disgrace of the former United Nations secretary-general when he was president of Austria. In the 1990s, he enlisted Bill Clinton's support in getting the Swiss banks to pay reparations on deposits made by Nazis with money stolen from Jews. Not many people can sign up the president of the United States in their cause. Even fewer could get Bill Clinton and Al D'Amato, the Republican chairman of the Senate Banking Committee and the president's mortal foe, to sign up for the same cause. Edgar managed to do that, with the help of his considerable powers of charm and persuasion, the influence of his office as head of the congress, and above all the wealth and power he represented as chairman of a global business empire, the Seagram Company.

In the days of *glasnost*, he could fly to Moscow on a Seagram jet and lobby Mikhail Gorbachev's closest advisers on allowing Russian Jews to emigrate to Israel and on granting them religious freedoms in the Soviet Union. The Soviet foreign minister, Eduard Shevardnadze, confirmed these stunning reversals in long-standing Soviet restrictions to Edgar months before announcing them at the Vienna meeting of the Committee for Security and Cooperation in Europe (CSCE) in 1988, and Edgar, in turn, personally informed the Israeli prime minister, Yitzhak Shamir. The World Jewish Congress took the lead in bringing new hope to Russian Jews after decades of repression under Communist rule – not to forget the frightful pogroms of the nineteenth century that drove many of our forebears, including Edgar's grandparents and my own, to migrate to Canada and the United States. Edgar had lots of help, as he would be the first to tell you, from the likes of his executive director, Israel Singer. But Edgar provided the leadership, he made the big phone calls, and he opened the important doors.

It was the Kurt Waldheim coup that really put the World Jewish Congress on the map. Long suspected of concealing his war record, the former UN secretary-general had returned to his native Austria to become his country's head of state. In March 1986, as Edgar noted in *The Making of a Jew,* the WJC released U.S. Army and UN documents listing Waldheim as a suspected war criminal – indeed, he was suspected of being a Brownshirt, one of Hitler's notorious Storm Troopers. In July 1986, the UN War Crimes Commission released a secret 1948 file recommending Waldheim be charged as a war criminal for murder and for putting hostages to death. The wartime documents were incriminating enough, but even better, Edgar and the WJC had art – a grainy photograph of a young man in a Nazi uniform, unmistakably Kurt Waldheim. That was the clincher in the court of world opinion. Waldheim was barred from entering the United States, and few, if any, nations agreed to receive an official visit from the Austrian head of state for the remainder of his six-year term, which expired in 1992.

In the 1990s, Edgar also served as chairman of the World Jewish Restitution Organization, whose primary objective was to recover Jewish property and investments that had been stolen from European Jews by the Nazis and later confiscated by the Soviet Communists and their satellite states. At the request of Israeli prime minister Yitzhak Rabin in 1995, Edgar led an international delegation to call on the president of

Switzerland and then meet with the Swiss Bankers' Association to recover Jewish holdings from numbered Swiss accounts.

The Swiss, as Edgar noted, spoke of the sanctity of secret Swiss
accounts and dragged their feet until Edgar got Senator D'Amato,
President Clinton, and First Lady Hillary Rodham Clinton involved in
the file. In the end, the Swiss government contributed the first 100
million Swiss francs to a restitution fund of 7 billion francs for the
surviving families. As Edgar pointed out, not only had the Swiss
banked stolen money and gold in secret accounts, they had also financed the activities of the Third Reich, perhaps even prolonging the
Second World War.

In the 1990s, Edgar also appeared to have found happiness on the
personal front with Jan Aronson, an artist who became his fourth wife.
Edgar had essentially grown up an agnostic Jew, but by the time of his
marriage to Jan in 1994, he had become not only a fervent advocate of
the Israeli and the Jewish cause, but also a highly observant Jew. His
wedding took place at the Orthodox Fifth Avenue Synagogue in New
York, in the presence of no fewer than four rabbis. As someone who has
attended most of Edgar's weddings, I was struck by how far he had
travelled from his unobservant origins in Montreal. Johnny Weinberg,
Seagram's valued investment banker from Goldman Sachs and one of
the assimilated Jews in attendance, told me it was the first time he had
ever been to "a Jewish wedding."

All the stars of Edgar's life appeared then to be perfectly aligned. He
was happily married. Seagram's business was in great shape – the profits from Seagram and the dividends from DuPont would simply go on
forever. And he had taken a global leadership role in the Jewish community. His father would have been very happy for him and extremely
proud of him.

And then Edgar, in a decision that foretold the fall of the Seagram
empire, allowed Junior to sell DuPont and buy MCA in 1995. Efer, as
Junior was called, had been named president and chief operating officer
in 1989, and by 1995 he was CEO as well as president, while Edgar remained as executive chairman and co-chairman of Seagram with
Charles.

Edgar was mesmerized by his son. There is no other way to describe
it. Edgar Jr is a very nice man, very diffident, a good listener, and not a
show-off in any sense of the word. He is anything but stupid. But he
had no business running Seagram, and if he hadn't been named Bronfman, he wouldn't have been. "Buying MCA represented an enormous

opportunity for my son, who was Seagram's CEO," Edgar later wrote in *Good Spirits*. Besides, Edgar added, both he and Junior had come to regard DuPont as "a boring investment."

I guess Barbra Streisand doesn't go to DuPont parties. It's also indisputable that MCA's hard assets, from Universal City to the Universal theme parks, were valuable real estate properties with a certain trademark value. But Junior would not leave well enough alone, and with his $10.4-billion purchase of Polygram, an astounding price for a record label, he took on a disastrous burden of debt that he ultimately tried to unload by selling Seagram itself to Vivendi in 2000. After it all ended so badly, with Vivendi stock sinking from a high of $83 when the merger was announced in June 2000, to an all-time low of $8.90 following the ouster of Jean-Marie Messier as head of Vivendi in the summer of 2002, Edgar Sr admitted that the responsibility lay with him and Edgar Jr. "It's one of those things where the buck stops here," he told journalist Brian Milner in 2003. "There's no place else. We can't look at somebody else and say, 'It was your fault.'"

It might well have been prevented in 1995 if only the board had simply nixed the sale of DuPont and the purchase of MCA.

In retrospect, I should have had an inkling – back in the 1980s – of the direction in which Junior would take the company. There were hints after he had joined Seagram but before we sold off Cadillac Fairview in 1987. On one occasion, Edgar assembled all the Cemp trustees and heirs in Toronto for a tour of the Eaton Centre, one of the jewels in the Cadillac Fairview crown, a shopping mall like no other. And Edgar Jr called at the last moment to say he couldn't make it because he was negotiating a film deal in Hollywood. I should have known.

There was a logical disconnect in Edgar's decision allowing Junior to go ahead with the sale of DuPont and the purchase of MCA. For years, Edgar had been saying that the ultimate achievement of his career had been getting hold of a huge stake in DuPont, one of the world's great companies, for a ridiculously low price. Then he went and sold it because his son wanted to go into the movie business. While the deal was very tax efficient for Seagram, the sale price was cheap, in relative terms – some 13 percent below its market price. Mind boggling.

Doing nothing was clearly not an option for Junior. But if we had done nothing, just think of where Seagram and the Bronfmans would have been today. Seagram would have been debt free, and the family could have bought back a lot of stock, ending up with an even larger position than their 33 percent share in 1995, and the dividends would have flowed to the family in the hundreds of millions of dollars. Forever.

After the MCA deal was done, Edgar wrote knowingly of Mr Sam that if his father had been alive, "he would never have approved." Edgar at least got that part of it right. As for the Vivendi merger, no one would have ever dared to suggest it to Mr Sam, except perhaps over his dead body.

∞

Mindel, always known as Minda, the "m" in Cemp, was the oldest of the Bronfman children, born in 1925, and in some ways the most like her father. She was ambitious, she was able, and she was angry her entire life. She was undoubtedly angry, at least in the subliminal sense, that there was no role for her in the family business. In those days, as she was coming of age at the end of the Second World War, that's how it was. The sons went into the business, the daughters got married, and some-times the sons-in-law were accepted into the business. Her husband wasn't – he wasn't even invited onto the Seagram board, which only in-creased her anger.

She was definitely angry, as was Phyllis, at their father for the way he had structured Cemp Investments when he set it up during the war. The "c" and "e" in Cemp, Charles and Edgar, were each given 30 percent of the holding, which was to pass on to their own children. The "m" and "p," Minda and Phyllis, got only 20 percent each.

It was a permanent bone of contention between the daughters and their father, particularly so for Minda. When she came to Montreal, she was always raising the issue with her father, to the point where Mr Sam, who was pretty good at intimidating people, was himself intimidated by his own daughter. He would call me and ask me to the Belvedere house for dinner on those occasions, and he once said to me, "You know, Leo, I love my daughter dearly, but goddamn it, she drives me crazy." She just wouldn't let go of the 30 percent for the boys and the 20 percent for the girls. She wasn't wrong about it, just obsessed with it. Phyllis agreed that it was fundamentally unfair, but didn't allow it to take over her life or poison her relationship with her father and brothers. Mr Sam would have me over just to have the head of Cemp in the room, so she could take it out on me rather than him. Or he would have me pick him up on a business pretext, just to get him out of the house.

I understood where she was coming from. And I rather admired Minda. She was bright, she was attractive, and she was tough. In today's world, she might well have been an extremely successful businesswoman. But back then, the best she could do was marry well and get away from her father. She did both in 1953, marrying the Baron Alain de Gunzburg, a Harvard MBA and the son of a titled French investment banking family. At the wedding, Mr Sam hosted a reception for two hundred people at the Ritz in Paris.

It was perhaps just a coincidence, though an interesting one, that both Minda and Phyllis married French businessmen and moved to Paris, undoubtedly to be as far out of their father's orbit as possible. And though I never heard Sam Bronfman refer to his first-born as the Baroness, I know he was happy that she had married "up." Given his fascination with breeding, it didn't get much better than the daughter of a whisky baron marrying the son of a real one.

The de Gunzburgs were not investment bankers in the American sense or merchant bankers in the British sense; they owned a small private bank with a few employees. The family title made them out to be like the Rothschilds, but they were small players in the world of Paris banking. That didn't prevent the de Gunzburgs from putting on airs, as only the French can.

When Sandra and I were married in 1957, we went to the south of France on our honeymoon, and then to Rome, Paris, and London. I'd never been to Europe, and I wanted to see the three great European capitals. When we got to Paris, Minda and Alain invited us to dinner. And dinner was announced in a manner that I'd certainly never heard: "Madame la Baronne est servie."

Alain was very arrogant in those days. He made sure I understood, then as later, that he was family and I was just an employee. He once told me I was lucky to have the job because his brothers-in-law had offered it to him. Actually, he had it the wrong way round. As Edgar wrote, Alain "proposed that he be named chief executive of Cemp Investments" – a proposal that was never considered, seriously or otherwise, by either Edgar or Charles.

Between Minda's exasperation over the division of the family trust and Alain's overreaching ambition to be accepted as a full partner by his brothers-in-law, it was inevitable that they would take an aggressive position in managing her money. And they did. At one point in the 1970s, Minda withdrew $30 million in capital allocations from her 20 percent share of Cemp. When I pointed out that this would draw down on her 20 percent principal, she replied that she didn't give a damn, that she and Alain were going to invest it and do deals on their own. I'm not aware of a single deal they did, though they looked at many. Minda was very bright, a graduate of Smith College, with a master's degree from Columbia University, and before marrying Alain she had worked for Lehman Brothers on Wall Street as well as at Time Inc. But that didn't qualify her as a dealmaker. Yet I'll give Alain credit for one deal he brought us – a stake in Club Med, the French vacation resort; when we later sold our position, Cemp made about $20 million on it. And the irony of it was that, given the structure of the trust, Minda's brothers made 50 per cent more on the deal than she did. Minda and Alain had two sons, Jean, a molecular biologist who became director of cancer research at the Curie Institute in Paris, and Charles, who obtained a master's degree from the Kennedy School of Government and managed the family investments in New York, both of them very nice young men.

After Mr Sam's death in 1971, there was a period when Edgar's management of Seagram was rather unfocused, to say the least, and in the mid-1970s Minda came to me to propose a putsch. She wanted me to join her in an effort to oust her own brother as chairman of Seagram. It could have been done. All the family's shares in Seagram were held through Cemp. There were seven members on the board of trustees – the four siblings and three advisers, the two lawyers, Laz Phillips and Phil Vineberg, and me.

She came to Cemp's offices at the CIL Building in Montreal and laid out the plot to oust Edgar, who she said was totally out of control. If the three outside trustees would join her, she would have a majority of four, and Edgar would be out, or at least would be facing a crisis of legitimacy on the Seagram board, having lost the confidence of his own family's trust.

I was stunned by the audacity of her scheme, and worried about the implications for the Bronfman family. As erratic as Edgar was in those days, his ouster would have caused the biggest family crisis imaginable and considerable turmoil for the Seagram brand name in financial markets. I told her, in no uncertain terms, that my answer was no and that I would be very surprised if Laz Phillips and Phil Vineberg, loyal family retainers for decades, would join in a palace coup. She never did anything more about it, and when I informed Edgar, he was clearly hearing about it for the first time, but he never did bother to express his thanks.

In 1984 Minda came to see me to confide terrible personal news. "I am here," she said, "to tell you that I have cancer of the liver." She was dying and she knew it, but she didn't want anyone else in the family circle, least of all her mother, to know about it. She swore me to absolute secrecy.

"Of course, I will respect your wishes," I replied, "but why are you telling me?"

"I am telling two people," she said, "you and Phil Vineberg, and I want you to rearrange my affairs so that when I die, I pay the least amount of taxes possible."

I thought, here is a very wealthy woman, facing death with great courage, and she is talking to me about taxes. But all the Bronfman children were like that, extremely tax oriented. Minda also said that she was still extremely upset that Charles had left Barbara and married Andrea Morrison. She started to cry about that and said, "I can't stand what Charles is doing." She added, with considerable bitterness, "The Bronfmans are monsters, we are all monsters." She didn't mean it, of course. I think she was trying to say that at some level she and her siblings had been prevented from leading normal lives, and now her own was about to end.

Some months later, in 1985, Sandra and I were in the south of France, where we had gone for intensive French lessons at St-Jean-Cap-Ferrat. We weren't there very long when I got a call from Charles saying that his sister had died. I phoned Alain with my condolences and told him we would be arriving the next morning in Paris.

"Please come right to the house," he replied. "Nobody else is invited but family, but I want you here." When we arrived at the de Gunzburg home the next day, Minda was laid out in a white gown on her bed. The coffin left from the house and the funeral cortège went straight to the cemetery, where she was buried in the de Gunzburg family crypt.

In 1986 Alain and his sons gave a generous $10-million endowment to Harvard to rename its Center for European Studies after her. A decade later, they donated another $5 million to the Minda de Gunzburg Center for European Studies. So her name lives on in an important way. The work of the centre was carried on by their friend and family adviser Guido Goldman, a Harvard professor and one of the most erudite figures I've ever met. Guido knew everyone. He once told me of being in the back of a limousine with Henry Kissinger and reminding his illustrious fellow-passenger that he had never criticized him when he was White House national security adviser or secretary of state in the Nixon and Ford administrations. *"Vat,"* Kissinger asked, "was there to criticize?"

∞

Phyllis is the last letter in Cemp, but she is by no means the least of Sam Bronfman's four children. In some ways, she is the most accomplished and independent. In others, she is the most like her father in that she had a clear vision of what she wanted to do and was very headstrong in her pursuit of it. Which also meant that, like her father, she expected things to be done on her terms, and could be extremely difficult to be around. Not to put too fine a point on it, Phyllis was very high maintenance. One of our frequent tasks at Cemp was settling with consultants she would hire, ostensibly for years, but then fire after a few months. At Cemp and later at Claridge Inc., the staff would dive under their desks when they saw her coming. She inherited some of her father's tyrannical traits.

In 1949, aged twenty-two, she married Jean Lambert, a self-described Paris business consultant, whom her brothers suspected of being a fortune hunter, not least because he had previously dated their older sister. Although she divorced in the mid-1950s, she always kept her former husband's name and made her own success as Phyllis Lambert rather than as Phyllis Bronfman.

And succeed she did, first as a maven and later as a doyenne of architecture. With her marriage ending in 1954, Phyllis flew from Paris to New York to challenge her father on a design by Charles Luckman for the proposed Seagram House on Park Avenue. She persuaded him to retain her, at the age of twenty-seven, as architectural consultant on the project. "Don't talk to me again until you've done it, and made your decision," he told her, as Michael Marrus recounted in *Mr Sam.*

Her decision to hire Ludwig Mies van der Rohe resulted in one of the great architectural achievements of modern times, one with the Seagram name on it. Knowing her father well, she recommended "the best," as he would have put it. More than that, she got her father's agreement to her own appointment as project director of the Seagram Building. In effect, she was put in charge of a development that would become a renowned legacy for the two most important men in her life, her father and her architect.

When I flew down to New York to attend the opening of the Seagram Building in 1957, I certainly noticed Mr Sam's great pride in his daughter for her unique role in the building's creation. If she hadn't insisted that he hire Mies, this architectural marvel would never have been built. Phyllis would go on to study architecture under the tutelage of the master and became an architect in her own right.

Five years later, after we had a disagreement with Skidmore, Owings & Merrill over wind shear in the design of the TD Tower in Toronto, I called Phyllis. "Okay, now it's your turn," I said. "It's up to me to hire the architect."

"It has to be Mies," she insisted, as I knew she would.

Apart from allowing us to associate with one of the premier architects of the age, Fairview's partnership with Mies gave us visibility and prestige, not only in Toronto, but across Canada and throughout North America. It was Phyllis who made our introduction to Mies, and Phyllis who deserves all the credit for our hiring him.

When she returned to Montreal from Paris in the 1970s, Phyllis became a heritage activist, campaigning hard to save Old Montreal, the historic area around the city's old port. Jean Drapeau, the legendary mayor of Montreal, took to calling her the Goddess of the Streets. She didn't just talk the talk, she also brought us an important restoration project, Les Cours le Royer, around the corner from Notre Dame Basilica in the heart of Old Montreal. We converted a disused warehouse into a highly sought-after condominium project. The premier of Quebec, René Lévesque, bought one of them.

At meetings of Cemp trustees, she would regularly criticize the Fairview and later Cadillac Fairview buildings and projects, and in the case of Place Montreal Trust in the mid-1980s, she organized the opposition, leading demonstrators with banners and placards in a protest on the project site on McGill College Avenue. What was I supposed to do? One of my principal shareholders was demonstrating against me, though not refusing any of her dividends.

At one point in the early 1970s, she got it in her mind that she wanted to be chief of design at Fairview Corporation.

"I think that is a really dumb idea," I said to Charles.

"Leo, she is our sister," Charles replied, "and we control the company – what can I do?"

He was right, and there was no denying either her talent or her taste.

I was a personal beneficiary of her good taste when she selected a paint-
ing by the renowned Canadian impressionist Marc-Aurèle de Foy
Suzor-Coté as the Bronfman family's gift to me on my fiftieth birthday.
The Suzor-Coté, *Bend in the Gosselin River,* hangs over the fireplace in
my study.

So I called her and she gave me a date when she could be in Toronto at our head office, and I assembled our top people, flying them
in first class from all over North America, the heads of all the divi-
sions, office, retail, and residential. She would be briefed on all our
projects, and the discussion would then focus on how to structure her
role and obtain her input on new buildings and shopping malls.
Everyone came to the meeting, except for one person. Guess who?
Phyllis.

I went to see Charles and blew my stack. "Listen," I said, "it has
taken me fifteen years to get this company to the point where it is now
one of the industry leaders in North America, and your sister is not going to fuck it up. You can decide. If she's in, I'm out. Life is too short
for this."

"I'll have to discuss it with Edgar," Charles said.

"Do what you want," I replied, "but I am not going to continue this
way."

At the next Seagram board meeting in Montreal, Edgar took me aside
and we went upstairs to Mr Sam's former office in the Seagram castle.

"I hear you are being obstinate on the question of Phyllis," Edgar began.

"Edgar, you can call it what you want, I don't think I'm being obstinate," I replied. "Let me ask you a simple question. You run Seagram,
right?

"Of course," he said.

"And how much interference do you brook in the running of Seagram?"

He held up his thumb and forefinger in the shape of a zero.

"That," I said, "is exactly how much interference I am willing to tol-
erate in the running of Fairview. You guys control it, but I have built it
to this position of pre-eminence."

"We will never discuss this with you again," Edgar said. And they
never did.

But there were times when I had to navigate murky waters between
the brothers and the sisters, whose relations were complicated by the
structure of the Cemp trust, as well as by Edgar's impulsive behaviour.

He once sold some Allied Signal stock we had been accumulating, without informing his siblings, or me, for that matter. Minda and Phyllis were understandably angry, and a family feud loomed, as even Edgar knew.

"Tell you what," I said. "I will take the blame and talk my way out of it."

After the Cemp trustees' meeting, Phyllis came to my office and said she needed to have a word with me.

"Not today," I replied, holding up my hand. "I've had you and your family up to here, and if I were you, I wouldn't talk to me today."

∞

Phyllis's greatest achievement – and her unquestioned legacy – is the Canadian Centre for Architecture (CCA), which she built around a railway baron's abandoned mansion in Montreal. Lord Shaughnessy had been the legendary head of the Canadian Pacific Railway, from the turn of the twentieth century through the First World War, and his house on Dorchester Boulevard, later Boulevard René Lévesque, was a historic as well as an architectural landmark. Phyllis bought it, saved it, restored it, and hired the brilliant architect Peter Rose to build the CCA around it, while she served as consulting architect. Rose's work, with its clean lines and generous use of space, evokes the minimalist style of Mies van der Rohe, and from the moment it opened in 1989 to the present day, the CCA has been hailed for its aesthetic beauty and for the importance of the work it houses. There are some 200,000 volumes in its library on the history, theory, and practice of architecture, and another 65,000 prints and architectural drawings in its impressive collection. In an ultimate tribute to the master, Phyllis staged the exhibition *Mies in America* in 2001. It aptly summed up her life's work.

In the calamitous denouement of the Seagram merger with Vivendi, the French conglomerate was forced to liquidate assets, including the cherished art collection Phyllis had curated in the Seagram Building. She likened the entire episode to "a Greek tragedy." But at least she had sold most of her own Vivendi stock well before disaster struck. Phyllis has keener investor instincts than has generally been known. After the swap of Seagram stock for Vivendi shares in June 2000, and very soon after the ninety-day lockup period expired, Phyllis sold most of her Vivendi position quite close to the top. She was acting on the advice of Arnie Ludwick, deputy chairman of Claridge, but it was her call, and she made the right one.

So that in the end, given the reversal of fortune suffered by her brother, Phyllis's original 20 percent share of Seagram in the Cemp trust may well have cashed out for more than Charles's 30 percent. Somehow, I think Minda would have approved.

5

Taking Toronto

The Toronto-Dominion Centre changed the skyline of modern Toronto. The Eaton Centre changed the shopping habits of Torontonians. We built them both, the TD Centre in the 1960s and the Eaton Centre in the 1970s.

At fifty-four storeys, the TD Bank Tower was not only the tallest office building in Canada and the Commonwealth when it was built, it determined the shape of the modern Toronto skyline, with the Big Five bank headquarters all clustered within a few blocks of one another at the south end of Bay Street. The TD Centre, designed by the renowned Mies van der Rohe, became the most prestigious office address in the country. And it made, it absolutely made, the TD into a national bank, where until then it had been regarded as a regional player in Ontario.

In time, the TD Centre would be expanded to five towers, sheathed in black, the largest office complex in Canada, and at 4.3 million square feet, one of the largest in the world. Once the TD had built a modern skyscraper, the other banks had no choice but to follow suit. First Canadian Place, Commerce Court, Royal Bank Plaza, Scotia Plaza, and eventually the Canada Trust Tower at BCE Place, all followed TD's lead.

Every time I fly into Toronto and look down at Mies's black towers, I think, we built that. Forty years after we unveiled our plans for the TD Centre in 1962, *Globe and Mail* columnist and architectural advocate William Thorsell called the completed vision "the best single architectural statement in Toronto" and "a certain national treasure."

As for the Eaton Centre, it was a daring concept for the 1970s. At a time when shopping malls were built in the suburbs, we decided to build one in the heart of downtown Toronto. It became the number one shopping mall in Canada and the number one tourism destination in Toronto. And the thing was, the Eatons didn't even want the family name on it. I had to talk them into it.

Even in the late 1950s, when I first started going there on business, it was apparent to the naked eye that Toronto was Canada's city of the future. The new 401 Expressway across the top of the city and the mushrooming growth of the suburbs made it very clear that Toronto was a city of almost limitless economic promise. We intended to get in on the ground floor of that boom. And we did.

The TD Centre also put Fairview on the map – it made our name, it made our company, and it took us to the big leagues of real estate development. Until then, we were just a regional player doing shopping centres and land deals out of Montreal. The TD Centre was the flagship for what became the largest real estate company in Canada and eventually one of the most important in North America. Wherever I travelled, to Houston, Dallas, Los Angeles, Washington, Philadelphia, or Atlanta – wherever we built – people said, "You built the TD Centre." Yes, we did.

In 1961 the TD's head office was a small six-storey building at the corner of King and Bay. This was known as the MINT corner after the four bank buildings there – the Montreal, the Imperial Bank of Commerce, the Nova Scotia, and the Toronto-Dominion. We had done a couple of small Toronto real estate deals with Wood Gundy, the investment banking firm, and one of their executives, Martin Wills, suggested we pitch the TD on building a new headquarters for them.

It was pretty audacious when you think of it. Who was I but a thirty-two-year-old kid? I had never financed or built anything remotely on the scale of what was being discussed. But I knew instinctively that if we could pull it off, it would make Fairview a player to reckon with. We had already been thinking big when we pitched for Montreal's Place Ville Marie, but lost out to Bill Zeckendorf, the New York developer who took a chance on a young architect named I.M. Pei, whose cruciform building became the signature of modern Montreal. If we couldn't build the tallest office tower in Montreal, we would try for the tallest in Toronto.

So Wills set up a meeting with the TD's chairman and CEO, Allen Lambert, whom I'd never met. He belonged to that generation of Canadian bankers who worked their way up from teller to the top. Allen had joined the bank as a clerk in Yellowknife in the Northwest Territories and ended up in the big corner suite in Toronto. He was one of those rare bankers who had both vision and a strong sense of community. The TD's fabulous collection of Inuit art, housed in the lobby of one of the bank towers, was Allen's personal project. After his 1978 retirement, he would keep an office in the TD Centre until his death in 2002 at the age of ninety-one. He was a remarkable banker, and a remarkable man, as I was to learn. He would also become a valued partner and a good friend.

I felt that I needed a bit of support for this meeting and asked Charles to come with me. After all, he was a Bronfman, and at least Allen Lambert would have heard of him. Martin Wills also came along, as did Noah Torno, a Toronto member of the Seagram board and a friend of Mr Sam's who had introduced us to Wood Gundy in the first place. Noah was always extremely helpful in opening doors for me in Toronto. Allen received us at the TD's head office, which looked as if it dated from the founding of either the Toronto or the Dominion bank, long before they merged in 1955.

We didn't come to the meeting with a plan, just an idea, and Allen had a very open mind. He thought that accumulating enough land to build a skyscraper would be a problem, and he was right about that. But he agreed to take the idea to his board, and they agreed to explore it further. Lambert liked the notion of being partners with the Bronfmans, which was pretty gutsy on his part. To some members of the Toronto financial establishment, the Bronfmans were still regarded as bootleggers. And the Bronfmans weren't Toronto money; they were Montreal money, and Jewish money at that. And finally, a prominent member of Allen's board was Cliff Hatch, the head of Hiram Walker, makers of Canadian Club, one of Seagram's biggest competitors. But Cliff approved the idea, and even said the Bronfmans were fine people, worthy competitors with whom the bank could do business. So the TD Bank came in with Fairview as fifty-fifty partners in the development.

We then began accumulating property as quietly as we could through A.E. LePage and Company, which Brian Magee and Gordon Gray built from nothing to a major player in the buying and selling of real estate. A lot of the land we were putting together was on Wellington Street, one block south of King, between Bay and York streets. The properties there were just small manufacturing buildings for things like the needle trade, and it wasn't hard to acquire them, provided the word didn't get out. As a matter of fact, I even bought part of the land assembly while I was in New York on other business. I simply walked into an office off the street, saw this guy, told him we were Fairview, that we wanted to build some stores on his vacant lot in Toronto, and he sold it to me on the spot. For the most part, we were paying about $15 a square foot, but in the end, to close on the last pieces of the puzzle, we went as high as $120 a square foot. And to give you an idea of how land prices went crazy in Toronto, the Reichmanns later paid $2,000 a square foot at the corner of York and Bay.

Now that we had the land assembly, the next question was the choice of an architect. Allen very much wanted to hire Gordon Bunshaft of the New York firm of Skidmore, Owings & Merrill, which had just built the new headquarters of the Chase Manhattan Bank, completed in 1961. If he was good enough for David Rockefeller, he was good enough for Allen Lambert. Besides, the bank's name was going to be on the building, so Fairview did not have a problem with TD choosing the architect. Allen and I went to New York, where David Rockefeller had arranged a tour of his new building for us. The Chase was monumental, sixty storeys of steel and concrete and 1.8 million square feet of space.

We hired Bunshaft and he came up with a design for a seventy-five-storey building encompassing the entire site. But it was to be built of exposed concrete, and that proved to be a problem with the engineers, who argued that you couldn't have a building of exposed concrete in a climate like Toronto's, where the temperature differential in winter could be as much as ninety degrees Fahrenheit between inside and outside. The building could literally shrink at the top, causing people at their desks to slide over to the windows. We had this conversation with Bunshaft and he said we were crazy.

We then brought in a guy named Paul Weidlinger, who was head of structural engineering at MIT, for another opinion, and he confirmed that we were right. Bunshaft was away from his New York office, over Christmas as I recall, and we wired him saying he had to do it in steel and make the tower smaller. He replied saying it would be the way it was, or nothing, so we send word back saying it's nothing.

Then I spoke to Phyllis Lambert. She, of course, strongly urged us to hire Mies van der Rohe. Allen Lambert and I flew to Chicago, met him, and hired him. And that is how Mies van der Rohe came to be the architect of the Toronto-Dominion Centre. What a coup it proved to be for us, and what an architectural legacy it has proven to be for Toronto.

When we first started clearing the site in 1963, Mies took Allen and me down there. There was nothing but rubble, but he walked us through it, explaining the concept of the plaza and why the building had to be set back from the street.

"Does it have to be that far back?" I asked.

"If you could visualize a fifty-four-storey building," he said, "you are going to end up telling me that I didn't push it back far enough."

And of course, when you look at the proportions of the site and Mies's realized vision, he was absolutely right. It is the plaza in front of the TD Centre, with all the open space, that makes the building. And the beautifully kept grounds on the plaza have been enhanced by Joe Fafard's wonderful bronze sculptures of cows lying in the grass.

Mies van der Rohe was a prince, very reserved and, like his buildings, very understated. But he had the gift of communicating very clearly what he was doing. One day, the head of the construction team called me up and said he'd just got an estimate for Mies's concept for the plaza and sidewalks, which he wanted done all in granite. It was going to cost a fortune. So I flew up to Toronto and met with Mies.

"You know," I ventured, "this is rather expensive."

"*Vell,* young man," Mies said in that soft German accent of his, "you are the boss and you call the shots. You have a choice. You can do it cheap or you can do it right."

What do you say to something like that? He was right, of course. And we did it right.

Mies once said to me that when you look at the great buildings of the world, you realize that if they didn't have the space around them that they did, you wouldn't even notice them. The Piazza San Marco in Venice, as Mies said, isn't as renowned for the cathedral as it is for the space. It's the same with St Peter's in Rome or the Louvre in Paris. It's certainly the case with the Seagram Building and the TD Centre.

When you look at the buildings from the later period of Mies's career, from the Seagram Building, to the TD Centre, to Westmount Square in Montreal, they all look the same. Each is a variation of the previous design; all of them are black towers set back from the street, with vast marble halls and huge windows in the lobbies. In the case of the Seagram Building, Seagram was actually sued unsuccessfully by the City of New York for extra taxes because of all the undeveloped office space on the site. While the TD Centre isn't as famous as the Seagram Building, it is a much grander design on a much larger scale, and it had a huge influence on the neighbourhood. And Westmount Square in Montreal, built while the TD Tower was underway, is a straight three-tower knockoff of the TD Centre, right down to the two-storey bank branch in the middle of the plaza.

It was also Mies's idea to put a retail shopping mall underneath the TD Tower. It was the first underground shopping mall in Toronto, and like the Place Ville Marie underground in Montreal, it sparked the building of an extensive underground passageway and retail network. Today in Toronto, you can take the Path, as it is called, from the Royal York Hotel and Royal Bank Plaza through the TD Centre to First Canadian Place and Scotia Plaza, all the way up to the Sheraton Centre Hotel across from Toronto City Hall.

From a construction point of view, two things made Mies's design easy to build and easy to lease. It was to be made of steel rather than concrete, and they made steel just down the road in Hamilton. And Mies's rectangular design for the building made it easier to rent because the space was squared off away from the elevators. We were breaking new ground in leasing in downtown Toronto, where space then went for $5 a square foot. We were asking $6, adding a premium for the prestige of the tallest building in the country.

Once we started building, it became evident that we had better get financing for it. Allen had turned the job over to one of his vice-presidents, who suggested a financing formula of 40 percent equity and 60 percent debt. I didn't know whether to laugh or cry. Come to that, as our lawyer Phil Vineberg pointed out, Cemp had more equity than the bank.

"Allen," I said, "that is not the way you do real estate deals. Real estate is a business of leverage, and I would suggest 10 percent equity and 90 percent debt."

Dick Thomson, later CEO of the TD but then Allen's assistant, suggested zero percent equity and 100 percent debt. I said that wouldn't look good either, that we had to put something in, and we settled on 5 percent equity and 95 percent debt. The TD and Fairview, as fifty-fifty partners, each put $6 million down on the deal. And when we sold our half share of the TD Centre in the liquidation of Cadillac Fairview in 1987, it was worth $500 million.

The only disagreement Allen Lambert and I had was over the elevators. When you have a bank as a partner, every one of its clients in the construction business wants in on the project. In the case of the TD Tower, the TD banked Westinghouse, a company that had a big elevator division in the United States but that couldn't crack the Canadian market, since Otis had the whole thing locked up in a virtual monopoly.

"We have to give the elevators to Westinghouse," Allen said.

"In that case," I replied, "we can't go to bid because if we go to bid and Westinghouse is not the low bidder, they are not going to get it."

I said we would see what provisions we had in our budget that might allow us to select Westinghouse without a bid process. But after thinking about it, Allen came back and said, "You're right, let's go to bid."

And Otis, not being fools, wanted to keep Westinghouse out of the Canadian market. One of the problems with being an elevator company in Canada is that the real money is in servicing, and without a critical mass of elevators to service, you can't make any money. Otis, determined to get the contract, cut their bid and may even have taken a loss on it, as the bid came in below our budget. The deal, though, was no small thing. There were thirty-seven elevators in a single building. And

Otis, now a division of United Technologies, is the leading elevator company in Canada to this day. Certainly, Westinghouse never had much luck cracking Otis's stranglehold on the market.

When all was said and done, the TD Tower cost $23 a square foot to build, excluding architectural fees and soft costs. The costs of buildings like that eventually went up to nearly $250 a square foot, which was about what it cost us to build Place Montreal Trust twenty years later in the mid-1980s.

Now that we had a building, we had to rent it. And though TD had its name on it, the bank initially took only 10 percent of the space. In a building of 1.3 million square feet, they took only 125,000 square feet, leaving us with nearly 1.2 million square feet to rent. No one had ever put that much space on the Toronto market all at once, and I had many sleepless nights over it. We were playing with big money without knowing how it would come out. But eventually we got it all rented, and then we built a second tower, a third, and a fourth. Mies van der Rohe died in August 1969, just as the second phase of the project was nearing completion.

The TD Tower itself was officially opened by Princess Alexandra in Canada's centennial year of 1967, and Ontario premier John Robarts hosted the famous Confederation of Tomorrow Conference on the top floor. The top-floor restaurant and bar, Stop 54, became a magnet for Toronto's financial community and for tourists.

I will always remember attending the topping-off ceremony with Charles Bronfman and Phil Givens, the flamboyant mayor of Toronto. We were standing on a plywood platform in the wind, fifty-four floors and 730 feet above the ground. I was never so scared in my life. Later, Phil Givens introduced me to Prince Philip during a royal visit to Toronto. "This is Leo Kolber," Givens told the prince, "he has the biggest erection in Toronto." Well, that was certainly one way of putting it.

Allen Lambert would later tell me many times that he could trace the remarkable growth of the TD Bank to the opening of the TD Centre. The tower gave the bank unique visibility, conveying bigness, wealth, and power. And we made sure that the integrity of the design wasn't compromised by putting a television tower on top. Ted Rogers, who was in the cable business even then, had approached Allen Lambert when we were building the first tower; he wanted to put a television transmission tower on it, like the one that was later built on top of Tower One of the World Trade Center in New York. Allen was quite taken with the idea, especially because Ted was going to pay us a lot of money.

"We can't do that, Allen," I said.

"What do you mean?" he asked.

"We would be taking a brilliantly designed building and putting a stick on top. It would stick out like a sore thumb."

Allen turned Ted down. Allen Lambert was a man of great taste, great discernment, and great class.

⊚

I later found out that when I turned forty in 1969, Charles phoned Allen and suggested the Bronfmans would be very pleased if I were appointed to the TD board of directors. Allen's reply was that at forty, I was still considered a bit young. Two years later, in 1971, I was named to the TD board, where I happily served for the next twenty-eight years, including a stint as chairman of the human resources committee. If you went back to the time I joined the board, you wouldn't find a VP of HR because no such post existed, but by the time I chaired the HR committee in the 1990s, the head of HR, Urban Joseph, was an executive VP, one of the top officers of the bank. We worked very well together, and it fell to me to advise Dick Thomson, who by 1998 had been chairman for twenty years, that it was really time for him to step down and make way for his designated successor, Charlie Baillie.

It was a very interesting learning experience for me, especially in the 1970s, getting to know what a great business banking can be. I remember saying that to Allen once, and he asked what I meant.

"I lend you a hundred dollars in a deposit," I said, "and you pay me practically no interest, then you turn around and lend it to someone at 6 percent interest, and that is all profit, minus your expenses, many of which you pass through to customers in service charges."

Allen and I developed a great partnership between the bank and Fairview and then Cadillac Fairview. In the early 1970s when the Bank of Montreal's Len Walker backed out of a deal to take a one-third interest in Pacific Centre when we were building it in Vancouver, I called Allen up and told him the story.

"Count me in for a third," he said. "It's a done deal." That's the kind of guy Allen was. His word was his bond.

Canadian banking owes a great deal to Allen Lambert, and so does the city of Toronto. In a tribute to Allen at his death in 2002, Bill Thorsell, in his *Globe* column, described the TD Centre as "the tallest building in a city just awakening to its new possibilities." Allen certainly personified the civic spirit of a Toronto that was becoming a world city, and the TD Centre was the architectural statement that defined the essence of a great city coming of age.

⌒

You wouldn't be able to build the TD Centre today. You wouldn't be able to build the Eaton Centre, either. You wouldn't be able to get the land for either one. We were very fortunate to secure the land for the TD Centre, an entire city block bounded by King and Wellington, from Bay to York streets. It was before the boom. It began the boom.

A few blocks uptown, Eaton's had been quietly accumulating land for years in the space between Queen and Dundas streets. They had been talking about developing it on and off for a decade by the time they came to see us at Fairview in 1970. But even then, they didn't have the entire parcel of land, and A.E. LePage and Fairview eventually accumulated more, about twenty additional properties. Once again, we were very fortunate to assemble most of a city block downtown.

We were about the fourth developer that Eaton's talked to. Brian Magee came to see me on the company's behalf at my house in Montreal, and we talked about the project late into the night.

"I'm willing to entertain the idea," I said, "but there are certain conditions without which I wouldn't touch this thing with a ten-foot pole. The first thing is that we will not touch the Old City Hall. We will build around it. I am not putting a bulldozer to the Old City Hall. I don't want to see the name Bronfman or Fairview associated with demolishing a heritage building."

I also told Brian we wouldn't demolish the old Salvation Army headquarters next to the Old City Hall, for the same reason.

"That's the easy part of my conditions," I said. "Now for the hard part. Eaton's has to close both the Queen and College Street stores and build a new store at the corner of Yonge and Dundas." Eaton's would have to commit to being an anchor tenant at the north end of the mall, while we would have Simpsons connected to the south end on the Queen Street side. It would work just as it did in the suburbs – the two anchors would magnetize the retail traffic in between them.

The Eaton family didn't have a problem with preserving the Old City Hall – they didn't want bad press any more than the Bronfmans did. But getting them to close two stores, including the Queen Street store right on the site of the proposed mall, threatened to be a deal breaker at first. Eaton's Queen Street store was a dump, "held together by paint and prayer," as John Craig Eaton, one of four brothers who had taken over the family business, put it in the *Toronto Star.*

I had one more condition. We would build two office towers over the mall, and Eaton's would have to locate its head office in one of them.

I had to admit it was asking a lot. But Eaton's finally relented, and in 1972 we began construction. Fairview had 60 percent ownership of the project, Eaton's had 20 percent, and Allen Lambert brought the TD Bank in for the final 20 percent. These were the same three partners that had built the Pacific Centre in Vancouver, which included a big Eaton's and the splendid Four Seasons Hotel.

It would be another five years before the Eaton Centre began to open in phases in 1977, and two more years before it was completed in 1979. First we built the galleria between the two future anchor tenants, with Eaton's and Simpsons as the final pieces of the puzzle at the north and south ends. The galleria was, and is, something to behold – at 866 feet it is nearly as long as three American football fields. In all, there was 1.6 million square feet, 1 million square feet for Eaton's flagship store and another 600,000 square feet in the galleria, with space for three hundred retail stores. And it was all under a vaulted glass atrium that soared more than 125 feet above the three levels of the mall.

The evident model for the huge solarium was the Victor Emmanuel Galleries in Milan. The architect, Eberhard Zeidler, was later quoted in Rod McQueen's book, *The Eatons,* comparing himself to a shipbuilder: "I build the ship, someone else sails it away." As always, Syd Bregman was our lead architect, and he brought in Zeidler as his partner on the project. It was the most imaginative architectural design for a mall I had ever seen. It was also extremely daring for a time when malls were built almost exclusively in the suburbs. Ray Wolfe, CEO of Oshawa Wholesale and a good friend, called me when he heard about it.

"You are making a terrible mistake," he said. "People will never come downtown."

"Ray," I replied, "people live downtown." There were dozens of high rises within easy walking distance, and the Toronto subway would run right underneath the centre.

In effect, if you build it, people will come. We built it, and did they ever come. The Eaton Centre was a spectacular success from day one. When we sold in 1987, the average sales were $750 per square foot, at the time the highest revenues per square foot in the world.

And to think I had to talk the Eatons into having their name on it. As the first phase approached completion, it still didn't have a name. I went to see Fred Eaton and proposed we call it the Eaton Centre. Cadillac Fairview was the majority owner, so I could have called it the Bronf-man Centre or the Fairview Centre, but the Eaton name had unique cachet and resonance in Toronto, and it made eminent sense to call it the Eaton Centre.

Fred was adamantly opposed, and I was shocked. "What if someone goes into another store and receives bad service?" he asked. "They will blame it on the Eatons."

"That may be true," I allowed. "On the other hand, this place is go-ing to be advertised in the papers, on radio and television, seven days a week. Every merchant in the mall is going to be advertising the Eaton Centre. Think of all that free publicity for Eaton's. I strongly suggest we call it the Eaton Centre."

Fred was still doubtful.

"Look," I insisted, "go talk to Allen Lambert and ask him what call-ing it the Toronto-Dominion Centre has done for him."

Freddie Eaton had no concept of the windfall of free publicity – worth tens of millions of dollars – he would be missing out on. The Eatons absolutely had to be talked into it. But I insisted because Eaton's was such a big brand name in Toronto – it isn't now, but it was then. Today, I could have sold naming rights to the place.

There is the story of the name of the building that got away. When Bill Zeckendorf was building Place Ville Marie in Montreal, he wanted to name the whole thing after the lead tenant, the Royal Bank of Can-ada. But Jimmy Muir, the bank's CEO at the time, was evidently con-cerned that Zeckendorf would use the bank's cachet to lure other tenants, and he demurred. So it became known as PVM instead, even though the bank's name was over the entrance to the building.

Earle McLaughlin, who succeeded Muir on his death in 1962, tried everything to re-brand the building with the bank's name. I ran into him once on a plane to Montreal from New York. He was sitting in one seat and had a maquette of the cruciform building in the other, and he ex-plained to me that he had spent the day with branding and signage con-sultants in Manhattan, trying to figure out some way to get PVM known as the Royal Bank Building instead. Technically, it is the Royal Bank Building at 1 Place Ville Marie. But if you were to get into a cab in Montreal and say, "Take me to the Royal Bank Building," the driver wouldn't have the faintest idea what you were talking about, although he might take you to the old Royal Bank Building on the rue St-Jacques. Place Ville Marie, that's different, everyone knows it.

Even the bad publicity about the Eaton Centre turned out to be good publicity. Michael Snow had created these sculptures of sixty Canada

Geese hanging from the glass ceiling of the galleria, "looking," as Rod McQueen later wrote, "as if they were about to come in for a landing." *Flight Stop* was the name of it. As part of the Christmas season in 1982, someone got the bright idea of tying red ribbons around their necks. Snow, who was very offended, sued us, and as I was informed by our lawyers, he had a very good case that we were demeaning his work. He hired the prominent Toronto litigation lawyer Julian Porter and the case was heard in the Supreme Court of Ontario.

There was no way I was going to settle. I wanted the publicity. Every television camera crew in Toronto came to the mall to shoot the story. People came by the thousands just to stare at the geese with the red ribbons. It went to court, where Porter argued hilariously, as Rod McQueen wrote: "I'm in no doubt that on Halloween there will be jack-o-lanterns hanging from all the geese and green ribbons on March 17." I loved every moment of it.

By the way, there was no equity in the Eaton Centre. Neither the Eatons, the TD Bank, nor Fairview ever put up a penny. It was financed 100 percent. When we sold Cadillac Fairview in 1987, the Eaton Centre was worth $600 million, and our 60 percent interest cashed out at $360 million. Which was a pretty good return on no investment. And for our $6-million investment in the TD Centre, we sold our half for $500 million. So for $6-million invested in those two Toronto landmarks alone, Cadillac Fairview walked away in 1987 with a profit of $854 million. Not bad. Not bad at all.

6

From Cemp to Cadillac Fairview

In the beginning, there were just the two of us, my secretary, Marion MacIlwain, and me, in an office in the Mount Royal Hotel. Every now and then, an accountant named Nat Gesser, who kept the books for my mother's hat shop across the street, would come in and write up a quarterly statement in longhand. We didn't even have Cemp's name on the door, and it wasn't yet called Cemp Investments, but Cemp Holdings, the trust established by Sam Bronfman in the name of his four children, Charles, Edgar, Minda, and Phyllis. The trust consisted almost entirely of Seagram stock.

When I was brought in as managing director in 1957, my job was to grow the net worth without putting up the Seagram shares as collateral. My first thought was real estate. My maternal grandfather had been a building contractor, and as a kid I used to spend summers hanging around his apartment building sites. Just out of law school in 1952, I had built five homes in the Town of Mount Royal, and since then I'd done some land deals with Charles and Edgar. So it was natural that I would look to real estate to make my first foray.

I had heard of this American concept called shopping centres. Though I had never even seen one, somehow I had the good fortune to latch on to the idea. In those days, shopping centres were not enclosed or air conditioned, they were outdoors and typically L-shaped around a parking lot. And they were always in the suburbs. We bought some land in the north end of Toronto and built our first mall, Parkway Plaza. Then, at the end of 1958, we bought seventeen properties from Principal Investments through Loblaws. Next we established Fairview Corporation as an operating subsidiary of Cemp and built another outdoor mall in suburban Scarborough, called Cedarbrae. It was a long strip shopping centre, but it needed a department store as an anchor tenant.

I went to see Eaton's, and one of the Eatons in charge of real estate basically blew me off, saying the space was too small for them even to consider. After all, they were Eaton's. So I literally walked across the street to the headquarters of Simpson's and, with no appointment, asked to see the president, Edgar Burton. I introduced myself as the representative of the Bronfmans, and to my surprise, they showed me right in to see him. I showed him the sketches for Cedarbrae and explained that we had space for a 100,000-square-foot department store right in the middle of the mall. He immediately took to the proposition, and called in his three top guys, including his brother, Allan, and told them Simpson's was doing my deal. The others didn't think it was a very good idea, but he overruled them and told them to get it done.

"I'm thrilled with your decision," I told him, "but why did you go against your guys?"

"Because," he said, "I can build a store at a very low cost, and all I have to do for my advertising is say, also at Cedarbrae." In those days, Simpson's took out full-page ads in the Toronto papers nearly every day, so they would be getting free advertising for Cedarbrae. It made a killing from day one.

That was the beginning of one of Fairview's two most important partnerships, the other being with Allen Lambert at the TD Bank. Edgar Burton and Allen Lambert had three things in common – they were visionaries, they had no trace of anti-Semitism, and they always worked on a handshake.

It was Edgar Burton who brought us Fairview Pointe Claire, the first of our big regional malls and the first enclosed one. It opened in 1964. Edgar was one of the first Canadian executives to have a private plane, an old DC-3 done up in style. One day when he was flying to the Maritimes, he gave a lift to Howard Webster, who owned things like the Windsor Hotel, Morgan Trust, and the *Globe and Mail*. Howard mentioned that he owned the corner of St John's Road and Metropolitan Boulevard in Pointe Claire, and Edgar knew right away that it was the best location for a mall on the West Island of Montreal.

Edgar called me up and said he had a handshake with Howard to buy the hundred-acre property. It was 40 cents a square foot, $1.6 million for the whole thing. He wanted to go in fifty-fifty with us, but also said he would get Eaton's to come in as the other anchor tenant in the deal. It was an offer made in heaven. Without an anchor, you don't have a shopping centre. Without two anchors, you don't have a regional. Edgar was not only bringing us the deal, he was delivering Canada's two premier department stores.

So Edgar flew in from Toronto, and I walked from my office to the Windsor Hotel, where we were to meet Howard for the closing. Howard had the head of Morgan Trust there, who said that regrettably they couldn't close the deal because the tax bill for Mr Webster would be much too high.

"Howard," Edgar said, "we shook hands on this deal." And Howard Webster, being very much a gentleman of the old school, took that very seriously.

"Why don't we recess?" I suggested. And I walked down the corridor with Edgar.

"Listen," I said, "if his problem is taxes, I can solve it."

"How will you do that?" Edgar asked.

"Instead of selling it to us, let him rent the land to us. So he gets a big fat income every year without having to worry about taxes. But we have to have an option to buy within twenty years."

We went back into the room and presented my plan to Howard and the guy from Morgan Trust, who was a retired colonel from the Canadian army.

"That is a brilliant solution," the colonel said. "It fits us perfectly, but we won't lease for twenty years without an escalation clause for inflation."

"Colonel," I said, "we were more than happy to pay you cash today, and we shouldn't be penalized for the fact that you can't sell. We have a deal, and you should honour it."

At which point Howard Webster spoke up. "The young man is right," he said, "do the deal."

And we did. We leased the land at 2.4 cents a foot for twenty years and built our first enclosed shopping centre for all of $7 million. Twenty years later, when we expanded Fairview to add a second level, we refinanced it and cashed out our original fifty-fifty positions, by then worth $25 million each for Simpsons-Sears and Cadillac Fairview, on an investment of half a million each. The rest of it had been financed.

The only problem was that I had no idea of how to do a lease with a department store without getting killed on the deal. Anchor tenants have unique space in malls, and their leases also tend to be uniquely advantageous to them. I said to Edgar that we would build his store, but he should design it. "You can do it in gold leaf or aluminum," I said, "that's up to you. You send me the construction bills every month, I will pay them, and your rent will be a net, net, net deal." In other words, Simpson's would pay the taxes, the air conditioning and heating, and the maintenance. "Your rent will be whatever our cost of long-term financing is, plus 2 percent, so we can make a margin." Edgar agreed, and we managed not to get fleeced by our department store anchor tenant, as was the case in so many U.S. malls.

∞

About two years later, just as we were completing Fairview Pointe Claire, Edgar Burton called to say he had his eye on another prime property in Ville d'Anjou, at the intersection of Metropolitan Boulevard and Autoroute 25 in the east end of Montreal.

I called Charles. "We are already making a killing in Pointe Claire," I said, "but we have got to do this one."

Charles and I had already discussed a vision where we would build regionals in the four quadrants of Montreal – the east end, the South Shore, Laval to the north, and Fairview on the West Island. And now Edgar was bringing us the second piece of the puzzle. This one became les Galeries d'Anjou, and we even got the municipality to rename the street adjacent to it Boulevard Galeries d'Anjou, which meant we got the mall's name on the expressway exit sign. Talk about free advertising. We later persuaded many other cities and towns across Canada to do the same for our malls in their jurisdiction.

It was Sam Steinberg, the grocery king, who brought us the third piece, Carrefour Laval, just across the back river in the sprawling new bedroom community of Laval, north of Montreal. He was the other Mr Sam, and earlier he had come to see me about Fairview. "I want to do business with youse guys," he said. That's the way he talked – "youse guys."

I gave Steinberg's an exclusive at Fairview, and Sam was very happy about it. "But in return," I said, "you've got to build the best goddamned supermarket in your chain." A couple of years later, I got a call from one of our people at Fairview in Toronto. He was hearing complaints from customers that Steinberg's was offering shoppers better prices in their satellite stores around Fairview.

"Sam," I said, "this is not nice. I give you an exclusive and you are not servicing my customers the way you do in your satellite stores. This is not right. And it's bad for my traffic."

Steinberg said it was his guys, not him.

"So, you are not the boss anymore?" I asked.

"Of course, I'm the boss."

"So change it."

"I can't."

"Sam, remember what you are telling me. Don't come and ask me for an exclusive again, because it ain't going to happen."

We were then building Galeries d'Anjou. I called the president of Dominion Stores in Toronto. "I am putting in two supermarkets in Galeries d'Anjou," I said. "Do you want to be in one of them?" He jumped at it. So we put in Steinberg's and Dominion, and when Sam found out, he went into a fury. He sent someone to see me to complain about it. "Tell him not to start up with me," I said. "I have got to protect myself."

Steinberg's had a real estate division called Ivanhoe, which later turned out to be the crown jewel of the company when it was sold at the end of the 1980s. Groceries are groceries, a low-margin business. Real estate is land, and as Mark Twain once observed, they ain't making any more. Michel Gaucher, a shipping executive who knew nothing about groceries, bought Steinberg's but later lost the company to Provigo, which in turn sold it to Loblaws. That was the deal Steinberg's had wanted to make in the first place, but Premier Robert Bourassa had stepped in and blocked it, because groceries were somehow deemed to be part of Quebec's *patrimoine*. While it was okay for Paul Desmarais to sell his Quebec forestry company, Consolidated Bathurst, to Stone Container of Chicago, it was not politically permissible for a Quebec grocery chain to be sold to an Ontario company. Bourassa persuaded Gaucher to buy the supermarkets, while the Caisse de Dépôt et Placement du Québec, the public pension fund, scooped up the real estate.

Anyhow, Sam Steinberg asked me to come see him at his office. We had to do business again.

"We have all this land in Laval," he began, explaining the location at the juncture of the Laurentian Autoroute and the new Autoroute 440. "I want to build a regional shopping centre, and I want to be your partner. Because you know how to do it, and we don't."

"Okay," I said, "let's agree on the price of the land, and I will come back in two weeks with my guys and give you a schematic. I will give you sketches, and I will give you some ideas on how it can be financed, and we will be fifty-fifty in it."

So we agreed that the price would be 40 cents a square foot and shook hands on it.

Two weeks later, I was back at Sam's office with my people, who had worked flat out on the presentation, from the sketches down to the financials. They even had a list of prospective tenants and a projected opening day. We went through the full presentation, and at the end Sam said, "Everything is fine except one thing."

"What's that?" I asked.

"The price is not 40 cents," he said. "It is 60 cents."

"Sam, we shook hands on 40 cents."

"I know," he replied. "I changed my mind."

"I don't do business with people who renege," I fumed. "If I can't trust your word, the hell with you."

I told my guys to pick up all our paper, and we walked out. When I got back to my office at the CIL Building, Steinberg's son-in-law, Leo Goldfarb, was on the phone.

"Leo," he said, "the old man has gone absolutely berserk."

"That's nothing," I said. "I am off the ceiling."

"I have to tell him something," Goldfarb said. "Can't you give me something to tell him?"

"Sure," I said. "But you have to give him the message just as I give it to you. Tell him I said to go fuck himself."

Two hours later, Goldfarb phoned again and we were back to 40 cents. And we built Carrefour Laval with Steinberg's and later Promenades St Bruno on the South Shore, completing our vision of building regional malls in each of Montreal's four quadrants. I used to say that if you built a first-class regional, which I defined as a million square feet or more, on the day you opened, it was worth $50 million more than what it cost to build. The four super-regionals in Montreal, each over a million square feet, were proof of that. To this day, they are the best malls in their areas, because they were the best built, in the best locations, with the best tenants.

In 1968, after we finished Galeries d'Anjou, Sam and Saidye Bronfman decided that they wanted to see it. So they climbed into the back of their big Cadillac on a Saturday afternoon and had their driver take them there. When I went to see Mr Sam the following Monday, he was going on about the place, which he called "Anjo" because he couldn't pronounce Anjou. "I couldn't believe my eyes," the old man said. "I never saw so many people shopping in my entire life. It was so packed I could barely walk." He was positively beaming. By then, he had overcome his initial reluctance about our real estate dealings and was taking a great deal of pride in what we were doing. It had become important to him that his sons had successfully branched out into another business.

There was a period of about twenty years, at Fairview and later at Cadillac Fairview, when most of the big mall projects were offered to us first. We built them all around the fast-growing suburbs of Toronto, from Don Mills Centre, to the Hillcrest Centre in Richmond Hill, to the Erin Mills Town Plaza in Mississauga. We built Polo Park and Portage Place in Winnipeg. We built Market Mall and Golden East Crossing in Calgary. We built in smaller centres, such as Owen Sound, Ontario, where we built the 250,000-square-foot Heritage Place, a lot of space for a town that size.

And in the early to mid-1970s, we built Pacific Centre in Vancouver, right downtown at the corner of Granville and Georgia, featuring a Toronto Dominion Bank tower as well as a renowned Four Seasons Hotel built over 1.3 million square feet of retail space. How did we get Four Seasons to come into a thirty-storey hotel over a mall? I picked up the phone and called Isadore Sharpe, and he said yes. He was building a reputation for being the best. And we already had ours for building the best.

Bill Rathie, the mayor of Vancouver, had called me and asked me to come out to discuss an important project that was pending there. So I flew out with my wife and of course fell in love with Vancouver, as everyone does. It may be the most beautiful city in the world. Mayor Rathie explained to me that the city was expropriating all this downtown land for a big commercial redevelopment, and he wanted Fairview to bid on it with other leading developers.

"Mr Mayor," I said, "we do not bid competitively."

He looked at me in complete surprise. "It is," he said, "going to be one of the great projects in Canada. How can you not compete for it?"

"Well, we happen to believe we are better than the rest of the developers, and it's not worth our time to spend millions of dollars preparing a bid to get beat out by 3 cents."

He saw my point, though I had to admit he had one, too. As a mayor, he could hardly not go to bid on a project of that importance.

"What do you suggest?" he asked.

"I think the fairest way to do it is to form a committee of councillors, visit malls, shopping centres, and banks across the country, and try to get a consensus as to who is the best developer in Canada, and invite that developer to sit down and negotiate the deal. I'll take my chances on that."

So he did, and that is how we got Pacific Centre. Then, right after his election, the next mayor of Vancouver, Tom Campbell, who had campaigned against us getting the nod in that way, flew to Montreal to see me.

"We want you to go ahead with the deal," he informed me.

"You surprise me," I said. "You have been fighting it all the way."

"Well, when I was in opposition, it made a good deal of sense to oppose it," he explained. "Now that I'm mayor, it makes just as much sense to support it."

So we built it, and to this day it remains one of the premier properties on the West Coast of Canada.

❧

Of course, the biggest development Fairview ever built was the TD Centre, by far the most valuable property in our portfolio, valued at $1 billion when we sold in 1987. That was absolutely at the top of the market – prices have never come back to those levels since. The rents we were getting per square foot when we sold were more than the building cost per square foot. Think of that as a concept – we were getting our money out every year, an annual return of more than 100 percent on our cost.

Following the success of the TD Centre, we did a number of other projects with Allen Lambert, nothing of landmark status but very solid properties nonetheless. Allen called me once and said he wanted to open a big branch at the corner of Bay and Bloor in Toronto and put an office building over it. But he didn't want to own the building, he just wanted the branch on the ground floor. He wanted us to build it, about 300,000 square feet. Not a big building, but not a small one either. Neil Wood, then our executive vice-president and chief operating officer in Toronto, expressed strong reservations about putting up a building without a lead tenant. But we got lucky – no sooner had we announced it than Ontario Hydro rented the entire building for fifteen years. It was a slam dunk.

In 1968 we joined with Cadillac Corporation to buy Canadian Equity and Development Limited, a company once owned by E.P. Taylor, the brewing magnate who also raced horses out of Winfield Farms – his thoroughbreds included the great Northern Dancer. We bought 80,000 acres outside Toronto in an area known as Erin Mills and essentially went on to build Mississauga. It was the biggest residential land deal ever in Canada.

Cadillac built homes. Fairview built shopping centres. It seemed like a good fit. We were supposed to have third partner, Marathon Realty, the real estate division of Canadian Pacific Limited, which originally came in for one-third of the deal. Ian Sinclair was building a huge conglomerate at CPL, but they had a very dense holding company culture, and we could never get answers and approvals out of them. Finally, I called Ian and said, "In the real estate business, you are sometimes called upon to make quick decisions. Your company doesn't seem to lend itself to that process." He graciously agreed to bow out, Cadillac and Fairview each took half, and we made a fortune on the Erin Mills development.

That was Fairview's first residential play, and it led to our eventual merger with Cadillac in June 1974. Once again, it seemed like a good fit. They were in residential real estate, we were in retail. They had industrial parks, we had office buildings. The merged company, Cadillac Fairview, would cover the waterfront in real estate. Eph Diamond, Joe Berman, and Jack Daniels – the Cadillac guys – were all extremely able and bright people. They were also real characters. They had named the company Cadillac in 1953 for no other reason than one of the partners drove one.

The Cadillac residential division came in very handy during the recession of 1981–82, the steepest economic downturn in half a century. We were carrying a ton of debt, losing a lot of tenants, and our stock price plummeted to about $5 a share. We had 10,000 apartment units in the Cadillac Fairview portfolio, which we sold in 1982 for $320 million, getting rid of most of our debt. While it might be an overstatement to say the apartment sale saved the company, it certainly restored the financial health of CF and allowed our share price to recover. By the time we sold at $35 a share, it had increased by a factor of seven in only five years.

The Cadillac guys had also started a cable company in the Toronto area, regarding it as something of a hobby rather than as an asset. When they built subdivisions, they would install cable TV and very generously turn the profits from the cable unit over to charity. Eventually, we sold it and remained a purely real estate player. Had we kept it, Ted Rogers would probably have bought it from us for a lot more than we got then.

The history of Fairview and Cadillac Fairview is more than a real estate story. It is the story of a world-competitive Canadian company. One of the reasons we merged Fairview with Cadillac in 1974 was to leverage the scale of the company in terms of our expertise and liquidity, and to move aggressively into the U.S. market. Basically, we were running out of things to build in Canada, a country of fewer than 25 million people in the mid-1970s and only 30 million by the turn of the new century. The entire Canadian market is smaller than the population of California. You could become a huge developer just doing things in California. In Canada, you couldn't. You had to go someplace else.

One of the things I learned from Mr Bronfman was that a home market like Canada was a good place to develop your products and sharpen your competitive skills. He spent most of his time in New York because that's where the market was. That gave me the motivation and mentality to think in those terms.

Because we had a reputation for building the best, we also attracted the best people in the real estate business. Outstanding young talent competed to join our firm. We paid them well and allowed them to do their jobs. When Neil Wood became president and COO of Fairview, I hardly ever bothered him about the design or details of a mall or office building. That was his job. My job as CEO was to bring the strategic vision and to have a good sense of the numbers. Later on at Cadillac Fairview, the corporation became more structured. As we grew, we created an executive committee that looked at every deal before going ahead. In the earlier days, Edgar Burton, Allen Lambert, and I had done deals as big as Pacific Centre on the phone or with a handshake. After the merger with Cadillac, Bernie Ghert, who had been with us at Cemp and then at Fairview as CFO, joined Cadillac Fairview as our CFO and gave us many years of exceptional service, going out as president and CEO when we sold.

In the late 1970s and the early 1980s, we began to move into the United States in a big way, building one of the largest real estate companies in North America. We organized the company into three business units: shopping centres headquartered in Toronto, urban development based in Dallas and Toronto, and industrial parks, located in Los Angeles. We had great people working for us – the best. Jim Bullock, the president of Cadillac Fairview Shopping Centres, presided over a vigorous period of growth in both Canada and the U.S. He developed nearly a dozen new malls in addition to the forty-two shopping centres we already owned, to give us nearly 30 million square feet in our system.

In Dallas, even as we were preparing to sell in 1987, Mike Prentiss as president of Cadillac Fairview Urban Development brought in seven new office towers and more than 5.3 million square feet of new space, in addition to the thirty-six buildings and 25 million square feet of office space we already owned in that division. In Atlanta, which was growing in the 1970s and 1980s the way Toronto had in the 1950s and 1960s, we built three huge regionals and two skyscrapers, the fifty-storey IBM Building and the first phase of Atlantic Center, a four-tower office complex that would eventually come in at 2.5 million square feet. In Dallas we built the sixty-storey Momentum Place, 2.2 million square feet that seemed to be a statement of the town's swagger at a time when *Dallas* was television's hit series and the Cowboys were known as "America's Team." In Washington we built a 1-million-square-foot building at 1001 Pennsylvania Avenue, on America's Main Street, as they called it, midway between the White House and the Capitol. We built towers on Wilshire Boulevard in Los Angeles and the massive 220-acre Fairview Park in suburban Fairfax County, Virginia, and everywhere we built, we built well.

Martin Seaton did an outstanding job running Cadillac Fairview Industrial Development. Again, even as we sold, he was developing nineteen new industrial parks and another 1.4 million square feet, in addition to the seventy-seven industrial parks and 6.2 million square feet already in our system. Developers don't get rich building industrial parks, and they certainly don't get architectural recognition for them. By their very nature, they are hidden from public view. But they generate good cash flow, and we made very good money on ours.

Our last project, Place Montreal Trust, was fittingly both an office tower and a mall, thirty storeys of granite and 615,000 square feet of office space over nearly 260,000 square feet of retail. It was completed in 1988, just after we sold. Many years later, I learned that René Viziau, who with his wife, Micheline, lives at and looks after my Mont-Gabriel home, had worked as a construction worker on the top ten floors of Place Montreal Trust. Also many years later, Stephen Bronfman and I led a group of local investors in a successful bid to buy it back for about 40 percent of what it had cost us to build it.

Just as in Hollywood there is always a script that directors and actors wish they had done, there is in the real estate business always a deal you wish had been yours. In my case, the deal that got away was the Irvine Ranch, 100,000 acres owned by the Irvine family in Irvine, California. While I was out there having a look at the land by helicopter and so on, I called my friend Mickey Rudin, whom I had met through Frank Sinatra. Mickey was Frank's lawyer, but he acted for lots of other people. He knew Joan Irvine, and set up a meeting between us at his office. She personally controlled about one-fifth of the property, so if I could get her on board, we had a good chance of getting it. We had bid it up to $280 million, and I put another $50 million on the table. Anyhow, we thought we had won the bid, but then Al Taubman, later the Sotheby's executive who went to jail, got involved with his own syndicate. He came to Toronto to see Eph Diamond and me and offered to go fifty-fifty. "Only if we can build the shopping centres," Eph said.

"What do you care what they build on it?" I asked. "Let's do it just for the land. It's one of the best land holdings I've ever seen."

Anyway, Eph voted on giving it a pass. Taubman and several other partners bought the Irvine Ranch for something like $370 million, and they made billions on the deal. That is the one that got away. And it kind of illustrates the problems of partnerships. If we had just been Fairview, rather than Cadillac Fairview, we would have done it.

And among the very stupid things I've done personally was to turn down an invitation to join the Augusta National Golf Club, where I believe I might have been the first Jewish member. With all the regionals and office towers we were building in Atlanta in the 1980s, I was spending a fair amount of time there. I became a good friend of Scott Hudgins, who was the local partner in our Atlanta projects. He was a prominent member of Augusta National and offered to put me up for membership. "I'll never use it," I said, declining with thanks. Of the many things I've regretted in my life, that is near the top of the list. Later Johnny Weinberg of Goldman Sachs and Sandy Weill of Citibank became the first Jews admitted to membership at Augusta. And imagine the vicarious thrill I would have felt as a Canadian in April 2003, when Mike Weir became the first Canadian, and the first lefty, ever to win the Masters.

In 1985 we noticed that Paul and Albert Reichmann of Olympia & York had been accumulating stock in Cadillac Fairview, enough that they had to declare their position as required by the Ontario Securities Commission. They actually acquired 15 percent of our company on the open market and became our second-largest shareholder. Naturally, we wondered whether they were planning to mount a hostile takeover bid. So I went to see Paul at O&Y's offices in First Canadian Place.

"Welcome to Cadillac Fairview," I began. "But tell me, why are you doing this? We have 40 percent of the stock through Cemp. Our partners have more. You are not going to get control."

"We have come to the conclusion that there is only so much real estate that Albert and I can do," Paul explained. "It is not a business that you can teach your children, either they have it or they don't, and we are not sure that ours do. So we're going to buy a lot of stock in your company." He gave me two reasons. One, he loved Cadillac Fairview's assets, and he was right about that – they were the best assets in North America. And two, he liked the way Bernie Ghert and I did things. "And we count on you and Bernie," he said. He wasn't even asking for seats on our board. I couldn't have been more relieved.

"Thank you very much," I said. "I appreciate your confidence and your investment."

Later, when we decided to sell, I went to see Paul again to give him an opportunity to bid on Cadillac Fairview. He made noises and a couple of manoeuvres, but I knew he would never give me our price, and he even admitted as much. Paul's reputation was that his word was his bond, and maybe it was. But whenever I shook hands with him on something, I would go back to my office and there would be a hand-delivered letter from his lawyer, telling me what he really meant, which would be not quite what I had thought he meant. Haggling over pennies per square foot has always made me crazy.

In *The Reichmanns,* the brilliant history of that family's meteoric rise and precipitous fall, Anthony Bianco wrote that I had negotiated an agreement with Paul pledging his participation in CF's sale to a third party, as long as the price was within reason. "The next day," Bianco wrote, "the board of Cadillac Fairview was meeting when a letter arrived from Reichmann altering the terms as Kolber understood them." There was no such thing as a done deal with Paul.

After we closed the sale of Cadillac Fairview in November 1987, Sandra and I took one of our frequent trips to London, where we always stayed in an apartment at 47 Park Street near the American Embassy in Grosvenor Square. Every morning, we would go for a long walk in central London, past Claridge's, Bond Street, and through to Hyde Park. And who did we bump into one morning but Paul Reichmann. He stayed at Claridge's whenever he was in London on the Canary Wharf project, which broke ground that very month of November 1987. He was a highly observant Orthodox Jew, and his idea of a walking outfit was a black suit, black tie, a yarmulke, and a pair of Reeboks. He was quite a sight to behold.

He stopped and greeted us, in his formal, courtly manner. "Good morning, Mrs Kolber," he said, nodding to Sandra. "How are you, Leo?"

We got to chatting and he asked where we were staying.

"47 Park Street," I said.

"What a coincidence," he said. "We used to have our office there. But we've arranged for our own building. By the way, have you ever seen our model of Canary Wharf?"

"No, Paul, I haven't" I said.

"It would my pleasure," he said, "if you would come to my office. We have an entire floor with a scale model. I want you, as one of the world's leading experts in real estate, to see it."

I said we would be delighted, and sure enough, he arranged for us to visit him the next day. O&Y had a beautiful eight-storey building on Greater George Street near the houses of Parliament at Westminster, and we were shown to Paul's gorgeous seventh-floor office. He offered us coffee before taking us up to the top floor by private elevator.

The model of Canary Wharf was stunning, a 10,000-square-foot maquette with moving trains and everything else. Paul, beaming with pride, walked us through the whole thing. It was going to be the biggest office project in the world, two-dozen office buildings when finally complete, vast retail and residential areas all around it, huge public squares, and lots of green space. At the heart of Canary Wharf would be a trio of neo-classical office towers designed by Cesar Pelli, with the tallest one, at fifty storeys, rising two hundred feet higher than anything ever built in London.

The vision was breathtaking. But there were problems with the realization of it. He was asking the financial services sector to relocate from The City, where it was happy, to the Docklands of East London, where there was no London Underground service and no assurance that Margaret Thatcher's government would agree to build the necessary tube spur. I can't imagine breaking ground on such an immense project without having a signed, sealed, and guaranteed agreement from the government that it would build the subway extension to get people there. There was also intense opposition from the British architectural establishment, including Prince Charles, then waging war on modern architecture. And the prospective tenants were mostly foreign-based firms like American Express, who in spite of Mrs Thatcher's Big Bang in 1986, opening British financial services to the world, were still regarded as interlopers in the close-knit circle of The City. Financing Canary Wharf was going to be one problem, filling it was going to be another.

"What do you think?" Reichmann finally asked.

"Paul," I replied, "I don't know nearly as much as you do about it, and I understand that because you are so off-location you have to create your own critical mass. You can't build just one building, you have to build twelve, because nobody wants to be there by themselves. It's not accessible by car, so you need rapid public transportation, which I don't know if you have yet. Aren't you a little bit worried about putting that much space on the market all at once?" I could see it was going to be a game of cutthroat on the rents.

"You are absolutely right," he said. "The concept is perfect, but I may be as much as ten years out in my timing. Still, we have the resources to see it through."

He didn't, as it turned out. When the real estate boom went bust in the early 1990s, O&Y got taken down, and Paul lost Canary Wharf to the banks in 1992. "In five short years," Anthony Bianco wrote, "the Reichmanns had squandered $10 billion, a reversal of fortune of a magnitude unequalled in modern history." Paul later managed to put together a consortium to buy it back in 1995, but only after losing his company over it. It must be said, though, that today Canary Wharf is a success. Paul was right – he was ten years out in his timing. In the end, his vision was vindicated. The World Financial Center, which he built in the shadow of the World Trade Center in Lower Manhattan, is another of Paul's unquestioned achievements.

Bob Campeau was another guy I knew in the commercial real estate business. He got his start building homes and government office buildings in Ottawa and went on to greater things such his signature building, Scotia Plaza, in Toronto, sixty-eight storeys of magnificent pink granite, a splendid office tower. He also went broke, first buying Allied and later Federated Stores for $11 billion in 1988, all of it with borrowed money, just before the real estate market crashed. I guess his wife liked shopping at Bloomingdale's, and Bob thought it would be nice if they owned it. In 1987 he sold his house atop Mont-Gabriel to me at the bargain basement price of $750,000. It was supposed to be a turn-key deal, but when Sandra and I arrived for our first weekend there, it turned out Bob had taken many of the paintings and most of the Quebec pine furniture. He later told me his wife wanted them.

∞

In 1986 the Bronfmans decided to sell Cadillac Fairview. Their reasons were never clear to me, since they made the decision at a meeting to which I was not invited. What I got was a phone call from our lawyer Bobby Vineberg, Phil's son. "The family," he informed me, "has made a decision to sell Cadillac Fairview." I was stunned. Not only did they not consult me, but neither Charles nor Edgar even bothered to call me. I was really pissed off. Why, I wondered, would they ever want to sell these gold-plated assets? But after thinking about it for a day or so, I talked to Sandra about it. "You know," I told her, "I have been stupid. If we can get the price I think we can get, this is a golden opportunity for me as a small shareholder to get a premium price with the other shareholders, and I will go on and do something else."

The stock was trading at $18 when the family decided to sell, and we got almost twice that when we closed the sale thirteen months later in November 1987. Charles and Edgar had the good sense to put me in charge of the sale, because, as chairman, I knew more about the company than anyone else. The first thing our president, Bernie Ghert, and I did was interview three investment banking firms, Salomon Brothers, Morgan Stanley, and Goldman Sachs. At Goldman, Johnny Weinberg was a valued adviser to Edgar Bronfman and later a member of the Sea-gram board. He had called Charles and Edgar and said he badly wanted to do the deal. Charles and Edgar then called me.

"Do you fellas want to be in charge or do you want me to be in charge of this?" I asked testily, perhaps still a bit sensitive from having been cut out of the decision to sell. "Maybe Goldman Sachs is the best, but I want to be the one to make that call. I want to see if they have the horses to do this. I'm not saying they're not a great firm – they are. But this is a particular kind of deal. It is real estate."

Then I called Weinberg. "Johnny," I said, "if you want this deal, you are going about it the wrong way. Don't call Edgar and Charles, call me. I am the guy in charge."

But when we went to see him for his presentation, Goldman Sachs blew us away. He had a team led by Ken Brodie and a woman named Robin Il-gin, and they proved to be in a class by themselves. Goldman won the presentation hands down. We also took on board a Canadian investment bank, McLeod Young Weir, but that was just window dressing. They eventually got a fee of nearly $10 million for doing practically nothing.

One day in the middle of all this, in the spring of 1987, I got a call from Ken Brodie at my Toronto office, asking if I could fly down to New York for dinner. So I agreed, and without so much as my passport or a change of clothes, grabbed a company plane. Ken took me to dinner with a guy named Neil Bluhm of JMB Realty Corporation from Chicago. They were one of the biggest real estate syndication and development companies in the world. I had wanted people to be clawing after CF, and Bluhm did. He put together nearly forty pension funds and institutional investors, mostly in the States, and offered an all-cash deal of Can$2.6 billion.

Then the stock market crashed. On October 19, 1987, the Dow fell more than 500 points, losing nearly 23 percent of its value in a single day. Ken Brodie called me at home.

"What do you think?" he asked.

"I think it's the best thing that could happen to our deal," I said.

"I agree," he said, "but tell me a bit of your thinking."

"First thing tomorrow morning," I said, "all kinds of *Fortune* 500 CEOs are going to be calling their pension guys in. They're going to look at the guy in charge of equities and say, 'You big *putz*, look what happened yesterday.' And a little guy at the back of the room is going to pipe up and say, 'Sir, I'm in charge of real estate equities, and they went up yesterday.' And the CEOs will all say, 'Aha, let's put more money in real estate.'"

And the next day, the California Pension Fund, which was already committed to $150 million, came in for another $50 million.

When all was said and done, the Bronfmans' share of the proceeds from the sale was $1.2 billion. The other shareholders, including me, all did very well. If you had bought 1,000 shares of Cadillac Fairview at the IPO price of $14.75 in 1974, you would have had 3,000 shares at $35.00 when the deal closed in November 1987.

I had nearly 3 million shares worth close to $100 million, but I wanted something more – recognition for thirty years of good work, of building a world-class company from nothing, and for doing the deal at the end. I went to Charles and asked for a 1 percent commission of $12 million, a very modest fee for putting together a deal like that. The money would be paid not to me, but to my foundation. Charles immediately agreed, as did Edgar, though he never did anything about it. Minda's family refused my request, and Phyllis, who had previously sold her shares of Cadillac Fairview, was not involved in the sale of the company. Charles, embarrassed that his siblings could be so cheap, put up $6 million himself. I gave $1 million to Bernie Ghert, who deserved it, and the rest to the Sandra and Leo Kolber Foundation. And then we all went home.

Years later, in March 2000, the Ontario Teachers' Pension Fund bought back most of the Canadian properties from JMB Realty, including the TD Centre, Eaton Centre, and Pacific Centre as well as the four land-mark regionals in Montreal. They also carried on the name of Cadillac Fairview. So what we built so well in one century endures in another.

7

Family

In the summer of 1956, when I was on a modest retainer with the Bronfmans to do land deals for them, Mr Sam asked me to go down to Daytona Beach in Florida, where he and several partners owned a fabulous stretch of about five miles of what would later become one of the most famous beaches in the world. For reasons that were unclear to me then, the old man wanted to sell, and my role was to find a buyer.

I went down to meet with prospective buyers, and a man named Sam Sair, from Winnipeg, also came along. It took a while to find enough buyers for five miles of beachfront, and we spent several evenings together in a Florida heat wave. We got to talking and Sam said that he and his wife had just visited Israel, where they met this young woman named Sandra Maizel from Montreal who was working there as a translator.

"Do you know her?" Sam asked.

"No, I don't." I had never heard the name.

"You really have to call her up and take her out," Sam said. "She is fantastic, brilliant, beautiful, speaks three languages."

When I got back to Montreal, I told my mother I had heard about this girl.

"What?" she said. "I thought you had taken out every single girl in Montreal, and here's one you haven't even heard of."

I looked her up, not in the phone book, but in the book of donations put out by Combined Jewish Appeal. Her father had given a few hundred dollars the previous year, which was pretty good for a man of his modest means. Then I made a cold call to her, explained that Sam Sair had spoken very highly of her after meeting her in Israel, and asked her out. She said yes, and while the rest isn't exactly history, she would become my lover, companion, and partner for forty-four years.

The Maizels were an interesting family, Zionists who had lived in Palestine before it was Israel. Sandra's father, Haim Maizel, a Polish Jew, was a graduate engineer from the Sorbonne in Paris, where his sisters had also attended university. Emigrating to Palestine before the First World War, he served in the Middle East with the Jewish Brigade of the Ottoman Army, which did not turn out to be the winning side. After spending some time as a guest of the British government, he emigrated to Canada via New York, where for a time he had a small electrical store.

In Montreal, he ended up working in his wife's family dress business, named Stella Dress after her. The Kornbluths had a very successful business, but for Haim, it was a long way from his engineering profession and even further away from working towards the building of a Jewish state. He hated every moment of it, and it showed. He was a very unhappy man, both a failed socialist and a failed capitalist. For her part, Stella tried to emulate Haim's academic bent by taking correspondence courses from the Hebrew University in Jerusalem. But Haim was not easy to live with; in addition to being unhappy, he was not in good health, suffering from ulcers most of his life. And as a result, Stella was not a very happy woman. The Maizels lived on the second floor of a modest triplex between Ducharme and Van Horne avenues, in Outremont.

Sandra was intrigued that I actually got on well with her father. He was a bit of an intellectual snob, the sort of person who looked down on people interested in money because he had none himself. And I, a young lawyer doing real estate deals for the Bronfmans, was certainly interested in money. Besides, I've never thought that intellectual and commercial interests were mutually exclusive. On the contrary, it is success in business that enables endowments of universities and the arts. In any event, Sandra and I had a courtship that was on-again, off-again. I would take her out to the wine cellar at Ruby Foo's and once even asked her sister Norah to join us. Norah ended up marrying Sam Freedman, who became dean of medicine at McGill and later vice-principal academic.

Sandra was in another league from anyone I had ever dated, very worldly and very smart. I'm not sure whether I pursued her because I was in love with her or because she was such a challenge – perhaps it was a bit of both. Whatever, after months of my asking her to marry me, she finally gave in and said yes, and I went to see her father to ask for her hand. He was delighted and warmly welcomed me to the Maizel family.

In September 1957, we were married in one of those Sunday-afternoon Jewish weddings at the Ritz-Carlton in Montreal. Charles and Edgar Bronfman were among my ushers, my brother Sam was best man, and my mother walked down the aisle with me. Haim Maizel paid for the wedding, but my mother chipped in and paid for the orchestra. Even at that, it was a stretch for the Maizels. Sandra had to pay for her own wedding dress, something she never forgot.

For our honeymoon, we went to Europe, which Sandra knew well but to which I had never been. We first went to the south of France, and then she showed me around Rome, Paris, and London. And so began her handling of my cultural education, which she would do for our lifetime together. By the time we got back, she was pregnant with our daughter. The first two bills I received in our marriage were for a diaphragm that didn't work and a pregnancy test that did.

Back in Montreal, we had no place to live, so we moved into the Mount Royal Hotel – where I had my Cemp office – while we looked for an apartment. We found one, furnished, for $200 a month in a building called the Park Ridge near the top of The Boulevard. Before long, we found a rental duplex on Lacombe Avenue in Côte-des-Neiges, so we were moving back into our old neighbourhood. It was right behind the Côte-des-Neiges armoury, so there were no neighbours over the back fence, and it was very private. Both the upstairs and downstairs were available – the owner was going to move into one or the other – and I said I would take the downstairs if I could get exclusive use of the back lawn.

"No problem," he said. "I have a country house, I don't need the back lawn, but it will be $250 a month instead of $225."

"You got a deal," I replied.

Now we had a house but no furniture. In those days, Eaton's would deliver furniture right from their College Street store in Toronto. Sandra went there, spent $10,000, and a week later a van rolled up and we had a fully furnished house.

Four years later, when Jonathan came along, we bought a beautiful house on Lexington Avenue near the summit of Westmount. Real estate was cheap then, even at the top of the hill – we got the house for $120,000 and put another $40,000 into it. I didn't want to carry a mortgage, so I borrowed the money from Cemp interest free, which in those days was legal.

I can't say it was a great marriage in the beginning. We had to make the adjustments all young couples do as they learn to share their lives. For a time, we went to a psychiatrist in separate sessions to try to iron out our differences. Sandra had a lot of things bottled up inside her, including some very creative impulses.

She found a way of expressing herself by writing poetry. Her first book of poems, *Bitter Sweet Lemons and Love,* published by McClelland and Stewart in 1967, received a good critical reception and actually sold over 2,500 copies, a bestseller for a volume of poetry in Canada. Edgar Andrew Collard, the distinguished editor of the Montreal *Gazette,* wrote that Sandra's poetry was "a triumph" and "a continual revelation of the richness, the variety, the unexpectedness, and the range of reality." In 1969 M&S published a second book of her poems, *All There Is of Love,* which also sold more than 2,500 copies.

But there was clearly something absent or missing in her own life, for in 1971 she became involved with another man, an Israeli she had met at a reception. I found out about it, as you always do, and was totally devastated. We eventually split up, and I bought a house a couple of blocks away on Summit Circle, where I live to this day. It was then a California house, with all the living space on one floor and a couple of bedrooms for the children. It was a spectacular place, all light and glass, designed by Fred Lebensold, the architect of Place des Arts in Montreal and the National Arts Centre in Ottawa. My son, Jonathan, remembers it as being like "the house on the cliff in *North by Northwest,* without the cliff, big glass windows all around."

I remember that as my bachelor summer, hanging around with Mordecai Richler, and he picked my brain about the Bronfmans, particularly Mr Sam, who died in July of that year. At the end of July, Sandra called and asked if the two of us could go to visit the kids at camp. She also asked if we could get back together.

"This can never happen again," I said.

And it never did. For the next twenty years, until she was stricken with a paralytic stroke, she was the best wife and the best partner any man could ask for. We had a wonderful life. We both had wanderlust, and we travelled more than any other couple I knew. We even went to Albania during the xenophobic rule of Enver Hoxa. The Swissair flight to Tirana was the only thing first class about the trip. The country was so poor that in the main department store in Tirana all the windows were boarded up. Together, we organized annual trips with Pierre Trudeau after he left office, beginning with our 1986 voyage from Moscow to Vladivostok on the Trans-Siberian Railway, in a manner fit for a czar. The next year, again with Pierre, we followed the Silk Road across the roof of the world, from Pakistan to China. Every year we would go to London for a week or ten days and see every play we could. During the decade I was a director of MGM, Sandra would usually fly out with me for board meetings in Los Angeles, where the studio put us up in a bungalow at the Beverly Hills Hotel. New York? All we had to do was hop on a company plane and we were there for a weekend of plays on Broadway.

It was as a hostess that Sandra truly excelled. She was the best organizer and the best party giver I've ever known. She had the best food, the best entertainment, and the best guests. Her table was known as one to get your feet under, for the quality of the conversation as well as for the quality of the food and drink.

For Jonathan's bar mitzvah in 1975, she organized a party and turned our garage into a disco for the kids. And she persuaded Danny Kaye to come. When Edgar Bronfman asked me to arrange a reception for Frank Sinatra following a concert in Montreal in 1976, she organized it in no time, and all the right people, both English and French speaking, were delighted to be invited. When Pierre Trudeau, as prime minister, called me and said he would be coming to dinner the very next night, Sandra wasn't the least bit flustered.

I've always had a thing about my birthday, and for my fortieth and later for my fiftieth, Sandra organized two spectacular evenings. I opened our front door on my fortieth birthday, and there was Danny Kaye, delivering an order of smoked meat. Since Danny and I shared the same birthday, she saw to it that we each got a cake with a candle. For my fiftieth birthday, she organized a black-tie dinner at the Ritz. Guests included Premier René Lévesque, Shimon Peres, who came all the way from Israel for the occasion, and Harry Belafonte.

When I was the honouree at an Israel Bonds dinner in 1985, Sandra organized the gala at the Queen Elizabeth Hotel, featuring Canada's new prime minister, Brian Mulroney, as the guest speaker and another surprise appearance by Danny Kaye. When Pierre Trudeau turned seventy in October 1989, Sandra organized a birthday dinner at our house for his family and closest friends. Afterwards, he wrote us a note calling it "a most civilized and delightful rite of passage into my state as a septuagenarian. Close family, close friends, great food, great wine and the spell of music so that all could join in song. A thousand thanks for the kind of evening I would like my children to remember us by." Sandra was so touched that she had Trudeau's note framed and hung in our country home at Mont-Gabriel.

For decades, Sandra worked tirelessly on behalf of the Montreal Symphony Orchestra, organizing one gala benefit after another. Danny Kaye gave two of his marvellous conducting performances, leaving Place des Arts in stitches. Luciano Pavarotti also performed with the MSO, as did another of the three tenors, Placido Domingo. Both our names were always on the program as chairs of the evening, but it was Sandra who did all the work. And unlike me, she actually had a highly developed appreciation of classical music and opera. While I worked at it, she knew it. When the MSO gave its annual concert at Carnegie Hall in New York, we would usually fly in for the weekend, and share a loge with Marie-Josée Drouin, who was then married to the conductor, Charles Dutoit. When the symphony toured Europe in 1987, we flew to Paris and joined the tour.

For all of this work with the MSO, Sandra received the Governor-General's Award for Volunteerism in 1994. It was a proud occasion, and a high honour, entirely deserved. Equally, in recognition of her voluntary activities and support of the arts, she was also named to the Order of Canada

She loved the movie business and worked with Edgar's film company, Sagittarius Productions. She later became a senior story editor with Astral Bellevue Pathé and worked on the development of the 1981 film *Porky's*, a significant box-office success whose cast included Kim Catrell.

Sandra eventually formed her own production company, and one of its animated features, *George and the Star*, was nominated for a Gemini Award in 1986. They got Paul Anka to write and perform the title song.

She also took very seriously her responsibilities as a director of the CBC from 1990 to 1998, and as a trustee of the National Film Board from 1999 until her death.

And she ran a very good house, decorating three of them, two in Montreal and one in Palm Beach. In the 1960s, she hired New York decorator Arthur Weinstein to do our Lexington house. Weinstein was a cousin of Charles's first wife, Barbara, which is how Sandra made his acquaintance. She was very happy with his work and hired him and his partner Don Shaw twenty years later to do our house in Palm Beach. Then, in 1987, they redecorated our Summit Circle house. The job took a year to finish, and we moved into a suite at the Queen Elizabeth Hotel for the entire period of renovations. Much later, I discovered that Sandra also had a sharp eye for antiques. A rolltop desk that she bought for something like $1,000 was recently appraised by Sotheby's at $50,000.

Most of all, she was a remarkable mother. If she had suffered an affection deficit from her own parents, she more than made up for it with Lynne and Jonathan. As much as I travelled, and I was usually on the road about two hundred days a year, Sandra always made it a point to be at home with the kids after school. And I always made it a point to be home on weekends. In those years, we rented a chalet at Chantecler in the Laurentians, and I would take the kids skiing on Saturdays. We were always exceptionally close as a family, and even when they were adults, our children would join us on our travels. Lynne and her husband, Barry Halliday, went with us on a trip to India in the late 1980s and often met us in London, where Barry is from. And Jonathan, on a world tour of his own in 1989, met up with us in Australia, and he accompanied us on some of our travels with Trudeau.

∞

Our children are as different as they could be. Lynne is very beautiful and brilliant, quite the brightest member of our family. Jonathan is outgoing and carefree, and for him the best has hardly been good enough. Not for a lack of his mother trying to instill in him the value of a dollar. I remember Sandra and I taking him, when he was only seven years old, to a store called Mr Lou's in the Snowdon neighbourhood of Montreal. I would buy the Sunday *New York Times,* and Jonathan would check out the toys in the back. He had his eye on a red truck, but was crying because he couldn't afford it – his allowance was only one dollar a week and the truck cost six dollars. "There's a way," Sandra said, "if you save your allowance for six weeks." She went back into the store, paid for the truck, and had them hold it. Six weeks later, he asked if it was time, and he came out of the store with a triumphant look on his face. It was pretty hard to teach kids about the value of money when we lived at the top of the hill, were driven around by a chauffeur, and flew everywhere on a private jet. As they got older, I would call a family council at the end of every year and say, here is what we have in terms of our worth. I wanted to be clear about it and to make the point that whatever we had, we owned as a family.

Both our kids always did well in school, though Lynne was the more studious one. Jonathan was the type who could ace an exam after pulling an all-night cramming session with his buddies. In any event, after graduating top of her class from St George's School of Montreal, Lynne went to Vassar, and later moved to New York, where she got into the Circle on the Square and became an accomplished actress and singer. Indeed, at the 1985 Israel Bonds dinner in my honour, Lynne sang the Canadian and Israeli national anthems, in French, English, and Hebrew. As any father can appreciate, that was quite a moment for me.

Like most women, Lynne has had to make choices between her career and her family, and she's always put family first. Lynne and Barry live in a large, comfortable apartment on Riverside Drive in New York, and they also own a country home on a lake in Connecticut. The lake comes in handy because Barry is an avid sailor and does all the outdoor pursuits, such as skiing and golf. They have a daughter, Olivia, who loves the outdoors as much as her father does. Olivia is like me in one sense – she doesn't have time for small talk on the phone, and cuts right to the chase. A real New Yorker. She's extremely bright, has a great sense of style, and can talk your ear off. She has sat in my seat in the Senate and made herself right at home.

Lynne has done an excellent job of combining family and career. She had a lead role in *The Rothschilds,* which had a long run Off Broadway. In 2000 she performed the songs of Cole Porter with the American Ballet Theater. The prima ballerina and others danced on stage while Lynne, dressed in an identical ballerina costume, stood off to one side and sang. The performance got a standing ovation from 2,500 people at the City Center. The guy sitting next to me said, "Wasn't that nice!" To which I replied, "That's my daughter," as any father would have. It was one of the proudest moments of my life. Then, in 2002, Lynne and several colleagues put together a musical revue called *Porterphiles*. The show featured unknown songs of Cole Porter and opened to strong reviews, with her picture in the *New York Times* on three occasions.

One of the reasons Lynne went to New York, she later said, was to be close to my mother, the hat lady, who had since married the man who made gift boxes for Tiffany's. As Lynne put it, her grandmother was a neat lady, "the height of cool." Lynne thought that wherever her grandmother lived "must have been the centre of the universe." In New York in the late 1980s, Lynne started dating Barry Halliday, who under the name B.H. Barry stages fight scenes and the like on Broadway and in the movies. If you've seen *Crazy for You* or *Kiss Me Kate* on Broadway or *The Addams Family* or the Civil War film *Glory,* you've seen Barry's work.

Once at a Penn and Teller show, Sandra and Barry were selected as participants from the audience. Afterwards, they both stepped outside the stage door for a smoke, and I figured out that he was the man dating my daughter.

"Are you B.H. Barry?" I asked.

"Yes," he replied.

"I'm Leo Kolber," I said. And that's how I met my future son-in-law.

Because of the nature of his business as a fight director, he would hire a lot of aspiring actors who made ends meet by waiting tables in Manhattan restaurants. So when we would go out for dinner with Lynne and Barry, the waiter or bartender was always buying drinks.

Since childhood, Jonathan had been fascinated with Israel. I think it
was partly because of the family history on his mother's side. He was
very close to his maternal grandfather, who filled his head with all his
war stories from Palestine. Since he also attended Jewish parochial
school, he was brainwashed on the subject of Israel, as he happily ad-
mits today. In high school, he often talked about going to university in
Israel, but I encouraged him to think of an Ivy League school. So when
he was about fourteen, I made him a deal – he could spend summers in
Israel if he would go to university in the United States.

One of the Ivy League schools he applied to was Princeton, and we
flew down for his interview with Avrum Yudevich, the head of Middle
East Studies, which Jonathan was planning to take as his major. Yudevich was a friend of Minda de Gunzberg, who had called him to put in
a word for our son. After the interview, we invited Yudevich to lunch.

"Your son is very bright," Yudevich said. "But I can't take him."

"Why not?" I demanded.

"Because he is Jewish."

"Excuse me," I said. "Here we are in 1980, and you, a Jew, are telling
me you can't take my son in Middle East Studies because he is Jewish."

"We are endowed by an Arab government," he said. "And we have a
Jewish quota."

Jonathan went to Harvard instead, where, indeed, he majored in
Middle East Studies, and he spent his junior year at the University of
Cairo studying in Arabic. He then worked as an entrance-level investment banker on the Canadian desk at Salomon Brothers on Wall Street.
The late 1980s was the era of the leveraged buyout, junk bonds, and
greed on Wall Street, and Jonathan jumped at the opportunity to get
away from it. He came to work with Charles Bronfman at Claridge in
Montreal before moving to Israel in 1991 and running Charles's investments there at Claridge Israel.

Charles and Jonathan did very well during the boom of the 1990s,
and at one point – before the stock market bubble burst in 2000 – were
ahead $600 million on their Israeli investments. Luckily, they had also
sold off some of their positions. During Operation Desert Storm in
1991, they bought a one-third interest in a big food company for $33
million, and in 1996 they sold it to Nestlé for $90 million cash.

As CEO of Koor Industries, Israel's largest employer, Jonathan had to
conduct a painful downsizing exercise, firing 6,000 people. But he took
$150 million of costs out of his system, restructured all of Koor's debt,

and returned the company to profitability in spite of the difficult operating environment in Israel. I've been very impressed by his skills in crisis management.

I'm also very impressed by Jonathan as a family man. He and Irit Kariv, a beautiful *sabra* whom he met within months of moving to Israel, have three children whom I don't see enough of because of the distance between us, and whom I worry a good deal about, as any grandfather would, living in Israel as they do in the time of the *intifada* terror. The oldest, Benjamin, is a very athletic kid who loves to play soccer and roller-blade hockey. The middle child, Daniella, is a gorgeous, hot-tempered girl. She's nicknamed Dilla because at her birth her older brother called her that, unable to pronounce her given name. The youngest one, Michael, keeps telling me, when I ask if he loves his grandfather, that he doesn't. He is going to be quite something. I have asked them all to call me Zaydeh, which is Yiddish for grandfather. That's how I addressed my own grandfather, and I've always considered it a very affectionate term.

After running a specialty food business for a number of years, Irit is focusing most of her time raising three children and running her home. She is extremely involved in helping to run a nationwide not-for-profit organization that takes care of the needs of displaced children who grow up in shelters. There are approximately eight thousand such children in Israel, and Irit has raised money and provided them with computers, additional educational services, and warmth. Her family are long established in Israel and, in fact, her grandfather was the mayor of Jerusalem before Teddy Kollek.

So my two children and four grandchildren are the light of my life. I call them the New Yorkers and the Israelis. While I regret the distance between us, my children were raised to have an international outlook, and so I can hardly resent that they do. We try to get together a couple of times a year, usually on a ski trip to my country house at Mont-Gabriel or to Courcheval in the French Alps, or sometimes on a holiday to our winter place in Palm Beach, which serves as a convenient staging ground for invasions of Disney World.

⌒

In the winter of 1991, Sandra and I drove up to our country home at Mont-Gabriel in the Laurentians with the intention of having a quiet weekend. She had just recovered from a bout of pneumonia and was looking forward to spending time at the mountaintop lodge, which had become our very favourite place since we had bought it from Bob Campeau in the late 1980s. In the 1950s, H.J. O'Connell, the construction magnate who developed Mont-Gabriel as a ski resort, built this great log house for himself. It's on top of the mountain, with a stunning view of the St Sauveur Valley that stretches out below the south side of the mountain.

After dinner, she complained of a terrible stomach pain, and hypochondriac that I was, I immediately called her doctor, who suggested she had taken too many antibiotics for pneumonia. Thanks a lot. In the morning, when she was feeling no better, and in fact quite a bit worse, I called our family doctor, Abe Mayman, in Montreal. "Drive right back to town," he said. "I will meet you at your house." He poked and prodded, and couldn't find anything wrong, but then suggested a second opinion from a gastroenterologist named Jacques Kessler from the Royal Victoria Hospital. The two of them stayed with her from eight in the morning until midnight. But during the night, after they'd gone, she kept having to go to the bathroom every twenty minutes, and then I saw that she was limping on one leg and had no movement in the other.

Meanwhile, a full-blown winter storm was raging outside. When I called Abe at five o'clock in the morning, he said he didn't think he could get his car up the hill to my place in the middle of a blizzard. I went to get him in my station wagon, and then we brought Sandra to the hospital. The X-rays showed that she had suffered a major abdominal bleed and then a cranial bleed as well. They needed to operate, fast. They contacted a neurosurgeon, Dr Gerard Mohr, who lived ten minutes from the Jewish General Hospital by car. "She is only going to last half an hour if we don't operate right now," he said. In the five-hour operation that followed, they essentially sopped up all the blood they could, and hoped her brain would absorb the rest. She was then wheeled into another operating room, since it turned out that her stomach had become gangrenous. Then, while she was in intensive care, she developed a staph infection.

Honestly, I don't know how she lived through all of this. She had suffered a massive, paralysing stroke. Since I had raised major money for the hospital, Sandra got their full attention. But the best medical minds, ranged in front of us for a consultation, could not agree on a prognosis. The best they could suggest was that we put her in the Jewish Rehab, where she remained for another six months. They didn't have either a private room or private nursing, but I arranged for both by way of a donation. Today there is the Sandra and Leo Kolber Wing of the Jewish Rehab, of which I'm extremely proud and which I regard as a testament to her courage.

When we finally got Sandra home, we had a head nurse named Ethelene Monrose stay with her. A remarkable woman, Ethelene went everywhere with Sandra during the final ten years of her life. If Sandra had a CBC board meeting, Ethelene went with her. When we went to New York for my granddaughter's birthday or for one of Lynne's concerts, Ethelene came along. She came to Israel with us twice. We had a staff of five nurses, three of whom stayed for the remaining ten years of her life. Sandra never really walked again without assistance, but at least she lived again.

For the first couple of years after the stroke, it was very difficult living with her. She was angry with me for keeping her alive. She kept saying that I wasn't being kind, that she would rather be dead. I got the house organized as both a hospital and a hotel. I'll acknowledge that very few people can afford home care of that quality, but I could, and no expense was spared. And as time went by, I would organize things so we could go to the movies together and even travel again. Because we owned Cineplex Odeon Theatres, I could call ahead to one of our cinemas in Montreal and have them cordon off part of a balcony.

We even managed two visits to Israel, for Jonathan's wedding in 1992 and later for a Seder on Passover and a visit with his children. It wasn't easy, partly because of her wheelchair and partly because she insisted on smoking during flights – cigarettes were one thing she refused to give up. I looked at chartering a plane, but it was difficult and prohibitively expensive to fly non-stop to Israel. So I called El-Al and asked about booking the entire first-class section of ten seats upstairs in a Boeing 747. Ten seats at $5,000 each, so it was $50,000 return fare. The Israeli consul-general in Montreal and his wife came along as our guests.

"I have a problem," I explained to the El-Al manager in Montreal. "My wife won't go unless she can smoke."

"Listen," he said, "it is your section of the plane, you can do what you like."

On the occasion of Jonathan's wedding, I genuinely believe she was happy to be alive. She sat there in her wheelchair and held court with the likes of Yitzhak Rabin and Shimon Peres. She was in her element, speaking Hebrew and talking politics. She was also very happy for Jonathan and, as always, openly affectionate with him. After that, she blamed me less for keeping her alive.

On September 5, 2001, I had been walking around inside the ropes at the Royal Montreal Golf Club, where Prime Minister Jean Chrétien was playing in a pro-am with Tiger Woods before the Canadian Open. I had to leave before the end of their game to visit Sandra, who had been hospitalized six days earlier with a blockage in her bowel. They took some X-rays at the Jewish General, but couldn't agree on the problem. Maybe she had a growth on her gall bladder, maybe not. Maybe they should do a colonoscopy, maybe not. Then they brought in a colorectal surgeon who thought she had a cancerous tumour in her bowel and recommended operating immediately instead of putting her through the trauma of a colonoscopy. So they did. They found no tumour, but took her gall bladder out anyway.

If they'd done the colonoscopy instead, they would have found nothing, and she would have kept her gall bladder. I was pretty underwhelmed by the diagnostic abilities of some of the best minds in the medical profession. Less than a week later, she died.

Jonathan flew home from Israel when he heard of his mother's health crisis. As it happened, he connected through Newark on the morning of September 11, landing in Montreal only minutes before the first plane flew into the World Trade Center. Since he called Lynne from the airport to say he had landed, we were spared the thought he might be on board one of the hi-jacked planes. Both our children managed to be with her at the end.

Sandra was an exceptionally brave person to have lived for ten years with the debilitating effects of her stroke. I was totally devoted to her, and while there were bad days, she soldiered on with great courage. She was only sixty-seven when she died. While it was a deliverance for her, and in some ways a release for me, her passing was a time of sadness and sorrow. She was the great love of my life.

8

Travels with Trudeau

I first met Pierre Trudeau at the Grey Cup in Montreal in 1969, the time he famously showed up wearing a cape for the ceremonial kickoff. I was chairman of Grey Cup Week, so Sandra and I had a suite at the Queen Elizabeth Hotel, and Trudeau came to a party there on the Saturday night before the game on Sunday afternoon.

It was first time I saw the effect Trudeau had on a room when he walked into it, though certainly not the last. At midnight, in swept Pierre, and I mean swept. He immediately became the centre of attention. He was brilliant. He was famous. He was also prime minister. And he had a commanding presence.

He didn't know me, but since I was the host, he came over to chat. It had been over a year since the Trudeaumania election of 1968, but he was still relatively new to his role as PM.

"You have my great sympathy for taking on this job," I told him.

"Why do you say that?" he asked.

"Because," I said, "you are the chief executive of the country, running a huge organization, but you can't choose your own executives, the cabinet. They are essentially thrust on you, and you also have all these geographical considerations."

"That's no problem at all," Trudeau said. But I knew he hadn't taken my point about the difference between running a government and managing a business.

Some ten years later, Marc Lalonde, Trudeau's Quebec lieutenant, asked me to become involved in raising money for the Liberal party. "The Jewish community doesn't give enough," Lalonde said.

"How much do you want to raise?" I asked.

"Fifty thousand dollars," he replied.

"Tell you what," I said. "You get Trudeau to come to my house for a fundraiser, and I'll get you a hundred."

So Lalonde, the one person who could deliver Trudeau, did.

"What do you expect me to do?" Trudeau asked when he came to the first fundraiser at my home.

"Well," I said, "I can tell you what I don't expect you to do. I don't expect you to make a speech."

"That's very good news. So what do you want me to do?"

"I want you to mingle and pose for as many photographs as possible, because I'll send these photographs as a memento of the evening, and this is what people will remember, having a picture with you."

Trudeau had an enormous appetite, and he always wanted to know what was for lunch or dinner. He was anything but indifferent about food. The first time he came to the house, almost immediately he asked whether we would be having something to eat.

"Yes," I replied, "it's a sit-down dinner." A sit-down dinner for one hundred couples outside on the back lawn.

"Well, what's for dinner?" he asked.

So I told him – caviar to start, followed by a full-course dinner, top of the line. "Can we afford that?" he asked. "I mean, can the party afford it?"

"We can't. I can," I replied. "I'm paying for it. Everything they pay goes right to the party."

"Oh," Trudeau said. "That's good."

We charged $1,000 a couple for those dinners at the house – a lot of money in those days. But because it was Trudeau and because he was prime minister, we never had any trouble getting people to come. They always sold out.

And Trudeau always showed up. One time he called ahead and asked if he could arrive about half an hour early, and said he needed the use of a shower. He showed up at the front door in blue jeans, covered in dust, with an RCMP officer carrying a garment bag.

This was not long after he had bought his home on Pine Avenue, the art deco mansion that the noted architect Ernest Cormier had built for himself on the south flank of Mount Royal. Among other commissions, Cormier designed the tower that became the signature building of the Université de Montréal on the other side of the mountain and the Supreme Court building in Ottawa. But the home Cormier built for himself would later become known as the Trudeau house. It had been unoccupied for some time when Trudeau bought it in 1979, and it needed a lot of work. Trudeau was doing some of it himself, and the day he came to our house for a shower, he had been scraping the floors.

In July 1982, when the Montreal Expos were hosting the All-Star baseball game at Olympic Stadium, Trudeau was invited to throw out the first pitch. This was appropriate, not just because he was prime minister, but because his father, Charlie Trudeau, had once owned the Montreal Royals, the Triple "A" team in the International League where Jackie Robinson broke baseball's colour line in 1946. Before the game – it is usually on the second Tuesday of July – I invited Trudeau to a barbecue at the house. Charles Bronfman was there, of course, and Bill Davis, then premier of Ontario, who had been very supportive of Trudeau in patriating the Canadian Constitution from Westminster. And there were business leaders, too. A New York banker immediately got into a huge argument with Trudeau about interest rates, which had recently peaked at 22.75 percent, and this in the midst of the worst economic downturn in half a century.

When I invited Pierre and his oldest son, Justin, to Opening Day in 1987, the *Globe and Mail* ran a picture above the fold on the front page. "See," I said to Pierre when I called him at his law office that morning, "you have to go to the ball game with me to get your picture on the front page." We shared a good laugh over that.

Trudeau often came to dinner. He knew the house from the fundraisers, he knew the hospitality, he knew us and liked us. Sometimes he would bring his boys, and occasionally we would go to Moishe's for steak or Milos for seafood. We had some memorable evenings with him at the house in the years after he left office as well, particularly two dinners in 1989. When Trudeau turned seventy in October of that year, Sandra organized a birthday party for him at the house. We had only his family and a few of his close friends, such as Marc Lalonde and Jacques Hébert, the senator who would later deliver one of the three eulogies at Trudeau's funeral. That night, we had a guy with an accordion playing French-Canadian folk songs, and everybody, including Trudeau, joined in.

In the summer of 1989, Jean Chrétien was getting set to run for the Liberal leadership, and Trudeau was giving him a hard time about Meech Lake. Trudeau was outspokenly opposed to the constitutional accord, writing in a famous newspaper article in May 1987 that it would put Canada on a "fast track to sovereignty-association," and calling Brian Mulroney "a weakling" and the premiers with whom he negotiated the deal "snivellers" who should be "sent packing." Trudeau had even come to the Senate in the spring of 1988, and appeared for seven hours in a committee of the whole, where he predicted that Meech would mean the end of Canada as we know it, "but if it is going to go, let it go with a bang rather than a whimper."

As for the Liberal leadership, Trudeau made it quite clear to Chrétien that, as he later put it, "my support is not unconditional" and might

very much depend on Chrétien's position on Meech. Chrétien was trying to walk a fine line between the Liberal party's Quebec wing, where
leadership delegates generally supported Meech, and the Trudeau wing,
notably in Ontario, which was violently opposed to it.

I was then raising money for Chrétien and doing my bit for his leadership campaign, and it was in the leadership context that he mentioned
that Trudeau was giving him a hard time over Meech.

"Do you want me to talk to him?" I asked Chrétien. "Maybe I can
help."

"That would be a big help to me," Chrétien said.

So I called Trudeau, and I said, "Look, Pierre, you are having this big
battle about Meech, but I want to help Chrétien because I think he can
win the next election and I think we should be helping him." And I
asked if he would come to dinner at the house to talk about it with
Chrétien. I told him I'd also invite Marc Lalonde, Michael Pitfield, who
had been clerk of the Privy Council under Trudeau, as well as Tom Axworthy, his former principal secretary, who was then working for
Charles Bronfman at the CRB Foundation.

It was a beautiful hot Friday evening in August 1989, which I remember well as the night of a lunar eclipse. Just about everyone, including
Chrétien, came alone and on time, most of them dressed in sports jack-
ets. Trudeau showed up late and wandered into the house wearing sandals, a grungy pair of shorts, and a T-shirt. We had drinks out on the
terrace, and I remember that Lalonde greeted Trudeau by saying he'd
just had lunch with Michel Vastel, the Quebec columnist. Trudeau got
quite angry and asked Lalonde why would he bother with someone
who had been so tough on him – when Trudeau appeared before the
Senate hearings on Meech Lake, he had testified entirely in English, and
Vastel had shouted down from the Press Gallery that he should speak in
French. My immediate thought was that the evening was not getting off
to a very promising start.

When we went in to dinner, Sandra presided at the table for the first
couple of courses, but then she discreetly withdrew so that we could
continue our discussion about Meech Lake and the Liberal leadership.
Trudeau was pretty hard on the people around the table who were asking him to ease up in his opposition to Meech. They got nowhere with
him. Around ten thirty, he got up to leave, and I walked him to the
door.

"You know, Pierre," I told him, "it's very easy for you to be critical
because you're not running for anything. But our friend Jean is running
for the leadership, and you really ought to support him."

He looked at me and said, "You're right, tell him I'm onside."

I walked him out to his car and the strangest thing then ensued. Because of the lunar eclipse and it being a Friday night, hundreds of people had driven up to the top of the mountain for a clear view of the night sky. People were just hanging out at the Summit, watching the eclipse, when out walked Pierre, and of course everyone recognized him immediately. They would later undoubtedly remember it as the night Trudeau showed up for the eclipse.

∞

Not long after Lalonde asked me to help with fundraising, Trudeau invited me to lunch at 24 Sussex. I just assumed others would be there as well, but it turned out it was only the two of us at the small table in the alcove of the dining room that overlooked the Ottawa River. He took off his jacket, sat down to a huge hot lunch, and devoured everything in sight.

He told me he didn't have any particular agenda. "I wanted to get to know you a bit," he said. "Do you have anything you would like to discuss with me?"

"Well," I said, "I am a Liberal, and you are the leader of the party, and I find that you are taking the party too far left. Your relations with the business community are lousy. And I don't think that is very productive. I think it is counterproductive."

"You know," Trudeau replied, "you have a point, but they are always tarring me with the socialist brush." He gave me the example of Jean de Grandpré, his classmate from law school, then the head of Bell Canada and later the founding chairman of BCE, who was always on his case. "I've given up on them," Trudeau said of the business community.

"Prime Minister," I replied, "I voted for you, I'm a Liberal, and I'm a businessman."

"Yes, I know all that," he said.

"Well, you certainly don't have a mandate from me to give up on the business community."

So he smiled, and he said, "You are right. I will try harder." He didn't, of course, but he was gracious enough to say that he would.

Then we chatted a bit about the nationalization of Petrofina and the creation of Petro-Canada, which I told him had a been mistake from my vantage point, a mistake later compounded by the NEP, the National Energy Program introduced by Marc Lalonde in October 1980. As a director of Bow Valley Investment, in Calgary, I knew firsthand how unpopular these policies were in the oil patch. "That's very interesting," he allowed, but while he was hearing me out, he certainly wasn't taking my views on board.

Trudeau's management, or rather his mismanagement, of Canada's finances was one issue on which we agreed to disagree. After he left office, I had no hesitation in telling him that he'd really "screwed up." Canada followed a lousy economic model under Trudeau. In Marc Lalonde's last year as finance minister, Canada ran a $38-billion deficit, or nearly 9 percent of GDP. When Pierre became prime minister in 1968, a century after Confederation, the national debt was $18 billion, an amount that included the cost of financing two world wars. When he left office in 1984, Ottawa's debt was more than $200 billion, an increase of more than 1,100 percent. But as I also discovered, Pierre would usually listen to an argument and always had a good argument of his own.

When the lunch was over, he had to get back to the House of Commons for Question Period and offered me a lift in his limousine. I thanked him and told him that if he was ever in Montreal to please come to my home for dinner.

"How about tomorrow night?" he suggested. "I'll call you tomorrow morning to confirm."

So I went back to Montreal and warned Sandra that we might be having the prime minister to dinner. "When?" she asked. "Tomorrow," I said. Not everyone could organize a dinner for the prime minister on such short notice, but nothing fazed Sandra. The next morning my phone rang at 9:00 a.m. sharp, and it was Trudeau himself calling, without his secretary placing the call and without going through the PMO switchboard. He asked me to have no more than four or five couples. "Let's keep it intimate," he said.

On at least one subsequent occasion, he asked Sandra if it would be all right if he brought a date. But on this one, he came alone. I had heard that he liked caviar, so Sandra got some of this great Iranian caviar, the kind that comes in the big blue box. We had a delightful evening, and when dinner was over, he said he had to leave early because he was taking his sons to an amusement park the next morning. And I had an extra box of caviar.

"I don't know what the rules are about giving something like this to you," I said, "but would you like a box of caviar?"

"I'd be delighted," he said. "Thank you very much."

He grabbed the box of caviar and left. In those days, there were no rules about that sort of thing.

As time went on, I would meet with Trudeau occasionally, and then in 1983, I lobbied him, through two of his closest associates, to name me to the Senate. There is a tradition in Canada that the party bagman is appointed to the Senate, and there is also a tradition of a Jewish seat from Quebec. I qualified on both counts, and besides, the Bronfmans were thinking of breaking up Cemp Investments and I thought the Senate would be an interesting place to spend part of my time. It's close to power, it's close to policy, there are a lot of interesting and informed people, and in those days it wasn't very demanding.

I decided to keep my lobbying circumspect. I made my interest known to Michael Pitfield, deputy chairman of Power Corporation and a Trudeau appointee to the Senate, whom I had befriended over the years. And I lobbied Marc Lalonde, by then the finance minister and the boss of the party in Quebec. As I've noted, it was he who had recruited me as the bagman in the first place.

Unfortunately, the other member of the Montreal Jewish community who wanted to be named to the Senate was Phil Vineberg, a brilliant figure who had been the Bronfmans' lawyer for many years. This situation was somewhat analogous to, and certainly an echo of, the time Laz Phillips was named to the Senate and his client, Sam Bronfman, wasn't. Mr Bronfman never really forgave Laz for accepting an appointment he had long coveted for himself.

Laz Phillips had initially been supportive of my candidacy, but Phil Vineberg was his nephew and also his law partner at Phillips Vineberg, our lawyers at Fairview and Cemp, as well as at Seagram. Laz explained to me that it was an awkward situation for him, and I told him that I perfectly understood his predicament. In any event, Phil Vineberg's many supporters lobbied vigorously for the appointment in the Jewish community, and he was clearly the preferred choice of the Canadian Jewish Congress and other organizations, as well as of prominent representatives of the community.

And I, as it turned out, was the choice of the only person who mattered – the prime minister. We were in Palm Beach over the holidays in December 1983. It was actually Christmas Eve, and I was just getting home from a round of golf when Sandra came rushing out to meet me in the driveway.

"You've got to call the prime minister," she said. "He's calling you. You have to call him back."

I knew it could only be about one of two things. Either I'd got it or I hadn't.

"I'm inviting you to join the Senate," Trudeau began. "But I have to tell you, you're not the first choice of the Jewish community."

"I'm aware of that, Prime Minister."

"But you're my first choice," he said with a light chuckle.

"Thank you, Prime Minister," I replied. "I'm honoured and delighted to accept."

At that moment, I couldn't help but think of Sam Bronfman and how I had got the appointment that he had sought as the crowning achievement of his career. I also thought of Laz Phillips and how neither one of us would have got there without the man who didn't – Laz as Sam Bronfman's lawyer and Leo as the guy who ran the family investments.

Now that I was actually being appointed to the Senate, I wondered how time-consuming it would be.

"How often do I have to go?" I asked.

Trudeau laughed. "Just show up once in a while," he said. "It's no big deal."

That was then, before senators were docked $250 a day for being absent. It later became quite a different place, very much more demanding and quite stimulating in terms of policy. In the later Chrétien years, I became chairman of the Senate Banking Committee, widely regarded as one of the best committees of Parliament because the members all came from the real world of business and finance, such as my friend Ian Sinclair, the former chairman and CEO of Canadian Pacific Limited. We were called to the Senate at the same time and sworn in together in January 1984, right around the time of my fifty-fifth birthday.

I've never regretted a moment of my twenty years in the Senate and have always been grateful to Pierre Trudeau for the opportunity to serve.

∽

Just a few weeks after my appointment, Trudeau took his famous walk in the snow on Leap Year Day and then announced his retirement. By the end of June he had left office, after four terms and more than fifteen tumultuous years as prime minister. His tenure exceeded Sir Wilfrid Laurier's, and only Mackenzie King and Sir John A. Macdonald served longer as prime minister of Canada.

At the time of his retirement from politics in 1984, Trudeau was a vigorous sixty-four years old. He returned to Montreal to raise his three sons, live in his art deco house on the hill, and practise law as counsel to the firm of Heenan Blaikie. He stayed fit, partly by walking to and from work every day. He had enough to do, but he was no longer prime minister, and it was clearly not an easy adjustment to private life after so many years in power.

Sandra and I kind of befriended him, making a point of inviting him on weekends to New York and, occasionally, London. In those days, I had the use of the company plane, so it didn't cost anything to invite Pierre along. In New York, we would usually take a suite at the Regency or Plaza Athenee, and he would be our guest in the second bedroom. We would go to a couple of plays, go out to dinner, that sort of thing, and he would usually bring a date.

On a couple of occasions, he was our guest at the Dorchester in London. One time when we flew in, he had this book, *Les Liaisons Dangereuses,* which he said was marvellous, and he insisted that we go see the play, *Dangerous Liaisons,* then being performed in London. He was right. It was marvellous. Another time, when we all landed in London from Moscow, Pierre had a lovely room at the Dorchester. The hotel had sent up a bowl of fruit as a token of welcome, and Pierre flashed that devilish grin of his and said, "This is what I'll have for breakfast so I won't have to spend any money." He was making fun of his reputation for being tight. But then, he *was* tight, as opposed to being cheap, and there is a difference. As for accommodations, he could stay in a royal suite or a dungeon, it didn't matter to him. He travelled light – he could be on the road for weeks with a pair of jeans and a couple of T-shirts. Once, in the middle of nowhere, he did his own laundry and hung it from a tree.

On that post-Moscow trip to London, he suggested we all go for a walk the next morning, but since Sandra and I had a couple of things to do, we decided to meet up with him for lunch at Cecconi, a very good Italian restaurant across from the Burlington Arcade. We got there a little early so that he wouldn't have to sit there on his own and told the maître d' that the former Canadian prime minister would be joining us. Pierre showed up wearing one of his grungy outfits, but they let him in anyway.

We had planned this stopover in London as a kind of cultural change after our trip to Moscow and a week-long train journey across Russia in October 1986. After the Russian trip, our travels with Trudeau became an annual event, until Sandra suffered her disabling stroke in 1991. In subsequent years, we travelled with Trudeau to Pakistan and China; Brazil, Peru, and Bolivia; Central America and the Galapagos Islands; and finally Vietnam, Laos, and Cambodia.

With one exception, these trips occurred in the fall. Trudeau always chose the destinations, and Sandra, Jack Austin, a friend and colleague from the Senate, and I always organized them. What became an annual rite of autumn passage began when I said to Pierre, "You love to travel. We love to travel. Let's go someplace." "There's nothing I love better," he agreed. He said there was one trip he had always wanted to take, and that was the Trans-Siberian Railway from Moscow to Vladivostok. Except that Vladivostok was a closed city.

So I went to see the Russian ambassador in Ottawa, and he said that they would be honoured to receive Mr Trudeau and that everything would be arranged, though Vladivostok remained a problem. I told Pierre it was a go, more or less, and asked him who else he would like to invite. He suggested Bernard Lamarre, the head of Lavalin Engineering, and his wife, Louise; and Paul Desmarais, the chairman of Power Corporation, who brought along his daughter-in-law Helene, who is married to Paul Desmarais Jr. Paul Sr's wife, Jackie, couldn't come.

The Orient Express it wasn't. But because it was Trudeau, the Soviets put on three cars just for us. A brand new dining car and a brand new sleeping car with private compartments. Sandra and I had one compartment for our luggage and one for each of us. And Trudeau had his own car, an entire car. It must have gone back to the czar's days because there was a large bedroom, a full bathroom with a bath, and a full sitting room with a boardroom table.

And every night after dinner, we would go sit at Pierre's table and get him in full flight on geo-politics as we roared through the Siberian tundra. It's a long journey, seven days and six nights. You leave Moscow in the afternoon, and you just keep on going. The Russians gave us a wonderful staff of three or four people, and every day at stops along the way, they somehow managed to find fresh fruits and vegetables, and they had an endless supply of caviar.

Trudeau was the only one with a bath, and so we all had to ask him if we could use it. And he said, "Okay, everybody can come and have a bath every day, but you have to clean up." So we all paraded into his car in our bathrobes and nightshirts every night and had our baths.

The company on that trip was very convivial. At dinner and afterwards, Trudeau would talk about politics, the Canadian and world scene. And he would regale us with anecdotes of Ronald Reagan and Jimmy Carter and all the people he had known at G7 summits, Commonwealth conferences, and bilateral visits. He said that Reagan, for example, was one of the nicest men he had ever met, but obviously not too bright. He said that whenever he met with Reagan, the president had all his talking points on three-by-five cards – he was totally scripted. So if Trudeau asked him about nuclear disarmament, Reagan would fish a card out of his pocket and read the answer. If he didn't have an appropriate card, Trudeau said, he would tell you an anecdote about Hollywood. But he would never extemporize. Trudeau liked Jimmy Carter very much, but shared the view that he micro-managed the American presidency. Carter would later lead the American delegation at Trudeau's funeral.

On the long train journey across Russia, Trudeau often said what a great country it was, extolling the virtues of the Soviet system. "Pierre," I said, "it may be the worst system that ever existed." The Soviet command economy was a complete mess and always had been. It was often said of the Soviet economy that everyone had a job, but nobody worked. Certainly nothing worked very efficiently.

More than twenty years earlier, Sandra and I had visited Russia, and on my return, Mr Bronfman, I guess because he had been born there, asked what I thought of the Soviet Union. "It's just an abject failure," I told him. "They can put a man in space, but everything else is a disaster." Small things. You couldn't get your tickets to the ballet done properly. Your hotel reservations would be all screwed up. They couldn't feed their own people, not because they couldn't grow enough food but because the supply management chain was always breaking down. If you went to the famous GUM department store to buy a couple of souvenir T-shirts, you would go to four different places in the store, one to pick out the purchase, another to get your bill, another to pay, and another to get it wrapped. It was one of the worst-run countries I ever saw.

But the Russians took very good care of us, from the moment we stepped on the plane in Montreal. The Russian ambassador came to the airport to see us off, informing us that as a special gesture in honour of Mr Trudeau, Aeroflot was going to fly non-stop from Montreal to Moscow.

"Doesn't it usually?" I asked.

"No," he replied, "normally we stop in Gander because the fuel there is cheaper."

When we got to Moscow, we stayed for a few days at the Intourist Hotel, where the Soviets put up all the foreign VIPs. On the second day we were there, Mikhail Gorbachev sent word that he had wanted to meet with Pierre but was regrettably detained by his briefings for the Reykjavik Summit with President Reagan on October 11 and 12. Instead, he asked if we could meet with Alexander Yakovlev, his closest adviser in those days of *glasnost* and *perestroika*. Yakovlev had previously been ambassador to Canada and knew Trudeau well.

Yakovlev received us in this huge office, not in the Kremlin, but in the headquarters of the Communist Party of the Soviet Union. He had interpreters there, whom he clearly didn't need because he kept correcting their English. "Pierre," he asked Trudeau, "is there anything we can do for you?" "Yes," Trudeau replied, "they won't let us into Vladivostok, since it's a closed city." "Ridiculous," Yakovlev allowed, and with a snap of his fingers, he commanded an aide to his side, and visas were arranged for us within half an hour.

In the event, Bernard Lamarre and I had to leave the train before Vladivostok, at Krasnoyarsk in Siberia, just north of Mongolia, and fly back to Moscow for some business meetings. And it was there that a funny thing happened. We arrived back in Moscow in the evening, and the next day was Yom Kippur. The eve of Yom Kippur, called Kol Nedrei, is a very solemn occasion in the Jewish faith. I'm not particularly observant, but I always like to go to synagogue for Kol Nedrei.

"Great," Bernard said. "I'll go with you." We were out to dinner with a diplomat from the Canadian Embassy, and because we had an embassy car with a flag on the hood, they allowed us through the police cordons at the main synagogue in Moscow.

Most of the congregation were quite elderly, and several of them noticed that we had arrived without yarmulkes, and suggested that we really should be wearing them. The Canadian diplomat had an idea. He had some hockey toques in the back of his car, and he ran to get them – three Montreal Canadiens toques, the *tricolore*, the red, white, and blue. And so you had these three guys going into synagogue in Moscow wearing these Montreal Canadiens toques. It was quite a sight.

The next year, Trudeau suggested we travel to Pakistan and China. He said he wanted to follow Marco Polo's Silk Road through the Karakoram Pass in Kashmir. It wouldn't be the last time that Trudeau told me he wanted to go to a place I had not only never been to, but had never heard of. So I went to see the Pakistani ambassador in Ottawa, and he contacted Islamabad. They replied that Trudeau must come and that everything would be looked after. Jack Austin asked if he could come along with his wife, Natalie. And our son, Jonathan, joined us, too.

When we landed in Islamabad, the entire Pakistani cabinet greeted us at the airport, and they told us that General Zia Ul-Haq would be receiving us for a private dinner. "I think we are pushing the envelope a little bit," Trudeau said as we were driven over to the president's office. Zia had come to office in a 1977 military coup that ousted the democratically elected president of Pakistan Ali Bhutto, the father of Benazir

Bhutto, who would herself later be elected president of Pakistan only to be deposed by another military coup. Not content with overthrowing the president, General Zia had him hanged in 1979, despite a worldwide wave of protest, particularly from Commonwealth countries such as Canada. Trudeau's discomfort in meeting with him was understandable.

But on a private level, Zia couldn't have been more hospitable or charming. He greeted us effusively before the dinner at his private office and informed us that our itinerary had already been arranged. Trudeau had his own ideas about driving out to the base of the Himalayan Mountains and setting out for China from there. But General Zia insisted that the army would fly us up by helicopter. Everywhere we went, General Zia would call by radiophone every night to see how we were doing. Less than a year later, he died in a mysterious air crash that also took the lives of several American officials.

We travelled in three Jeeps through the Hunza Valley and across the Gobi Desert. The Hunza Valley is breathtakingly beautiful, the inspiration for the legend of Shangri-la, and in the capital, Karimabad, we met the Mir of Hunza, Ghazanfar Ali Khan, a man with a Harvard education. He wanted to know how he could get a visa to Canada. There were guest houses with no electricity but with perfumes from Paris. And in Gilgit, we went to a polo match where they used a sheep's head, or a goat's head, as a ball. It was very rough, and very exciting.

By the time we approached the Chinese border, we were at 16,000 feet, and the air was so thin that they gave us all some oxygen. A glacier had recently melted, resulting in a lake across our path. General Zia sent the Pakistani Army Corps of Engineers to build rafts to take us across. When we got to the other side, we encountered a small yellow school bus that had been stranded there. It turned out that the eight tourists on board were all from Quebec, and of course they recognized Pierre. Here we were, high in the Himalayas, in the highest mountain passes in the world, in the most isolated and rugged terrain imaginable, and we ran into these people from Quebec, all doing doubletakes when they first saw Pierre and making a huge fuss over him. So we arranged for the rafts to take them to the other side of the lake, and then resumed our way to the Chinese border.

The border crossing at the Kunjerab Pass was a little hut in the Himalayas, normally open only a few hours a week. Not only did the Chinese government send a doctor, they even sent a representative from the Bank of China so that we could exchange dollars for yuan. And then we drove for another twenty-four hours. The entire Himalayan mountain range covers nearly 600,000 square kilometres, and it seems to me that we drove through all of it.

Western China converges on the borders of Pakistan, Afghanistan, and Russia. Gradually descending the snow-capped Pamir Mountains to 10,000 feet, we stopped in a Tadjik town called Tashkorgan, where the hotel was basically a cement hut of two storeys divided into rooms. No toilets, no electricity, no water, and no heat. The place was filthy, and we all slept in our clothes. But the locals put on an evening of wild dancing for us. They were all dead drunk.

Eventually, we found our way to Beijing, where the Chinese staged a dinner in Trudeau's honour at the Great Hall of the People. In a country where institutional memory is measured in centuries, they well remembered that Trudeau had been the first Western statesman, and Canada the first Western country, to recognize the People's Republic of China. This was in 1970, even before Henry Kissinger's ping-pong diplomacy opened the way for President Nixon's historic visit in 1972. For Trudeau's dinner, the Chinese turned out everyone who had been an ambassador to Canada since recognition, and since all of them had been accredited to Trudeau's government, he knew and remembered them all. It was a nice touch, and Pierre was clearly delighted.

Then I chartered a plane so that we could fly out to the Three Gorges of the Yangtze River, where the Chinese were going ahead with controversial plans to build the world's largest hydroelectric dam. When completed, after about twenty years, the $24-billion project will, as reported by the *Asia Times*, "tower 575 feet above the world's third longest river ... its reservoir will stretch 350 miles upstream and force the displacement of close to 2 million people." A lot of lush land – and spectacular scenery – was going to be submersed, and Pierre thought it was sad that they were doing this, but he also understood their need for new energy sources.

Finally, we ended up in the southern port city of Canton, now called Guangzhou, a major centre for international trade and higher education. The Chinese put us up in a hotel that was better than anything I've ever seen in New York. They gave us the royal suite on the top floor of a forty-storey hotel – it was really a cluster of suites within a master suite. Everyone had their own living room and library, with a staff to look after each couple. Altogether, it was quite a journey.

There were always significant logistical challenges in organizing these trips, but the most difficult to arrange was the one to Vietnam, Laos, and Cambodia in November 1990. Since the Vietnam War, the Americans still had no relations with the Vietnamese, and for that matter, neither did Canada. So Sandra and I spent a few days in Mexico City getting the whole trip sorted out with the Vietnamese Embassy there. Neither did Canada have relations with Cambodia, but I managed to arrange visas through the good offices of Yves Fortier, then Canada's ambassador to the United Nations, where Cambodia did have a delegation. Trudeau was accompanied on this trip by Nancy Southam, a close friend who would be with him through the palliative care phase of his final illness in September 2000.

In Cambodia, we were invited to meet the prime minister, Hun Sen, and Trudeau was very uneasy about that. In the 1970s, at least 2 million Cambodians had died in the genocide practised by the Pol Pot regime during the forcible evacuation of the cities. The country was still coming out of the darkness of Khmer Rouge rule. Hun Sen may not have been a despot, but neither was he a great democrat, and in the car on the way over to meet him, Trudeau wondered why we were seeing him. "Well, we are guests in this country," I replied, "and he extended an invitation to you." "What can I possibly say to him?" Trudeau asked. "You've met leaders from all over the world, in all sorts of circumstances," I assured him. "If you want, I'll do all the talking." And that's pretty much how it turned out.

In Brazil in February 1990, we had a lot of fun attending the Carnival in Rio. After that, the Brazilian Air Force flew us in a small plane deep into the Amazon jungle. The Amazon Rainforest has been called the last frontier on Earth, and as Leslie Taylor has written, "If Amazonia were a country, it would be the ninth largest in the world." Deep in the rainforest, we met the Yanomani tribe, one of the last great "primitive" tribes in the world. Very few tourists ever meet them. Everyone goes around naked, and they live in one big community hut. Whether it is sex or going to the bathroom, it is all done communally. The day we were there, the men were all away hunting, so the women served us lunch in the hut.

We also went to Peru and Bolivia. La Paz, the capital of Bolivia, is so elevated that the poor live in the heights of the city and the more affluent live down below, where the air is easier to breathe. It's the only city I've ever visited where the rich people don't live on the hill. For this trip, I had the company plane for a couple of weeks, so it was a little easier to organize.

We also flew to Nicaragua, Costa Rica, and the Galapagos Islands, 1,000 kilometres or 600 miles off the coast of Ecuador. In Managua,

Nicaragua, a meeting was furtively arranged with President Daniel Ortega, the leftist Sandinista leader whom Ronald Reagan had tried to oust by lending active support to the "Contra" rebels. After much delay, Ortega met with us at a secret location, in a room with the curtains drawn. This was just before the elections held under the Arias agreement, that would see the defeat of Ortega and the Sandinistas by a centrist-right coalition.

The Galapagos Archipelago consists of about thirteen volcanic islands, some of them millions of years old and some still being formed. The Galapagos is nature's number one preserve. As you go from island to island, you have to shake the sand from the previous island off your boots so that you won't contaminate the next one. As Dr Robert Rothman has written, "Charles Darwin was the first to make a scientific study of the islands in 1835 ... and in later years maintained that the Galapagos was the source of all his ideas and research."

The Galapagos was one fantastic place for swimming and scuba diving, and Pierre was an expert at both. One day we were all frolicking with some sea lions that swam playfully around at fantastic speeds. It was a terrific moment. Sandra just went over to our son, Jonathan, and gave him a hug and a kiss on the cheek. She was very demonstrative with our kids. And Pierre walked over and said, "You know, Sandra, I wish I could do that more often with my kids." I'm sure he did. Perhaps he just wished he could be more affectionate, more often.

Our travels with Trudeau sadly came to an abrupt end in 1991, after Sandra's stroke. It happened that she later received the Governor-General's Award in recognition of her volunteerism on behalf of organizations such as the Montreal Symphony Orchestra. It's an important honour, and a major black-tie event before two thousand people and television cameras at the National Arts Centre in Ottawa. While she was physically incapacitated, her mind was still working quite well, and she wondered if Trudeau would introduce her, either live or on video. He had lunch with me and explained that there were some things he didn't do: he didn't do prefaces, he didn't do introductions. He wrote her a nice long letter of apology, but he wouldn't do it.

There were other things he didn't do – he didn't visit hospitals and he never visited Sandra. That kind of cooled things between us. He didn't go to funerals either, though there were notable exceptions, such as the funeral of his closest friend, Gérard Pelletier. Then Trudeau lost his youngest son, Michel, in a terrible avalanche in British Columbia over Christmas of 1998. He was never the same after that. As strong as he was, as deep as his faith was, like any parent, he couldn't recover from such an unnatural and terrible loss.

The last time I saw Pierre was on his eightieth birthday in 1999. Prime Minister Chrétien was giving a dinner in his honour at 24 Sussex. I flew up to Ottawa with Trudeau on a plane provided by Power Corporation, and it was a very memorable evening. By that time, it was clear that he was not himself, not well. Less than a year later, in September 2000, he died, and a grieving nation recognized what a different and remarkable leader he had been. When he was buried with full national honours from the Notre Dame Basilica in Old Montreal, I was invited to go to the church on Place d'Armes with the Desmarais family. They first gathered at the Power Corporation offices a few blocks away, and there was a question of whether there would be a collection. Paul Desmarais, who was like Trudeau in that he never carried any money, fretted that he had no cash. I gave him a couple of $100 bills. There was no collection, as it turned out, but Paul forgot to return my money. A few days later, I got an envelope by courier from John Rae of Power. Inside were two crisp $100 bills. Trudeau would have enjoyed that.

In 1993, when he brought out his autobiography, *Memoirs,* he signed my copy with an inscription I'll always cherish: "Leo, intrepid companion of our travels." I don't know about the intrepid part, but I was privileged to be his companion on our travels.

9

Prime Ministers, Premiers, and Pols

When Charles Bronfman bought the Montreal Expos as Canada's first team in Major League Baseball, he asked former prime minister Lester B. Pearson to become honorary chairman of the club. Pearson was a great baseball fan, so much so that when he visited Hyannis Port after his election in 1963, President John F. Kennedy had one of his close aides, Dave Powers, give the PM a quiz on baseball statistics and trivia. He passed with flying colours. As he wrote in the concluding volume of *Mike,* his admirable memoirs, "I am not sure whether President Kennedy was impressed by my grasp of North American and international affairs, but I certainly know that Powers was impressed by my knowledge of baseball."

By the winter of 1972, Mr Pearson had been diagnosed with cancer, and Charles decided to fly him down to spring training in Florida with us on the company jet. I ended up sitting alone with him in the front of the plane, while Charles sat at the back with a couple of his Expos partners.

There I was with a former prime minister, father of the Canadian flag and Nobel Peace Prize laureate, as a captive audience for three hours. Of all the people he had met in his life, the one who intrigued me most was Nikita Khrushchev, the Soviet strongman of the 1950s and early 1960s, who rose to power after the death of Joseph Stalin in 1953 and remained in office until his ouster by Leonid Brezhnev in the bloodless Kremlin coup of 1964.

"I wonder if you could tell me about him," I ventured, "because he's the kind of personality I've always been interested in – rough, tough, and untutored." Khrushchev had once famously banged his shoe on the Soviet delegation's desk at the United Nations General Assembly. It wasn't very elegant, but it certainly got the world's attention.

"I met him on a visit to Russia when I was foreign minister," Pearson replied. In fact, he was the first NATO foreign minister to visit the Soviet Union, in 1955. Khrushchev invited him to his summer dacha on the Black Sea near Yalta. "We went to dinner, and they started giving toasts with vodka," he recalled. "One after another." Eighteen toasts in all, with Khrushchev checking on his guests to make sure they were "bottoms up" every time. As Pearson recalled in his memoirs, "We even drank to the Canadian wheat surplus ... [and] President Eisenhower's recovery from his illness."

"By midnight," Pearson told me "Khrushchev was so addled that his bodyguards had to help him walk out." He added that he himself was able to walk out to his car under his own steam, but when awakened early the next morning by a Canadian embassy official, felt somewhat the worse for wear. "So I asked him," Pearson recalled, "how he thought it had gone the night before. 'Oh,' he said, 'Khrushchev was very impressed with you.' 'Really,' I said, 'with my position on NATO?' 'No, he couldn't care less about Canada's position on NATO. He was impressed with the way you handled your vodka.'"

It was Pearson, as prime minister, who had put Laz Phillips in the Senate, having previously passed over Sam Bronfman, but we didn't discuss that. He led Canada through five tumultuous years of change from 1963 to 1968, and I believe he has a place in history in the first rank of Canadian prime ministers. He brought in the Canadian flag, negotiated the Auto Pact – the forerunner of free trade – and established the Canada Pension Plan, with an opting-out formula that led to the creation of the Quebec Pension Plan, itself the foundation for the Caisse de Dépôt et Placement du Québec, which by the twenty-first century had grown to $135 billion in assets. He set Canada on the road to universal health care by bringing in Medicare, and he governed with the last balanced budgets the country would see for thirty years. He presided over Canada's centennial celebrations in 1967, a time of unique optimism in the country that, in a way, made it possible for Pierre Trudeau to become Liberal leader when Pearson stepped down the next year.

There's a famous picture of Mr Pearson at the cabinet swearing-in on April 4, 1967, with three future Liberal prime ministers – Trudeau, John Turner, and Jean Chrétien. As it turned out, I would become closely involved with them all.

In the 1984 Liberal leadership campaign, I supported Turner, to the considerable chagrin of Chrétien. After the Liberals lost the 1984 election, Chrétien asked me to come to his office in the East Block. He said he had it on good authority that I had given money to Turner for a trust fund to provide for his financial security after he left Ottawa.

"If you can prove it," I said, "I will give $50,000 to a charity of your choice, and if you can't prove it, you will give $1,000 to a charity of my choice. So now you're on your own. Prove it." And the odds were 50 to 1.

I had honestly believed that Turner was the guy who could win the election for us after Trudeau left. I was wrong about that, but I was one of a group who encouraged Turner to return to politics from Bay Street in 1984, and we were prepared to put together a retirement fund for him, something I believe had been done for Mr Pearson. I had breakfast with Turner and offered to do something like that for him, and he turned me down flat. He thought it was inappropriate. So it's not that I didn't want to give money to him or raise it for him, but I never did in that sense, because he wouldn't accept that kind of donation. And Chrétien never took the bet.

After he became leader, Turner called and asked me to become chief fundraiser of the Liberal party. After Brian Mulroney swept the country in the election of September 4, 1984, Turner was trying to rebuild the Liberal party, including its finances, by raising money and paying down debt. During his Bay Street years, John and I were on the Seagram board together, and I'd come to know him quite well.

We went to dinner at Mamma Teresa's, an Italian restaurant in Ottawa and a big hangout of politicians, consultants, and journalists. He had a steak, a salad, and a few "scotcheroonies," as he liked to say, and we agreed that I would become the chief bagman for the party. But I insisted that for a period of at least six months I would be in charge of spending the money as well as raising it. He said, "Fine, give me a couple of paragraphs and I will read it out tomorrow at caucus." Caucus came and went, but he said nothing. "Weren't you supposed to say something?" I asked. "Iona Campagnolo," he said of the senator who was then party president, "got to me and said it would be too much power in one man's hands."

"I'm not going to let you down, John," I said. "I will raise the money. I will collect two and a half million dollars. But you are going to spend three and a half million. There is no control on the spending. Believe me, I see it, because I sit on the committee."

And in the next nine months, my executive assistant, Herb Metcalfe, and I traversed the country five times, from Vancouver to Newfoundland. It wasn't easy. It is never easy raising money for a party that is just going into opposition, as opposed to a party just coming into government as the Tories were. But we raised the $2.5 million. And sure enough, the party spent more than we raised.

We worked at it three full days a week. It helped that I had the company plane to get us around the country. It also helped in terms of access that I was running the Bronfman investments and had built shopping centres and office buildings in every major city in Canada. You don't schlep around the country asking people to write $25,000 cheques, usually from their companies but in some cases from themselves, unless you're seeing all the right people. And we saw them all.

When it was over, I was down in New York for a weekend with Sandra, and Herb called to say that Turner had fired him. Why? Apparently, because he and his wife, Isabel, had included some Tories at a party at their house and Turner had got wind of it. So I called Turner and lit into him.

"You simply can't do this," I said. "You can't fire my assistant. The least you could have done was consult me first. What you've done is just plain stupid. And I am tendering my resignation over the phone. Goodbye."

Not long after that, Turner called me into his office and asked me to stay on, but I declined. He then asked if I would at least accept a farewell party at Stornoway, the opposition leader's residence, which I did.

"While I'm here, John," I said, "I want to give you some advice, totally unsolicited."

"What's that?" he asked.

"There are people you've discarded in the party, and there is no room for grudges in politics. You've got to bring everyone into the tent."

He just said something like, "That's the way it is in politics." So there it was. I was out. And that was the last I heard from Turner in quite some time. Then in September 1988, my secretary, Peggy Gaon, informed me that I was invited to lunch at Stornoway. I thought it was a bit strange, not that I wasn't on speaking terms with John, but we hadn't exactly been getting along since I had quit as chief fundraiser. I figured there would be a lot of people there, but when I got to Stornoway for lunch on September 19, it turned out that it was just Turner and I. It was a beautiful late summer day, and we sat out in the backyard.

Finally, he asked, "So, whaddya think?" He was referring to the coming election.

"I read in the papers that Brian's going to call the election in a couple of weeks," I said. "And I can tell you, John, that you are going to get your ass handed to you in a sling. We might do better than the last time, but we have no hope of winning."

Turner obviously disagreed. "If I can get my message on free trade across," he said, "I have a chance at forming a minority government."

"First of all," I replied, "free trade is necessary for the country. It's our only hope of survival, in my view. And if your best hope is a minority government after two tries, what are you doing it for?" And I added, "If I am right, you are going to hurt the country, you are going to hurt the party, and most of all, you are going to hurt yourself. Because if you lose two elections, your currency is going to be so badly debased you will never get it back in business."

I didn't have a mandate from anyone and I was basically thinking out loud, but I suggested to Turner that if he resigned before the election, I could get him back on the board of Seagram and a couple of other top boards.

Only eleven days later, on September 30, Mulroney dropped the election writ. It turned out that there was later a putsch inside the party to replace Turner with Chrétien in the middle of the campaign. The Liberal party looked like it was imploding. Then Turner pulled it together and scored impressively in the October 25 English-language debate, telling Mulroney he had "sold us out" on free trade. The polling numbers moved up, and for a brief time, it looked as if Turner might even win, but then as John Duffy would write in *Fights of Our Lives,* his critically acclaimed book on crucial Canadian elections, Turner became "trapped in his own crusade" and couldn't move on to other issues, while Mulroney barnstormed the country furiously for the last three weeks of the campaign and successfully transformed it into a referendum on free trade. On November 21, Mulroney won his second consecutive majority, nothing like his 211-seat landslide of 1984 but still a big majority of 170 ridings in what was then a 295-seat House of Commons.

One of the reasons I was such a strong supporter of free trade was that the Bronfman companies were all essentially free traders in goods, services, and investments. All of them had grown well beyond their Canadian origins to take advantage of growth and market opportunities in the United States. Seagram was number one in North America in liquors and wines, and number two worldwide. We built Cadillac Fairview into one of the largest real estate companies in North America. They were proud Canadian companies, and big winners in the U.S. That's been my experience, and the numbers under free trade prove it was a good thing for Canada. Since the implementation of free trade in 1989, Canada's exports to the U.S. grew from $100 billion a year to $350 billion in 2002; and world exports as a share of our output have grown from 23 percent to 45 percent of Canada's gross domestic product. More than half of Canada's non-governmental output is in exports to the United States. It's no coincidence that companies such as Alcan, Bombardier, and Nortel Networks all have about 95 percent of their sales outside Canada.

My concern for Turner's viability on Bay Street proved to be well founded. Though he returned to the practice of law in Toronto and did well enough, he never again sat on the board of an important Canadian company. Not only did the business community not agree with his position on free trade, on some level it never forgave him for it.

∞

Not long after Turner bowed to the inevitable and announced his resignation in May 1989, Johnny Rae came to see me on behalf of Chrétien. Then as later, John was an executive at Power Corporation, and he was going to be running Chrétien's leadership campaign. "I need twenty friends to give $10,000 each for Jean's leadership campaign," he said. He was looking for seed money. I took out a cheque book, wrote him a personal cheque for $10,000, and sent him on his way. And I was very pleased to do it. I supported Chrétien from the beginning of the 1990 leadership race. I believed his time had come, and I believed he could bring us back to power in the next election.

Since leaving politics in February 1986, Chrétien had been doing very well in a commercial law practice with Lang Michener in Ottawa and as a partner in Gordon Securities on Bay Street – in fact, better than he had expected, as he explained when he came to see me one day at Cemp's offices on the top floor of CIL House in Montreal. He'd phoned one mid-afternoon to say he was across the street at Place Ville Marie and wondered if he could drop by for fifteen minutes. He ended up staying three hours. He said he was bringing in a lot of business. "I'm getting cheques for ten, fifteen, twenty thousand dollars," he said, and he seemed quite surprised by it.

"You're the former minister of finance," I said to him, "why should you be surprised?"

"The one thing I can't believe," he said, "is the amount of tax I have to pay."

"Jean," I said. "You were the minister of finance and you didn't know what the marginal tax rates were?"

"I didn't realize they were that high," he replied.

"Not only that," I said, "but you are paying it as a resident of Ontario. Those of us who live in Quebec pay higher."

"Well," Chrétien said, "if I ever get into power, it will never be more than 50 percent."

It turned out that Chrétien, with Paul Martin as finance minister, not only balanced the budget and began to pay down the federal debt, but in the October 2000 budget brought in the deepest tax cuts in Canadian history. Chrétien also cut the taxable portion of capital gains from 75 percent to 50 percent. In essence, our Liberal government cut the capital gains tax in half, something I had been pushing hard for as chairman of the Senate Banking Committee. I made one of my few interventions in caucus about it. There are members who speak every week, but I can count on the fingers of one hand the number of speeches I've made in caucus over a twenty-year period. As I explained to caucus, when you lower personal income taxes, something like 88 cents on the dollar is saved or spent and only 12 cents is reinvested, where if you lower capital gains, the effect is just the opposite. Most of it gets reinvested. Canada desperately needs more working capital. And somewhat to my amazement, when I sat down, I got a big ovation.

After I spoke, the PM told the caucus, "I want you guys to listen to Leo on this, because he is right." It was Chrétien, as much as Martin, who made that happen.

The restoration of a sound and sensible fiscal framework was probably the number one achievement of the Chrétien years, and that was because of the partnership between Chrétien and Martin. Paul couldn't have balanced the books without the strong support of the prime minister, who kept skating the spenders into the boards.

Chrétien easily won the leadership over Martin at the Calgary convention on June 23, 1990, winning 57 percent of the delegate votes, including mine, on the first ballot. But at some level, though Chrétien and Martin made a formidable team for years, they never got over the bad blood of that leadership campaign. Chrétien, in particular, never forgave Martin for running such an aggressive campaign against him, especially on the issue of Meech Lake, which Martin supported and Chrétien opposed. Chrétien was genuinely troubled by the distinct society clause, and he also wanted to win the favour of the Trudeau wing of the party.

They often spoke disparagingly of one another, and Chrétien was occasionally very rough on Martin in caucus. Paul would just sit there, taking it stoically. Eventually, things just got out of hand between them, and Chrétien fired Martin on Sunday, June 2, 2002. This brought the leadership issue to a head later that summer, when Chrétien finally tried to head off a caucus revolt by announcing the timetable for his retirement in February 2004.

For most of the 1990s, I was pretty much an absentee senator. Not to put too fine a point on it, my attendance record stank. When Sandra was struck by her disabling illness, I basically stopped showing up for a few years. But once we got her care regularized at home, I began to take an interest in the Senate again. And by 1999 I realized that I had five years left in the Senate before my mandatory retirement on my seventy-fifth birthday in January 2004. I decided that I didn't want to be remembered just as a bagman who never showed up. I wanted to leave my mark, and I thought the best way I could do that would be as chairman of the Senate Committee on Banking, Trade and Commerce. Banking was one area where I had expertise that no one else in Parliament had – I'd been a senior director of the Toronto-Dominion Bank for more than twenty-five years, and I was going off that board, so there would be no conflict with being chair of the banking committee. And in any event, in my experience, senators rarely felt conflicted. Furthermore, I had run the Bronfmans' investments for more than thirty years and had built the largest real estate company in the country. So I also knew all about banking issues from the vantage point of customers.

Just as I had discreetly lobbied Trudeau through senior associates for my appointment to the Senate, I now made my interest in the banking committee chairmanship known to Chrétien through his chief of staff, Jean Pelletier. And there was a telephone call from the prime minister to our leader in the Senate, Bernie Boudreau from Nova Scotia, who would later resign to run unsuccessfully in the 2000 election. That's what got me the chairmanship. Without that call I wouldn't have got it. Jack Austin from British Columbia was senior to me, and he wanted it badly. But Jack didn't have anything like the expertise in finance and banking that I have. And I think I've proven that on the committee during my final four years in the Senate. Unfortunately, my appointment kind of strained what had once been a very close relationship – Jack and his wife, Natalie, had come along on most of our trips with Trudeau. But as with my original appointment to the Senate, I was again the choice of the only person who mattered – the prime minister. I believe the banking committee has done some significant work. In 2002 and 2003, for instance, we took a good look at the question of large bank mergers as well as at some of the corporate governance issues arising from what became known as "Enronitis" – the malaise of corporate ethics that shook public confidence in markets and business leadership in North America.

Chrétien was good to me in other ways. Some time after my wife's stroke, when she was able to get out again, the PM and his wife, Aline, phoned to invite us to a small dinner at 24 Sussex. There was only one other couple, Dick Thomson and his wife, Heather. It was an intimate evening in Sandra's honour, and I was deeply moved. He included me in a parliamentary delegation that accompanied him on a visit to Israel in April 2000. He invited me to dinner with the Queen on her golden jubilee visit to Canada in October 2002, and seated me and Mona Golfman, the new lady in my life, at a table right next to hers. He would invite me to his summer cottage in Shawinigan, a beautiful place on a very pristine lake. We would play golf at Grand-Mère, and in this setting, he was always a very informal and accessible guy.

Most of all, Chrétien worked very hard raising money for the party. He was absolutely first class at that. If it weren't for him, our debt would have been double the $3 million we had nationally in 2002, with another $2 million in Quebec. It's amazing to me that a party could be $5 million in the red after nearly a decade in government. But that also tells you something about the Liberal party – we are apparently even better at spending money than we are at raising it.

But by the summer of 2002, it was increasingly apparent that Chrétien's time as Liberal leader and prime minister was coming to an end. At our summer caucus in the Saguenay, he was facing a full-scale revolt. Two senior Quebec cabinet ministers, Immigration Minister Denis Coderre and Justice Minister Martin Cauchon, had the idea of circulating a loyalty letter to the PM. It blew up in their faces when they were only able to obtain the signatures of barely more than half the number of Liberal MPs, six of whom later said they'd never agreed to it.

With all the leverage and power of appointments in the PM's pleasure – from naming cabinet ministers, parliamentary secretaries, and committee chairs, to choosing who dines with the Queen – only half the caucus was onside. It was devastating. On the Senate side, Laurier Lapierre circulated a loyalty pledge signed by forty-eight out of sixty-two Liberal senators, including me. But of course, we all had the luxury of job security and of not having to run for office. I didn't mind signing, but I thought the whole idea was insulting.

When the PM arrived in Saguenay on August 21, he vowed to fight a leadership review that would require that he win a double majority of both card-carrying Liberals and delegates at a convention scheduled for February 2003, a review he appeared destined to lose on both counts. "It's not about power, it's about responsibility," he said, trying to put it on the high road, adding, "I don't think Canadians like what they have seen from us this summer." Less than twenty-four hours later, he announced his retirement.

I never thought Chrétien intended to fight the leadership review, because it would have cost at least $2 million, and he never raised a penny of it in the spring and summer of 2002. John Rae, who was ostensibly running the PM's effort to win the review, came to see me once in June 2002, but didn't ask me to raise any money on behalf of the PM. He didn't even ask me for a personal donation. That's when I knew the game was over.

Besides, the time had come for Chrétien to leave. Yogi Berra was wrong. When it's over, it is actually over, and in Chrétien's case, it was over. I also thought he made an error, in terms of a smooth transition as well as of his own legacy, in deciding to take eighteen months to leave, by far the longest political transition in Canadian history. The convention itself was later set for November 2003, fully fourteen months after Chrétien's retirement announcement.

After the Saguenay caucus, I enthusiastically joined a group of senior advisers and fundraisers for Paul Martin's leadership campaign. I had known Paul well during his business career as CEO of Canada Steamship Lines in Montreal. As a member and later chair of the Senate Banking Committee, I had the opportunity to work with him on a number of tax and banking issues when he was minister of finance. On the big issue of balancing the budget, paying down debt, and cutting taxes, he did a superb job, one that uniquely prepared him to become prime minister. He inherited a deficit of $42 billion and a national debt that had reached $583 billion by the time he balanced the books in 1998.

He never looked back, giving Canadians their deepest tax cuts in history in the budget of October 2000 – $100 billion over five years. And he resisted the pressure to resume spending sprees the country could ill afford, insisting that we pay down some of the debt, more than $46 billion by the time he left Finance in 2002. In the Martin years, Canada's debt as a percentage of GDP was reduced from 71 percent to 49 percent. Canada went from worst to first in the G7 in management of its fiscal framework. His legacy as finance minister is unmatched in modern times.

However, on a couple of issues, I thought Paul's political antennae were rather too sensitive to public opinion, keeping him from making the tough leadership decisions. I strongly disagreed with Paul's decision to kill the proposed bank mergers in 1998. The decision to disallow the bank mergers at the end of the 1990s was a big mistake, depriving Canadian banking of the critical mass of assets and operational economies of scale it needed to succeed in the era of globalization. In 1975 the largest Canadian bank, the Royal Bank of Canada, was the twenty-third largest in the world as measured by assets. By 2002, its successor, RBC Financial Group, had fallen to fifty-third place. As RBC president Gord Nixon pointed out in a thoughtful speech I attended in Montreal in May 2002, "The market capitalization of a single Dutch financial institution, ING Group, is now almost as big as Canada's five largest banks combined." In fact, the largest foreign player in Canada, HSBC, had a market value of U.S.$110 billion, more than the market cap of Canada's Big Five, and you could throw in the sixth, the National Bank, for good measure.

I hope that Martin, as prime minister, will revisit the issue of bank mergers, as we revisited it on the Senate Banking Committee beginning in late 2002 when John Manley, Martin's successor at Finance, sent me a letter asking us to clarify "the public interest" in the rules on mergers.

I like Manley. I liked the way, as foreign affairs minister, he instinctively said the right things about standing with the Americans in the wake of the September 11 terror attacks and the way he pointed out the "glaring inadequacy" of our defence capacity and how we were "trading on a reputation that was built two generations and more ago – but that we haven't continued to live up to." There's a straight-talking side to Manley that I find very appealing, and he was my second choice for Liberal leader. My former assistant, Herb Metcalfe, a prominent Ottawa government affairs consultant, was one of Manley's top campaign advisers, and at Herb's request, I was happy to host a dinner for Manley in December 2002. When Manley pulled out of the leadership race in July 2003, I can't say it came as a surprise. He had a shortage of warm bodies and cold cash – two essential elements in a leadership game. It was the smart thing to do, keeping Manley whole for the next race.

I also hope, and have every reason to believe, that Martin will reaffirm Canada's strong support of Israel, which became increasingly ambiguous at the end of the Chrétien years, especially after the wave of suicide bombings that began with the Palestinian *intifada* in the fall of 2000, and continued with ever more deadly results, and recriminations from the Israelis.

At the outset of the Liberal leadership campaign in October 2002, I had eighteen members of the Montreal Jewish community for a breakfast for Paul at the house, and before they raised a nickel on his behalf, they understandably wanted to know his position on Israel. They were quite satisfied, as I was. Later, in December, I hosted a fundraiser on his behalf. It was a sit-down dinner at my house, and Paul took one course, from the soup to the coffee, at each of the tables. And then he took questions. His command of issues, across the broad spectrum of the policy agenda, was quite impressive.

Raising money for his leadership campaign was not a problem for Paul. In the spring of 2003, he held a cocktail at the Chateau Champlain in Montreal – a thousand people at a thousand dollars a head – and they raised $1 million in the one evening, a record for a single fundraiser in Canada.

Paul will be the fifth Liberal prime minister I've known, four of whom I've had the opportunity to work with. But I've also known a sixth prime minister – Brian Mulroney.

I first knew Brian and Mila Mulroney socially in the 1970s. They were a charming, good-looking, and fun couple. And Sandra, who gave the best parties in Montreal, would often invite them. This was after his first, failed run for the Conservative leadership in 1976, when he became president of the Iron Ore Company. They bought a house on Belvedere Road, near the summit of Mount Royal, not far from our place on Summit Circle, and they were frequent guests at our house. They were there for parties where Frank Sinatra, Danny Kaye, and Robert Charlebois came to the house, and occasionally Brian would sing a song of his own.

In 1983, on Brian's second try for the Tory leadership, his bagman, Senator Guy Charbonneau, came to see me for a donation and we gave $50,000 to Brian's campaign. Then, after he won, we gave him another $50,000 to help defray his campaign debt. I discussed it with Charles and we agreed it was not only a smart move, but the right thing to do. We liked Brian. We liked his pro-business mindset. We liked that he was perfectly bilingual. And we liked his strong support of Israel. So there I was, a Liberal bagman, donating $100,000 to a Conservative. We may not have been the biggest single donor to Brian's campaign, but we were certainly one of the biggest.

Then I helped Mulroney sort out a problem he had with Eddie Goodman, one of the most powerful Conservatives in Toronto, who was very close to the government of Bill Davis at Queen's Park. By April 1983, it became apparent that Davis himself would not run for the federal Conservative leadership. Brian was trying to win some support in the Davis camp, but he was encountering pretty stiff resistance from Goodman. Eddie was our Toronto lawyer at what was then Goodman and Goodman. When I was running Cadillac Fairview and we had an issue with Queen's Park, I could be inside Davis's office in five minutes if Eddie was handling it.

Brian asked if I could smooth things out with Eddie, so I called him up. Eddie had a famous lisp, and he started screaming about Brian, how he had been involved in setting up a trust fund for Claude Wagner to bring him from the bench into politics as a Conservative candidate in the 1972 election.

"He handled the whole thing and he denies it," Eddie shouted into the phone.

"Eddie," I said, "there's no room for grudges in politics, so be a good fellow and at least meet with him."

"If you want me to, I will," he said.

"Here's what I'll arrange," I said. "I'll bring Brian to Toronto for lunch in my dining room at Cadillac Fairview, and I'll just join you for coffee."

So I picked Brian up, flew him up to Toronto on the company plane, and left him in the dining room with Eddie. They spent two hours together, and made friends, or at least made peace. That was my other contribution to his leadership campaign – helping to get Fast Eddie Goodman onside.

As prime minister in May 1985, Mulroney came to speak at an Israel Bonds dinner in Montreal where I was the honouree. When the dinner committee had approached me about it, I had said I would accept provided they could get the new PM as the guest speaker, which they managed to do, probably because Charles Bronfman was chairing the dinner. I was delighted and particularly pleased by his strong statement of support for Israel.

Canada, he said, was committed "unshakably to the preservation of the state of Israel." I must say that in his nine years as prime minister, he never wavered in his support for Israel, and I also have to say that Israel never had a better friend as prime minister of Canada. I was also grateful for his continued support of Israel after he left office, particularly when Israel came under attack in the Human Rights Commission of the United Nations. In a particularly pointed and pertinent speech to the United Nations Association of Canada in October 2001, Mulroney said, "Stripped of their intellectual pretensions, these ritual denunciations of Israel are a pernicious form of racism. And the ultimate irony of the attempts to isolate Israel at the UN is, of course, that the modern state of Israel was born at the UN." Exactly. When he was named Man of the Year by the Jewish National Fund in 2003, an honour long overdue, I was delighted be one of the co-chairs of the tribute.

Brian also appointed Sandra to the board of the CBC, and while it obviously suited his purpose to name her to a board he otherwise packed with Tories, she was more than qualified. She knew the film and television industries top to bottom, as a writer and as a producer, and she knew both the English and French sides of the Canadian cultural equation. She was a good board member and gave Mulroney no reason to regret appointing her.

After her stroke in 1991 and until he left office in June 1993, the Mulroneys would often call, usually every second Saturday evening, to ask how she was doing. They would keep her on the phone for about half an hour, Brian on one line and Mila on an extension, and just bring her up to date on the inside of politics and the social life of the capital. Those calls meant a lot to Sandra, and they meant even more to me.

When Mulroney had his troubles over the Airbus Affair in 1995, I sympathized with him in his predicament. Eventually the government had to settle the case on his terms, with $2 million in costs and an apology to him and his family for the trouble they had been put through. The strain of the Airbus episode took a visible toll on him, but I was delighted with his vindication.

In April 1987, when President Reagan came to address a joint session of Parliament, I had a very good seat among the senators seated on the floor of the Commons, and Sandra had an even better one, looking directly down at Ronald Reagan from the Senate Gallery of the House. I could see why he was called the "Great Communicator." I never saw anyone give such a compelling scripted performance. Even when interrupted by the NDP's Svend Robinson, shouting, "No Star Wars!" Reagan didn't miss a beat, replying that he felt right at home with a heckler.

Afterwards, as we made our way back to the Senate side through the Hall of Honour in the Centre Block, the official party swept past on their way out. Brian noticed us standing there, stopped, and brought President and Nancy Reagan over to meet us. "Mr President," he said, "I want you to meet a very good friend, Senator Kolber and his wife. He is not a Conservative, but he is a good friend."

That's how I've always felt about Brian – he isn't a Liberal, but he is a good friend."

∞

I met René Lévesque, indirectly, through Phyllis Lambert. At her insistence, we got involved in the restoration of several buildings, called Les

Cours le Royer, behind Notre Dame Basilica in Old Montreal. It was a non-profit thing for us, a way of doing something for the community and for the restoration and revival of the old city, a cause close to Phyllis's heart. It is a first-class development, it was Phyllis who got us involved, and it is entirely to her credit that we were.

The rehab resulted in a unique mix of lofts and apartments, and Lévesque bought one of them not long after he became premier of Quebec in 1976. The residential real estate market was then quite depressed, mainly because of his election, and he got it at a very good price. But it turned out that it was very noisy in Old Montreal, particularly in the summertime, especially on Place Jacques Cartier, the main square of the old city, directly behind Les Cours le Royer, where thousands of people hung out at night. Eventually, Lévesque got tired of the noise and sold, but by this time the market had recovered and he made, I was told, about $50,000 on the deal.

Apparently, it was the most money Lévesque had ever made on any deal in his life, and he was quite grateful. He sent word through the architect of Les Cours le Royer, Maurice Desnoyers, that he would like to come by my house for a drink to say thanks, which was very nice of him, but quite unnecessary. So we set it up for him to come by on a Sunday afternoon. He arrived at four o'clock with Corinne Côté, to whom he was not yet married, and his friend Yves Michaud, whom he had named Quebec's delegate-general in Paris.

Many years later, in 2000, there would be a famous encounter between Michaud and me. I ran into him in the barbershop of the Chateau Champlain and asked him if he was still a separatist. He just exploded and he said, "You always think the Jews are the only ones who have ever been persecuted." Then, in an interview on French-language radio, he essentially repeated his comments while recounting the incident. The upshot of the whole affair was that Lucien Bouchard resigned as premier of Quebec in January 2001, partly because he was completely fed up with the xenophobic wing of the Parti Québécois. Bouchard then joined Davies Ward Phillips Vineberg, the Montreal office of the firm that had represented the Bronfmans for more than half a century.

Anyway, Lévesque came for an hour and stayed for more than four hours, and clearly enjoyed himself. We showed him and Corinne around the house. There was a lot of Quebec art on the walls – a Suzor-Coté and others – and a lot of Quebec fabrics and furniture in the living room. Lévesque was very pleased that Québécois artists and artisans had such prominence in a house that received a lot of Canadian and foreign visitors.

I didn't vote for Lévesque, of course, but it was hard not to like him. And perhaps because of his background in journalism, he was a good listener. At one point, I told him his language policies worked against him because they were keeping people out of the stores. "What do you mean?" he asked. I explained that we owned Fairview Centre in Pointe Claire, where 90 percent of the clients were English speaking, and Bill 101 required that signs be exclusively in French. "It's going to cost you money on the sales tax," I told Lévesque, "because we are scaring away shoppers. It's not good for us, not good for anybody." He gave me one of his trademark shrugs and said we could agree to disagree.

He had several large martinis, and we gave them a tour of the wine cellar. I brought up a bottle of Romanée-Conti, 1966, which is considered the best of all the Burgundies. "I know you have rules about gifts," I told Lévesque, "but I strongly suggest you accept this." Lévesque looked at it, then looked at Michaud, who said, "Don't be a damn fool, take it." And so he did.

We invited René and Corinne to my fiftieth birthday party in January 1979, an incredible event that Sandra staged at the Ritz. Shimon Peres flew in from Israel to be there. Lévesque, sitting at our table, said he very much wanted to meet with Shimon, and I said we would set it up the next time he was in town.

The next time Shimon visited was in August, and we arranged to fly up to Quebec City on the company plane. Shimon, a voracious reader, had noticed a biography of Lévesque in his hotel suite the previous evening, and he read it before going to bed. It turned out that we saw Lévesque on August 24, his birthday, and Shimon wished him all the best. Lévesque was pretty impressed. There were just the three of us, sitting there for two hours in Lévesque's office in the forbidding concrete building known as the Bunker. Lévesque was most interested to know how Israel handled the language issue – that was his main agenda item for the meeting. Shimon didn't quite catch his drift and said there was really no problem. Finally Lévesque came to the point and asked, "What language are your signs in?"

"In whatever language people want them in," Peres replied. "They could be in Arabic, they could be in Yiddish, they could be in Hebrew, they could be in French, in English, anything you want."

Then Lévesque asked what language people would be served in when they went to a government office. "They can be served in Hebrew, Arabic, or English?" he asked incredulously. "And there's no problem?"

"None at all," Shimon replied. Lévesque was quite taken aback. I assume he was looking to draw a parallel between Quebec and Israel, the official language of the majority and the languages of cultural communities. In fact, Quebec finally adopted a solution somewhat similar to the Israeli experience in 1993, when Robert Bourassa's government passed Bill 86, allowing signs in other languages provided French was the priority and predominant language.

Danny Kaye came to conduct the Montreal Symphony, with all proceeds to the orchestra's pension fund. Sandra and I were hosting the event, and I invited Lévesque to come and sit in our box at Place des Arts. Everybody else wore black tie, but Lévesque came in a rumpled suit and Wallabies. As a war correspondent for the Americans in the Second World War, Lévesque had seen Danny entertain the troops. He greatly admired him and asked if he could meet him backstage after the concert. But he kept asking how much we were paying him. Sandra repeatedly explained that Danny did these benefits for orchestras and wasn't being paid anything. "Mr Premier," she asked, "why are you so doubtful?" Lévesque just couldn't believe that Danny wasn't getting paid. But he stayed for the reception, which was very unusual for him, and had a great time.

The thing I liked about Lévesque was that you could be very blunt with him and, within reason, he was never offended. Before Danny came on at the symphony gala, I tried to explain to Lévesque why some Holocaust survivors in the Jewish community had an apocalyptic view of him and his party. "These people come from a place where they were thrown out," I explained, "and now they think you want to throw them out of Quebec." He didn't like what I said, but at least he listened.

From time to time, I would go to see Lévesque on a business problem or a community issue, and we always got along very well. I can't say we were close friends – we weren't. But I really liked him.

I knew Robert Bourassa in both his political lives as premier of Quebec. It was partly because of him that I advised Charles to get out of the broadcasting business. Bourassa had brought in Bill 22 in 1974, making French Quebec's official language, and a year later the bill became the focus of anger in the English community of Montreal, stirred up by a talk radio host named John Robertson at CFCF, one of several Montreal radio and TV stations we owned through a company called Multiple Access. Because of all the heat the radio station was generating, we were getting a lot of heat back from the Quebec nationalists. They were taking two names in vain, Bronfman and Seagram, that it was my job to protect. I thought, who needs this? And Charles agreed.

Then the regulator, the Canadian Radio-Television Commission, denied our request to buy a few radio stations in northern Ontario, on the grounds that we weren't local or regional owners. That did it for me. If we couldn't grow our broadcasting business, we would get out, and before long we sold at a nice profit.

Bourassa's defeat in the 1976 election was attributable in part to his being deserted in droves by "angryphones," English-speaking voters in the Montreal region. So complete and utter was his defeat that no one imagined then that he would ever make a comeback. Except him. And he did, regaining the Quebec Liberal leadership in 1983 and serving another two terms as premier, from 1985 to 1994. By the time of Bourassa's return to politics, the rules of fundraising had changed considerably. Lévesque had passed a law banning donations by corporations and trade unions to all Quebec political parties, and he would later call this the proudest achievement of his premiership. Individual donations were permitted but limited to $3,000, and were made public on an annual basis.

Lévesque had every reason to be proud of the integrity and transparency of the new rules, but it wasn't hard to raise money, especially with the PQ as the adversary. When Bourassa returned as Liberal leader, he asked me to do a fundraiser for him, and I had no trouble getting forty people to come to lunch in the Cemp dining room at $3,000 a head. We raised $120,000 in one small lunch.

But I was somewhat taken aback by his apparent indifference to the loss of head offices suffered by Montreal. When I raised this with him once, his reply was that "for every one that leaves we have two coming in," which wasn't even close to the truth. His comment had nothing to do with reality, but he made it as if it were fact. Yet I liked Robert, he was a very nice man, and in private he was utterly charming and good-humoured, far from his public image as an underfed accountant.

After Bourassa retired at the beginning of 1994, I had no involvement with the Quebec Liberals until the spring of 1998, when Daniel Johnson resigned and Jean Charest was drafted as his successor. While the draft was indeed spontaneous, it was not without encouragement. For example, the PM's office asked a number of us to call Charest and urge him to do it. So I did. I told Charest, who was then Conservative leader in Ottawa, that he didn't really have a choice. If he turned it down, he would be seen as not answering the call for Quebec and

Canada. The Liberals and the federalists were looking for more than a leader, they were looking for a saviour to run against the charismatic Lucien Bouchard in the election expected in the fall of that year.

"In my opinion, if you don't do this," I said, "you may hurt your political career for a long time."

"I think you may be right," Charest replied.

"If you decide to do it," I said, "I'll put my money where my mouth is and organize your first big fundraiser."

So when he accepted the leadership, he took me up on it. I organized a small committee for a cocktail party, and we had no trouble raising over $750,000 at $3,000 a head. One prominent member of the Montreal Jewish community had nine members of his family give $3,000 each. That's how easy a sell Jean Charest was in Montreal in those days, and not just in the Jewish community but among francophones, anglophones, and allophones as well. It was the most successful fundraiser the Quebec Liberals ever had – there's never been one like it before or since.

Oddly enough, when the fundraiser was over, that was the last I heard from Charest for quite some time.

The expectations of Charest were far too high, and he lost the 1998 election, though he managed to win the popular vote. Subsequently, he worked hard not only at learning the issues, but at building a campaign organization. As they went into the Quebec election in 2003, I was impressed that the Liberals had a war chest of $6 million as an opposition party. In contrast, the federal Liberals, a party in government, were nearing $6 million in debt. It's hard to figure. It probably goes back to Lévesque's campaign finance law. Wealthy people can donate on behalf of every member of their family of voting age. It's actually a very efficient, as well as a very democratic, way to raise money.

Charest, Mario Dumont of the Action Démocratique du Québec, and the PQ's Bernard Landry, the three political leaders who squared off in the Quebec election of April 2003, were the latest in a long line of Quebec politicians I've known. And I was delighted that Charest won the April 14 election with 46 percent of the popular vote against 33 percent for Landry and the PQ and 18 percent for Dumont and the ADQ. By the early spring of 2003, against the distracting backdrop of the war in Iraq, Charest had recaptured the mood for change, performed brilliantly in the leaders' debate, stormed down the homestretch, and was a thoroughly deserving winner of the election.

The first Quebec premier I ever saw, though I never met him, was Maurice Duplessis, at the peak of his powers in 1948. Charles Bronfman had season tickets for the Canadiens. Duplessis had seats very close by, and on Saturday nights he would arrive with a girlfriend he had in Montreal. His routine was that they would have dinner at the Ritz, come to the game just as it started, leave five minutes before the end so as to beat the crowd, and then head back to the Ritz, where he stayed when he was in Montreal. One night we were walking along Sherbrooke Street, when the premier's motorcade pulled up with these police outriders on motorcycles. Duplessis got out of the car, peeled out a thick roll of bills, I don't know whether they were fives or twenties, and gave one to each cop. Try that today!

Among the other provincial politicians I've known, Bill Davis was a particular favourite of mine, in and out of office. He was premier of Ontario for fourteen years, from 1971 to 1985, and he was one of the most successful politicians I've ever met. If we were inaugurating a major shopping centre or shopping mall in or around Toronto, Bill would sometimes come out for the opening and speak in that delightful bafflegab of his. He really understood the people of Ontario. He wasn't known as Brampton Billy for nothing.

When Davis retired in the winter of 1985, Eddie Goodman called and asked me if I could advise the premier on how to handle corporate directorships and other aspects of his transition from public to private life. Bill has a winter home in Fort Lauderdale, and Eddie had one in Palm Beach right next to mine. Bill drove down one day for a game of tennis with Eddie, and afterwards I went over to have a coffee with him.

"Look, you are going to be in big demand," I said, "so, first of all don't sell yourself short. Pick your spots, don't take small companies, and take your time. Don't be in a rush."

I suggested that a bank was a must for him, and predicted that the Canadian Imperial Bank of Commerce would ask him to join their board, as they did. I told him that Seagram would invite him onto our board, as we did, and that Paul Desmarais would put him on the board of Power Corporation, as he did.

"Then," I added, "sit back, savour your achievements, savour your reputation, and in time accept another two or three boards if you want to." Which is pretty much what happened. Bill joined the Toronto law firm of Tory, Tory, Deslauriers and Binnington, and collected about half-a-dozen first-class directorships. We served together on the Seagram

board, and both retired at the same annual meeting, around our seventieth birthdays, at the end of 1999.

∞

Of all the politicians I dealt with at the municipal level – and in the real
estate development business that was a lot – the most fascinating by far
was Jean Drapeau, the powerful mayor of Montreal for nearly thirty
years, from 1954 to 1957, and from 1960 to 1986. Drapeau was the
mayor who brought Expo '67 and the 1976 Olympics to Montreal. He
built the city's fabulous subway, the metro, which redrew the development map of downtown Montreal. He brought Major League Baseball
to Montreal with the Expos in 1968. And even before the Expos,
Drapeau led an attempt to win a National Football League franchise for
Montreal.

Which was how I first met him in the mid-1960s. Drapeau called
Charles one day and asked him to a highly secret meeting he would be
holding in his office on a Sunday morning. Charles said he would be
out of town but asked if I could attend on his behalf. So I showed up at
the mayor's office at City Hall, five minutes early for a ten o'clock
meeting. Sam Steinberg was there – the two of us representing the Jewish community – as well as some blue-chip members of the francophone
and anglophone business establishment.

Drapeau began the meeting by saying he wanted to bid on an NFL
franchise, but he needed $10 million up front and needed our help. The
silence was eloquent, and at a certain point Sam Steinberg jabbed me in
the ribs and said, "This is really embarrassing for the mayor."

"Well," I replied, "what would you like to do about it?"

"I'm ready to pledge a million," he said, "are you?"

"Sure."

"Announce it," he said.

"You announce it. You are the elder statesman here in the Jewish
community."

So Steinberg said, "Mr Mayor, Steinberg's is in for a million, and the
Bronfmans are in for a million."

Do you know how much they raised that morning? Two million.
That was it. Everybody else had to go home and think about it. And it
never happened. But Drapeau delegated a member of his executive committee, Gerry Snyder, to work on it, and I went with him to Cleveland,
Pittsburgh, and a number of other cities to watch NFL football games.

Nearly twenty years later, I had frequent dealings with Drapeau over a concert hall we were going to build for the Montreal Symphony Orchestra, free of charge, in the mezzanine and basement level of Place Montreal Trust. We eventually built the project, a thirty-storey office tower over a mall that occupied an entire block of McGill College Avenue between Ste-Catherine Street and de Maisonneuve Boulevard. But we never did build the symphony hall.

The project bogged down over a dispute that involved one of my own four principal shareholders, Phyllis Lambert, an activist on heritage Montreal issues, picketing her own company. The office tower, it turned out, would slightly impede the view of Mount Royal. In Montreal, no building can block out the Mountain, just as in Washington, D.C., no building can be taller than the Capitol Dome. And Phyllis led the opposition.

The building and shopping mall were also going to crowd the sidewalk, and Phyllis was not the only one upset about that. At the time, Montreal had no master plan for its development, and McGill College was far from what it has become today, with its broad sidewalks, buildings set back from the street in the style of Mies van der Rohe, and a median strip festooned with flowers. We played a role in all of that. When the Montreal Board of Trade and la Chambre de Commerce de Montréal suggested a consultative process on the development of McGill College, we agreed, and Cadillac Fairview paid for the hearings.

There were no bigger boosters of the MSO than Sandra and me, as attested by the symphony holding a concert in her honour in December 2002, a year after her passing. For years, Drapeau had been trying to get the MSO its own hall. The Salle Wilfrid Pelletier of Place des Arts, the orchestra's home since 1963, was acoustically challenged and not always available to the symphony. And it was the mayor, not me, who first suggested a concert hall at Place Montreal Trust. Then, when the heat started, he disappeared.

And there was plenty of heat. Our proposal to put a concert hall in a mall and office complex met with widespread outrage and editorial indignation. The symphony deserved its own home, the critics howled, and we agreed. We were offering one, for free, at no cost to the taxpayer. Not one cent of public money would have been spent on it. But the critics retorted that it should be a stand-alone architectural statement, forgetting, it seemed, that there is not one window inside the MSO's old rental hall at Place des Arts.

The proposed location was the best in Montreal, in the heart of downtown, one block north of Place Ville Marie, one block south of

McGill University, on a majestic avenue that joined the Mountain above to the city below. It was right on the McGill College metro stop, one of the busiest in the city. And we were going to provide all the parking to symphony patrons.

And then there were questions about the acoustics. We brought in Zubin Mehta as a consultant. He had been the MSO's first world-renowned conductor in the 1960s, and had gone on to greater fame with the Los Angeles Philharmonic and the Israeli Philharmonic orchestras. His brother Zarin, who would become general manager of the New York Philharmonic, was then the general manager of the MSO, and he, too, was closely involved. Zubin Mehta introduced us to some of the world's great acousticians, and all I can say is that I'm satisfied that it would have been a world-class hall in that sense.

But the outcry, largely from people who had never been to a concert, or editorialists who had never donated a nickel to the MSO, was such that we had to abandon the symphony hall, though we built Place Montreal Trust, the last major Cadillac Fairview project in Montreal before the company was sold in 1987. In 2002, the Quebec government announced the latest in a series of projects as a home for the symphony, a 2,000-seat concert hall that would cost taxpayers $100 million. It would be finished by the year 2006, twenty years after we would have completed a world-class hall at no cost to taxpayers. A final irony: a $140-million office tower was to be built over the concert hall as a home for two thousand provincial civil servants.

In 2002, Charles's son, Stephen, and I were among a group of investors who bought back Place Montreal Trust. It's still an outstanding building, but it would have been even better with a symphony hall, which would have provided the MSO with a permanent home and resolved many of the orchestra's financial problems.

Still, it was the abortive plan for a symphony hall that brought me in frequent and close touch with Mayor Drapeau. For a period of about six months I was seeing him a couple of times a week. I would usually meet with him late in the afternoon, come right to the point, and try to wrap things up within fifteen minutes. Then I would get up and thank him for his time, and he would say, "No, sit, let's talk." And he would talk and talk.

It was then that I realized why he got to work at six in the morning and left at midnight. He had longer meetings than anyone I ever met. So I would sit down, and he would launch into a brilliant dissertation on some political topic, and he would keep me for another hour and a half.

If there was an American presidential election in the offing, he would dissect it. If there was a referendum or an election coming up in Quebec, he would tell me exactly what was going to happen. He was a brilliant politician and an astute observer of politics.

Looking back on the prime ministers, premiers, and pols I've known, I realize that I've been quite privileged to have known them all. Six prime ministers of Canada. Several premiers, mostly in Quebec. And one mayor of Montreal, in a class by himself.

10

The Bagman

It was Marc Lalonde who got me involved in fundraising for the Liberal Party of Canada in 1980. He was then minister of energy in the Liberal government and Pierre Trudeau's Quebec lieutenant. As such, he was the boss, and I do mean boss, of the government and the party in Quebec. Everything the Trudeau government did in Quebec, every project, every grant, every appointment, crossed his desk. Every dollar that was spent, every patronage plum, was approved by him. Lalonde wasn't just dispensing patronage and pork in Quebec, he was also fighting the separatist government of René Lévesque. And he wanted my help in raising money for the party.

I went to visit him at his Montreal home on a Sunday afternoon. For a man who wielded great power, he lived in remarkably modest circumstances, in a duplex on Légaré in the Côte-des-Neiges district of Montreal.

He said he wanted my help in raising money from the Jewish community and that $50,000 was the figure he had in mind. I told him that if he could deliver Trudeau, and only Trudeau, to my house for a fundraiser, I could make his life easy and raise twice as much. The next day, Lalonde called me back with a date. It was the first of four such evenings we had with Pierre, once every year until he left office in 1984. He was always very gracious, very willing to pose for pictures. Trudeau was fundamentally a shy man, and so he wasn't particularly good at working the room. But he had such personal magnetism that the room worked him.

So that was my initial involvement with political fundraising. Then, after the Liberals lost the 1984 election, John Turner asked me to become the chief bagman for the party, and in 1985 we founded the Laurier Club, where for $1,000 a year members had special access to the

Liberal leader. It was a pretty tough sell in the beginning, since the Liberals were in opposition until 1993. After that, it became much easier, with cocktails at 24 Sussex and breakfasts with cabinet ministers.

I promised Turner that I would raise $2.5 million in corporate donations from CEOs across the country, and in nine months we got it done. My assistant, Herb Metcalfe, and I made 235 corporate calls, soliciting donations of $25,000 from each corporation to help the party pay down its debt and get back on its feet after the devastating defeat of 1984. Not everyone gave, but nearly everyone agreed to see us. Not because I represented John Turner, but because I represented the Bronfmans, and because Cadillac Fairview had office towers and major shopping malls in nearly every Canadian city from coast to coast. So when Herb would call for an appointment, hardly anyone declined. I also had the use of a company plane, and that made getting around much easier. And wherever we went, there was always legitimate business I could also do on behalf of Cadillac Fairview.

That was the enjoyable part of the experience, getting around the country and learning a lot about it. One of the things I discovered was the regional nature of Canada, how different the issues were from one city and one province to the next. I was struck by something Trudeau had told me, that Canada was basically not governable, because, as he said, "when you do something for the West, they scream in the East, and when you do something for the East, they scream in the West." Sir Wilfrid Laurier put it more succinctly a century ago: "This is a difficult country to govern." Wherever we went, people had different lists of complaints about Ottawa. In Toronto, they would say Ottawa wasn't focused enough on reducing the deficit. In Calgary, the oil patch was still furious with the Liberals over the National Energy Program. In Vancouver, they looked west across the Pacific, not east across the Rockies. Every city had a different perspective and different priorities.

One CEO was quite up front with me when he asked, "What do I get for my twenty-five grand?" – a reasonable question to ask someone who's collecting for an opposition party, with no access to sell.

"You get an investment in the democratic process," I replied. "You get the satisfaction of knowing that you've contributed to the well-being of the two-party system." In those days, there were three national parties in Canada, but the New Democrats were the party of the left, and only the Liberals and Conservatives had ever formed governments, which remains the case to this day. The Tories had then recently come into office, and there was nothing very subtle about their fundraising techniques. Not only did they sell access to Prime Minister Mulroney and cabinet members through their 500 Club, but suppliers and consultants to the government, as well as crown agencies, also understood that it would be in their enlightened self-interest to donate to the Tory cause.

When the Liberals were in office, both under Trudeau and Jean Chrétien, I would tell a prospective donor: "I can guarantee you access in most cases to a cabinet minister, but once you get in the door, you're on your own." Cabinet ministers see lots of people, and they usually saw them faster after I'd put in a phone call, but I couldn't guarantee that donors would get what they wanted from the government. No one can guarantee that, not within the law at any rate.

As I also discovered, some business leaders have pretty short memories. Near the end of the Trudeau years, I got a call one day from two high-powered financiers who wanted an appointment with Marc Lalonde, then the minister of finance. I got them an appointment for nine o'clock the next morning, and they thought I was a genius. It turned out Lalonde didn't do what they wanted, but at least they got to make their case. Three months later, I wrote one of them asking him for a $1,000 donation, and he called me back, swearing he would "never give the Liberals another goddamn cent."

"Did you get your appointment?" I yelled back into the phone. "Did you get it fast?"

"We couldn't believe how powerful you were," he replied.

"Do you think I'm powerful because of my good looks or because I raise money for the party – which? – just take a guess!"

The guy couriered me a cheque the next day.

Another time a Jewish businessman from Montreal, a *shmatte* guy, called me up about some imported line of clothing that the government was holding up on the docks. This happens all the time. Governments are very good at slowing down imports when they want to send a message to the exporting country.

"Why don't you call your member of Parliament?" I suggested.

"I don't know who it is," he said, which was a typical reply.

So I made the call to the minister of revenue, who was in charge of Canada Customs, and the goods were released the next morning. The *shmatte* guy was very grateful. Then I wrote him a few months later asking for a donation to the party, and he wouldn't give me a cent. He was a real jerk about it.

The Liberal party itself has always had this attitude that fundraising was a necessary evil. And as the bagman, I became quite accustomed to being sneered at by Liberal colleagues. Fundamentally, most MPS worried about raising enough money for their own campaigns and couldn't care less about the national party. That was the attitude when I was chief fundraiser, and it remains the attitude to this day. If Liberal MPs and riding associations were required to turn over their surplus cash to the party, we would be out of debt in a big hurry, though being Liberals we would soon find new ways of digging the party even deeper into debt. In 2003, after three consecutive election victories and ten years in government, the Liberal party somehow remained several million dollars in debt.

Jean Chrétien tried to do something about this when he ordered every member of the Liberal caucus to raise $30,000 for the party. One woman, who shall remain nameless, a junior cabinet minister, came up to me and said, "Leo, how on earth do I raise $30,000?"

"You're in the cabinet, right?" I replied.

"Of course."

"And you're running a department with a budget of, what, millions of dollars, right?"

"Right."

"And you're asking me how to raise $30,000, is that right?"

"Right."

"Well," I told her, "you call sixty people and ask for $500 each. Or you call thirty people and ask for $1,000 each. Or you call six people and ask for $5,000 each. That's how."

Pierre Trudeau had the worst attitude about fundraising. He basically wouldn't do it, except for the big annual dinners and private events like the ones at my home. He had also ordered his cabinet ministers not to get involved in fundraising because he wanted to avoid the appearance of any conflicts of interest. Jean Chrétien was different. He was a workhorse for the party, indefatigable at doing fundraising dinners all across the country. If it weren't for him, the Liberal party would be millions of dollars deeper in debt. In 2002 alone, the *National Post* reported, he was scheduled to do no less than fourteen dinners across the country,

Chrétien even opened 24 Sussex for Laurier Club cocktails, something Mulroney had declined to do for the Tory party's 500 Club. And in the months before the 1997 election, Chrétien also agreed to host a series of small dinners at the prime minister's official residence.

Following the near-death experience of the 1995 Quebec referendum, Trudeau's former principal secretary Tom Axworthy got together with former clerk of the Privy Council Michael Pitfield and me for a discussion of how the federalists could improve their message and communications in the event of another referendum. Axworthy was then working for

Charles Bronfman's CRB Foundation as executive director of the Heritage Project on Canadian history, and Pitfield was deputy chairman of Power Corporation. After some discussion, Tom suggested we send Gordon Ashworth, former national director of the Liberal party, to Washington to see how the Democrats and Republicans used new technologies to communicate. Ashworth spent some time with the Democratic and Republican national committees, and came back with some recommendations, including a targeted voice mail campaign that measured the listener response to the message. We presented his findings to the Liberal high command, including Chrétien's chief of staff, Jean Pelletier, and his special adviser, Eddy Goldenberg, and they were quite enthusiastic, but the PM was lukewarm to the plan and nothing more ever came of it.

But then in the winter of 1997, only a couple of months before the election call, Pelletier and Goldenberg asked to see me after a Montreal fundraiser and said they needed to raise an additional $1.5 million in the hope of winning more seats in Quebec, which had been swept by the separatist Bloc Québécois in 1993.

"The only way I can do this quickly," I told them, "is if you give me access to Sussex on seven different nights for small dinners with the prime minister, groups of no more than ten people." The dinners started at six, and would go on until nine thirty, so the guests would have three and a half hours with the prime minister at his residence. The guest list was the top tier of the Canadian business establishment, and nobody turned down an invitation to dinner at 24 Sussex. The PM was very relaxed in this setting and very forthcoming with the guests.

Nobody was asked for money to go have dinner there – that would have been pretty cheesy. But afterwards I called the seventy guests individually, explaining our strategy of pushing back the separatists in Quebec, and we raised the $1.5 million extra cash for the spring campaign. We also had a better result in the election of May 1997, largely because the Bloc's charismatic founder, Lucien Bouchard, had quit federal politics to become premier of Quebec, and partly because the Liberals were able to hire more organizers and increase their media buy because of the extra money we raised.

Of the many fundraisers held at my house, the most publicized was one in Chrétien's honour for which he failed to show up. It turned out he was busy that Sunday afternoon in May 2002, firing Art Eggleton as minister of defence in a weekend cabinet shuffle.

The political minister for Quebec, Justice Minister Martin Cauchon, had asked me to put on the event, again for the purpose of raising money for the Quebec wing of the party, which in spite of being in office nine years at that point, was itself $2 million in debt. I said I would put on a dinner at $10,000 a couple, but only if the PM came as the guest of honour. Chrétien readily agreed. As always, in addition to paying for myself, I would pay for the event, about $50,000 for the food, drinks, music, and setting up a tent for a sit-down dinner for forty in my backyard. It was the first time I had organized one of these things on my own, and the first since the death of my wife the previous September. It was one more reminder of how much I missed Sandra and how good she had been at putting these dinners together.

Chrétien wasn't a draw the way Trudeau had been, though as prime minister he wasn't a hard sell, either. But $10,000 a couple *was* a hard sell. And somehow the word got out. First, *National Post* social columnist Gillian Cosgrove ran an item on the upcoming event in her Saturday column. By the following Thursday, it had moved to page one of the *Post,* headlined "Secret Liberal fundraiser." It wasn't secret at all, only private, but it was now all mixed up with the Liberal ethics, sponsorship, and conflict-of-interest controversies.

"Mr. Kolber has been a key fundraiser for the Liberal party for years," wrote the *Post's* Ottawa bureau chief, Bob Fife. "Holding the fundraiser at a private residence of the party's chief fundraiser leaves the perception that the $10,000 contribution entitles them to special favours from Mr. Chrétien, opposition critics said."

John Reynolds, House leader of the Canadian Alliance, the official opposition, was predictably shocked and appalled. "It is an exclusive club, it's to buy access to the prime minister," he complained. "If I was a businessman and somebody said, 'Listen, if you want to do business in Quebec, you have to be in with the Liberals, and here is the way to do it: for $10,000 you can get a private dinner with the prime minister, get your picture taken and you have access.'"

Conservative leader Joe Clark jumped into the fray, demanding that Chrétien reveal the names of the people attending, and wondering aloud, as the *Post* reported it, "whether any of the people attending the fundraiser [were] also seeking federal advertising contracts or government sponsorship programs." As if Paul Desmarais Jr, Stephen Bronfman, or any of the people who attended would be looking for government contracts.

By Friday, May 24, two days before the dinner, the story was the main headline on the front page of *Le Devoir.* "10 000 $ pour avoir accès à Chrétien," blared the headline over the story, which did not fail to mention that my house was in Westmount. By the morning after the dinner, the *National Post* torqued the story even higher, referring to "a fundraising party in a mansion atop Montreal." There was more. "The streets near Mr. Kolber's Summit Circle house in the wealthy Montreal suburb of Westmount," reported Graeme Hamilton, "were clogged with limousines and luxury cars."

All the ingredients for a media game of gotcha were there: a "secret" event at $10,000 a couple, at a house on top of the hill, with the street "clogged" with limousines, and privileged access to the prime minister. It was the media equivalent of a drive-by shooting.

Except for one thing – the PM was a no-show. He called to apologize that he couldn't make it because of the cabinet shuffle. Actually, the late-afternoon timing of the cabinet shuffle could easily have been moved up. My own sense was that with all the heat the dinner had drawn, Chrétien was advised to give it a miss and so scheduled the cabinet shuffle to conflict with it. Even then, he still could have made it. But he sent John Manley, the deputy prime minister, in his place. Four other senior cabinet members, all from Quebec, also showed up.

I must admit that Chrétien – even *in absentia* – could have done without the media circus on the sidewalk outside my house. I could have done without it myself. Some of the guests later said they saw themselves on television walking into the dinner. In all, the evening cost me $100,000 – $50,000 for the dinner and another $50,000 to pay my own way and buy tickets for four others who otherwise couldn't have afforded it. I wasn't bothered by that. But I was pretty annoyed by the whole flap.

There was more incoming media flak in mid-June when the PM hosted a huge garden party for the Laurier Club under a tent at 24 Sussex. One of the television networks even hired a helicopter to fly over the PM's residence and get footage of the event. "About 1,200 Liberal members of the so-called Laurier Club who contributed a maximum of $1,000 to the party were invited to a garden party at 24 Sussex," the *National Post* reported, "where they mingled with the prime minister and cabinet ministers."

Once again, Joe Clark was scandalized, suggesting that the PM was in violation of the Official Residences Act, which limited the use of such residences to representational public events. "24 Sussex Drive belongs to the people of Canada, not to the Liberal party," Clark thundered in the House of Commons the next day. "How can the prime minister defend using 24 Sussex Drive as a prop and lure for a Liberal fundraising event?"

I've always played within the rules of fundraising, but I must admit that all the negative coverage associated with these legitimate fundraising events does give the impression that big money buys privileged access to politicians. Perhaps to the surprise of many, I was strongly supportive of Prime Minister Chrétien's initiative to improve the image of fundraising by ruling donations from corporations and trade unions virtually off limits. And I said so publicly when introducing Chrétien for the last time as prime minister at the Laurier Club's annual cocktail in Montreal in February 2003.

By then, Chrétien had introduced his campaign finance reform bill. It had caused a huge ruckus in the Liberal caucus, and the party's president, Stephen LeDrew, had called it "dumb as a bag of hammers," thereby assuring that Chrétien would never name him to the Senate, a traditional reward for an outgoing president of the party in power.

Chrétien was essentially adopting the Quebec model of political financing. In 1977 René Lévesque outlawed corporate and union donations in Quebec, limiting individual donations to $3,000 and requiring them to be disclosed. At the time, the Parti Québécois thought they would be putting the Quebec Liberals out of business, but the legislation instead allowed them to be reborn, for it meant they could never again be called the tools of the corporations.

Chrétien's legislation allowed small businesses to donate up to $1,000 to candidates in their ridings, and capped individual donations at $5,000. This meant that rather than buying a table at a dinner for $5,000 in the name of Power Corporation, Paul Desmarais could donate $5,000 himself and another $5,000 on behalf of his wife. As could his sons, Paul Jr and André. Theoretically, the Quebec model could generate a lot more cash and allow more members of the public to participate in the process of funding political parties in a much more transparent process. And in future, the new rules will also apply to party leadership campaigns, where there have never been effective limits or full disclosure. For example, in December 2002 I raised $150,000 for Paul Martin's campaign with a dinner at my home, with fifteen couples at $10,000 each. Under the leadership rules, he had to disclose the donations within a month of receiving them, but not how or where the money was raised. For that dinner, we didn't have the press camped on my doorstep, and it didn't make any news.

According to the rules that were finally announced in February 2003, six months after the campaign had begun, candidates were permitted to raise $4 million after that date, but could spend whatever they had previously raised. A classic case of closing the barn door after the horse has got out.

With the reform to campaign financing, there will be better financial controls and better rationalization for spending, in both general elections and leadership campaigns. And this is long overdue in a game in which there have been virtually no outcome tests until now. This is particularly true of leadership campaigns, in which the very nature of the fundraising game is like betting on a horse race – even a prohibitive favourite can stumble down the stretch. But by then, all the money has been committed and spent. In any leadership campaign, even successful ones, there are always unpaid bills at the end of the day, for polling, phone banks, cells phones, and even for room service.

But at least a new party leader has the leverage to pay off debts. It is the unsuccessful candidates, and ultimately their creditors, who are left holding paper rather than cash. Even Paul Martin, clearly the front-runner from the outset of the 2003 Liberal leadership race, was faced with the challenge of organizing a national leadership campaign as a backbencher, rather than as a cabinet minister with a big staff and access to executive jets for travel on government business that could be combined with a leadership tour. Fortunately for Martin, he would have no difficulty raising as much as $10 million for his leadership campaign. Unfortunately, he would also have no difficulty spending it. The Martin campaign was a big operation, with a frightening cash-burn rate.

As one who has been in the fundraising game as long as anyone in Canadian politics, I regard Chrétien's campaign finance reform legislation as an important initiative, one for which he will be well remembered, as Lévesque has been.

∽

I've sometimes been asked about the difference between raising money for a charitable cause and fundraising for a political party. There are two main differences. The first is the tax break. Charitable donations are 100 percent deductible, whereas political donations are deductible up to a certain percentage – prior to Chrétien's 2003 campaign finance reform, up to $1,100, and after, up to $5,000.

The second difference is that when you go to see someone on behalf of the symphony orchestra, you don't have to listen to a speech. When you canvass someone on behalf of a political party, you have to listen to a big harangue about how lousy your policies are. After the *intifada* started up in the Middle East again in 2000, I got an earful from the Jewish community about the Chrétien government not being supportive enough of Israel, and this was from guys who weren't even writing cheques.

My standard reply was, you want to influence policy? Get involved in the political process at some level. Donating to a political party is one legitimate way of doing it. It opens doors. It gets you a hearing. Always has. Always will. When people in the Jewish community, particularly in Montreal, asked me what Chrétien had done for them lately, I told them that he had defeated separatism and that the value of their houses had gone up significantly as a result. When people invested in the stock market asked me what the Liberals had done for them, I would remind them that Chrétien had reduced the capital gains tax by 50 percent and that they stood to keep a lot more of their profits.

Because the Jewish community gives so much to Jewish charities, it's difficult to raise Jewish money for non-Jewish organizations such as hospitals and universities.

When I was deputy chairman of a capital campaign for McGill University, I approached a wealthy Jew whose son attended McGill.

"No," he said, "I give money to Hebrew University."

"That's in Jerusalem," I replied. "Your son goes to university in Montreal."

"I give to Israel," he said.

That attitude is unfortunately still prevalent and remains a mystery to people outside the Jewish community. Even as a Jew, it is something of a mystery to me. While it is important for Jews to support CJA and Israel, it is equally important that they support worthy causes in the communities we are part of. In 2003, for example, Paul Desmarais and I were honorary co-chairs of a fundraising campaign for the Montreal Symphony Orchestra. My role was essentially to deliver major donations from the Jewish community.

There is fundraising, and there is Jewish fundraising. Jewish fundraising is to fundraising as military music is to music – loud, brassy, and inescapable.

Over the years, I've raised tens of millions of dollars for a host of causes, from political parties to symphony orchestras, from hospitals to universities, from Canada to Israel. Raising money for the Jewish community, and for Israel, is different than raising money in the genteel Gentile world.

First of all, Jewish fundraising is a hierarchy of philanthropy. And it is a very high-pressure business. The richer the donor, the bigger the donation expected of him. It goes back, in a sense, to the biblical practice of tithing, of a man giving 10 percent of his income to those less fortunate than himself. It also goes, in the Jewish community, to a sense of solidarity. If wealthy Jews don't give according to their means, at levels arbitrarily set for them, they are practically shunned socially within the community.

Thus in Montreal, Combined Jewish Appeal annually raises more money than Centraide, the local United Way, though Jews now comprise less than 5 percent of the city's population of 2 million people. The generosity of Montreal Jews, widely acknowledged throughout North America and Israel, dates from Sam Bronfman's election as president of the Canadian Jewish Congress in 1939, and accelerated after the founding of Israel in 1948.

The pressure tactics of CJA are legendary in the community. Talk about four thousand years of Jewish guilt – it's all there in fundraising techniques. For years, I had been donating $300,000 to CJA, most of it in my own name, but $25,000 in the name of my wife. Within weeks of her death in September 2001, they called me and asked if I would maintain her donation with mine. For decades, applicants to the Elm Ridge Golf Club would be asked flat out how much they had given to the Jewish community's annual fundraising. If the number wasn't big enough, they didn't get in. It was that simple. And once you make a pledge, they expect to see the money. There is the story of the three men marooned on an island in the Pacific Ocean, a Catholic, a Protestant, and a Jew. The Catholic makes a big bonfire and the Protestant writes "help" in big letters in the sand, in the hope of being sighted. The Jewish guy is lying on the beach, taking some sun. "Don't you want to be rescued?" they ask him. "I made a big pledge to United Jewish Appeal," the Jew replies. "Don't worry, they'll find me."

On many occasions I've been asked by asked by Gentile friends why it is that Jews are so generous to Jewish charities, out of all proportion to their numbers in the community. I can't think of any answer other than the one I've always given: we take care of our own.

But sometimes we do such a good job of taking care of our own that there's a perception we take care only of our own. This isn't so, though we need to do a better job of getting out the message. The Jewish General Hospital is a case in point. Founded as a 50-bed community hospital in the 1930s, it had grown by the end of the century to 630 beds, the third-largest hospital in Quebec. By the beginning of the twenty-first century, only 28 percent of the hospital's clientele were Jewish, the remainder being English- and French-speaking patients – Christians and members of Montreal's Arabic and Muslim communities.

Yet while 72 percent of the hospital's clientele is non-Jewish, about 90 percent of its donations still come from the Jewish community. So the Jewish community, in looking after its own, is heavily subsidizing the health care of the larger population of Montreal.

During my two-year term as president of the Jewish General in the mid-1990s, I had occasion to explain to Jean Rochon, the health minister in the Parti Québécois government, that our hospital had more francophone than Jewish patients. He was aware of that, but said that in a round of health care cuts, he was ordering two hundred beds closed, nearly one-third of our capacity.

"You are the minister," I replied, "and if you order us to close two hundred beds, we will. But I am not just taking your word for it. You will have to write me a letter requesting it. Please note that when we receive the letter, we will close the beds and publish your letter in every single newspaper in Montreal. So when people complain, they will come to you, not me."

"Well," he protested, "I didn't mean right away."

He never explained what he really meant, and we never closed a single bed.

A couple of reasons the Jewish General attracts such a diverse clientele are the high quality of its medical staff and the fact it has kept up with some of the more technological advances of modern medicine. I've played a small role myself, on at least a couple of occasions as the result of undergoing tests on outdated equipment. Once, while president of the Jewish, I was undergoing tests prior to prostate surgery. They took three samples, but after the third one, there was apparently a problem.

"Of all people to have this happen to," said Dr Steve Jacobson. "The machine broke."

I was lying there, naked on a table, wondering whether it was a set-up. I couldn't help laughing.

"How much would a new one cost?" I asked.

"One hundred thousand dollars," Steve said.

So I bought one for the hospital. On another occasion, while undergoing a colonoscopy, I was discussing the procedure with Albert Cohen, the head of gastroenterology.

"How old is the equipment?" I asked.

"Ten years old," he replied. "We are sadly out of date. We just don't have the budgets in Canadian hospitals for new equipment." He said it would take $250,000 for new colonoscopy equipment. So I paid half, the hospital foundation paid half, and when I recently had another colonoscopy, the difference was night and day. It was, literally, the difference between colour and black and white.

Another time, I went to the Jewish for an eye examination, found that some of their equipment was also inadequate, and subsequently had it replaced. And because my father died at an early age of a heart attack, it meant a lot to me to help out the cardiology department.

I don't know whether being a hypochondriac has helped keep me alive and in good health this long, but hopefully it's been good for the hospital.

11

Hooray for Hollywood

The Hollywood connection began with a sixty-second Polaroid.

In the late 1950s, a noted New York stock analyst named Sam Steadman recommended we take a position in Polaroid, even before it became one of the Nifty Fifty, the great growth stocks of the era. Edgar thought it was a good idea and took it to his father.

"We have a whisky business to run," Mr Sam said dismissively. "What are you giving me with Polaroid?"

Then Edgar, in a brilliant move, brought Sam Steadman to his father's palatial office in the new Seagram Building. They showed Mr Sam the camera, took a picture, and in sixty seconds it was developed. Mr Bronfman was astounded, but since he'd seen it himself, he became a believer, and Edgar bought a big block of stock.

So Polaroid was one of the things in the Cemp portfolio when I became managing director in 1957, and when we eventually sold the stock in the mid-1960s, we made at least $20 million on our position, a lot of money in those days. We were looking to reinvest it, and one of my analysts at Cemp, John Wanamaker, brought me an idea. "Leo," he said, "this is a steal." It was Paramount Pictures. And he was right – it was a steal. In those days, the entire capitalized value of Paramount Pictures was something like $60 or $70 million, with Famous Players' distribution and exhibition business in Canada basically thrown in for free. So after I spoke to Charles and Edgar, we started accumulating Paramount, and before long – using our $20-million profit from Polaroid – we ended up with about 30 percent of Paramount.

When Mr Bronfman heard about it, he simply went ballistic. He brought the three of us, Edgar, Charles, and me, in for a talk. "I don't want you in the goddamned movie business," he began. "We have got whisky. We have got real estate. We have got oil. What the hell else do you want?"

But we wouldn't let go of the idea, and we did something to try to persuade him. We brought in Steadman's partner and Edgar's father-in-law, John Loeb, who was a pillar of Wall Street and a leading figure among the "Our Crowd" Jews Mr Sam so admired. Loeb's brokerage and investment banking firm, Carl M. Loeb, Rhoades & Company, was one of the most conservative in New York.

Loeb came with three of his guys to the executive floor of the Seagram Building and made a presentation to Mr Bronfman, Edgar, Charles, and me. They concluded, as we had, that it was a terrific buy. For all of twenty millions bucks, we had acquired 30 percent of one of the great Hollywood brands, one with a storied film library at a time when television, starved for movie titles, was the fastest-growing medium in history. Though it was then making very few movies on its Hollywood lot, it was a vertically integrated company in production, distribution, and exhibition, in addition to the film library. This was decades before anyone had thought of a word like "convergence."

When I think about it, it would have saved us a lot of trouble later on, with Edgar Jr going Hollywood, if we had been in the movie business when he wanted to get into it. It would have saved us billions and billions of dollars, $5.7 billion to be exact, the cost of buying MCA in 1995. Ultimately, it might have saved the Seagram empire, instead of Hollywood being the root cause of its downfall.

But even with John Loeb's strong recommendation, Mr Bronfman was having none of it, and so we began to look around for a buyer for Cemp's position in Paramount. When it got around that our block of Paramount stock was for sale, I got a call from Charles Bluhdorn of a company called Gulf & Western Industries, which he had leveraged into other businesses from modest origins in auto parts. An Austrian immigrant with a sharp accent, Charlie was a wild man on the telephone, shouting that he was going to buy our stock for such and such a price. Since my instructions were to sell, we eventually negotiated a price that left us with a handsome profit but was still a steal for him. "He landed the studio," as Dennis McDougall observed in *The Last Mogul,* his history of Lew Wasserman's Hollywood, "by offering more than he could afford for less than what the studio was worth."

Which is how, in 1966, Gulf & Western gained control of one of the great names in Hollywood and went into the movie business. Paramount's franchises would include *The Godfather* and, later, such television shows as *Entertainment Tonight*. Which is also how Edgar, and eventually Junior, came back with plays for Hollywood studios that eventually led to disaster for the Bronfman dynasty.

Two years later, in 1968, Edgar made the acquaintance of a guy named G.M. Levin, a real estate developer who built shopping centres in New Jersey. Levin had a block of stock in Metro-Goldwyn-Mayer, another venerable Hollywood studio. The stock was selling in the low 40s and Edgar, in one of his Edgar moments, offered him around $60 a share, without knowing where the money was coming from.

The next day, he called me. He needed the money to buy Levin's MGM stock.

"What did you pay?" I asked.

"Sixty bucks a share," he replied.

"Are you crazy?" I yelled.

Then I went to see his father and told him the story.

"Mr Bronfman," I said, "it is not my money, it doesn't belong to me, but there has to be a semblance of business sense. We cannot overpay for things like this. And Edgar can't do things like this without consulting us."

"You are absolutely right," he said. "It won't happen again."

The millions it cost to get Levin's block of MGM stock was money I didn't have on hand. At Cemp, we had plenty of capital, and great net worth, but no cash. If one of Mr Sam's four children wanted a large amount of money, it usually came out of capital allocations, which is to say a one-time payment drawn on his or her capital, resulting in a dilution of equity at current valuations.

So when Charles needed money to buy the Expos, it came from capital allocations. When Phyllis wanted money to build the Canadian Centre for Architecture, it came from allocations. When Minda wanted money to make investments with her husband, it came from allocations. But when Edgar needed money for his MGM stake and didn't want to do it from allocations, we had to find a way to do it through Cemp Investments, especially since Mr Sam would never approve it as a Seagram acquisition.

So I had to get the money, fast. I called up Arnold Hart, chairman of the Bank of Montreal, our bankers at Cemp and Fairview.

"Could I come and see you?" I began.

"What for?" he replied.

"I have to borrow some money."

"I don't do that," he said. "You have to do it through your branch." This was in the days before private banking and wealth management.

"Arnold," I said, "if I go to the branch, they won't have the faintest idea of what I'm talking about."

"Sorry," he replied, "that's how it is."

So I called Bill Nicks, president of the Bank of Nova Scotia, made an appointment to see him, caught the next plane to Toronto, and told him what I needed and what for.

"Sure," he said. "How many years do you want it for?"

He wrote the loan out in longhand, initialled it, signed it, as I did, and we had a deal. I flew back to Montreal with a loan for Edgar's MGM stock in my pocket.

This, then, was the origin of the legendary exchange between Edgar and his father.

"So, Edgar," Mr Sam is supposed to have asked, "you're spending $40 million to get laid?"

"Dad," Edgar famously replied, "it doesn't cost $40 million to get laid."

Anyway, we were now in the movie business, with a 15 percent stake of MGM. James M. Linen, the CEO of Time Inc., asked Edgar if they could come in for another 5 percent, and together our 20 percent gave us four seats on the board. Edgar became non-executive chairman, I became a director representing the Cemp interest, and Time had another two seats. We were able to take control of the board and fire the CEO, Bob O'Brien. Edgar brought in a guy named Bo Polk, former head of General Mills, who knew as much about the movie business as we did.

Less than a year later, in 1969, Edgar was approached by representatives of Kirk Kerkorian, offering to buy us out with shares in Trans-America Corporation of San Francisco. Kirk was an interesting man, an authentic war hero, an Armenian American who had flown in the RAF Ferry Command in the Second World War, flying Mosquito bombers built by de Havilland in Canada over to Scotland via Gander, New-foundland, or Goose Bay, Labrador, and Iceland. Eventually, he would catch an Atlantic jet stream known as the "Iceland Wave" and fly non-stop from Labrador in just over seven hours – turboprops going at jet speed. Kirk later told me that while based in Montreal, he had lived in Town of Mount Royal, the same suburb where I built my first five houses in the early 1950s. He was very well paid for the work, $1,000 per trip, and he made thirty-three crossings of the Atlantic. At war's end, Kerkorian returned to his native California, and with some of his wartime savings, bought a single-engine Cessna and hired out to fly people to a little town in the desert called Las Vegas. Kerkorian became one of the great builders of modern Las Vegas, acquiring land and selling it to casinos like the Flamingo and Caesars Palace, before building his own resort, the International, at the end of the 1960s.

At the same time, Kirk got all lit up on the idea of buying MGM. When Edgar refused to sell, he simply accumulated the stock until he

had more than we did, and he won control of the studio in 1969. It
didn't even take a proxy fight. The Bronfman family was stuck with 15
percent of MGM, whose share price had plunged since we bought it.
"Why are you spending all of your time for 15 percent of the stock?"
Mr Sam asked Edgar, who had to admit, as he did in *Good Spirits,* that
his father was "absolutely right."

Edgar's siblings sold at a loss, but the two of us stayed in. I had
bought some of Cemp's MGM stock for myself. "Listen," I told Edgar,
"in for a dime, in for a dollar." There was no point in selling at $8. If
we were going to lose we might as well lose the whole thing. Eventually,
we sold our stock at a good profit because of the MGM Grand Hotel
and Casino in Las Vegas, which proved to be one of the greatest cash
cows in history, bringing the studio's stock all the way back to where
we had bought it in 1968, and then some.

Kerkorian had asked me to remain on the MGM board, which I was
delighted to do, since I had developed some friendships in Hollywood,
particularly with Danny Kaye. Kirk fired Bo Polk, of course, and
brought in Jim Aubrey, previously president of CBS, and one of the
most unpleasant people I ever met. But one of the most pleasant parts of
the MGM experience was getting to know Cary Grant, a friend of Kirk's
whom he brought on the board.

Cary Grant was a very nice man, obviously a screen legend by the
time we met in 1970, the year he finally received his honorary Oscar for
his brilliant career. Not only had he been a great screen idol, with the
best light touch in the history of Hollywood, he was also a very smart
businessman. As an actor, he had struck out on his own at a time when
the studios owned the talent, and as the biggest box office draw of his
time, he was able to dictate terms by working for a percentage of the
gross in addition to his payment up front, becoming the highest-paid
actor in Hollywood history. He had also been smart enough to go out
on top, in 1966, with his last film, *Walk, Don't Run.* His co-star, Jim
Hutton, won an Oscar as best supporting actor and graciously thanked
"Cary Grant, who keeps winning these things for other people."

In retirement, Cary served on the board of Fabergé. At MGM board
meetings, he was a very good listener, but he was invariably supportive
of whatever happened to be Kirk's position.

We got to be friendly, and it would cause quite a commotion on the
Cemp switchboard whenever a man called up saying he was Cary
Grant, in that Cary Grant voice, and it actually turned out to be Cary
Grant. It happened once to Sandra when we were staying at the Beverly
Wilshire in Los Angeles during an MGM board meeting.

"Hello, is Leo there?"

"He's out," she said. "Who's calling?"

"It's Cary Grant."

Of course, she thought it was someone impersonating Cary Grant and hung up on him. Only when he called back was she convinced that he really was Cary Grant. He was used to people hanging up on him because he said he was Cary Grant.

"Leo," he once told me after a board meeting, "I like that sport jacket you're wearing."

I was stunned. The most elegant man in the history of Hollywood, who wore his own clothes in such stylish thrillers as *It Takes a Thief* and *North by Northwest,* was complimenting me on a sport jacket.

"Where did you get it?" Cary asked. I gave him the name of the store in Hollywood, and Cary said it was on his way and that he'd pick one up on the way home.

Cary, Danny Kaye, and I all happened to share the same birthday, January 18, and we got into the habit of calling one another to exchange birthday greetings.

I had a difficult time getting my mind around the way a movie studio ran as a business, because it wasn't run as a business. It was run as a bet. At MGM, film projects were subject to board approval, and we gave a go or no-go based on a one-paragraph synopsis. Take *The Sound of Music*, which we didn't make, as an example. The synopsis would read: family flees Austria, starts a choir. Who would put any money into that? Then, every movie is called a director's movie, because it is the director who is supposed to bring it in on time and on budget. But how do you tell that to David Lean?

The British director was justly celebrated for his wide-screen epics, *Bridge on the River Kwai, Lawrence of Arabia*, and *Doctor Zhivago*. Altogether, his films won twenty-seven Academy Awards, and he won two Oscars as best director. He was also famous as a perfectionist. When he was shooting *Ryan's Daughter* for MGM in Ireland in 1969 and 1970, he spent months on a storm scene. Unhappy with the Irish coast for a climactic explosion scene, he decamped to South Africa with the entire cast and crew to get what he wanted. Not satisfied with the look of Irish villages, he built his own in Dingle Bay, on the country's western shore. The costs were driving us crazy, and we kept having to put another million or two into the movie. Our only other choice was to shut down production, and we weren't about to shut down David Lean. In the end, *Ryan's Daughter* recouped its cost and went on to win two Oscars, though it fell far short of both the blockbuster success and the critical acclaim one would expect for a David Lean film.

I decided I wanted to see for myself how Lean was spending all this money on a movie, so I flew over to Ireland with Sandra to visit the film on location. Robert Mitchum and Sarah Miles were the nominal stars, but the real star of the picture was unquestionably the director, who proved to be courtly and hospitable. David agreeably spent quite a bit of time with us, not only allowing us to visit the locations during shooting, but over a long dinner explaining his vision of the movie and his definite *auteur* view of the director's role in every picture. In Kevin Brownlow's 1996 biography, the cover picture is of David directing a scene from *Ryan's Daughter*. He's on a beach, shooting the perfect storm.

∞

Kirk Kerkorian was somewhat reclusive, even then, but in a private rather than an eccentric way. And he was secretive in the way of all smart businesspeople, keeping his plans to himself until he was ready to reveal them. So I wondered what he was up to in 1971 when he called a special meeting of the MGM board without informing the directors of the reason we were being summoned to Los Angeles.

It turned out that Kirk had a big idea – to build the world's largest hotel and casino in Vegas. It also turned out that he had a conflict of interest in that he owned the land he wanted to sell to MGM to build what would become the MGM Grand, named for *Grand Hotel*, one of the studio's classics from the 1930s.

But Kirk had ethics. Though he was a hard-nosed businessman, he was also an honest one. He had charts, he had sketches – at twenty-six storeys and 2,084 rooms it would indeed be the largest hotel in the world. What he didn't have precisely was the cost – it turned out to be $107 million. Nor was he sure how much it would make. But he was sure that the board had to approve the deal quickly, that very day, because he was concerned about an imminent hike in the price of steel. He wanted to transfer the land to MGM at a price fixed by an independent assessor. It was all on the up and up, except that Kirk and the inside directors couldn't vote on it.

That left the two outside directors, a New York lawyer – Arnold Daum – and me. I asked for a recess and adjourned with Arnold to the next room.

"Leo, you can't do this," Arnold said. "If anybody at Harvard Business School ever heard of this, they would laugh you out of the room. This is no way to approve a deal."

"You know, Arnold," I replied, "I'm going to tell you something. The one thing Kirk seems to know is gambling – he sure doesn't know about making movies, nobody does, but he knows about gambling. Maybe this is our way out of the damn movie business. Kirk has a lot more to lose than we do. So what the hell, let's do it."

Then Arnold and I went back into the room and cast the two deciding votes in favour of building the MGM Grand. Kirk moved quickly. The ground-breaking ceremony was in 1972 and the Grand opened in 1973. In its very first year, it earned a net profit of $40 million. In 1986 Kirk sold the MGM Grand, as well as a namesake built in Reno, to Bally Corporation for nearly $600 million. He then sold MGM to Ted Turner of CNN, but later bought it back minus its fabulous film library, which included *Gone with the Wind.* Ted had coveted and was determined to keep that part of the business to build his specialty cable channels. Subsequently, Kirk sold MGM for $1.3 billion in 1990 and then reacquired it for the same price in 1996, only to put it in play again in 2002. Meanwhile, MGM had built a new Grand that opened in 1990 at a cost of $1 billion, on a scale that dwarfed the original next door. As the *Las Vegas Review-Journal* described it, there were "5,000 rooms, eight restaurants, a health club, a monorail, the 15,000-seat MGM Grand Garden, and a theme park as big as Disneyland when it opened in 1955."

Kirk not only had the vision, he had the raw courage of a wartime aviator who had successfully ferried fighter planes across an ocean, while a majority of pilots ditched and perished in the icy waters of the North Atlantic. He simply knew no fear. With the cash flow from the Grand in the 1970s, MGM stock recovered to more than the price we had paid for it. Edgar and I actually made money in the end, something over a million dollars in my case and a lot more in his. Altogether, we did quite a bit better than we would have at the tables, when we finally cashed our chips and went home. But before we did, Edgar saw the MGM Grand for himself on a trip to Las Vegas, a weekend in June 1975 that included a memorable night out with Frank Sinatra.

"I've never seen it," Edgar said one day. "Why don't you arrange it? And we'll go out for a couple of days." And so we did, flying out from New York on the Seagram plane. One of Edgar's best friends, a man by the name of Bill Green, came along on the plane. And Bill was a great friend of Sinatra's.

We landed in Vegas, where we were met by three stretch limos from the MGM Grand, checked into these huge suites they had given me as a director and Edgar as an important shareholder of the company, and went down to dinner around eight o'clock on the Friday evening. Bill Green joined us and informed us that Frank, who would be opening at Caesars Palace the next night, was inviting us to join him for drinks after dinner over at the Dunes.

The Dunes was across the street from the Grand, and Caesars was kitty-corner. So after dinner, around ten o'clock, we walked over to the Dunes and asked for Frank. They showed us into a private room, set up with a bar, and there was Frank, accompanied by Barbara Marx, to whom he was not yet married. Obviously, Sinatra was well known as a late-night guy, and he was looking for a little action.

"Frank," I suggested meekly, "I'm told that the MGM Grand, of which I am a director, has a private room upstairs for gambling. Would you like me to lay it on?"

"I would love that," he said. "I've never even heard of it."

"Give me five minutes," I replied. So I went to the phone, called the Grand, and asked for the night manager. I introduced myself, told him what I had in mind, and informed him that we were bringing Frank Sinatra over. He asked for fifteen minutes to set it up, and said he would meet us at the door. We were about a hundred yards away from the MGM Grand, but there was no such thing as walking, not with Frank. There were three stretch limos to take us across the street, and there were a couple of bodyguards with guns. At the Grand, the private gambling suite was set up for blackjack, which was what Frank wanted, and the hotel laid on an open bar with a huge dessert table. Even in Miami I'd never seen anything like the displays of food they put on in Vegas.

There was a busboy, an old African American, who was looking after the room. Frank remembered him from one of his earlier appearances in Vegas, asked him how he was doing, and gave him a $100 tip.

Frank carried a lot of cash. I believe that since his credit had been cut off at the Sands back in the 1960s, Frank always made a point of carrying enough cash to cover his losses at the tables. He pulled out an envelope with crisp $100 bills and asked for $10,000 in chips. Edgar signed a chit for $10,000, and Bill Green signed for $5,000. So there was $25,000 on the table, and ten minutes later, it was all gone. By Nevada law, I wasn't allowed to gamble at the MGM Grand, not only because I was a director of the company, but because my name was on the state gambling licence.

"Hit me," Frank said, and promptly lost another $10,000. Edgar and Bill also equalled their losses. So just like that, the house was ahead $50,000. We stayed on until one in the morning, when jet lag caught up with us and we finally all said our goodnights.

By this time, Frank had knocked back several V.O.'s – he actually drank our stuff, and not just to be polite to Edgar – and he was still looking for action. Back at Caesars, as I learned later, he found it, and then some. Somebody said something that triggered Frank's famous temper, and then he turned on Barbara and called her a bitch for not coming to his defence. She ran off crying to their suite, and when he got back there, she was packing up her cosmetics, throwing them all in a bag. She announced that she was leaving, that she was going to call the Kolbers and spend the night with us over at the MGM Grand. She did call, too, but thankfully I had asked the hotel operator for a no disturb on the phone. Frank now knew he was in trouble with Barbara and summoned the night manager. "Who owns the fucking jewelry store in the hotel?" Frank yelled, demanding that he be summoned to open his store at three o'clock in the morning. So Sinatra bought Barbara a bauble for $25,000, and they kissed and made up. All in all, it was an expensive night out for Sinatra.

In October 1976, Frank was scheduled to sing in the round at centre ice in the Montreal Forum. It was during one of his triumphant comeback tours. Edgar called from New York to say he would be flying Frank up on the Seagram jet. "It would be nice," he said, "if you could give a little reception for him at your house after the concert. You know, two hours or so, and then he'll fly back to New York after midnight."

Sandra was delighted to arrange a late-night buffet, and we had no trouble getting people to come. Everybody who was anybody in Montreal wanted to meet Sinatra. He had asked who was coming, and when I showed him the list he was visibly impressed that it started with the chairman of the Royal Bank of Canada. Brian and Mila Mulroney, then a rising young power couple on the Montreal scene, were among the guests. Brian later remembered arriving early and, seeing Frank standing alone at our wet bar, striking up a conversation with him. In the 1980s and 1990s, they would see a fair amount of each other in California, where Frank was close to Ronald and, especially, Nancy Reagan. Interestingly, Frank didn't sing at the house that night, though Brian sang *When Irish Eyes Are Smiling,* while the great Québécois star Robert Charlebois sang a few songs in French and I, dancing a *hora,* favoured the guests with an off-key rendition of "Hava Nagela."

For all his reputation as a barroom brawler, I have to say Frank was the essence of a gentleman any time I saw him. The night he came to our house in Montreal, he went around and had a nice word for everyone, and obligingly posed for pictures with everyone who asked. Some time after that, I was in Calgary attending a board of directors meeting at Bow Valley Industries when a secretary burst excitedly into the room and said that Frank Sinatra was on the phone for me. He had tracked me down through my Montreal office.

"Leo," he began, "how are you? How's the family?" Frank wasn't Italian for nothing. He always asked about the family.

"Fine, Frank, what's up?"

"Listen," he said, "can you do me a favour? I want to take the train from Montreal to Vancouver on a private car. I hear they do that."

"Give me a couple of days," I said. "I'll get back to you."

I called Ian Sinclair, chairman of Canadian Pacific Limited, the parent of the Canadian Pacific Railway, which ran the famed Canadian from Montreal to Vancouver. The train was world renowned for its comfort, service, and view of the Rockies from the observation car. Sinclair, who was known as "Big Julie" for the fear he struck in corporate hearts around CP, said he would have one of his guys get right back to me. And it turned out that Frank was right – they had these beautifully reconditioned private cars that slept small groups and rented out for about $25,000 a trip. They just attached the private car to the Canadian. So I called Frank up, and he was delighted.

"As my gift," I said, "I'll put on a case of V.O. and a case of Chivas." Everything was arranged, but about two weeks later, Frank called back to say he had changed his mind and was cancelling the trip.

One of the delights of the decade I spent on the MGM board was that it got me to Los Angeles six times a year for the bi-monthly board meeting. Sandra loved the movie business, she dabbled in it herself as a writer and producer of several small films, and she would often accompany me on these trips to Hollywood. The studio usually put us up at the Beverly Hills Hotel, which was, then as now, the class of Hollywood hotels, and they would always set us up in one of their famous bungalows.

Those trips usually gave me an opportunity to renew what had become a close friendship with the comedian Danny Kaye. I had first met him in the mid-1960s, when he came to Montreal to entertain at Place des Arts. Mr Bronfman, who was giving a lunch for him at his home on Belvedere Road, called me at the office to ask if I would like to come. Would I? I'd been a fan of Danny's for many years and loved his Emmy-winning variety television series, *The Danny Kaye Show,* then in the middle of its run from 1963 to 1967. After the lunch, I drove Danny back to his hotel and on the way asked whether he would like to come by my house for a late dinner if he was free after the performance that night.

He started dictating the menu to me in the back of the car, the first time I heard of his complete fascination, even obsession, with food. "I'd like Swiss cheese, but it has to be thinly sliced," he said, "and corned beef, also thinly sliced. And not too many people – five or six couples at the most."

It was the first of many times Danny would be a guest in my house and the beginning of a friendship that endured until his death of a heart attack in 1987.

After his performance in Montreal, he was going to another charitable function in Toronto, accompanied by Paul-Émile Cardinal Léger, the charismatic archbishop of Montreal. I suggested he take the company jet, and Danny, an accomplished pilot, was delighted. Though he wasn't licensed to fly in Canada, he schmoozed with the pilots and suggested the cardinal sit in the co-pilot's seat. He called me from the private hangar at Execaire in Montreal. "I'm taking the priest with me," he said in Yiddish.

Danny logged thousands of hours in the air travelling on behalf of symphony orchestras and UNICEF, the other great cause of his life. He had been involved with UNICEF since 1954 and was so identified with it that when the United Nations Children's Fund won the Nobel Peace Prize in 1965, he was asked to accept it. His work with symphony orchestras had begun at the suggestion of the great conductor Eugene Ormandy, and Danny was quite a sight on the podium, conducting *Flight of the Bumblebee* with a fly swatter. *Live from Lincoln Center: An Evening with Danny Kaye and the New York Philarmonic* won a Peabody Award in 1981. He made classical music accessible to a wider audience while raising millions of dollars for orchestras and their musicians' pension funds. Two of those benefits were with the Montreal Symphony Orchestra, which Sandra and I chaired. Born in 1913, the youngest son of an immigrant Ukrainian tailor, David Daniel Kaminsky had come a long way from his humble origins as a Brooklyn Jew.

Danny liked to tell a story on himself of the time he flew into Vancouver for a benefit and was recognized by the immigration official. "Danny Kaye, I can't believe it's you," the officer gushed.

"It's me," Danny said.

"I'm one of your biggest fans," the officer continued. "Wait till I tell my wife I met you."

"That's very kind of you," Danny said.

"By the way," the officer asked, "do you have any identification?"

Danny once conducted a benefit with the Los Angeles Philharmonic and invited Sandra and I to fly out for it. The performance was followed by a reception at Danny's home in Beverly Hills, and somehow we arrived before most of the other guests, except for one famous musician, who was standing by himself in the living room. I went up and introduced myself to Jascha Heifetz, the virtuoso violinist. He made no attempt at pleasantries and was extremely curt. "If I have offended you in some way, I apologize," I said, and moved on. Itzhak Perlman, the renowned violinist, arrived a bit later, and when I described the incident to him, he laughed. "Don't worry about it," he said. "He's like that with everyone. He's my mentor and he treats me the same."

Danny had a way of turning up unannounced, as he did when he showed up delivering smoked meat at the front door as a surprise at my fortieth birthday party, his birthday as well. Danny didn't just simply arrive, he made an entrance. "Am I in the right house?" he shouted. "Where am I?" In 1985, when I was the honouree at an Israel Bonds dinner in Montreal, Sandra called Danny and got him to come as a surprise. He burst into the ballroom of the Queen Elizabeth Hotel yelling, "Where is Kolber, where is Kolber?"

The madcap, frenetic aspect of Danny that we saw in movies like *The Court Jester* wasn't an act. That was Danny, always improvising some crazy way of attracting attention. And if he wasn't the centre of attention, he would simply leave the room. Fundamentally, he hadn't changed since he broke in on the Borscht Belt in the 1930s, running through dining rooms, waving his arms, and yelling gibberish at the hotel guests.

One time in New York, when he was starring in *Two by Two* on Broadway, we were on our way to "21" for a late-night dinner, when Danny jumped out of the car and started directing traffic, waving his arms madly in all directions. He created a huge traffic jam, one of the craziest and funniest stunts I ever saw. He also loved to go to the Stage Deli in New York, owned by Max Asnas, who was a great fan and always wanted him to eat for free. Danny insisted that he be charged at least $1.50 for a pastrami sandwich. He once grabbed a bill for $2.50 from me. "Don't pay it," he said, tipping the waiters $50 as he left the table. "This is outrageous," he said in a loud stage voice and walked out, pretending to be in a great huff. Danny made great exits, too.

But what Danny really enjoyed was eating in and making dinner for his guests. He was a gourmet cook. His specialty was Chinese cuisine, and in the kitchen of his Beverly Hills home, he had every pot and pan in existence. He could whip up anything on a moment's notice, from the main course through dessert. One night I was at his place and he picked up the phone and called his neighbour, Kirk Douglas.

"Kolber is here from Montreal," Danny yelled into the phone. "Come on over for dinner. It is informal."

Five minutes later, in walked Kirk Douglas, wearing silk pajamas and a bathrobe.

"See," he said, "I am informal."

But like many great comedians, Danny was also a profoundly serious man and, politically, a very courageous one. At the height of the Communist witch hunt in Hollywood, he had flown to Washington with Humphrey Bogart and Lauren Bacall, and other brave souls, to protest against the conduct of the House Un-American Activities Committee.

As I later learned, he was also a scratch golfer. He took up the game later in life, and proceeded to become very good at it, just as he was a very good pilot, a very good cook, a very good guest conductor, and a very good spokesman for UNICEF. He had long since conquered Hollywood, pretty much the top of the mountain for a Brooklyn Jew in show business. He had taken London by storm – his shows at the Palladium broke all records from one decade to the next. He had been in the movies. He had been on television. He had sung with Bing Crosby, played with Louis Armstrong, danced with Fred Astaire, and even done drag with Laurence Olivier in a *Night of a Hundred Stars* charity benefit.

His other interests, from cuisine to conducting, from golf to goodwill ambassador, gave a broader definition and meaning to his life. There may have been bigger stars, but none had his multiple talents as a song and dance man, as a comedian and serious actor who could make audiences laugh and weep. And very few had his experience of a wider world. How many people in Hollywood have a share of a Nobel Peace Prize? Truly, he was Hollywood's renaissance man, and I was privileged to be his good friend.

∽

One day in the mid-1970s, I had a call from Taft Schreiber, a ranking executive at MCA, the talent agency that had grown into a film and television business in association with Universal Studios. Only Jules Stein and Lew Wasserman were senior to Schreiber in the MCA hierarchy.

Hired as an office boy in the late 1920s, he eventually opened their Hollywood office and then remained with MCA until his death in 1976. He died as a result of complications from a routine prostatectomy – someone had given him the wrong blood type in a transfusion.

Taft's great coup in the 1940s had been to bring Jack Benny into the MCA stable at a time when he was the biggest radio star in America. Benny went on, of course, to become America's biggest television star in the 1950s. In order to shelter its clients' incomes, MCA had perfected the creative accounting technique of incorporating their stars, thereby maximizing their expenses and minimizing their marginal tax rates. Schreiber and Stein set up a trust fund when another MCA client, Ronald Reagan, ran for governor of California in 1966. Taft was also a close supporter of Richard Nixon when he was in the White House.

For some reason, Taft was calling me as an MGM director to see if I could help straighten out a problem between the two studios. When it turned out I was able to be helpful, he was very grateful and asked if I would come to his house for dinner the next time I was in town with my wife.

When we got to Taft's house, he said, "We are going to Chasen's for dinner, where I've arranged for you to meet two special people." At the restaurant, they showed us to the back, where Jack Benny and George Burns were waiting in a booth. Benny was then well into his seventies, and Burns must have been about eighty, just at the beginning of his second career. Like a couple of duelling fiddlers, the two of them kept us in stitches for the next two hours. It was a memorable night out.

My next encounter with MCA was far more businesslike, much less pleasant, and brought me in contact with Wasserman himself, whom Jack Valenti, the redoubtable Washington lobbyist for the film industry's Motion Picture Association, had once called "the Zeus of Mount Olympus" in Hollywood.

It has been said that Lew had all the warmth of an undertaker, which I think overstated his charm. He was more like the cadaver, the coldest man I ever met in half a century in business. It was Garth Drabinsky who brought me into Lew's world – one more thing I have to thank Garth for.

Drabinsky owned a film exhibition company called Cineplex, and he was a pioneer of the multi-screen cinema that revolutionized movie-going in the 1970s and 1980s. Garth was one of Cadillac Fairview's tenants in the Eaton Centre in Toronto, and his eighteen-screen Cineplex in Canada's number one mall was the flagship of his upstart chain. We had never met when, in 1983, I received a cold call from him.

One thing about Garth – he never lacked for *chutzpah*. Or, to give him his due, for vision.

Garth later recalled our first conversation in his memoir, *Closer to the Sun*. "Leo, we have never met," he said. "But I want you to know I think you are an asshole."

"Why?" I was supposed to have replied.

Which, had such an exchange ever occurred, would have been an interesting conversation between a landlord and a delinquent tenant. Garth had issues of cash-flow management, which meant he was often late with the rent. And as it later turned out, his accounting principles were not generally accepted. Eventually, he lost his company to us at Claridge Inc., successor to Cemp, and to Lew Wasserman and MCA.

But I admired Garth's nerve, and I liked the way he went for it, so at the end of our first conversation I invited him in for a meeting at Cadillac Fairview's head office in the south tower of the Eaton Centre. He took me through some of his brief but turbulent corporate history, which included his building the Beverly Center Cineplex in L.A., which within months of its 1982 opening became the largest-grossing movie complex on a per-seat basis in North America, as well as his ongoing struggle to break the duopoly of Famous Players and Canadian Odeon, whose virtual stranglehold on film distribution in Canada was a major cause of Garth's uneven revenue stream. In a business that was all about putting bums on seats, getting exhibition rights to hot films was everything.

Finally, I asked him what he wanted and what he was going to do for money. "Come to think of it," Garth said, "I could use $5 million."

I was intrigued by the possibility of investing in Cineplex. It seemed like it might be a good fit for us. Cadillac Fairview built and owned shopping malls in Canada and the United States. Cineplex built and ran multi-screen theatres in both countries. And in both Canada and the U.S., most new movie screens were going into malls, many of which were undergoing retrofits to accommodate the trend. Cadillac Fairview had the locations. Cineplex had the concept. And Garth, I had to admit, had the moxie. When I discussed it with Charles Bronfman and Jimmy Raymond, the president of Cemp, they agreed that it was a good fit, and a few months later we invested $3.7 million in Cineplex.

"Garth," I told him, "you build us a great company."

With his new infusion of equity, Garth went on a building and buying spree. In 1984, with $12 million in bridge financing from Cemp, he was able to close a deal to buy out Canadian Odeon, in a single master stroke tripling his capacity to nearly 450 screens. By the end of the year, he had re-branded the company as Cineplex Odeon, a smart move, since Odeon had a lot of brand equity with moviegoers. Then, in 1985, he got involved with MCA when he was invited to design a movie complex right on the lot at Universal Studios in Burbank.

Which was where Lew Wasserman and Sid Sheinberg came in. Garth went to the fabled Black Tower to take them through his $14-million proposal for the Universal Cinema, and at the end of it Lew asked if he "would consider taking in an investor" in Cineplex Odeon, namely MCA.

Since Cemp and its close associates were Garth's biggest shareholders, he informed us almost immediately and kept us advised of developments. I must admit I thought it was a good idea at the time, that having MCA associated with Cineplex Odeon would work at a lot of levels, from the equity it would bring to the table, to the synergies it would bring to the business. Mind you, this was before "synergy" became a big business buzzword in the 1990s, just before the year of "convergence" in 2000.

When the two parties met in L.A. in January 1986, they finally agreed that MCA would buy a one-third interest in Cineplex Odeon for $106 million, payable in 1.5 million shares of MCA stock, with an option to buy more shares not to exceed 50 percent control of the company, an option MCA exercised within months. With the proceeds from the sale of the MCA stock, Garth was able to retire a significant amount of debt and leverage his ambitiously acquisitive business plan. He was on a roll. By his own account, in May 1986, "Cineplex Odeon's equity soared to $274 million and total assets reached $530 million. As for the circuit, Cineplex Odeon had 1,176 screens, 395 of them in the key locations that made Cineplex Odeon into a blockbuster in the exhibition business."

Then it sank in a Florida swamp, down the road from the fantasyland that is Disney World in Orlando, where MCA owned a huge parcel of land. Since the early 1980s, Wasserman and Sheinberg had wanted to build a theme park that would become Universal Studios, Florida. They wanted Garth to build it for them, with Cineplex Odeon's money, as well as their own. Garth went for it, and we went along with it. It was a huge mistake.

They agreed that MCA and Cineplex Odeon would each put up $65 million and together borrow another $90 million to build a 130-acre theme park. By the time it finally opened in 1990, it had cost $700 million and cost Garth his company.

By 1989, Wasserman and Sheinberg had soured on Drabinsky and rebuffed his bid to buy back MCA's equity. They wanted him out. Because of Investment Canada restrictions on foreign ownership of cultural industries, MCA had only one-third of the votes on the Cineplex Odeon board, even though it had half the common shares. If Garth could buy out Claridge's 30 percent, as he offered to do for $125 million, he would retain control of Cineplex Odeon and we would have been very happy to be out.

When Lew and Sid got wind of Garth's $17.50 a share offer in March 1989, they moved to block it with the Securities and Exchange Commission on the grounds that MCA hadn't been given an opportunity to bid on our shares. It's not that Cineplex Odeon was important to them. But in their world, being outmanoeuvred by Garth meant a loss of face, something they simply wouldn't permit. Nobody was going to make *schlemiels* out of them.

Since Seagram shares traded on the New York Stock Exchange, subject to jurisdiction by the SEC, we were sensitive to MCA's allegation. My job was protecting two names, Seagram and Bronfman, and I didn't want either one of them tainted by litigation. There was also a regulatory hitch in that the Quebec Securities Commission forbade the sale of a controlling block of stock owned by a group of more than five shareholders without its permission. And there were clearly more than five of us, with all the Bronfman family trusts and close investors, including me. By now, there were two warring camps, Garth and his partner, Myron Gottlieb, on one side and Lew and Sid on the other. And we, as the other major shareholder, were unhappily stuck in the middle.

In November 1989, I flew to Los Angeles with Sandra, who was a Cineplex Odeon director, along with Jimmy Raymond and Bob Rabinovitch, later president of the CBC but then a senior executive with Claridge. Garth and Myron Gottlieb came along with us on the plane, and they made a case for selling off non-core assets to pay down the huge debt incurred in the Orlando theme park fiasco.

In L.A., I tried to make peace with Wasserman and Sheinberg on Garth's behalf, but to no avail. They insisted that he had to go, and I informed Garth that he was out. I told him that if he went quietly, we would sell him a couple of assets so that he could start over. He had bought the Canadian rights to *The Phantom of the Opera* and spent millions restoring the historic Pantages Theatre in Toronto, which became a remarkable musical showcase. In the 1990s, Livent was a very hot theatre company, and Garth a highly successful impresario whose honours included a well-deserved Tony award for his Broadway production of *Kiss of the Spiderwoman*.

But Garth's tragic flaw, his apparent inattention to the generally accepted principles of accounting, again proved to be his undoing. In October 2002, Drabinsky, Gottlieb, and two associates were charged with massive fraud by the RCMP, accused of having "misrepresented the health of the company" from the time of Livent's founding in December 1989 until they lost it in 1998. The aggrieved parties in the alleged $500-million fraud included three Canadian chartered banks; Southam Inc., then owned by media magnate Conrad Black; and Hollywood super agent Michael Ovitz, who had invested in Livent. As a condition of posting bail, Drabinsky and Gottlieb were required to surrender their passports. Not that they would be travelling to the U.S. anytime soon. Previously indicted on sixteen counts of fraud by a New York grand jury, Drabinsky and Gottlieb refused to respond to the charges and were, as the *National Post* reported, "considered fugitives in the United States, where there are warrants for their arrest."

In his book, Garth was pretty hard on me, and that's fair ball. I understand that he lost a lot in the Cineplex Odeon saga. We lost a lot, too. There was plenty of blame to be shared around the table, by Garth as an entrepreneur and by the Claridge group as investors. He thought that my "vacillations, indecisiveness and lack of spine had led directly" to his ouster. Not content to go after me, he took a run at Sandra, saying, "How I disliked that woman. I always felt she was a phony." This was in 1995, long after she had been incapacitated by a paralysing stroke. Evidently, Garth felt a need to kick a woman in a wheelchair.

My own sense is that it was more Garth's mismanagement and miscalculation – and his overreaching in taking on the Universal theme park in Orlando – that proved to be his undoing. And that began, in retrospect, when he accepted, and we approved, Lew Wasserman and Sid Sheinberg as our partners.

They would remain our partners for seven more years, until Seagram bought MCA and, in the bargain, the Bronfmans acquired their half interest of Cineplex Odeon. But by then the Cineplex infrastructure was wearing as thin as the carpets in its theatres, and the concept of many small screens was being overtaken by larger ones, with more Dolby sound, seats that felt like first class on planes, and café lattes as well as espresso machines in the lobbies. Even as Garth's vision of theatres as a destination was being vindicated, his theatre designs were rendered obsolete.

We merged with Loews Theatres in 1998, creating Loews Cineplex, one of the world's largest exhibition companies. It eventually filed for bankruptcy protection in 2001, but Gerry Schwartz, who had something of a Midas touch with Onex Corporation, a Toronto holding company, acquired it and brought it out of Chapter 11 bankruptcy in the U.S. in 2002.

In March 1995, Edgar Bronfman Jr flew to Palm Beach to brief his uncle Charles and me on the play he was about to make for MCA. He was on his way to Japan, where he would conclude his secret talks with Matsushita to buy 80 percent of MCA for $5.7 billion. And the talks were secret, right to the end. Lew Wasserman read about them in the *Wall Street Journal* on March 31, just like the receptionists and mail boys at the Black Tower.

The Japanese electronics manufacturer, makers of Panasonic, were very unhappy with their 1990 purchase of MCA for more than $6 billion and the assumption of its debts for a further $1.3 billion. They retained Wasserman and Sheinberg as senior executives of the company, but discovered that while Japanese industry functioned on just-in-time inventory management, Hollywood worked on a hurry-up-and-wait basis. The Matsushita purchase of MCA was one of the first media convergence plays between makers of pipeline and producers of content, and the unhappy experience all round should have been a warning that these fundamentally different businesses can never be successfully merged.

Once again with Edgar Jr, I returned to the charge that if we were going to buy MCA, we didn't have to sell our DuPont stake, we could borrow the entire amount and service the debt with our DuPont dividends. Junior said that the DuPont sale wasn't related to the MCA play, which was the silliest damn thing I ever heard. "We're selling DuPont because it is the right thing to do," he said, "not because we are buying something else." He actually seemed to believe what he was saying. DuPont, he added, was just "a commodity play." Some commodities. Nylon. Dacron. Teflon. Textron. As it turned out, the stupidity of it was breathtaking.

One thing I'll say for Junior – he negotiated a price that was good for us and fair for the Japanese, allowing them a face-saving exit. And as Dennis McDougall noted in *The Last Mogul*, "MCA's hard assets alone – its library, theme parks and real estate – were easily worth $5.7 billion."

But two things bothered me. We did not have to sell DuPont to do this deal, since we could easily have financed it with DuPont dividends. And we were going Hollywood again, the lowest-margin business this side of fast food, with a lot higher maintenance of the help. Kids flipping burgers did not have agents, did not come with entourages, and did not travel in private jets. Even Junior understood that. "Hollywood," he said at the time, "is the dumbest town in America."

I guess he felt he could change that – he thought he knew the town. In 1970, at the age of fifteen, Junior had gone to work as a gofer for producer David Puttnam, who was shooting a movie called *Melody* for Edgar's Sagittarius Productions. By 1981 Junior had produced his own movie, *The Border*. He had also dabbled in song writing, and one of his songs had even been recorded by Dionne Warwick. He had shown a nice sense of ironic humour in incorporating his song company under the name Boozetunes.

Once we acquired Universal, the next conversation was, who would run it? Junior was quite taken with Michael Ovitz, the super agent whose Creative Artists Agency, CAA, had tied up much of the talent in Hollywood the way Wasserman had in MCA's heyday. Ovitz had been involved as a middleman in both MCA deals with Matsushita, Lew selling it in 1990 and Junior buying it in 1995.

Now Junior was in talks with Ovitz to bring him in to run the studio, but Ovitz was asking for an unheard-of salary and signing package of $250 million up front. And Junior was going to go for it. The Ovitz story even made the cover of *Newsweek* in June 1995 as practically a done deal – shades of Edgar naming Junior the heir apparent in *Fortune* back in 1986, without the family or board having been informed.

But Ovitz's deal was going to come before the compensation committee of the Seagram board, which Charles and I sat on, and this was where we both finally stepped in.

"Charles, I don't care what you think, I'm telling you right now I'm voting against this," I said. "This is criminal, you can be put in jail for this." So we flew down to New York, had a meeting with Edgar in which we made our opposition unequivocally clear, and kiboshed the Ovitz deal. In Hollywood, the MCA spin machine put it out that Wasserman had nixed the deal. Nonsense. Lew wasn't even in the loop. Charles vetoed it.

Mike Ovitz was obviously an incredibly successful agent. But there is a difference between representing talent and running a diversified entertainment company, as Michael Eisner discovered after he hired Ovitz to be his number two at Disney and learned that he knew nothing about being a chief operating officer. Then Disney had to pay Ovitz more than $100 million to go away after only a year on the job. Even Junior had an intimation that Ovitz knew nothing about running a real business when they were in talks about Ovitz taking charge of MCA. Junior told him he would have authority over everything except treasury, and Ovitz apparently asked what treasury was.

With the purchase of MCA, Seagram sold off its interest in Time Warner, in which it had invested $2.3 billion, having gradually built its stake from 5 percent in 1993 to nearly 15 percent in 1995. But Time

Warner CEO Gerald Levin put in a poison pill and even denied Seagram the seats on the Time Warner board to which it was entitled. Edgar found himself in the position his father had spoken of in regard to MGM in 1968 – investing all that time and money for 15 percent of a media company over which he had no control. In that sense, the MCA deal allowed Seagram to sell off its Time Warner shares, and at a nice profit.

Junior ended up running the place, and he made two smart decisions. He threw Sid Sheinberg and his son off the lot after three of the films they made, in a production deal with Universal, all turned out to be turkeys. And he renamed the company Universal Studios, on the very sound basis that MCA had no brand equity with customers. One thing Edgar Jr had learned well from his father, and from his grandfather before him, was the importance of the brand.

As for Lew Wasserman, we hadn't seen the last of him. Junior graciously renamed the Black Tower for him, and Edgar insisted he join the Seagram board as a signal of continuity and amity between the old and the new management groups. Wasserman served on the Seagram board between 1995 and April 1998, when he went off at age eighty-five. I can't say that he ever contributed much to our discussions, but he certainly looked impressive, and inscrutable, behind his trademark horn-rimmed glasses.

Thus began the Bronfman family's third venture in Hollywood, the one that led to the demise of the Seagram empire. Perhaps the ultimate disaster of the Vivendi-Universal merger could have been averted had Junior been content to own the Universal he bought, as opposed to the one he tried to build. But that was never his intention, as became clear when he paid more than $10 billion to buy Polygram Records. If only we had held on to Paramount Pictures way back when.

The unloading of our DuPont stock and the MCA deal signalled the beginning of a bad period between Charles and Edgar. As Edgar recounted one conversation in his memoir, *Good Spirits,* Charles finally confronted him in his own elegant way.

"I thought as we got older we were supposed to get closer and be better friends," Charles began.

"Well, that's what's happening," Edgar replied.

"No, it isn't," Charles said.

"What are you talking about?"

"MCA."

Finally, Charles had put the issue on the table with his brother, saying he hadn't said no because he hadn't "wanted to start a family feud."

"There probably would have been one," Edgar replied, "but if you had said no, we wouldn't have made the deal."

If only.

At the end of 2002, the *New York Times* reported from Los Angeles that Hollywood had just completed its most successful year ever, with ticket sales of $9 billion across North America. All the studios in Hollywood had a combined gross of $9 billion.

A single company, DuPont, had revenues in 2002 of $25 billion, more than two and a half times the combined studio revenue in Hollywood in the best year in its history. Seagram's dividend from DuPont stock would have been nearly $350 million, and its forgone dividends from 1995 to 2003 totalled $2.5 billion.

Sam Bronfman had been right in his premonition – empires have indeed come and gone, including his own.

12

Authors and Artists

Mordecai Richler got it wrong – the best revenge is to outlive someone, as Sam Bronfman used to say. Solomon Gursky, the central character in his thinly disguised novel on the Bronfmans, said that "Gerald Murphy got it wrong – living twice, maybe three times, is the best revenge." And Solomon did, living the life of a Canadian bootlegger, a British peer, and an Israeli intelligence official. Gerald Murphy was the friend of F. Scott Fitzgerald, the model for Dick Diver in *Tender Is the Night,* who once said, "Living well is the best revenge."

Oh, Mordecai! He was such a great writer, though not always a great human being. Now that he is dead, I've finally got around to reading *Solomon Gursky Was Here.* Sandra read it when it came out in 1989, and urged me not to. We were in the book as Harvey and Becky Schwartz, a couple of Jewish social climbers. Harvey worked for the Gurskys, running their investment trust and real estate company, and Becky wrote a bad book of columns entitled *Hugs, Pain, and Chocolate Chip Cookies.* How close is that to home? In fact, Harvey's home was a big house on Belvedere Road in Westmount. It doesn't get any closer than that.

In *Solomon Gursky Was Here,* Mr Sam became Mr Bernard, Bernard Gursky, who came out of the prairies, built a liquor empire in Montreal during Prohibition in the United States, and froze his brothers, including Solomon, out of the business. The other brother, Morrie, was a ringer for Allan Bronfman, educated and cultivated – Bernard even threw an ashtray at him. Morrie, like Allan, never got around to telling his children that his brother had forced him out of the business. The brothers lived in adjoining mansions at the top of Westmount, and their children had their own hockey rink. Eleanor Roosevelt came for tea during the Second World War. All true. Bernard's sons, Lionel and

Nathan, were born in 1929 and 1931, just as Edgar and Charles were. I don't know why Mordecai bothered to change the names. "I made the Gurskys up out of my own head," Mordecai insisted in his author's note. Please.

When he gave a reading from *Solomon Gursky* at the Montreal Jewish Public Library after it came out in 1989, he was asked whether it was about the Bronfmans. He replied, as the Montreal literary columnist Joel Yanofsky later recounted, "I will not have seven years of my work reduced to gossip."

"Seriously, who was *Solomon Gursky* about if not the Bronfmans?" Yanofsky asked in an appreciation of Mordecai in *Maisonneuve* magazine. "Richler had even lifted a line from Peter C. Newman's book about the Bronfmans, and plunked it down in his novel. When Mr Bernard, the engagingly vulgar character Richler modeled after Bronfman patriarch Samuel, is asked if he gets ulcers, he replied, 'I don't get ulcers, I give them.'" Precisely.

Harvey Schwartz was a relentless ass-kisser, not to mention a paranoid hypochondriac who wore argyle socks. There was a time when Mordecai and I saw a good deal of one another, but then he used something in a television play that I had told him privately about Sam Bronfman's death, and that ended our friendship.

Mordecai first came to see me with Michael Spencer, head of the Canadian Film Development Commission, to get my advice on building a movie industry in Canada. At the time, I was on the board of MGM, and I believe as the only Canadian on any board of a Hollywood studio. Mordecai brought Spencer to lunch at Cemp's mahogany-panelled offices, which also made an appearance in *Solomon Gursky Was Here*. He described them perfectly as part of the Gursky Tower on what was then Dorchester Boulevard, later Boulevard René Lévesque, in Montreal.

"Here is what you should do," I told Spencer. "Build two sound studios, state of the art, one in Toronto and one in Montreal. Then lease them out to Hollywood producers at cut rates, with one condition, that the director hires Canadian crews. In that way, in five or six years, we can develop the best film crews in the world. You will build a reputation for Canada that way, and the film industry will seek us out.

"On the other hand," I said, "if you continue handing out $200,000 to everybody with a script idea, you will just piss it all away." Which, unfortunately, was what happened, initially. I knew enough about movies by then to know that you make them with bankable stars, and then the issue of where they're shot becomes a question of comparative cost

advantage. This, by the 1990s, proved to be exactly how the film industry grew in Canada, to the considerable annoyance of the crafts' and actors' unions in Hollywood. For example, *My Big Fat Greek Wedding,*
Nia Vardalos's runaway hit produced by Tom Hanks and his wife, Rita
Wilson, was shot in Toronto, which passed for Chicago. Montreal has
passed for New York in dozens of features.

In any event, Mordecai and I became good friends and hung out a
good deal together during my bachelor summer of 1971, the period of
my brief separation from Sandra. On Friday, July 10, Sam Bronfman
died, and I got involved with organizing his funeral, to the point of going to Paperman's Funeral Home with Edgar and Charles and choosing
a casket for the old man. Charles and Edgar were going to go for a pine
box, and I could tell by the look on Mr Paperman's face that he could
see a big sale slipping away.

"You can't do that," I said to Charles, pointing out that his father
would be lying in state for two days at Samuel Bronfman House of the
Canadian Jewish Congress. So we chose a bronze one instead for
$12,500, the equivalent of about $50,000 today. Mordecai came over
to the house that night to kind of commiserate with me. I poured him a
few single malt whiskies and told him the story of the coffin. Then I forgot about it.

Flash forward to a year or so later. Sandra and I, back together, were
lying in bed on a Sunday night watching a CBC teleplay by Mordecai.
Some guys were playing golf, one of them died on the course, and they
schlepped him around in a golf cart. And one of them said that, as had
been done for Sam Bronfman, they would have to spend $12,500 on a
casket for him. There was only one place Richler could have got that –
from me, in my own home.

I was furious with Mordecai. "Look," I told him, "I can't sustain a
friendship where I have to watch every word I say. What kind of friendship is that?"

He got very nasty about it, as only Mordecai could, and that was the
end of our friendship. We never spoke again. Whenever we were at the
same party, which happened with some frequency, he would go out of
his way to avoid me. And instead of being his friend, I became a character in one of his books. But now that I've finally read it, I must admit, it
was a very good book, perhaps his best ever. So in a certain sense, I was
flattered to be in it, even if the caricature was highly unflattering. Argyle socks, indeed.

I'll also give Mordecai credit for being a good husband and father. He
was madly in love with his wife, Florence, and once told me he couldn't

understand men who cheated on their wives. He also raised five highly accomplished children, journalists and writers in their own right, which proves that the apple doesn't fall far from the tree. Another thing I'll say for Mordecai is that he didn't have an ounce of pretension in him, literary or otherwise. A year after Mordecai's death, his friend Jack Rabinovitch, sponsor of Canada's Giller Prize, recalled in *Maclean's* that when Mordecai received an honorary degree from McGill in 1975, he referred to the Jewish quota in his address. "If you were Jewish you needed 75 percent to get into McGill, but if you were Gentile you needed only 65 percent," he said. "I want you to realize this, I would not even have made it as a Gentile."

Peter C. Newman was another author I got to know well. We became acquainted when he was writing the first volume in his series that began with *The Canadian Establishment*. For some reason, he got it into his head to do a sequel on the Jewish establishment in Canada, and I tried to talk him out of it by pointing out that no such establishment existed. So he wrote a book about the Bronfmans instead. Published in 1978, it was called *Bronfman Dynasty: The Rothschilds of the New World*. I had no quarrel with the title, but some of the content was quite contentious.

I was also concerned, in the aftermath of young Sam Bronfman's 1975 kidnapping, for the safety of Charles's children and my own. It's fair to say I was a bit paranoid on the subject. Newman was then editor of *Maclean's,* and I went to see him at his Toronto office. "If anything happens to a Bronfman or a Kolber kid because of someone reading this book getting the wrong idea," I said, "I will cut your balls off." I must admit to being highly unpleasant about it. On the whole, I liked Peter and liked what he was trying to do in his work, making business and businesspeople more interesting to read about. By and large, he succeeded in that.

Newman's publisher was Jack McClelland of McClelland and Stewart, who had also published my wife's books of poetry. Jack was a friend, and he agreed to let me have an advance look at the galleys, something he probably shouldn't have done. Charles Bronfman, Phil Vineberg, Sandra, and I divided up the manuscript and began marking up the errors. Newman was anxious to get the book out in time for the Christmas season, but he agreed to make some of the changes we insisted on.

"As this volume was going to press," Peter explained in his author's note, "Jack McClelland, my publisher, received word from Charles Bronfman that he had somehow obtained a set of early galleys from, as he put it, 'an unnamed source.'" Whatever the source, Newman acknowledged "a professional obligation to correct any possible errors of a purely factual nature." He did, and got his book out for Christmas.

On Christmas Eve, Jack McClelland sent me a copy signed by himself as publisher. "Dear Leo," his dedication began. "This is a collector's copy – one of a kind." On page 212, he wrote, "you will find some copy that escaped our editor initially but that appears only in this copy." It was about me, describing me as a "rambunctious and carefree six-footer with shocks of heavy black hair," an intense and driven business executive who was transformed to "a zesty big guy" at home. If only.

Until then, Newman had often called me for background on business deals and business leaders, and always respected confidences in the way he used any information I gave him for his books or his column. After our run-in over the Bronfman book, I didn't hear very much from him again.

Looking back, it seems to me that there were always writers in the vicinity of the Bronfmans, either writing for them or writing about them. A.M. Klein, the socialist poet, made a good capitalist living for many years as Sam Bronfman's speechwriter. He apparently complained that the work was demeaning of his dignity, but never stopped cashing the cheques. Mordecai Richler put him in *Solomon Gursky* as well, as L.B. Berger, the father of the narrator, Moses Berger, a dissolute writer who bore more than a passing resemblance to Mordecai himself. And in that way, I imagine, Mordecai settled a score with the Bronfmans on behalf of A.M. Klein.

As Sam Bronfman neared the end of his life in the late 1960s, Charles and Edgar hired a writer named Terence Robertson to do an authorized biography of their father. Robertson interviewed Mr Sam extensively, as well as his wife and children and close members of the family's business circle, including me. But the family couldn't get the book out of him. He wrote a manuscript that was apparently quite incoherent, and then he disappeared. In January 1970, he was found dead, a suicide, in a hotel room in New York.

But his interview transcripts survived and proved to be useful to Michael Marrus when Charles and the family hired him many years later, in 1989, to write the authorized biography, *Mr Sam*, that was published to generally positive reviews in 1991. Marrus, a University of Toronto historian and a specialist in Jewish history, had only one condition – that there be no conditions. He wanted to be free to write the book without interference or review by the family. As Marrus elegantly put it, these were "terms which kept the project's sponsors at a congenial arm's length." Charles was as good as his word, and I was among the many people Marrus interviewed for his biography. He captured the scope of Mr Sam's ambition, the sweep of his life, his vision as a business leader, his leadership in Jewish affairs, and his utter devotion to Saidye Bronfman.

In the winter of 2003, I heard that Charles himself was hard at work on his memoirs, in collaboration with the renowned British historian Martin Gilbert. They had apparently struck up a friendship in Jerusalem, where each spends a part of the year. Gilbert's 1998 book, *Israel,* which came out on the country's fiftieth anniversary, is a masterful popular history of that country. But he's best known, of course, for his epic biographies of Sir Winston Churchill.

Only a Bronfman could engage Churchill's official biographer as his own.

In the late 1950s, Sandra and I flew to Los Angeles on one of those old prop aircraft with a forward lounge in first class. She went up front to have a smoke and ended up meeting Sammy Cahn, the songwriter who wrote "Three Coins in the Fountain" and "High Hopes." He worked with Frank Sinatra and had won several Oscars for best song in a film. Somehow, we struck up a friendship with Sammy, and when Sandra organized my fiftieth birthday party at the Ritz in 1979, guess who was leading the orchestra? Sammy Cahn.

Harry Belafonte, then a good friend, flew in for the party from New York, and we even did a duet together at the microphone, though I didn't hear any requests for me to do an encore. Harry and I were close enough friends that he invited us to a couple of his political soirees in New York, close enough that I once loaned him $100,000 to help finance a movie he was producing in Jamaica.

"Harry," I said, "this is a risky undertaking. How about if I just come in as your partner, and if it doesn't turn out, you won't owe me anything?"

He insisted that the picture would make money, and he wanted to own all of it. It didn't. I never asked him for my money back, but unbeknownst to me, the impresario Sam Gesser, who booked Harry's concerts in Montreal, reminded Belafonte that he owed me a hundred grand. Harry then had his accountant call me.

"Harry wants to pay back your money," he said.

"Thank you."

"It has been three years," the accountant noted. "What rate of interest do we owe you?"

"I don't charge my friends interest."

"That's very generous," he said.

Harry paid me back the $100,000 and I never heard from him again.

As a young man, I bought season tickets for the Montreal Symphony at a time when they played at a place called Plateau Hall in Parc Lafontaine. It was more of an auditorium than a concert hall, and the orchestra was anything but the world-class ensemble it later became. I would take my mother, or occasionally a date, and tried very hard to develop a taste for classical music, something I have failed to do over a period of nearly fifty years. Sandra, who really appreciated the classical repertoire, did her best to develop my appreciation of classical music, getting me to listen to recordings over the years, from 78 RPMs, to longplaying albums, to tapes, and finally to CD-ROMs.

From the moment the MSO hired the dashing young Zubin Mehta as its conductor in 1961, it began to arrive as a serious orchestra. When it finally got an appropriate concert hall in 1963, the 3,000-seat Salle Wilfrid Pelletier at Place des Arts, Sandra and I were in the black-tie audience on opening night. And for all the years that followed, including the nearly quarter century that conductor Charles Dutoit brought the MSO Grammy awards and world acclaim, we were fervent supporters of the symphony. When the MSO sold out Carnegie Hall, as it did every year, we always flew to New York to be in the audience. And we organized any number of fundraising galas with Danny Kaye, Luciano Pavarotti, and Placido Domingo, among others.

Zubin Mehta's brother, Zarin, was the managing director of the MSO in those years, before he went off to run the Ravinia Festival in Chicago and ultimately become head of the New York Philharmonic Orchestra, the real big time. Placido Domingo was doing an MSO benefit at the Montreal Forum in 1986, and he packed the place. Zarin asked if I could put on a small dinner for him afterwards, and we were delighted to organize a midnight supper on a warm evening in our backyard. Pierre Trudeau came, as did Paul and Jackie Desmarais and Zarin and his wife, who had been Zubin's first wife. Placido couldn't have been nicer or friendlier, posing for pictures with everyone. He didn't sing at the house, though I believe Jackie Desmarais might have. She tends to do that. When Paul ran into an acquaintance at Caroline Mulroney's wedding, he asked, "Have you seen my wife?" "She hasn't sung yet," he was assured. "Don't worry," Paul said, "she will."

In November 1987, after a stressful year of selling off Cadillac Fairview, the Bronfmans walked away with $1.2-billion profit and I cashed out my stock for nearly $100 million. After thirty years of hard work, it was a big payday for me.

"Let's disappear for a few weeks," I said to Sandra.

"As it happens," she said, "the MSO left yesterday for Paris." This was the start of a tour behind the Iron Curtain, and she had been invited to go along.

We got on a plane that very night, flew to Paris, and took a car to the Plaza Athénée. Walking through the lobby, we ran into Mila Mulroney and her assistant, Bonnie Brownlee. They ended up sitting right in front of us at the concert that night at l'Opera de Paris, so I leaned over and invited them to join us for dinner the next night at the Tour d'Argent. My daughter, Lynne, and her husband, Barry, were flying in from New York, and Mila and Bonnie made a table for six.

At the Tour d'Argent, the deal is that you have drinks downstairs and then they take you upstairs to your table, with Notre Dame de Paris and all of Paris at your feet. It is one of the most breathtaking views in the entire world, and the Tour d'Argent is certainly one of the best restaurants.

"This is the table they gave Brian and me the last time we were here," Mila said as we were seated at the best table in the house. She was impressed. I was impressed with the bill – $3,000 for dinner for six. What the hell! I had just cashed a big cheque. I could afford to buy the prime minister's wife and her assistant dinner at the Tour d'Argent. I'll never forget Mila and Brian's many calls and expressions of kindness after Sandra's stroke. Later, after they left 24 Sussex and returned to live in Montreal, they even gave a dinner in Sandra's honour. It was entirely unnecessary and typically generous of them.

Anyway, we followed the orchestra throughout Eastern Europe, beginning with East Berlin, where the Berlin Wall still divided East and West. It would be two more years before it fell. We went to Leipzig, Prague, and finally jumped off to Rome. Everywhere it went, the MSO was acclaimed with great ovations. The tour was a triumph from beginning to end. I remember thinking then that the Montreal Symphony had truly come a long way from Plateau Hall and that we had been privileged to accompany them on part of the journey.

13

Anti-Semitism and the Jewish Mosaic

I first experienced the sting of anti-Semitism when we moved from a Jewish neighbourhood off Park Avenue at the foot of Mount Royal to a Gentile one in Notre-Dame-de-Grace in the west end of Montreal. My father had inherited a house on NDG Avenue, and my mother transformed it into a little jewel of a home. But it meant that instead of going to a school where the enrolment was 98 percent Jewish and 2 percent Gentile, the class was now 98 percent Gentile and 2 percent Jewish.

Many times during my years at West Hill High during the Second World War, I was chased home from school by people calling me a "dirty Jew." I once had a friend named Morley Pinkney, who later became an Anglican priest, and we used to play outside together. I once asked him inside for a soft drink. And he said, "I'm not allowed to go into your home." When I asked why, he replied, "Because you are Jews." I had never heard anything like this before, and while I won't say it was an awakening, it was certainly a discovery.

The Montreal into which I was born, then a city of one and a quarter million people, was composed mostly of a French Catholic majority, a powerful English Protestant minority, a primarily Irish enclave of English Catholics, and a Jewish community of about 65,000 people, by far the largest, most affluent and influential such community in Canada – influencial within the community, that is. While Montreal was, even then, Canada's most cosmopolitan city, its Jewish component was more tolerated by the other groups than encouraged by them to become an integral part of the economic and social life of the city. As Edgar Bronfman has written in his impassioned memoir, *The Making of a Jew,* "Anti-Semitism was palpable in Montreal. There were restricted hotels (no Jews or dogs) and Jews were not welcome on the boards of banks or of McGill University … the powers that were had little, if any social contact with Jews, and very little business dealings, except occasionally on a professional level, and what little contact there was occurred because of charitable endeavours."

One of the reasons the Jewish General Hospital was built in Montreal in the 1930s was so that Jewish doctors would have a place to practise medicine and perform surgeries. They were not well accepted or accredited at the English hospitals in Montreal, the Royal Victoria and the Montreal General, which in those days reflected the exclusionary attitudes of the WASP establishment that built them, endowed them, and funded their ongoing activities. Both my grandfathers were involved as donors in the initial fundraising campaign for the Jewish General, and half a century later I became its president.

Built with community funds in the middle of the Great Depression as a small hospital with fifty beds and six doctors, "the Jewish" had by the turn of the twenty-first century become the third-busiest hospital in Quebec, with 50,000 emergency cases and 23,000 bed patients a year, and with 550 affiliated doctors and over 1,000 nurses on staff. Ironically in view of its origins, the Jewish General is now a McGill teaching hospital, accounting for 20 percent of the medical training and 30 percent of the research of all the adult hospitals affiliated with McGill. In my own time, the university enforced quotas against Jewish students and was associated with English teaching hospitals that wouldn't accredit Jewish doctors.

In the very year "the Jewish" opened, a disturbing incident occurred involving the appointment to a French-language hospital of a Jewish doctor who had graduated first in his class from a French-language medical school. McGill sociologist Morton Weinfeld recounted the episode in *Like Everyone Else ... but Different,* his illuminating book on the Jewish community in Canada. "In 1934," Weinfeld wrote, "Dr. Samuel Rabinovitch, a top graduate from the Université de Montréal's medical school, was awarded an internship at Montreal's Notre Dame Hospital. In protest, all his fellow interns walked out, soon joined by interns in other Catholic hospitals. Eventually, the young doctor resigned his appointment. More telling, the interns' strike enjoyed support from all sectors of Quebec society, including *Le Devoir,*" which alleged that Catholic patients would find it "repugnant" to be treated by a Jewish doctor. Dr Rabinovitch left Canada and, as Irving Abella later wrote in *A Coat of Many Colours*, a history of Jewish life in Canada, he "went on to a distinguished career in the U.S." before returning to Montreal on his retirement in the 1980s.

Anti-Semitism was not a new phenomenon in Quebec or elsewhere in Canada. The first known Jewish immigrant to Canada was deported back to France in 1739, on the orders of King Louis XVI himself, for refusing to convert to Catholicism. Esther Brandeau had slipped into port at Quebec City disguised as a man. She'd taken the name Jacques La-Farge and claimed to have shipped out to New France to begin a new life.

"Under the French, Canada's first colonizers, Jewish settlement was strictly barred, indeed all non-Catholic settlement was prohibited," Abella wrote. "Thus, from the moment the French settlement began in the early 1600s, to the capture of Quebec by the British in 1759, Jews were forbidden to enter New France."

Jewish settlement was tolerated under British rule, but when Ezekiel Hart, scion of a Jewish merchant family in Trois-Rivières, won a by-election in the Quebec legislative assembly in 1807, he was prevented from taking his seat on the technicality that he had crossed out "in the year of our Lord 1807" on his election papers and simply signed his own name and the year. When he was re-elected in a subsequent by-election the following year, this time swearing the oath on a New Testament, he was prevented from taking his seat on the grounds that since he was a Jew, his oath on the New Testament was not credible or binding. Finally, the assembly voted 18 to 8 in favour of a resolution affirming that Jews "cannot sit nor vote in this House." And at the end of the nineteenth century, the Dreyfus Affair, the trial of Jewish army officer Alfred Dreyfus for treason, resulted in almost as many anti-Semitic recriminations in Quebec as in France. It also led, as Irving Abella wrote, to the founding of the *Jewish Times*, a militant voice in defence of the beleaguered Jewish community in Quebec and Canada.

The origins of French Canada as a theocracy, a union of church and state, were more apparent than ever in the 1930s when, as Abella observed, "the Roman Catholic church and its allies in the French Canadian nationalist movement were aggressively anti-Jewish." The clerical and secular elements of anti-Semitism were personified by the Abbé Lionel Groulx, the brilliant orator who was most effective at rallying French Canadian opinion against Jews. And since the 1930s were a period of economic hardship, the success of Jews as merchants was highly visible and made them all the more convenient as scapegoats.

The Catholic Church and the Quebec nationalist movement, with the complicity of the French press, organized boycotts of Jewish merchants in Montreal. "If we do not buy from them, they will leave," suggested the newspaper *Action catholique*. The church sponsored an "achat chez nous" campaign that was quite unambiguous in what was meant by "chez nous." And the Société St-Jean-Baptiste ended rallies with the pledge "I promise that under no circumstances shall I buy from a Jew."

Things were hardly any better for Jews during the Depression years elsewhere in Canada. "In 1933," as the former prime minister Brian Mulroney reminded a University of Toronto conference on anti-Semitism in 2003, "Toronto witnessed the Christie Pits riot – anti-Semites terrorized a Jewish baseball team in a street battle that went on all night."

My own anecdotal experiences of growing up Jewish in Montreal certainly fit the description of anti-Semitism as later defined by the Anti-Defamation League in 1989, as "simply a hostility directed at Jews solely because they are Jews." As Dr Karen Mock has written, "Anti-Semites are antagonistic to Jews for who they are and what they represent, and this antagonism has an ancient history."

I had no awareness of institutionalized anti-Semitism in my own adolescent life. I was unaware, for example, that in 1939 the government of Canada turned away the *St-Louis*, a boatload of desperate German Jewish refugees, sending them to certain death in Europe. Canada was closed to Jewish immigrants before and during the Second World War, and when asked how many Jews would be allowed into Canada after the war, a senior immigration official notoriously replied, "None is too many." The quotation became the title of Irving Abella and Harold Troper's damning indictment of Canada's official indifference to the plight of Jews under the Nazi regime.

Even before the war and the Holocaust, the Canadian prime minister of the day, W.L. Mackenzie King, wrote in his diary: "The sorrows which the Jews have to bear at this time are almost beyond comprehension. Something will have to be done by our country." Tragically, nothing was. But King also wrote admiringly of meeting Chancellor Adolf Hitler in 1937, sizing him up "as one who truly loves his fellow man."

"The impression King formed of the Fuehrer was not only absurd, it was calamitous," the noted journalist Bruce Hutchison would later write in *The Incredible Canadian,* his best-selling biography of Mackenzie King. "It distorted all King's thinking on the human tragedy now about to open."

Canada ignored not only the plight of the Jews, but also the protests of many Canadians and the pleadings of the press. A prominent Montrealer, William Birks, called the government's closed-door policy "narrow, bigoted and short sighted." Socialist leader J.S. Woodsworth said he felt "helpless and ashamed" as a Canadian. The *Toronto Star* and the *Winnipeg Free Press* both condemned Ottawa's "cowardly policy."

Why did Mackenzie King do nothing? Because of political expediency; because he was afraid he could not carry his cabinet on an open-door policy, particularly his senior Quebec minister, Ernest Lapointe. As Abella noted in *A Coat of Many Colours*, "Accepting Jewish refugees, [King] told his sympathetic cabinet, would undermine Canadian unity ... strengthen the forces of Quebec nationalism, and bring about bloodshed in the streets." Abella added, "King was influenced in these views by his Quebec lieutenant, Ernest Lapointe, who kept the bug in his ear about the dangers of alienating his province by opening Canada's doors to Jewish immigration, no matter how limited."

While the doors of Canada were closed to one persecuted minority, Canada became a prison for another, as the government forcibly dislocated, wrongfully incarcerated, seized the property of, and disenfranchised thousands of loyal Canadians of Japanese ancestry.

Sam Bronfman was certainly well aware of the Holocaust. As president of the Canadian Jewish Congress during the Second World War, he was uniquely positioned in Canada to know what was going on in Europe and he made sure the Canadian government knew about it at the highest levels. He managed to persuade Ottawa to take in a thousand Jewish orphans from Europe, with a guarantee of finding Jewish homes for them. But Canada, like the United States, could have, should have, done much more.

During the entire period of the Nazi reign of terror, from 1933 to 1945, a grand total of five thousand Jewish immigrants were admitted to Canada, on a proportional basis only half as many as were allowed to enter even the United States, which practised a similar policy of turning its back on Jews. The policy of excluding Jewish immigrants was ruthlessly enforced by the openly anti-Semitic deputy minister of immigration, F.C. Blair, with the full knowledge of the prime minister. How many Jews perished as a result of this policy of indifference will simply never be known. In his speech to the international anti-Semitism conference in 2003, Mulroney blamed Mackenzie King for contributing to the deaths of "countless Jews."

Mr Sam and Mrs Saidye, as they were known, were strong supporters of the war effort and rallied the Jewish community across Canada to serve the twin causes of democracy and saving European Jewry from extinction. As Edgar Bronfman later wrote of his father in *The Making of a Jew*, "He believed that Canada, the inheritor of English libertarianism, had made it possible for Jews to live as *almost* equal citizens under the

Union Jack." As Edgar also noted, "it was easy to understand that the Jewish community was very supportive of the war." Neither his father, nor any of his friends, "would have ever dreamed of doing anything that would make that community look anything less than super-patriotic."

Mr Bronfman used to say to me, "My boys don't understand anti-Semitism, you do." And I did, from an early age. "You have to tell them what the real world is," he would insist. Edgar and Charles, as Mr Bronfman said, lived "an extremely sheltered and privileged life." It bothered him a lot that they didn't seem to understand it, though in fact they caught on soon enough when they were sent away to Trinity College School, a high Protestant prep school in Port Hope, Ontario, where they were the only Jews on campus.

Previously, Edgar and Charles had attended Selwyn House, a WASP boys school, and while they encountered no discrimination to speak of, Edgar later wrote in *Good Spirits* that it "created great confusion in our lives." The Bronfman boys, he wrote, had two sets of friends, "the WASPs at Selwyn, and the Jews from synagogue, whom we saw only on Saturdays and Sundays."

Charles and especially Edgar encountered no such confusion in their lives at Trinity, where they were treated badly from the outset, an experience they may not have shared with their father. "Both Charles and I were forced to spend two unhappy years in this den of intolerance," Edgar wrote, recalling that he "constantly overheard comments denigrating Jews."

When I entered McGill as a sixteen-year-old freshman in the fall of 1945, there was a quota system for the number of Jews accepted by the university. A perfect score on the university admission exams was 1000, and if you were a Jew, you needed a score of 750 to get in, while if you were a Gentile, you needed only 650. My score was 775, so I got in, no problem, but a lot of young Jews didn't, and it was a real bone of contention in the community.

While McGill was not alone in discriminating against Jewish applicants, its quota system was, as Abella observed, the "most notorious." For years, as Abella wrote in *A Coat of Many Colours,* "it was an open secret that standards of admission for Jewish applicants were far higher than for anyone else." Sir Arthur Currie, commander of Canada's troops in the First World War and principal of McGill between the wars, evidently worried, as Abella put it, "that so many Jewish students would qualify that there would scarcely be room for non-Jews." It is a measure of how much things have changed for the better that Bernard Shapiro was named principal of McGill in 1994 without any fanfare over his being a

Jew. Sam Bronfman had to put in a lifetime of striving and success before being named to McGill's board of governors, but it passed unnoticed when Bob Rabinovitch, who worked for Charles as chief operating officer of Claridge Inc., was named chairman of the McGill board in 1999.

It was Sam Bronfman, as I later learned, who was instrumental in persuading McGill to end the Jewish quota some years after the Second World War. Cyril James, the principal of McGill from 1939 to 1962, went to see him and actually had the nerve to ask why the Jewish community didn't contribute more to McGill. Mr Bronfman conceded the point and said he would spearhead a fundraising effort in the community, but that in return McGill would have to end the Jewish quota, which it did. There were still quotas in medicine, but they were territorial or geographical quotas; in other words, so many med-school students would be admitted from outside Quebec and so many from outside Canada. But the Jewish quota was over.

When we closed our first big deal at Cemp Investments, a $7-million land package we bought from the Bennett family and Principal Investments, we met on a Saturday morning at the National Club in Toronto. Archie Bennett, the patriarch of the Bennett family, called me and said, "You understand that at that club Jews aren't allowed." They closed the deal with us, Jewish investors and their Jewish lawyers and managers, at a club where Jews weren't permitted. This was in December 1958, to give you an idea of the extent to which anti-Semitism still existed in the Canadian business community. Later I became a member of that club, though I never used it very often.

There was one time, in 1981, when anti-Semitism actually worked in our favour in a business deal, and that was the deal we didn't do to buy St Joseph Lead. Seagram had just sold Texas Pacific Oil and Gas for $2.3 billion, and we were casting around for a company in which to invest the proceeds. Edgar held these business seminars in New York, where we would discuss various industries and specific companies we might invest in. Finally, it was decided we would make a hostile bid for St Joseph Lead, a big mineral and natural resource company. Happily and fortuitously, the St Joe board didn't want Jews to have anything to do with their company, so they kept upping the price, and finally we walked away from it. Felix Rohatyn, the man who saved New York from bankruptcy in the 1970s, was advising us on the deal, and he took me aside and asked just what it was the Bronfmans wanted.

"Well, Felix," I said, "number one, they want not to overpay."

But, bottom line, St Joe didn't want to sell to Jews. And if St Joe Lead wanted Jews, we would have been poor a long time ago. It was the best

With the family – Sandra, Lynne, and
Jonathan, and Danny Kaye. For once,
it seems to be Sandra's birthday, not mine!

In October 1976, Frank Sinatra came to
the house for a reception after a concert,
and couldn't have been nicer, posing for
photos like this one with us and one of
Lynne's friends.

A family photo with Brian and Mila Mulroney in 1985, when the prime minister spoke at an Israel Bonds dinner where I was the honouree.

Sandra gets set to go flying with the Israeli air force.

With Luciano Pavarotti backstage at Place des Arts at a symphony benefit chaired by Sandra and me. While both our names were on the program, she did all the work.

Danny Kaye with Sandra, Marie-Josée Drouin, then married to Montreal Symphony conductor Charles Dutoit, Charles Dutoit, and me, at our home following another one of Danny's benefit concerts in the mid-1980s.

With David Lean, on location on the set of *Ryan's Daughter* in Ireland in 1970. As a member of the Metro-Goldwyn-Mayer Inc. board, I wanted to see how the great director was spending all our money. The answer was, with no trouble at all.

MATILDA! Harry
Belafonte and I sing
up a storm at my
fiftieth birthday at
the Ritz in 1979.

Sandra chats with
Rudolf Nureyev.
Pierre Trudeau
and I join the
conversation.

Stretching our legs during a stop along the Trans-Siberian Railway, a week-long journey from Moscow to Vladivostok in October 1986. Pierre Trudeau strikes his gunslinger pose while Paul Desmarais, Sandra, Louise Lamarre, and I look on.

Sandra with Pierre on board one of the three private cars the Russians put on the train for us – a day car and diner, a sleeper for the rest of us, and a private car for Trudeau.

With one of our stewards as I'm about to take my bath in Trudeau's private car.

With Jack Austin, Pierre, and President Zia of Pakistan at a private dinner in Islamabad in 1987. We took the Silk Road, across the top of the world, through Kathmandu and into China.

Taliban man: On our trip across the wilds of Pakistan, I bought a hat and tried to blend in with the locals. To no avail.

With Trudeau, from one island in the Galapagos to the next.

Pierre trying to teach me how to scuba dive
in the Galapagos Islands in 1990. I'm afraid
it was quite hopeless.

Pierre in his favourite garb:
shorts and sandals.

With Nicaraguan president Daniel Ortega, Pierre, and our son, Jonathan.
The meeting was held in a secret location, with the curtains drawn.

Sandra was known for a table to get your feet under, for the good food, good wine, and good talk. She's chatting here with Pierre Trudeau at a party we gave for his seventieth birthday in October 1989.

With Jonathan at the same dinner, one of many such nights.

My mom, Luba, and me at my home in the 1990s. She was then in her nineties, but still remarkably alert and fit.

My younger brother, Sam, the funniest man I know, and my grandson Benjamin.

With Sandra by the shore of the Mediterranean Sea in Tel Aviv in 1990.

My granddaughter Olivia checks out my desk in the Senate Chamber in Ottawa.

My gang: My grandchildren – (left to right) Benjamin, Daniella, Michael, and Olivia – with Mona Golfman, the new lady in my life, on a ski trip to Courchevel in the French Alps in 2003.

With daughter-in-law Irit, a real Israeli *sabra* and the mother of three great kids.

With my son-in-law, Barry Halliday, a great skier and a great guy.

With my daughter, Lynne, an accomplished singer and actress, as well as a great mom to my oldest grandchild, Olivia. There's nothing quite like the closeness between dads and daughters.

The picture is, for once, worth a thousand words.

deal we never did. Instead, under Edgar's leadership, we got 20 percent of DuPont, the best deal we ever did.

I had several experiences, as late as the mid-1970s, involving golf clubs in Toronto that didn't admit Jews, even as guests, let alone as members. After Neil Wood became president of Cadillac Fairview, following the merger of Fairview and Cadillac, he joined the Lambton Golf Club and he discovered that he couldn't invite me as his guest, even though I was his boss and we were paying for his membership. Neil was very embarrassed, and he wanted to resign.

"Not on your life," I said, and asked him for a list of directors of the club. One name, Cecil Forsythe, leapt off the page. He was the head of Great-West Life's Toronto office and had been doing business with us as a lender to Fairview Corporation from our first shopping centre projects in Ontario. It turned out that he was going to be in Montreal for an insurance convention. I called and invited him for lunch and a round of golf at Elm Ridge, which by the way was as exclusively Jewish as other clubs were exclusively Gentile, some of them to this day. But at least he could come as my guest. Neil joined us, and Buddy Rothschild, who worked for me, rounded out the foursome. Since he was a two handicap, Buddy was also the ringer in the group.

It turned out that Forsythe was not only a terrific golfer, but a lovely man, and as we were driving back into town to drop him at his hotel, he thanked me for a great day.

"Not at all," I replied, "what a pity you can't reciprocate."

"What do you mean?" he asked.

"Jews aren't allowed at Lambton," I reminded him.

"Leave it with me," he said.

And he got it changed. Did it make a big difference in mindset? Not really. But to his great credit, Forsythe got it changed. And it is in a succession of such little victories over discrimination that larger victories are won.

There was another incident, about a decade earlier, around the time we were negotiating the deal for the Toronto-Dominion Centre for the first of what would become five towers. Allen Lambert, the TD chairman, and I became quite friendly, and eventually he asked if I played golf. "Oh, yes," I said, "and you?"

"Absolutely," he replied, "let's have a game."

"Great," I said. "Let me invite me you to Oakdale. I'm not a member, but some of my staff are. It's a Jewish club."

"No," he said, "I've invited you. I want you to come to the Toronto Golf Club."

"Allen," I said after a slight pause in the conversation, "that would be very nice. But I have to remind you, and I don't want to embarrass you, but they don't allow Jewish guests."

"That can't be," he said.

I explained that when there was a tournament at Oakdale, most clubs in the Toronto area gave its members reciprocal privileges for a week, but the Toronto Golf Club wouldn't.

"They don't want Jews there," I said simply.

Lambert, very upset, buzzed his secretary and in my presence, was connected with the secretary of the Toronto Golf Club. "I want to come next Tuesday," he said, "and I have a guest, Mr Kolber, who is of the Jewish faith – is there a problem with that?"

As Allen listened, his face grew beet red, and then he said, "Okay, I hear what you are saying. We will be there."

I later learned from Dick Thomson, who would become Allen's successor but was then his executive assistant, that Allen had actually been told he couldn't bring me as his guest. "Allen was really pissed off," Dick told me. "They had said, 'No, you can't bring him.'" And that when I left, Allen called back and said, "Listen, you have your line of credit with me, and you have your annual meeting at our offices. You had just better not cause any trouble, because I am bringing him."

And he did, bless him. Eventually, they changed the policy of excluding Jews there, too.

But it was a long struggle. Mr Bronfman never belonged to the Mount Royal Club, citadel of Montreal's "anglostocracy," as author William Weintraub put it. His son Charles was one of the first Jews admitted when he joined in 1970. I've been a member there since 1977, and I regard it as the finest luncheon club in Canada. "Names that were unheard of a generation ago," as the prominent lawyer Heward Stikeman, himself a pillar of the Montreal establishment, wrote in his 1999 centennial history of the Mount Royal Club, "now take their place on the membership list."

Over the years, I've given a lot of dinners there, for business and political fundraising, to the point where the members of the exclusively Jewish Montefiore Club started getting on my case. Sorry, I would tell them, but the Montefiore isn't as good as the Mount Royal.

But on one occasion I really annoyed them. I gave a lunch at the Mount Royal for Shimon Peres when he was prime minister of Israel in 1986, and invited everyone, including all the movers and shakers in the Jewish community. One of them came up to me after the lunch and said, "You know, Leo, he is the Israeli prime minister, he should have eaten at the Montefiore Club."

"Like hell," I replied. "They discriminate against us, do we have to discriminate against them?"

There are still anti-Semitic practices in places such as Palm Beach, where I've had a winter home for many years. To this day, the Everglades Club is notorious for barring Jews. I play at the Palm Beach Club, which is predominantly Jewish, although we have a few non-Jewish members. In fact, Paul Desmarais of Power Corporation and his wife, Jackie, are members at the Palm Beach Club, and I believe one of the reasons they joined is that they could not invite their Jewish friends to the Everglades, where they are also members. Former prime minister Brian Mulroney, to his credit, refused an honorary membership with playing privileges at the Everglades because of its anti-Semitic policy. Indeed, if memory serves, Paul Desmarais had difficulty getting into the Everglades because of the objections of John "Bud" McDougald, who probably opposed his joining for two reasons. He undoubtedly thought of Paul as a French-Canadian social climber from Sudbury who had tried to wrest control of Argus Corporation from him.

But discrimination in Canada certainly wasn't confined to Jews. The growth of the separatist movement in Quebec in the 1960s and 1970s was largely rooted in a very real sense of grievance, not least over senior management jobs in business and commerce being closed to francophone Quebecers. Discrimination doesn't have to be based on colour, or even religious affiliation; it can also be a matter of language and culture, as it was, either real or perceived, in Quebec.

I would like to think that my experience as a member of a cultural minority made me more sensitive to the situation of French-speaking Canadians in general and francophone Quebecers in particular. At Fairview Corporation, we did business in French as well as English long before it became the law under the Parti Québécois government's Bill 101 in 1977.

At Fairview, we made a conscious effort to attract major francophone retailers to our malls, and we executed leases in French long before it was required by law. It was more than the right thing to do, it was also good for business. If you have a mall such as Galeries d'Anjou in the east end of Montreal, in a neighbourhood that is 90 percent French speaking, it simply increases retail traffic when people can not only shop in French, but buy from francophone merchants.

When I was chairman of the Grey Cup Week committee in Montreal in 1969, there was a question on both sides of the linguistic divide of whether we should conduct our meetings in English or French. I said people would speak their language of choice. And it worked very well.

That's also been my experience over several decades of involvement with the Montreal Symphony Orchestra, an exemplary institution in terms of outreach to a bilingual and multicultural community. The orchestra could never have built its international reputation, under conductors such as Zubin Mehta and Charles Dutoit, without the strong financial support of the French, English, and Jewish communities in the city, all joined in a common cause.

Edgar has written that New York is the best place in the world, outside of Israel, for a Jew to live. But I consider that Montreal today is equally cosmopolitan and just as tolerant of many cultures and faiths. In a city of 3.4 million people, the thirteenth-largest metropolitan area in North America, there are still 85,000 Jews, both English and French speaking, from the most orthodox and observant to the more liberal and permissive. A lot of Jewish money left Montreal in the exodus following the election of the PQ in 1976, and again after the close call of the 1995 referendum. By the turn of the century, there were many more Jews, much more Jewish money, and a lot more Jewish influence in Toronto than in Montreal. The Jewish community of Toronto had become nearly twice as large as the Montreal community, though Montreal Jews continued to be much more generous on a per capita basis in support of Combined Jewish Appeal.

But it would be wrong to say that there is anything like a Jewish establishment in Canada either in the business community or in the political domain. There is a Jewish establishment on Wall Street, with venerable names in investment banking such as Loeb, Lehman, and Goldman Sachs, the assimilationist Jews of largely German extraction. There is a Jewish establishment in Hollywood, and has been from the building of the studio system by the likes of Goldwyn, Mayer, and Warner Brothers. In 1996, according to Lew Wasserman biographer Dennis McDougall, the top five Hollywood donors to the Democratic party were Jews – David Geffen, Wasserman, Steven Spielberg, Jeffrey Katzenberg, and Sid Sheinberg. The sixth-largest donor was also Jewish – Edgar Bronfman Jr. There is nothing like that in Canada, and there never has been.

I had this conversation many years ago with the author and establishment chronicler Peter C. Newman, after the first and very successful volume of *The Canadian Establishment* came out in 1975. Himself a Jewish émigré from the former Czechoslovakia, Newman told me he wanted to do the second volume on the Jewish establishment.

"Peter, that is a nutty idea," I said. "There is no such thing." And I took him through it. "Where do you see Jews on bank boards? Where do you see Jews in politics? Do you think because there are a couple of hundred dress and suit manufacturers in Montreal, each of them millionaires, but not multi-millionaires, that is an establishment?" No, it is just a bunch of *shmatte* guys. You see them at Moishe's in Montreal, enjoying a good steak. It's where the rag trade hangs out, but it's no establishment.

In *Like Everyone Else ... but Different,* McGill sociologist Morton Weinfeld makes the very good and interesting point that "historically, Jewish fortunes were made in areas like retail trade or real estate, not the traditional sources of wealth and power of the Canadian establishment of the time."

Weinfeld reminds us that John Porter, in his 1965 classic *The Vertical Mosaic,* found that less than 1 percent of the nearly 1,000 directors of the top 170 Canadian corporations were Jewish. Porter's associate, Wallace Clement, in a 1972 follow-up study, found a slight improvement in that 4 percent of directors of the top 113 companies were Jewish, but that 25 of them came from only six families, one of them being the Bronfman family. And Peter Newman, in his first volume of *The Canadian Establishment* in 1975, looked at 171 CEOs, of whom 10, or 6 percent, were Jewish.

There is also a difference between wealth and power. In 1996 the *Financial Post* found that seven of the fifty wealthiest Canadians were Jewish, or 14 percent of the names on the list. In April 2000, the *National Post* listed ten Jews among the fifty wealthiest people in the country. Those figures, Weinfeld reckoned, were comparable to the Jewish percentage on the *Forbes* 400 list of wealthiest Americans. Yet back in 1986, Weinfeld noted, a study found "that Jews comprised only 7.4 percent of the senior executives in America's largest businesses, much less than the 23 percent range for wealth." In Canada, Weinfeld found that in 1991 "22 percent of Jews lived in households with over $100,000 incomes, three times the rate for non-Jews." But again, wealth does not mean power. There is also a stereotype of wealthy Jews that belies poverty among Jews. As the McGill Consortium for Ethnicity and Strategic Social Planning observed in an analysis of the 1991 census, "One out of six Jews, 15.7 percent, lived below the Statistics Canada poverty line or were marginal to it in 1991. The corresponding figures for all Canadians was 18.6 percent." Just as the Jewish community was becoming demographically representative of the larger Canadian population, the authors concluded "so do the Jewish poor become more similar to the Canadian poor."

Jews on bank boards? I was among the first when I was appointed to the board of the TD Bank in 1971. To this day, there are very few. Mr Bronfman was named to the Bank of Montreal board only in 1962, and Charles later replaced him. Laz Phillips made the Royal Bank board in the 1950s, and later Mitzi Dobrin, Sam Steinberg's daughter, was appointed after the Royal's chairman W. Earle McLaughlin said in the mid-1970s that he would appoint a woman when he could find one qualified for his board. In the predictable furor that ensued, he quickly found Mitzi.

Jews in politics, in the federal cabinet, or the Senate? Herb Gray was the first Jew appointed to the federal cabinet and that was only in 1969. Barney Danson joined him in the 1970s. Gray's longevity was such that he was one of only two Jews in Jean Chrétien's cabinet more than thirty years later, the other being Elinor Caplan. Herb, Bob Kaplan, and Jack Austin from the Senate made three Jews in Trudeau's last cabinet in the 1980s, though none of them was in a position to influence financial or foreign policy. During the Mulroney years, Gerry Weiner was minister of citizenship and later secretary of state, minor portfolios.

But in 2003, there were five Jews in the Senate – Jerry Grafstein, Richard Croft, Jack Austin, Mira Spivak, and me. And I have to say that's more than a fair and representative number from the Jewish community from across Canada – nearly 5 percent of the seats in the Senate coming from a community with only 1 percent of the population of Canada. I have held what has come to be known as "the Jewish seat" from Quebec, the one Laz Phillips got after Mr Bronfman didn't. And I became the first Jewish chairman of the Senate Banking Committee, an important first, especially in the sense that nothing much was made of it.

With Irwin Cotler from the House of Commons side, I've tried to put together a bipartisan group of Jewish MPs and senators – we call it "the Jewish caucus" – so that we can present a united front and be more effective on issues concerning the community, particularly the government's policy on Israel.

Jews in the public service? Mickey Cohen was deputy minister of finance under Pierre Trudeau, and Stanley Hartt was deputy in Finance under Brian Mulroney, before becoming his chief of staff. Indeed, Hartt was the first of three consecutive Jewish chiefs of staff to Mulroney, followed by Norman Spector and Hugh Segal. Mulroney later appointed Spector as Canada's first Jewish ambassador to Israel and representative to the Palestinian Authority, partly to make the point that Jews should not be precluded from that sensitive post. Later, Chrétien appointed David Berger, another Montreal Jew, as Spector's replacement in Tel Aviv. And Segal would become the first Jew to seek the leadership of the Conservative party, running second to Joe Clark on the first ballot in 1998. In the Canadian foreign service, for generations home of the best and the brightest of Canada's public servants, Allan Gotlieb became the first Jew to serve as undersecretary of state and later, in the 1980s, the first Jew to serve as Canada's ambassador to Washington. And Mulroney brought in Simon Reisman, the legendary trade official who had negotiated the Canada-U.S. Auto Pact in 1965, to be Canada's ambassador and chief negotiator in the Canada-U.S. trade talks that resulted in the Free Trade Agreement in 1987.

There's never been a Jewish finance minister. There's never been a national Jewish leader of either of the two leading Canadian parties, much less a Jewish prime minister, yet there has been measurable progress. David Lewis led the federal NDP in the early 1970s, while his son Stephen was leader of the party in Ontario and became leader of the opposition in a minority legislature in 1975. In British Columbia in 1972, the NDP's Dave Barrett became Canada's first Jewish premier.

In Quebec, Stanley Hartt's father, Maurice Hartt, was a prominent Liberal member of the legislature in the 1940s when they were in opposition to Maurice Duplessis. In a famous exchange in the Quebec legislature, when Duplessis heckled Liberal leader Adélard Godbout for having a Jew as his spokesman, Hartt pointed to the crucifix over the Speaker's throne and replied, "There is a Jew who has been speaking to you for 2000 years and you still don't listen to him." In the 1970s, Victor Goldbloom was a senior minister in the Bourassa government, occupying the important portfolio of municipal affairs, in which he had oversight over the construction of the 1976 Olympic installations. And in 1985, Herbert Marx would become Quebec's first Jewish justice minister in the reborn Bourassa administration. Lionel Groulx must have been spinning in his grave. And in Ontario, Larry Grossman was provincial treasurer in the Davis government in the 1980s and, briefly, the leader of the Tory party in the 1987 election.

In Chrétien's office, Eddy Goldenberg and Chaviva Hosek were important advisers, but not particularly on what Mr Bronfman used to call "Jewish business," and that's as it should be – they had national responsibilities, not a Jewish constituency. The last two clerks of the Privy Council during my Senate years were Jews – Mel Cappe and Alex Himelfarb, and carrying a brief for the community wasn't their role, either. David Zussman, president of the Public Policy Forum, an Ottawa think-tank, was an influential outside adviser to Chrétien, but again he never advanced a particularly Jewish agenda, nor was that his role. Bob Rabinovitch, appointed by Chrétien as CBC president, cannot be accused of a pro-Israeli bias, given the CBC news coverage of the Middle East conflict, in which Palestinian terrorists are styled "militants," to the chagrin of the Jewish community, whose protests have been in vain. As Morton Weinfeld has pointed out, "Jewish politicians and public servants have to negotiate a delicate balance between competing claims."

Jews in the judiciary? There are plenty of Jewish judges at the superior court level, but very few on the courts of appeal. Yet I was delighted in July 2003 when Prime Minister Chrétien named Morris Fish from the Quebec appeal court to the Supreme Court, the first non-francophone appointed from Quebec in fifty years and only the second Jew ever to serve on the country's high court. The first had been Bora Laskin, the distinguished chief justice at the time the Charter of Rights and Freedoms was adopted in 1982.

Jews influencing public policy from the business community? Gerry Schwartz may be the exception that proves the rule of very little Jewish business influence in Ottawa. He's not only won the respect of Bay Street with the success of his holding company, Onex Corporation, but he's been Paul Martin's most important fundraiser, and with his wife, Heather Reisman, he will be a power behind the scenes in the Martin government. Gerry is a genuine player because he has chosen to leverage his business success into political influence in a way that very few members of the community ever bother to try. Izzy Asper, with his hawkish stance on Israel, has sought to exert an influence as the owner of the CanWest newspapers and the *National Post*.

For a time, in the heyday of Olympia & York in real estate in the 1980s, Paul and Albert Reichmann were forces to contend with in the interconnected world of business and politics, as well as in the Jewish community of Toronto, where they favoured Orthodox Jewish causes with their philanthropy. Nor were they afraid to go to the top to facilitate the building of Canary Wharf, their massive $20-billion project in London's Docklands. When they couldn't get approval from the British bureaucracy for a subway extension to the inconvenient Canary Wharf site, they persuaded Brian Mulroney to speak to Margaret Thatcher about it, and in 1989 it got done.

When Mulroney visited Moscow in November 1989, Albert Reichmann was part of the delegation as Canadian chairman of the Canada-USSR

Business Council, and apart from trade deals and joint ventures, Reichmann persuaded the prime minister to make a private visit to a *yeshiva* where the rabbi and his students were threatened with eviction. As Anthony Bianco observed in *The Reichmanns*, "Albert Reichmann's highly visible role in the Mulroney trade mission and his chairmanship of the Canadian-Russian Trade Council considerably enhanced his standing within the Canadian business community. For the first time a Reichmann brother had donned the mantle of a corporate statesman."

If there had been resistance by the Canadian establishment to Sam Bronfman, it crumbled under the sheer weight of his money and his persistence in kicking down the door. By the next generation, Charles was a full-fledged member of the establishment, sitting on important boards such as Bank of Montreal and Power Corporation, becoming a leading benefactor of McGill and Université de Montréal, and playing a full leadership role in the Jewish community. But then in 1997 he left Montreal to live in New York, Palm Beach, and Israel, essentially abdicating the Bronfman family's role in the Canadian business and political establishment and his own pre-eminent role in the Montreal Jewish community. As Peter Newman observed in his 1998 book *Titans,* the third volume in his series on the Canadian establishment, "It wasn't the sale of the house that had Jewish Montreal upset, but its owner's departure."

There are a lot of reasons why the Canadian Jewish community has so little economic and political clout in Canada relative to its wealth and education, and the primary one is that the community is reluctant to involve itself in national and provincial politics, and generally doesn't get involved with causes, unless the cause is Israel. I know, because I was the chief Liberal bagman for several years and actively involved in fundraising for more than two decades. If you were to ask, how can you have clout without contributing? Well, that is a very good question. I was a Jewish guy with a certain amount of clout, because I collected as well as contributed, and because I represented the Bronfmans.

There is an urban legend that the Jewish community has powerful political connections in Canada because it votes heavily in favour of the ruling Liberal party, because it supposedly contributes generously to the Liberals, and because it is perceived as having high-powered lobbies through the Canada-Israel Committee and the Canadian Jewish Congress.

Actually, only the first part is correct – the Jewish community votes for the Liberal party, big time, particularly in my home province of Quebec. As Morton Weinfeld has written, "The historic Jewish support for the Liberal Party is not hard to explain. It begins with the fact that the highest periods of mass Jewish immigration took place under Liberal governments, first under Wilfrid Laurier and later under Louis St. Laurent and Lester Pearson. (The restrictive policies of Mackenzie King's Liberals were either unknown, forgotten or forgiven.)" Seeking a haven from the extremes of the left and the right of their own experience in Europe, they "found their home in the Liberal Party," which Pierre Trudeau once described as "the party of the extreme centre."

But as I can personally attest, the myth of Canadian Jews being major contributors to the Liberal party is just that – a myth. And when members of the community would complain to me about Canadian policy on the Mideast, as they often did after the resumption of the murderous *intifada* terrorist campaign in 2000, I would ask how they could expect to influence policy without contributing, in one way or another, to the political process. It is not enough just to vote; if you want to influence outcomes, you have to get in the game.

As for the so-called Jewish lobby, I can only say I wish it were as effective as its opponents imagined it to be. When Ottawa, under intense pressure from Washington, finally branded Hezbollah a terrorist organization in December 2002, even the CBC's Eric Sorensen on *The National* attributed the decision to "the latest in a series of pressure tactics" from "the Jewish lobby," as if its influence was somehow pervasive and sinister. Washington sources had branded Hezbollah "terror's A team" in a *New York Times* report in which its leader in Lebanon, Sheik Hassan Nasrallah, was quoted as denouncing "a plan by the United States and the Zionists to control the region," and warning of their "dangerous and satanic goals." This is the voice of reason that Lebanon championed, on Christmas Day 2002, when it asked Ottawa to drop its Hezbollah ban by once again distinguishing between its military and political wings. Ottawa's action was not motivated by "the Jewish lobby" so much as dictated by the necessity of falling in line behind George W. Bush in the war on terrorism.

In truth, the influence of the Canadian Jewish Congress has been in decline since Mr Bronfman's day. And the Canada-Israel Committee, established for the purpose of being a powerful coordinative voice in matters of mutual interest, has actually been quite ineffective. In terms of my own anecdotal experience with CIC, it is quite disorganized. On Prime Minister Chrétien's official visit to Israel in 2000, I ran into Rob Ritter, executive director of the CIC, in the lobby of the King David Hotel in Jerusalem, and he wasn't even aware I was on the trip, nor did he offer to brief me on the committee's agenda for the visit. I was one of two Jewish parliamentarians on the trip, and I had some private time with the PM on the plane, but I wasn't in a position to advance the CIC's position because I had no idea what it was.

There is no "Jewish lobby" in Ottawa, certainly not in the sense that there is in Washington, where there is indeed a powerful Jewish presence. The American Israel Political Action Committee, in striking contrast to the CIC, is one of the most powerful lobbies I've ever seen. AIPAC has a lot of money, and with that money, it can directly influence electoral and political outcomes in six or seven states, including New York, California, and Florida, three of the most important states in terms of the House of Representatives, not to mention their importance in the Electoral College, which ultimately elects the president. Jews in Canada have nothing like that kind of influence. And Jews in the Liberal party have nothing like the presence or influence of Jews in the Democratic party in the United States, where, as David Frum observed in *The Right Man,* his 2003 best-seller on George W. Bush's White House, the previous Bill Clinton administration was filled with Jews: "His closest friends and most trusted aides were Jewish, his administration was crammed with Jewish appointees, both his nominees to the Supreme Court were Jewish – even his most famous girl friend was Jewish."

As for the perception that the Jewish community in Canada, 330,000 people in the 2001 census, is some kind of monolithic machine, that is not to know Canadian Jewry very well. By the very nature of the Diaspora, Canadian Jews come from all over Europe and Africa, and represent all points of the economic, political, religious, and linguistic spectrum. There are uptown Jews and downtown Jews, as the wealthy and working-class segments used to be known. There are pro-Zionists and anti-Zionists, pro-Labour and pro-Likud, Orthodox and progressives, English and French speaking. There is no such thing as a Jewish melting pot, much less a Jewish establishment.

But there is a Jewish mosaic. And there is a Canadian establishment in which Jews, in my lifetime, have become fully integrated.

In any event, I believe I may have talked Peter Newman out of writing a book on the Jewish establishment, and he decided to write one on the Bronfmans instead. But that is another story.

14

Israeli Friends and Friends of Israel

In the summer of 2002, while spending a few days in Palm Beach, I received an urgent call from Nancy Rosenfeld, who works for Charles and Stephen Bronfman on their Jewish philanthropies.

She said the Israeli government was about to close its consulate-general in Montreal as an austerity measure, while keeping open its delegation in Toronto. For the Jewish community in Montreal, this would be a double blow. For one thing, the Israeli consular office was a symbol of the community's close connection to Israel and a rallying point for pro-Israeli demonstrations during crises in the Middle East. For another, it meant that, in Israeli eyes, the Jewish community in Montreal was less important than the one in Toronto, a blow to their civic as well as their Jewish pride.

And indeed, the 2001 census revealed that the Jewish population of Montreal continued to decline steadily to 85,000 ethnic Jews, while the Jewish community of Toronto continued to grow to about 160,000, nearly twice the number in Montreal. Those numbers spoke of the inexorable toll that a quarter century of political uncertainty had taken on a community that was ultra-sensitive to any form of nationalism, however democratic the movement might be. In Quebec, René Lévesque and his successors in the Parti Québécois were nothing if not democrats, and anything but anti-Semitic, although the Jewish community could have done without being harassed by Quebec's notorious language police for English-only labels on imported *matzo*. And as it had been the PQ's intention to break up one country while in the process of creating another, thousands of Jews preferred a future in Canada to one in Quebec.

Diminished as it might be, the Jewish community in Montreal was still among the most important in North America in terms of its generosity to the Israeli cause, having one of the most vital community infrastructures anywhere outside Israel. The Jewish "campus" in the Snowdon district of Montreal, with the Canadian Jewish Congress headquarters at Cummings House and the Saidye Bronfman Centre across the street as the nerve centre of cultural activities, was a thriving hub of community activity. Moreover, Quebec accounted for about 40 percent of Canadian trade with Israel, with whom our country had a free trade agreement. Finally, Montreal was the one city in North America with a significant French-speaking Jewish population, mainly Sephardic Jews, accustomed to dealing with the Israeli consulate in French.

Frankly, I don't like to get involved in Jewish community issues, which are usually proof of the old adage: two Jews, three views. But the closing of the Israeli consulate was an exception – it was an emotional issue that struck a nerve with the entire Jewish community.

So I called Shimon Peres, the Israeli foreign minister, my oldest and closest friend in Israel. The Pereses are family to us. We are family to them. When my son, Jonathan, spent his summers as a student in Israel, he would often spend weekends with Uncle Shimon and Auntie Sonia.

Shimon explained that it was an economy measure, pure and simple, that they had to take costs out of the system, and closing either Montreal or Toronto would achieve that.

"Why are you keeping Toronto open and closing Montreal?" I asked.

"I spoke to Charles Bronfman," he replied, "and Charles said, 'Look, there are more Jews in Toronto, keep that one open and close Montreal.' "

"I can't believe he would say that," I told Shimon.

Then I called Charles, and he had kind of a change of heart, especially after speaking to Steve Cummings, the head of the Federation of Jewish Community Services in Montreal and point man on the consular file. But then, nothing. I was told by the consul-general in Montreal, who was preparing to close his office, that it was a *fait accompli*. So then I spoke to the Israeli ambassador in Ottawa, Haim Divon, a lovely man who didn't seem to be in this particular loop.

Enough already. I called Shimon again with an offer he couldn't refuse. If he would keep both the Toronto and Montreal delegations open, I was authorized to tell him that the Jewish community in Montreal would subsidize the cost of "their" consulate by U.S.$200,000 a year for the next three years. We would also talk to the leadership of the community in Toronto about matching Montreal's donation.

Shimon put one of his officials on the line. "Can you put that in writing?" he asked. I immediately faxed it to Shimon's office. And so it was done, and the consulate-general in Montreal remained open. In my first phone call, Shimon had said he would do nothing until he heard back from me and we settled it one way or another. As always, he proved as good as his word.

⊗

From the time I met Shimon in 1958, he always struck me as the best and the brightest of a remarkable generation of Israelis who had dedicated their lives to the service of their young country. This extraordinary group included Teddy Kollek, later mayor of Jerusalem, but then head of the Prime Minister's Office under David Ben-Gurion, the founding father of Israel.

As a young man in my twenties, I was pretty much of an agnostic on Israel. My world was Canada. I grew up in a household that, while obviously Jewish, was certainly not Zionist, so I didn't even hear the arguments for a Jewish homeland. But all that changed when I met Sandra. A whole new world opened up to me. She had already lived there, and with her fluent Hebrew, she worked as a translator. Her father was a leader in the Zionist movement and had fought for the Turkish Empire in the First World War. So when we flew to Israel as young newlyweds, it was new terrain for me but familiar ground for her. And it marked the beginning of friendships that have endured a lifetime, and of the dual allegiance that millions of Diaspora Jews feel for the Israeli nation as well as their own.

With Sam Bronfman's official seventieth birthday looming on the horizon, the family suggested that I go to Israel in 1958 to see if I could find something appropriate they could contribute to by which they could honour their father. So we went. It was my first trip to Israel, and we stayed in Ramat Gan, which was then on the outskirts of Tel Aviv. Because I was representing the Bronfmans, I was received by Teddy Kollek, who as head of the Prime Minister's Office saw to it that we met all the right people, including Shimon, at the time director-general in the defence ministry.

Teddy formed a committee of three, including himself, to take us around and help us decide what we might donate in Mr Bronfman's name. The other two were Avraham Biran, director of the Department of Antiquities, and Yigael Yadin, a former army chief of staff, from 1949 to 1952, and an outstanding archaeologist – he was a professor at the Hebrew University. Many years later, Yadin would serve on a five-person commission of inquiry to determine what went wrong for Israel in the early days of the 1973 Yom Kippur War, when the Egyptians and Syrians attacked without apparent warning on the holiest Jewish day of the year, a day on which Israeli reservists were home with family. The commission, as Robert Slater noted in *Warrior Statesman,* his biography of Moshe Dayan, "absolved Golda Meir and Moshe Dayan and laid the blame on Chief of Staff David Elazar, recommending that he quit." It was shocking – the person who bore political responsibility, Defence Minister Dayan, was absolved, while the general who had carried out his orders was blamed. When Yadin later came to dinner at our house, I asked how he could be party to such a whitewash. He made it very clear that the commission was not about to blame Dayan, who, whatever his failings in the Yom Kippur War, remained the dashing general with the famous eye patch, hero of the Sinai Campaign when he was chief of staff in 1956 and, as defence minister, brilliant strategist of Israel's victory in the Six Day War in 1967 – its greatest triumph. Israel being rather short on heroes in 1974, Yadin frankly conceded that the commission was not about to destroy the reputation of the greatest Israeli war hero of them all.

Teddy took us to a site in Jerusalem near the Knesset and said he envisaged putting a world-calibre archaeological and biblical museum there. He said the United States government had already contributed about $750,000 to the project. Sandra and I were quite taken by the idea, so we sat down with Teddy to discuss the bottom line in all major donations – what you get for what you give.

Teddy spelled it out. For $2 million they would call it the Bronfman Museum, named after the entire family. For $1 million we would get a large wing called the Samuel Bronfman Archaeological and Biblical Museum, a wing devoted to archaeological and biblical artefacts, of which there was no shortage in Israel.

Back in Montreal, I met with Mr Bronfman, and he asked for a recommendation as between a donation of $1 million and $2 million.

"Well," I said, "I would certainly not give two million, I would only give a million."

"Why are you being so cheap with my money?" he asked.

"I am not being cheap," I replied, "but my firm belief is that if the whole thing is called the Bronfman Museum, it will never grow to what you want it to be or to what Israel would want it to be."

"Why not?" he asked.

"Because people aren't going to give their prized possessions and artefacts, and whatever, to something named after you. But if you just have one wing, and the rest is called the Israel Museum or whatever, I'm sure Jews all over the world would contribute to it."

"You know, you are right," he said.

And for $1 million, we got the Bronfman wing of the Israel Museum, a magnificent pavilion. Just as I had predicted, others gave generously to the museum. The American impresario Billy Rose donated a sculpture garden. "If there's a war," he jokingly told his Israeli hosts, "you have my permission to turn the sculptures into bullets."

In his budgetary allocation for the National Museum of Israel in 1960, Prime Minister Ben-Gurion told the Knesset it would be built "in the city of King David, amidst the timeless Judean Hills." And so it was, on a twenty-two-acre hill called Nave Shaanan, or Tranquil Habitat. When we went to the dedication ceremony of the Bronfman Archeological Museum in 1962, Ben-Gurion himself attended and gave Mr Sam the famous lecture about how you are not truly invested in Israel unless you or your children are living there.

Back in 1958, Mr Sam had asked me a very interesting question: "Who was the most impressive person you met in Israel?"

"No question," I replied, "it was Shimon Peres."

I think he was pleased by my answer. He had met Peres back in 1951 when Shimon was the twenty-eight-year-old head of procurement for the Israeli defence ministry and had come to Montreal and Ottawa from New York on a shopping mission. It was on this trip that Mr Bronfman had helped him get some armaments at half price, for $1 million rather than the $2 million the Canadian government had been demanding.

Shimon was born in Poland in 1923 and immigrated with his family to Palestine, as a child. He founded an early Israeli kibbutz in the Jordan Valley in 1943 and played a critical role in the 1948 War of Independence as head of arms purchases. He was a senior defence official when I first knew him in 1958, and much later became defence minister. On his watch, he approved the daring raid on Entebbe in 1976, enabling the rescue of Israeli passengers aboard an Air France flight that had been hijacked by Palestinian terrorists.

Subsequently, Shimon served in several governments as foreign minister, finance minister, and twice as prime minister. And in 1994 he received the ultimate accolade as co-winner of the Nobel Peace Prize with Yitzhak Rabin and Yasser Arafat for, as the Norwegian Nobel committee put it, "their efforts to create peace in the Middle East." Shimon was a bit like Abba Eban, who had been foreign minister in the Ben-Gurion government, in the sense that he was clearly the most worldly and Western Israeli public figure of his time, and also in the sense that he had trouble getting elected Labour leader.

Improbably, Peres lost the Labour leadership in 1977 to Rabin, who then proceeded to lose the election to Menachem Begin and the Likud coalition on the right. Shimon finally replaced Rabin as Labour leader and was poised to win the 1981 election against an unpopular Begin government. Then just two weeks before voting day, the Israeli air force bombed the Iraqi nuclear reactor and destroyed it, a daring feat reminiscent of the lightning Entebbe raid. The resulting surge of national pride was enough to re-elect Begin and Likud. The next election in 1984 resulted in a stalemate and a government of national unity in which Shimon finally attained his great ambition to be prime minister. But after two years, the power-sharing arrangement saw him become foreign minister again under Yitzhak Shamir.

Shimon finally became prime minister for a second time in the tragic circumstances of Rabin's assassination at a peace rally in November 1995. Peres should have been a lock to win election in his own right in 1996, but fate again intervened against him with a Palestinian terrorist bombing campaign that shifted votes decisively to the right in favour of Benjamin Netanyahu and Likud. Bibi Netanyahu was everything Peres was not – charismatic, telegenic, and a gifted communicator, even a bit too slick for some Israeli tastes.

When Ehud Barak, a former chief of the Israeli Defence Forces and the most decorated soldier in Israel, led Labour back to power in 2000, he shunted Shimon aside to an economic portfolio to keep him as far away as possible from the peace process, a file Barak understandably wanted for himself. He tried valiantly to reach a comprehensive settlement with Yasser Arafat, but when the Palestinian leader walked away from a very good deal that included shared jurisdiction of East Jerusalem, the peace process was doomed. The *intifada* that erupted in the wake of Ariel Sharon's provocative visit to the Temple Mount in Jerusalem in September 2000 was a death blow to Barak's government, ultimately resulting in Sharon's election in 2001.

I had first met Ehud Barak when he was Israeli chief of defence staff. I had gone to Israel at the invitation of Charles Bronfman's foundation, whose vocation was to get Jewish youth from throughout the Diaspora to spend at least one summer vacation in Israel. One night, on a beach on the Mediterranean Sea, we had a *cum sitz*, where people come and sit and talk. It was Ehud who was doing most of the talking, and he made a brilliant *tour d'horizon* of Israeli politics and the perpetual impasse with the Palestinians.

"Maybe you should become prime minister," I suggested.

"God forbid," said his wife. "That would be a horrible thing."

When I saw him in the spring of 2000, he had become prime minister and the leader of Labour. I was accompanying Jean Chrétien on a visit to Israel, the one where he jokingly said he didn't know whether he was "in North, East, South or West Jerusalem," which neither the Israelis nor the Palestinians found amusing. That was just prior to the summer talks at Camp David, where Arafat walked away from a deal that would have seen most of the West Bank and many of the Israeli settlements handed over to the Palestinian Authority. Barak may well have had trouble selling the deal in Israel even without the *intifada*.

He had been generous as only Israel's most decorated soldier could have been. With the collapse of the peace process and the onset of the new terror campaign, his government was clearly doomed to lose the elections he called in 2001. Yet I believe he will be remembered for taking worthwhile risks for peace. A comprehensive settlement, if one is ever achieved, will certainly look a lot like the one Barak offered at Camp David. And I definitely count Ehud Barak as a friend.

As we negotiated the Bronfman museum donation, Kollek and I became good friends. He had enormous energy and the best set of political skills of anyone I ever met. He was mayor of Jerusalem for thirty years, and he not only reached out to the Arab Israelis of the city, but became one of the best-known mayors in the entire world. He had an incredible memory and wonderful people skills. Dining out with him was an event – like having dinner with the King of Jerusalem. When Sandra and I first met him, we told him that she was three months' pregnant with our first child. Six months later, we got a telegram from him, asking, "Why haven't I heard the good news yet?"

He had an enormous appetite. On business trips he would schedule four breakfast meetings and actually eat all four breakfasts. One time at Charles Bronfman's house, he devoured three huge bowls of cherries in a single sitting. And on a visit to Montreal with Ben-Gurion in 1959, he visited us and our baby daughter, Lynne, at our small duplex and devoured a huge breakfast.

"Have you ever met Ben-Gurion?" he asked.

"No, of course I haven't," I replied.

"Come," he said, "you will meet him."

"Come on, Teddy, he is a very busy man."

"No, he is not doing anything," Teddy insisted. "He is just reading."

I later learned that Ben-Gurion was an omnivorous reader and that whenever Teddy or Shimon travelled abroad, they would be given a list of the latest books to buy in America or Britain.

And so we drove down to the Ritz-Carlton Hotel where the Israeli prime minister was staying. Teddy asked us to wait for a minute in his room across from Ben-Gurion's suite. "Okay," Teddy said presently, "BG will see you."

So in we went, Teddy, Sandra, and me, and Ben-Gurion was alone in his suite, sitting by a window for better reading light. From his first comments, it was clear that Teddy had given him a quick briefing on me.

"I understand you work for the Bronfmans," Ben-Gurion began.

"Yes, sir," I replied, knowing he was going to dinner at Mr Sam's that night.

"How much money do they have?"

I kind of coughed, gasped, and then mumbled something unintelligible, at which point he turned his back on me and began talking to Sandra. Teddy had briefed him that she had family in Israel, had worked there, and spoke Hebrew. He spoke to her in Hebrew, completely ignoring me. He was fascinated by her father's career as a Zionist and military figure and by the story of how Sandra's family came to the United States and Canada.

He never said another word to me, except goodbye. So I spoke one sentence to him, in which I coughed and gasped, and Sandra spoke to him for an hour.

I have met most Israeli prime ministers, at least the Labour ones, from Ben-Gurion to Barak. Yitzhak Rabin came as prime minister to my son's wedding to Irit Kariv in Tel Aviv in 1992. The entire Israeli cabinet turned out that day. On November 4, 1995, as Rabin was winding up a speech at a huge peace rally in Tel Aviv, Jonathan and Irit were standing on the podium. "Let's get out of here," Jonathan said to her, "it's going to be a madhouse." It was, though not in the way he meant it. A few feet in front of where they had been standing, Rabin was assassinated by an Israeli extremist.

Among the Likud prime ministers, I met Netanyahu once at Charles's house, but I can't say I knew him. In any event, I have been a Labourite all my life. Liberal in Canada, Labour in Israel. I'm a socialist at heart, a strange kind of socialist, but a socialist in my own way. My idea, when Israeli leaders like Peres came to Montreal, was to introduce them to more than just the leadership of the Jewish community. They already had those votes. I wanted to build support for Israel across the broader Canadian spectrum, among business and political leaders in Montreal and across Canada. The Israelis will tell you that they can only count on three or four friends in the world and that they regard Canada as their most reliable and generous friend, after the United States.

From 1948 to 1977, Labour was the government party of Israel. But Likud has been in power in most of the years since, and that reflects the changing composition of the Israeli nation. Founded by European Jews with an essentially Western and liberal outlook, Israel now has a new majority from a wider Diaspora, predominantly on the right, in favour of retaining the West Bank and maintaining the settlements there, with the support of Orthodox Israeli Jews and other religious factions of the right. One of the hopeful developments of the 2003 election was the breakthrough scored by the non-sectarian Shinui party, which attracted thousands of voters fed up with both Labour and Likud, parties of old men and old ideas on both the left and the right. Many Shinui voters were equally annoyed with the entitlement claims of Orthodox Jews in Israel, who refused to pay taxes, as well as to be subject to the military draft. Shinui's strong showing in the 2003 election was a warning to the two leading parties, as well as a small harbinger of hope.

One of the great Israeli personalities, and one of my great friends, was Pinchas Sapir, who was finance minister under Golda Meir. In her 1975 autobiography, *My Life,* Meir wrote, "I personally couldn't have imagined heading a cabinet without him." She would later say of him, after he became chairman of the Jewish Agency, which managed the relocation of Diaspora Jews to Israel, that he was "Israel's most successful fund raiser."

Was he ever. He had no scruples when it came to hitting on people for investments or donations for Israel. "When Sapir meets a Jew abroad," Golda wrote, "he says 'how much money have you got?' And the funny thing is, the man tells him!"

Once Sapir called me from the airport after his plane had landed in Montreal and said he had to see me at my office right away. He was on his way to an Israel Bonds dinner at the Windsor Hotel and knew my office was only a few blocks away. So he stopped in and started telling me about a big piece of land near Tel Aviv.

"You are in the real estate business," he said. "You should get involved in developing it." We were talking about $300 million, and it was going to be a huge development.

"When do you want an answer?" I asked.

"Now," he said.

"You know, Pinchas," I replied, "normally we spend more than ten minutes thinking about $300 million." But to him, as Israeli finance minister, $300 million was just another number to be crunched.

Edgar Bronfman and I were once asked to meet him at his hotel in New York, and he walked in, very apologetic for being five minutes late. "You'll have to excuse me," he said, "I was talking to the prime." He never referred to Golda as the prime minister, always as "the prime."

"I hope everything is all right," I said.

"Fine," he said. "I was busy buying sugar, and I needed to tell the prime about it." There he was, minister of finance, buying sugar on the commodities market. "Israel needs sugar," he explained, "what can I tell you?"

He was very hands-on as a politician and very connected to the Israeli people. Every Saturday afternoon, he would hold court at a place in Tel Aviv called Café Lilith. He would sit at a table drinking coffee while supplicants would line up to tell him their problems. He always had an aide there, keeping notes. That's how he kept in touch with the people.

One time I finally said to him, "Wouldn't you like to be prime minister? You seem to do everything else."

"If I thought there was any chance of my becoming prime minister," he replied, "I would jump out that window."

It was a window in the St Regis Hotel in New York. Sandra and I had just checked in for the weekend, when the phone had rung. "Leo, it is Sapir," he began, "I am over at the Essex House and I want to talk to you about something."

How he found us, I'll never know. He had a way of doing that. I was once in the Polo Lounge of the Beverly Hills Hotel, when I got a page. It was Sapir, calling from Cincinnati.

He once came to Montreal to speak at a fundraiser for Combined Jewish Appeal at the Montefiore Club. Then, as now, they had a hierarchy of giving, and in order to be invited to hear Sapir, men had to have pledged $30,000 and women at least $10,000. Apparently I had given enough to be invited but Sandra hadn't, and so I went alone. When I got there, the first thing he did was ask, "Where is Sandra?"

"She didn't give enough, so she couldn't come," I said.

"Don't be ridiculous," Sapir said, "you get her here right now."

So I did, and as she walked through the front door of the Montefiore Club, a woman who shall remain nameless said to her, "You have no right to be here," and Sandra started to cry. I've never forgotten that woman's stupid and unnecessary slight.

Pinchas Sapir had every reason to be pleased with the Bronfmans' role, both as donors to Israel and investors in the country. Whenever there was a military emergency, Sam Bronfman would not only sharply increase his own donation to Israel, he would call on the community leadership, as he did in the Six Day War, to do the same. And beyond his donation of the Bronfman wing of the Israel Museum, he donated a village. This was a program in the 1950s whereby, in return for a quarter of a million dollars, donors got a village named after them. The village named for him was Evan Shmuel, which means Stone of Samuel. And before my next trip to Israel, he said to me, "I know they have built this town, go have a look at it, and tell me what it is like."

For most of these visits to Israel, our hosts were a retired Israeli army colonel named Nachman Karni and his wife, Sara. Nachman had lost an arm in one of the Israeli wars, but that didn't prevent him from getting around and showing us the entire country. But even he had trouble finding Evan Shmuel, which was basically on a back road to nowhere. Eventually we found it, and I took some footage of it with an 8 mm movie camera. It turned out to be the cultural centre for several neighbouring immigrant communities, African Jewish communities. I hadn't even been aware of their existence. Years later, in the famous 1991 Operation Solomon, the Israelis would transport fifteen thousand Ethiopian Jews to Israel in a single day's airlift.

When Mr Bronfman flew to Israel for the dedication of the museum in 1962, we took him to see his village. The village children gave a performance of these African native dances, in his honour, in the middle of nowhere in Israel. The old man loved it.

But it was Charles who invested the most, both financially and emotionally, in Israel. In groceries.

In the 1950s and 1960s, the Israelis were trying to persuade Westerners to invest there, as well as support Israel by buying bonds. At the time, investing in Israel was very controversial, especially among more observant Jews in Montreal and other Canadian communities. I remember being at a presentation when a guy showed up with $100,000 in bonds and stock certificates, but walked out when he heard that he would make money on them. When I asked him why, he said, "I don't want to invest in anything that makes money in Israel – that is immoral."

"How will Israel succeed if it doesn't create enterprises?" I asked.

"Not with my money, they can't," the man said, and he walked out. It's a strange mentality when you look back on it, but almost understandable in terms of nation building.

So Charles decided to do his part by founding a supermarket chain with a group of North American Jews, including Bert Loeb from Ottawa, Ray Wolfe from Oshawa Wholesale, and a couple of others. Super-Sol means super-store in Hebrew, and it took off right away. They had no competition, except from the army stores. Super-Sol stores were very clean – always an issue in Israel – and very well run. Or so Charles thought.

Then one day in 1964 he called me at Cemp and said, "We have a real problem with Super-Sol."

"I have nothing to do with that," I replied. "What's the problem?"

"The balance sheet looks healthy," Charles said, "but we can't pay our bills. Something is really wrong."

He asked if I would fly over to Israel and look into it. Of course I would. But what did I know from groceries? So I called Sam Steinberg, who knew all about groceries, and explained the situation. He said there was a Chicago family named Waxenberg that had just sold their grocery business and that the son, Maynard Waxenberg, lived in London. I asked if he would call him and ask him to come to Israel with me. Steinberg said he would be delighted, Waxenberg agreed, and I flew out with Sandra and an accountant named Cecil Vineberg. We picked up Waxenberg in London and flew on to Israel.

The managing director and the chief accountant met us at the airport, and we stopped at the main store on Ben Yehuda Street in Tel Aviv.

"How much was your inventory and when did you last do it?" I asked.

"A month ago," the managing director replied, "and it was about 150,000 pounds worth."

Waxenberg whispered in my ear: "If there is 150,000 pounds worth of inventory in this store, you can use my head for a football." And sure enough, when we paced off the floor space, we realized the store would do well to hold about half that much inventory.

"What is the most expensive thing you sell in the store?" I asked.

"Olive oil," the manager replied.

"Show me where you sell it," I ordered, and he showed me a space of about three feet. I calculated the price of olive oil, paced off the entire store, multiplied as if only olive oil was sold in the store, and still did not come up with a number that would show 150,000 pounds worth of inventory. Clearly, something was wrong.

"I want inventory taken Saturday night after the close of business of our five stores," I said to the head of our outside accounting firm.

"In Israel," he replied, "it takes three months to prepare an inventory."

"Do it, or you're fired," I ordered. So it was done. I went to one store, Sandra to another, Vineberg, Waxenberg, and a guy who worked for us there covered the other three, and then we all brought the inventory sheets to Super-Sol headquarters at two in the morning. We asked for the sheets from the previous inventory. Cecil looked at the old sheets for maybe twenty seconds and said, "Leo, these have been tampered with – zeros have been added." Sure enough, 10 cases had become 100, and 100 cases had become 1,000. Early the next morning, we brought in an Israeli handwriting expert who confirmed that zeros had been added to the previous inventory and that the handwriting was different. It was quite simple, really.

So we called in the two senior managers at four o'clock in the morning. "There are two possibilities," I said, "either you guys knew or you didn't know. If you knew, you are both crooks, if you didn't know, you're both incompetent, so either way you're both out."

It was later discovered that two of the company's directors had taken excess cash out of the company and reinvested it, not in the company's name, but their own. The investments all went *muhullah*, which means belly up in Yiddish, and they didn't put the money back – they hid the losses by overstating the inventory. As Michael Marrus noted in *Mr Sam*, "It emerged that Super-Sol's manager in Israel, together with … Ottawa businessman and community leader Bertram Loeb, were involved in serious wrongdoing in the management of the company, leading to its near-collapse and criminal prosecutions in Israel."

But I was the one who blew the whistle.

I turned to our lawyer, Joshua Rottenstreich, and I said, "I want to see the minister of justice first thing in the morning." It turned out he was a Canadian named Dov Joseph, and he was only too happy to see me. I told him the story and he said, "What do you want from me? I had two murders in Haifa last night."

"Jews will stop investing here if they get stolen from," I replied. "I want you to get the police to arrest the bastards, that's what I want."

"You've got to treat Israel as a country like any other country," he said.

"Do you think this would happen in Turkey?" I yelled at him. "We invest here because we are Jews."

In a very angry state, I went to see a friend who was a colonel in the Israeli army. "Look," I said to him, "I have to go back to Montreal, but would you keep an eye on this situation for me? Because I'm telling you someone is going to torch the Super-Sol headquarters. Their only way out is to burn the records and the building along with it."

A few weeks later, the phone rang on a Sunday afternoon, and it was Jack Brin, whom I had put in charge of the place. "I don't know how to tell you this," he began, "but the head office burnt down." It was, as they used to say, a very successful fire.

∞

As I write, in the spring of 2003, Israel is approaching the fifty-fifth anniversary of its nationhood, declared in May 1948. As a Canadian Jew and as a Liberal, I have long been quite proud of Canada's role in the birth of Israel and of the Liberal party's role in recognizing it. Canada was not only present at the creation, it was one of the midwives at the United Nations and later in that year one of the first countries to recognize the Israeli state.

Lester B. Pearson, a future Nobel peace laureate for his role in creating the UN peacekeeping force in the Sinai, wrote these words in Canada's official recognition of the Israeli state on Christmas Eve in 1948: "The State of Israel has, in the opinion of the Canadian government, given satisfactory proof that it complies with the conditions of statehood. These essential conditions are generally recognized to be external independence, and effective government within a reasonably well defined territory."

Or as Martin Gilbert, the official biographer of Sir Winston Churchill, put it in the introduction to *Israel,* his sweeping history of the Jewish state on its fiftieth anniversary in 1998, "Israel possesses a strong will to succeed and prosper, to maintain its vigorous and fulfilling daily life, and to confound the critics who point to both external and self-inflicted problems as insoluble."

In other words, a light unto the nations.

15

Management and Leadership in Business

I think I am a reasonably good manager, but I'm not a detail guy and never have been. The big picture has always been what interested me. If you read the business autobiographies, from Lew Gerstner of IBM to Jack Welch of GE, or if you look at the success stories in a book like *In Search of Excellence,* the common thread is the importance of having a vision. But you can't have the vision and be the one executing it. That's why they have CEOS and COOS – the chief executive officer should have the vision, and the chief operating officer should implement it.

I had the vision, for example, of building the super-regionals in the four quadrants of Montreal. But the strategy is only the half of it; the real challenge is carrying it out. And I was extremely fortunate in having Neil Wood as president and COO of Fairview. In my view, he was the best executive in the real estate industry. Neil was a Harvard MBA, a big strapping guy of six foot six, and not only did we make a great team, we made a real Mutt and Jeff combination. He was a towering figure in the industry in more ways than one.

I could say, "Neil, here is the deal, invite me to the opening." That's a bit glib, but it's also how good he was. What I wanted was monthly progress reports on projects, as well as the financials of costs versus budget. We would never start a building until we had about 70 to 80 percent of the costs tied down. The vision and the financials are the two main responsibilities of a CEO.

Neil left to go out on his own some time after the Cadillac-Fairview merger in 1974. There was a bit of a cultural clash with the Cadillac guys. Oddly enough, I never heard of any major deals that he did after that. But his operational skill set, for building and running retail malls and office buildings, was unique in my experience. Then we were equally fortunate that Bernie Ghert, who had joined us from Cemp as CFO, was ready to step in as president and COO. Later he became president and CEO, a role in which he remained until we sold in 1987. Succession is one of the major tests of corporate governance, and thanks to Bernie, we passed it with flying colours.

One important management test is the managing of a senior executive's time. I've always had a fetish about punctuality, as my own children would be the first to tell you. I would make dinner reservations on a Saturday night, and at six thirty I would be ready to go, asking my daughter why she was still in her bathrobe. "Dad, we're not leaving for another half hour," Lynne would say, "we just have to put on clothes." And at quarter to seven I would be pacing, impatient to leave. Jonathan used to say that if we were going to a restaurant, I would have calculated in advance how many minutes it took to get there.

One time I was giving some of the Cemp guys a ride from Montreal to Toronto on a company plane. I used to distribute my schedule to our senior executives, and anyone who had to be where I was going was always welcome to come along. We were supposed to be wheels up at eight o'clock this particular morning, but one of our executives was late, held up in rush hour traffic. I told the pilots to leave without him. He finally got there as we were taxiing, but we left without him anyway. He was never late again. If Charles or Edgar was offering me a lift on a company plane, I always got there half an hour before the scheduled departure as a courtesy, and expected the same from my own staff.

But it wasn't about being a control freak – it was about managing my time. I had so many appointments and meetings in the course of a normal day that if I started running fifteen minutes late for the first one, I would fall hopelessly behind. The company planes, which I had the use of for thirty years, gave me the additional flexibility of scheduling meetings in two and sometimes three different cities on the same day. Breakfast in Montreal, lunch in Toronto, dinner in New York, Washington, or Dallas. But it also meant that my schedule was even more intricate. I couldn't keep pilots waiting at the hangar, and I couldn't be late for an appointment in another city.

For more than thirty years, I have kept my own calendar in *Economist* annual diaries, the ones beautifully bound in red leather. I've kept them all, and today they line a complete shelf in the study of my home in Montreal. At the end of every year, I would add up how many days I was at home, how many weekends we were in the country, and how many days I was, as I always wrote on the back page, "out of town." There were very few years when I was not out of town at least two hundred days or more. Over a thirty-year period, I spent more than six thousand days on the road, or nearly twenty years of my life.

That's why managing their time is one of the most important jobs of senior management. The only time I would ever fall behind was when I had a meeting on a development project with Jean Drapeau, the long-time mayor of Montreal. He would often keep me waiting for half an hour, and then keep me in his office for an hour longer than scheduled while he analysed some political situation or another. I learned to schedule him last in the day.

If there was one thing I was good at, it was delegating. I was also good at taking advice. At both Cemp and Cadillac Fairview, I encouraged people to give me their true assessments of investments and projects – that's what I was paying them for, to tell me what I needed to know, not what they thought I wanted to hear. I am the kind of guy who doesn't live easily without answers.

And I was good at numbers. In all our real estate ventures, I could compute the numbers in my head without ever looking at a spreadsheet. I don't know where I got that gift, but it sure came in handy.

When I was a kid spending summers at my grandparents' place at Préfontaine, there was a hotel called the Mohawk on the Rivière-du-Nord, the kind of clapboard place that can be found in most small towns in the Laurentians north of Montreal. The owners of the hotel, the Itscovitch family, also had a hall across the street where they had dances on Saturday nights. When we were about twelve years old, a bunch of us used to hang around the front door, begging them to let us in. Ira Itscovitch, the son of the owner, used to work the door and was always refusing to let us in because of our age.

"Come on, Ira," I pleaded one night, "let us in."

"I'll tell you what," Ira said. "I'll give you a mathematical problem, and if you answer it correctly, the four of you can come in for free."

"Terrific," I said. "What is it?"

"How many twos go into five?" he asked.

My three buddies immediately said two and a half.

"No that's not it," I said "he wouldn't be asking if that was the answer, it's too obvious." I explained to them that two went into five ten times. I hadn't yet studied algebra, or permutations and combinations, but that was the correct answer all right.

"Ten," I said to Ira. "Two goes into five ten times."

Ira nearly fell on his head, and then he let us in. The next day, he came to see my mother. "Luba," he said, "this kid has a gift for mathematics. He should go to an advanced school."

I never did study math, but I have an extremely good mind for numbers, which was very helpful in running our business. In the early days at Cemp and Fairview, people would come to meetings with calculators, but I always crunched numbers in my head.

As a college student, soon after my father died, I once went to a gastroenterologist named Louis Notkin, and he assured me that I did not have cancer. "How can you be sure?" I asked. "Because," he said, "cancer is my brother." Meaning, he saw cancer every day and knew it like his own brother. I have been living with numbers all my life, and they are my brother. I can look at a balance sheet and see inside the numbers.

My son, Jonathan, says I'm very numeric and analytical, with a clear focus on how to measure success, which is money. Either the company makes money or it loses money, makes a good return on equity or doesn't, pays a dividend or doesn't. There is no bullshit about it. Except for EBITDA. That *is* bullshit. Earnings before interest, taxes, depreciation, and amortization. It's like saying you'd be running your household budget in the black if you didn't have to pay interest on your mortgage. EBITDA is one of the reasons valuations got out of whack in the 1990s, and one of the reasons we've had a crisis of corporate governance. By 2003 corporate America was rushing to restate its earnings. But by then the damage had been done, not only to investor portfolios, but also to confidence in markets and business leaders.

It was Bob Campeau who first mentioned EBITDA to me when he asked us to come in for $100 million on his deal to buy Allied Stores. "You should see the EBITDA," he said. "The what?" I asked. "The EBITDA," he repeated. I had no idea what he was talking about. Apparently, neither did he.

Let me illustrate. Let's say you go out and borrow $1 billion in your business, and you pay 6 percent for the money. You invest the money in a new division of the business, except it doesn't do so well, and you get only a 3 percent return. So what are the salient numbers now? You've borrowed $1 billion dollars, and it is costing you $60 million a year to service it, but you only have $30 million in cash coming in. An intelligent, logical calculation would conclude that you are losing $30 million a year. But that's before EBITDA became fashionable – the interest doesn't count, so your EBITDA has actually gone up $30 million. Go figure.

Edgar Bronfman Jr. was very big on EBITDA and used to talk about it at Seagram board meetings, especially in regard to Universal Studios. I kept arguing against using EBITDA in our statements, and I kept losing the argument. Then in late 2002, I saw an article written by Warren Buffet, the great oracle of investing, urging business to do away with the nonsense of EBITDA.

There's another bit of valuation nonsense called IRR, the internal rate of return. According to IRR, you discount back your cash, and that is your return, but it presumes you are eventually going to sell and is predicated on what your selling price will be in five or ten years' time. Every real estate IRR calculation between 1987 and 1992 was proven to be wrong, because the real estate market tanked and the IRR disappeared. Whenever we bought something at Cadillac Fairview, my guys would always tell me what the IRR was, and I kept saying, "Don't tell me about the internal rate of return, I want to know what the cash on cash is." That is to say, when you buy a building, it brings in so much money, then you deduct all the expenses, including the financing costs, and the cash that's left is cash on the cash you put in. Cash on cash.

We always ran our financial affairs at Fairview and Cadillac Fairview in the most conservative way possible. Our policy was to be above reproach in our accounting methods, and our books were pristine. For example, if we owned a piece of vacant land in our housing division, we had the option in the tax code to either write off the carrying charges each year or capitalize it. We always wrote off everything, because I always thought it was the most fair and representative way to decide. In the long run, it always paid off.

In the real estate development business, there is nothing more important than relations with suppliers and contractors, from the consulting architects down to the plumbing and electrical subcontractors. They are the ones who bring a project in on time and on budget. And they are the ones who build in quality. I always insisted that we pay our bills on time and take a 2 percent discount for cash when it was offered. Some very successful developers have bad reputations with their suppliers because they don't pay for months, sometimes forcing them into court to settle. I know of one wealthy developer who deliberately ran his business that way, virtually inviting suppliers to sue him, because as he once said, "I can hold out in court longer than they can." But the word got around on him – don't do business with him. Reputation is everything; integrity is at the heart of trademark value.

We also went out of our way to nurture good relations with the tenants in our malls. We encouraged them to form tenants' associations and to work on joint promotions in their communities as well as in their malls. We understood that their success as measured by sales was our success as measured by sales per square foot and overall retail traffic. For our part, we advertised our super-regionals as "the Fashion Centres," and it became part of our branding. We had something like six thousand tenants in our malls in Canada and the U.S., and while it was important that they paid the rent on time, it was equally important that they chose to rent from us. Because we had the best locations and the best anchor tenants, we also attracted the best brands in retail, whether local or national. In a sense, the Fairview and Cadillac Fairview brands meant that we were trusted.

There's a tendency for people in the real estate business to get over-leveraged, as the Reichmanns and Bob Campeau did. We never had that kind of exposure at Fairview and Cadillac Fairview. When it turned out we had too much debt at a bad moment, as interest rates peaked at 22.75 percent in the scary economic downturn of 1981–82, we sold our entire apartment division to pay down debt. Both our balance sheet and our stock recovered as a result. My biggest priority was to sleep well at night, and while we may have made less money than others in the real estate business, we also lost less in the downturns.

But the real estate industry, by its very nature, is highly leveraged. If you ask how we were able to build Fairview Corporation without putting up any of Cemp's Seagram stock as collateral, the answer is simple: we put up the land we were building on as collateral. And as we grew, our cash flow enabled us to put up the 5 percent cash investment we usually needed to put in. So real estate can be a very good business: it requires very little cash up front; the property itself can be used to secure financing; and it throws off cash every month. If you can get to the first level, however you define that in growing a business, the easier the rest is going to be, because you have cash flow to back you up. Some developers will only give the covenant of the next project. But as Fairview and Cadillac Fairview became brand names, our regularized cash flow became our best financial guarantee and got us financing at the prime rate. We never had to pay prime plus, because of the trademark value of our brand.

∽

During the bubble era, and since, business executives have been spending far too much of their time talking to analysts, time taken away from running their business.

All this stuff about visibility "going forward," this next quarter and the next quarter, that's bullshit, too. Though I made my share of presentations to financial analysts, beginning with our IPO in 1974, I never talked to analysts on a quarterly basis and I certainly never spoke to them as a group in a quarterly conference call. Did a company make its earnings number this quarter, did it beat its "consensus number" or beat the "whisper number" and offer good guidance on earnings "visibility" for the next quarter? It's all hype and hogwash, and has nothing to do with running a business. I don't care what kind of genius you are; if you are planning only for the next three months, you are not doing your job. Many CEOs are forced to think very short term, and I don't know of any business that ever grew properly with short-term horizons. I never worried about making this quarter or the next quarter. I worried about making my next five years.

Then they have these earnings estimates known as first call, second call, and actual results. And if you miss your number by even 1 percent, your stock gets pounded. You might as well be betting on football – did you beat the spread or not?

What is the appropriate horizon? That's harder to say, but it sure helps to have confidence in the product you are making or the service you are providing. Take Seagram, for example. They would make big quantities of scotch and lay it down for twelve years. How did they know what the sales of Chivas Regal would be in twelve years? They didn't. But they had confidence in the product and its branded value.

In my day, I never heard of analysts running anything. Now, they have become the tail that wags the dog of business. If your quarter was down a bit, there could be any number of reasons, from weather to war. The two important questions should be: are your assets in place and growing, and what is the state of your balance sheet? Business would do well to adopt an attitude towards analysts along the lines of "We're too busy running our business to talk to you. If you like us, buy; if you don't, sell."

Good investment tips usually come from brokers, not from books. But one thing that's always bothered me about investing is that people talk about "playing the market." It's not a game, and if you look at it that way, you're going to get hurt. It's not Monopoly, it's your money. It's one thing for the day traders and short sellers to "play" the market, but it's no place for the average investor looking to build a retirement nest egg. You should never open a margin account – playing with the house's money is a good way to lose yours. If your broker advises it, you should change brokers.

I've lived through a few bear and bull markets since the 1950s, as well as the tech bubble that burst in March 2000. How crazy was it? There was a start-up stock named Certicom – they made wireless security software – that at one time had a market value greater than the Bank of Montreal. One day, shortly before the bubble burst in March 2000, its stock went up $35 on the Toronto Stock Exchange on nothing more than the news they would be listing on the NASDAQ. Did it have anything to do with the fundamentals of their business, of their technology, of their revenue stream, even of a path to profitability? No, it was entirely about the bubble. Last I looked, it was a penny stock.

The long bull market of the 1990s saw the greatest inflation of valuation in history. And not just among the techs such as Nortel Networks, which at its peak in 2000 was trading at $124.50, over a hundred times trailing earnings, and had a market value of $375 billion, more than the Big Three automakers combined. I'm happy to say that I sold 36,000 shares of Nortel at $122, and sorry to say that I held on to 36,000 more and watched them sink as low as 67 cents at the bottom of the bear market in October 2002. But in the bubble era, even one of the biggest blue chips on the Dow, GE, was trading at sixty times earnings. It took nearly ninety years for the Dow to reach 1000, and another fifteen years to get to 2000 in 1987. It was at 3000 when the first George Bush left office in January 1993, and surpassed 10,000 on Bill Clinton's watch. A lot of those inflated values got wrung out of the system, and when the Dow retreated below 8000 in 2002 and 2003, GE had plummeted from $60 in the bubble to a low of $21.

But it was still the same company it was at $60, and the low 20s would have been the wrong time to sell. You shouldn't run for cover too quickly.

Let me explain with an example from Cadillac Fairview. In 1982, at the time we sold off thousands of apartments to reduce our debt, our stock was in the tank at five bucks. One of the original Cadillac partners came to see me in a bit of a panic and asked if Cemp wanted to buy a million of his shares.

"Well," I said, "we are not sellers, but we are not buyers, either."

I asked him what the problem was. He replied that his entire family investment was tied up in 2.5 million CF shares. He was worried about losing everything.

"I think this is the wrong time to look at selling," I said. "We're going through a hard time but it's going to get better. If the real estate business goes to hell, maybe we'll go to hell with it, but I doubt it, because our assets are pure gold."

He sold a million shares for $5 a share and tendered his remaining 1.5 million shares for $35 a share when we sold the company only five years later. The decision to sell when he did cost him $30 million.

In a market correction, my sense would be to ride it out if you can. The stock of good companies always comes back in the next bull market. And by that I mean companies that make profits in recessions, pay dividends, have a good return on equity, and trade at a reasonable multiple of earnings. Companies like DuPont, come to think of it. The next time you see GE closing in on $60, though, you might want to think of asking your broker if it's a good time to sell.

But I've generally made it a rule not to give people advice or tips on the stock market. It goes back to Sandra's Uncle Irving, in the late 1950s. We were at some family gathering, when he mentioned that he was in the market, and asked if I had any tips.

"Buy Columbia Pictures," I advised. "It is about $16, and I just bought a thousand shares." The stock went up to $28, and I sold. In those days, there was no capital gains tax, and $12,000 profit for me was a pretty good score. So I called him up and said, "Irving, I can't tell you what to do, but since I told you to buy it, in good conscience I have to tell you I am now selling it."

"Good," he said, "I will do the same." And the stock kept going up to $34. We were going to a family funeral, and Uncle Irving was driving, and I was in the back seat with my wife.

"See that genius in the back seat?" he asked the guy sitting in front with him. "He tells me to buy the stock at $16, and then he tells me to sell at $28, and it is now $34."

He was giving me the business, but I learned a good lesson – don't give people stock tips. A month later he called and asked what stock he should buy. "This conversation is over," I said, and hung up.

But I couldn't always avoid giving people investment advice. Charles once gave me a birthday gift of a photograph of me by the great Yousuf Karsh, renowned for his wartime portrait of a glowering Winston Churchill. Karsh had snatched the cigar from his hand during a brief sitting in the Speaker's chamber in Ottawa following his famous "some chicken, some neck" speech to the House of Commons in 1941. During his remarkable career, Karsh also photographed every American president from Herbert Hoover to Bill Clinton. After our session, during which he did the best he could, given the subject's obvious limitations, he called and asked if he could bring his wife, Estrilla, to dinner. Thinking we might discuss some of his famous portraits, I was delighted. But Karsh, as it turned out, had another agenda. He wanted stock tips and investment advice.

∞

Investing is a lot like beauty – it is in the eye of the beholder. And it has a lot to do with your age. At my age, I am interested in two things. First, preserving my capital so I can leave my kids a significant sum that will make their lives, and my grandchildren's lives, easier. Second, I don't want to lose what I've got. So I take an aggressively conservative investment outlook. I have a certain amount of money invested in extremely liquid positions, where I try to invest in dividend situations in both common and preferred shares, because the tax on dividends in Canada is only 33 percent, as opposed to a 50 percent marginal rate on regular income. So that suits my purpose. If I were forty, I would be thinking differently, and if I were thirty, even more differently, in terms of the investment risks I would be willing to take.

Occasionally, I still dabble in real estate, because it is my first love in business and what I know best. If you asked me what I looked for by way of return, the answer would be a number of things. I like to buy real estate that can be sold at a good profit after a few years. The real estate market in Canada has never recovered fully from the crash of the 1990s – in fact, it has never recovered to where it was when we sold Cadillac Fairview near the top of the market in 1987. In 2002 a group of investors, including Stephen Bronfman and me, bought Place Montreal Trust for less than half of what it cost us to build it in the late 1980s. It cost about $240 a square foot to build, and we bought it back for $100 a square foot. There are tenants who got space practically for free just to fill the building, but their leases are coming due. So at some point, we hope there is going to be a nice return.

For example, a few years ago, a group of us bought the office building in Les Cours Mont Royal, the renovated Mount Royal Hotel where I had my first office in 1957. We bought it at $40 a square foot, and it had cost about $100 a square foot to renovate. We sold at $80 per square foot. We doubled our money in three years.

I look for properties that throw off cash on cash, which again is the rent they bring in minus expenses and financing costs – the cash you take out on the cash you put in. I evaluate real estate opportunities by ballpark numbers, cash on cash, cost per square foot versus rent per square foot. Fundamentally, that's all there is to it. Real estate is something I understand, because it's in my blood, because I've been in it all my life, because I know what to look for.

But I would not have been a good venture capitalist. If someone had brought me a new discovery, a new patent, a new medicine, I wouldn't have had the knowledge, or the patience, to deal with that.

In my personal finances, I've never carried a mortgage or ever owed much in the way of debt. I realize that is a very privileged thing to be able to say. I know that the vast majority of people carry mortgages on their homes. The Bronfmans lent me the money for my first house, interest free; I paid it off and that was the end of it. I am congenitally unable to have personal debt. It has been years since I owed anything to a bank. If you look at my balance sheet, you see assets and no liabilities.

In terms of my cash flow for the last decade, I've had my salary from the Senate, a consulting retainer from Claridge, and rental income from real estate properties. But essentially I'm one of those very few fortunate people able to live off my investment income. I think it was one of the Rockefellers who said that you have achieved complete financial security when you're able to live off the interest on your interest. I can't.

But my sense is that after $100 million, it doesn't make any difference how rich you are, you have everything you would ever need to live extraordinarily well, and then some. You also have the opportunity to give something back. The Sandra and Leo Kolber Foundation, small by the standards of most charitable organizations, is appropriate and proportionate in terms of my means. I've tried to focus the foundation's endeavours where it can make a difference in my own community. In 2002 the foundation endowed a theatre as the headquarters for the Montreal International Film Festival. I thought of it as a fitting memorial to my wife, who loved movies, and loved Montreal.

I was head of Cemp Investments and chairman of Fairview Corporation and Cadillac Fairview for thirty years. I was on the boards of Seagram and the Toronto-Dominion Bank for twenty-eight years. I was on the board of the Montreal Expos for twenty-two years. I was on the boards of MGM and DuPont for more than ten years. I was chairman of Cineplex Odeon after the ouster of Garth Drabinsky, and for a time I was chairman of Claridge Inc., Charles Bronfman's investment holding company.

Altogether, that's more than 150 years of service on various corporate boards. From my experience, I would make two observations about boards of directors. First, it is very difficult for a board to go against the will of a CEO. And second, boards are very interesting in terms of different corporate cultures, and highly stimulating in terms of the people you meet.

On the first point, Seagram itself offers a very good example of the difficulty of overruling a CEO. As we saw in the sale of DuPont and the purchase of MCA in 1995, and again with the merger of Seagram and Vivendi in 2000, these were deals Junior wanted to do, and he did them, in spite of the strong opposition of Charles, who was co-chairman of the board and chairman of the executive committee. At the time of the Vivendi deal, there were thirteen outside directors, as against six insiders, five of them members of the Bronfman family. The composition of the board was similar at the time of the DuPont sale and MCA acquisition.

On the second point on the nature of boards, it was fascinating to observe the different corporate cultures and standards of corporate governance. And it was equally fascinating to get to know people from the diverse worlds of real estate, banking, consumer products, chemical and plastics, movie production, and film exhibition. Thanks to Charles, who invited me onto the Montreal Expos board from the club's inception in 1968, I even got to know something of the wonderful and financially weird world of baseball. And thanks to Kirk Kerkorian, whose circle of friends included movie stars and war heroes, I became acquainted with fellow MGM directors Cary Grant and Omar Bradley, the five-star general who directed the American ground forces under the command of Dwight Eisenhower in the liberation of Europe. And Cary Grant, because we shared birthdays, made it a point of calling every January 18. We had some enjoyable evenings out together. He was not only one of the most enduring stars in Hollywood history and a very smart businessman in his own right, he was also a very nice man.

Kirk's decision to diversify out of Hollywood, taking MGM into Las Vegas with the MGM Grand, proved to be one of the great business visions of the twentieth century. But in the film production side of the business, there was hardly a picture we made that came in on budget or later covered its costs. It is not a rational business to begin with, except for the notion of bankable stars. In the late 1960s and early 1970s with a yearly budget of, say, $50 million for film production, we based our decisions about what movies to make and what directors to assign on synopses of one or two sentences. There wasn't one member of the board, including me, who knew anything about making movies. But Kirk knew about gambling and he had nerves of ice. Before he gave it up, he would bet $50,000 on an NFL game and go to bed without knowing either the score or, more importantly, whether he had covered the spread.

I found out that a bank board wasn't all that different from the board of a Hollywood studio, in terms of what directors knew about the investments they were asked to authorize. At the TD Bank, they would bring every credit over $2 million to the full board. I remember sitting in a board meeting where they brought more than two hundred credits to the board for review. And we basically looked at them the way the MGM board approved a movie, based on a couple of lines written down and no real discussion. We were spending about ten seconds reviewing each credit. Finally, I put my hand up and said to Allen Lambert, "Mr Chairman, this is crazy. Not only do I not know how to document this loan, I am being given about ten seconds to approve it."

Allen agreed, and they changed the process so that the only credits brought to the board were director related. If you were an officer or director of another company and that company's credit was bring reviewed or a loan was being proposed, then you would step out of the room while the board discussed it. I believe that is still the protocol at the TD Bank.

For a long time, the typical bank board in Canada was too big to be functional. At thirty-five and forty directors, with so many members from each region of the country and appropriate gender balance, it wasn't a corporate board – it was a cabinet, more of a sounding board than an effective decisional body. Nowadays, bank boards are much smaller, often with less than twenty members, enabling them to function like the cabinet committee on priorities and planning, where the real policy decisions are taken in Ottawa.

Serving on the DuPont board for a decade, until we sold our interest in 1995, was one of the great experiences of my life. It wasn't just that they took such good care of their directors, which they did to the point of overdoing it – each director would have an office and a secretary during board meetings at head office in Wilmington, Delaware. It was the culture of the company that was truly impressive. DuPont was very R&D intensive. The reason they invented so many products and processes, from Nylon to Teflon, was that they invested in their development. DuPont would spend about $1.2 billion a year on R&D, about $200 million of that on medical research alone. There are many leading American universities and hospitals that don't put that much effort into research. And when you take the comparison further, there is also something of the difference between pure and applied research, between hypotheses and solutions. But when you think about it, all research, to be of any value in the real world, has to have a practical application.

Though Seagram was DuPont's most important shareholder, with nearly 25 percent of the stock and four members of the board, we never interfered with the running of the company. And thanks to Charles, who served as our ambassador to DuPont, we got along very well with senior management, such as Ed Woolard, CEO at the time we sold our shares back to the company. Charles was very good at representational events – for example, he'd get couples from DuPont and Seagram together for memorable dinners in Palm Beach. That wasn't one of the reasons Charles was so upset about the decision to sell DuPont. But I'm sure it was one of the things he missed, simply because he was so good at it.

The Seagram and DuPont boards were similar in one respect in that both companies were reliable harbingers of the economy. We used to say at Seagram that when some of our premium brands were slumping, it was a sign that the economy was weak. If sales of Chivas Regal were off in one quarter, that was always a sign of flat or negative growth in the economy.

The Montreal Expos board was simply a lot of fun for a long time. And then it wasn't, when Major League Baseball's costs started getting out of whack, which was why Charles made the very smart decision to sell and get out of the game in 1991. But for twenty-three years it was a small part of the great ride of my life. Charles put up the money to buy the expansion franchise against my strong opposition, probably the worst advice I ever gave him.

For as long as Charles owned the team, we would usually fly down to spring training together and hang out. I can still vividly recall standing behind Charles, Mayor Jean Drapeau, and Quebec premier Jean-Jacques Bertrand at the first Opening Day in 1969. Those early years at Jarry Park were the most fun in the team's history, the era when the team was known as Nos Amours, when the city of Montreal had a wonderful love affair with baseball.

Thanks to Charles, the Expos were one more positive in my life. And the baseball team was a very positive thing for him – it allowed him to emerge from the shadow of his famous father and do something important completely on his own. When he sold, he even made a decent return on his money, more than he would have on a twenty-year bond. At some level, I believe owning the Expos gave Charles a comfort level with being a public figure and a community leader. His commitment to a united Canada, through the efforts of the CRB Foundation's Heritage Project, was second to none. His contribution to Canada was uniquely recognized when Prime Minister Mulroney named him to the Queen's Privy Council for Canada, an honour normally reserved for cabinet ministers. So when he became the Honourable Charles Bronfman, an honour the father never even dreamed of was conferred upon the son.

⚭

Corporate governance has become very trendy since the bubble burst on the stock market in 2000, and particularly since the Enron, World-Com, and Tyco scandals. This is what happens in a corporate world driven by greed rather than by enduring corporate values. Insider trading is rampant, conflicts of interest abound, ethical standards abate, and the generally accepted principles of accounting go out the window.

In the blowback from these scandals, there has been a tendency to legislate corporate governance, notably with the Sarbanes-Oxley Bill in Washington. But there are laws against being a crook already on the books, and there are certain laws of common sense that should have prevailed in the governance of these companies at the board level.

Consider the example of WorldCom. Bernie Ebbers, the CEO, went to his board and repeatedly borrowed $400 million to cover his losses in the stock market, this at a time when he was getting margin calls on his own stock. That should have set alarm bells ringing everywhere, but no, they loaned him the money. He should have been kicked out so fast he couldn't see the door.

At WorldCom, it turned out that they cooked their books by writing off billions of dollars of operating costs as capital expenditures. As the *Christian Science Monitor* reported in its online edition in June 2002, "WorldCom booked as capital expenses, rather than ordinary maintenance, some of its expenses on the company's telecom network ... this gimmick improperly boosted cash flow $3.8 billion over the last five years." Any first-year accounting student would have flunked out for making such an assumption.

At Tyco, Dennis Kozlowski allegedly took from his own shareholders when he bought paintings for the company and put them in his own home, to say nothing of the hundreds of millions of dollars of misstated earnings that beat down Tyco's shareholder value. At Enron, Ken Lay and his fellow executives urged employees to hold on to their stock on the way down, even as they were selling off their own positions. Thousands of employees, heavily invested in their own company, lost everything. Lay and his colleagues should all go to jail. That would be the best deterrent to executives robbing their own employees and duping their shareholders.

There are certain aspects of corporate governance that can be legislated or regulated, notably conflicts of interest. But equally, these are also matters of simple common sense. For example, if a brokerage firm is doing an IPO through its investment bank, its analysts shouldn't be touting the stock to its retail customers. If an accounting firm is doing a company's books, it shouldn't be doing management consulting with the same firm. Arthur Andersen paid the price of doing both with Enron and World-Com. One of the five largest accounting firms in the world, Arthur Andersen, went out of business because its trademark became worthless in a matter of months. Such conflicts should be outlawed by the law of common sense, to say nothing of the law of the land.

As long ago as the early 1990s, the Korn Ferry annual survey of executives ranked succession as the most important issue of corporate governance. This is particularly important when sons or daughters are taking over the family business from the founding parent. It's one thing when the family business is privately held and quite another when it becomes a public company.

In my own experience, bringing children into the family business is usually a mistake. My son works with Charles Bronfman as CEO of Koor Industries in Israel. But Jonathan Kolber is not family, though Charles is his godfather and my oldest friend. And Jonathan, in my admittedly biased judgment, has proven his mettle, not during the bubble years, but during the correction since 2000. He had a solid professional formation before moving to Israel in 1991 – a Harvard undergraduate degree, an entry-level position on Wall Street, and an apprenticeship with Claridge in Montreal. By the time he moved to Israel, he had paid a significant amount of dues. He also knew the corporate culture of his shareholder and had, from the time he sat on his maternal grandfather's knee, a knowledge of the market he was moving into.

Seagram was quite a different model, a publicly listed company long before Edgar and Charles succeeded their father. There wasn't just a shareholder, there were *the* shareholders, including employees who bought the stock.

Neither Edgar nor Charles would have taken over the family business without the encouragement of Mr Sam. While it was always clear that Edgar was the heir apparent, he also paid his dues, working his way up from assistant blender to the corner office. There was no aspect of the liquor and beverage business, from blending to aging, from bottling to marketing, that he did not know. He also knew America, our most important market, and as a Canadian who had grown up next door to the U.S., he knew a good deal about local sensibilities in markets around the world. He grew Seagram's core business steadily for two decades following the death of Mr Sam, and he diversified out of booze, as well. He deserves all the credit for our selling Texas Pacific Oil and Gas at the top of the market in 1981 and for subsequently turning our bid for Conoco into a huge stake in DuPont.

But Edgar's fatal flaw was his hero worship of Edgar Jr, a high school dropout who was unqualified to take over the business. In fairness to Edgar Jr, he made several good moves in spirits and beverages, making Seagram Wine Coolers the dominant player in that growth segment and acquiring Tropicana, a premium orange juice that, among other things, could be mixed with Seagram vodka brands. But it's clear that Junior wasn't content to run a consumer products company, that he had his eye on building an entertainment conglomerate. Which was fine as far as it went, except that he was playing with other people's money, not just his own or even the Bronfman family fortune, but money that belonged to the shareholders. Bottom line, he had no business running the business.

He was by no means unique in this respect. Interestingly, the *New York Times* ran a piece in its business section early in 2003, when Ted Rogers named his son to take over his communications and cable TV business, noting that it was a particularly Canadian thing that sons and daughters came into the family business, even when publicly held. That's a fair observation. Izzy Asper brought his children into the top positions of CanWest. Ken Thomson has brought his son into his media empire. Paul Desmarais brought his sons into Power Corporation, though it must be said they were well trained for the management roles they assumed and had strong management support from the likes of Robert Gratton, head of Power Financial, CEO of their financial services holdings across North America.

If family owners insist on bringing their children into the family business, they might look at imposing disciplines, as the Schlumberger family has in France, where the children must spend time working in another business before they are accepted into the family business of supplying the oil industry worldwide.

For myself, I come back to the example of the greatest hockey player I ever saw – Maurice "Rocket" Richard. What were the chances of the Rocket's sons succeeding the Rocket on the ice? None. The odds against have been the same in business, and always will be.

16

The Senate Banking Committee

In October 2002, I received a phone call from Kevin Lynch, the deputy minister of finance, asking if the Senate Committee on Banking, Trade and Commerce would help out his minister, John Manley, with the touchy issue of large bank mergers, a game that was again afoot in talks between the Bank of Nova Scotia and the Bank of Montreal. In Canada, large, or Schedule 1, banks must be widely held, with no shareholder holding more than 20 percent of the voting stock. Small, or Schedule 11, banks are typically regional or subsidiaries of foreign banks, and may be closely held.

Manley wanted the Senate Banking Committee, and the House Finance Committee under Sue Barnes, to examine the question of large bank mergers by determining "the public interest." In essence, Manley and Lynch, with the approval of the Prime Minister's Office, were punting a big political problem to us.

Mergers had been on the public policy agenda once before, in 1998, when the Bank of Montreal and the Royal Bank of Canada announced their intention to merge, followed in short order by a merger announcement between the TD Bank, of which I was then a director, and the Canadian Imperial Bank of Commerce. Just like that, the Big Five would have become the Big Three, with only Scotiabank on the outside looking in. Paul Martin, then finance minister, was extremely annoyed at the very idea of mergers, perhaps because he reportedly heard about the Royal-BMO deal on the radio rather than on the phone from Royal chairman John Cleghorn, his neighbour in the Eastern Townships. The powerful Ontario Liberal caucus was dead set against mergers from the get-go, as were consumer advocates and small business groups.

In 2002 the finance ministry suggested what appeared to be a more transparent and intellectually rigorous process. When I received a letter from Manley on October 24 formally asking the banking committee to look into mergers and the public interest, it was obvious that we would hold hearings. I was determined to get out in front of the merger curve by holding our hearings quickly and getting our report out before the year-end holiday recess, and thus well before the Commons Finance Committee's report. We began hearings on November 25, a month after receiving Manley's letter, and got our recommendations and report out within two weeks of concluding them on November 29.

I wanted the Senate committee to set the agenda for the discussion, not just within the government, but also with the news media. I knew that we were much more likely than the Commons Finance Committee to be supportive of mergers, frankly because none of us had to face the voters, and because many of us on the committee had experience in the financial services sector and knew the issues on both sides of the debate.

On one side were critical mass and economies of scale to make Canadian banks world-competitive in a global industry; on the other, the issue of service and the availability of credit, especially to small business, in the retail banking sector. Thus, the pros and the cons. The briefs on both sides were quite predictable. But I thought that it was time, nearly five years since the last merger debate, for a thorough airing of views, and I was convinced our committee could make a significant contribution to an important issue. I also thought that if my committee could frame the discussion on our own terms, we could move it forward quickly to where I wanted it to come out – approving a limited number of mergers and restricting political oversight to the financial regulators, where it belonged.

That's exactly what we recommended, in what may have been a record time of only six weeks. We published a unanimous report on December 12, nearly four months ahead of our deadline of March 31, 2003, recommending bank mergers be permitted if they passed the regulatory test, removing parliamentary review while leaving the final word with the finance minister. We went even further, recommending the government "undertake a review of barriers to entry into the financial services sector for domestic and international competitors and take other actions – including tax changes – that would foster competition." In other words, open up Canadian financial services to foreign competition.

Unanimity is very important in the traditions of Senate committee reports, where bipartisan consensus is the rule rather than the exception. This was the case in 2002 with the report out of Colin Kenny's Senate Defence Committee that recommended Canadian forces be recalled from overseas for two years, during which time the mission would be redefined and the forces re-equipped and brought up to strength. It was the case with Michael Kirby's committee and its recommendation, after three years of study, to reinvest billions of dollars in public health care. And it was very much the case with my committee, though we are able to move with unusual speed. This was partly due to the rapid emergence of a bipartisan consensus, as well as to diligent staff work by my executive assistant, Steve Campbell, and the committee clerk, Denis Robert, to say nothing of our two outstanding staff researchers – June Dewetering, on loan from the Library of Parliament, and Kelly Bourassa, assigned to my own staff – both gifted writers who brought a very complex issue into a clear focus. June and Kelly were at work on the draft of the report even as we were conducting the hearings, which is how we were able to get it out so fast.

It would be more than another three months before the Barnes committee reported, predictably recommending mergers be permitted with the caveat that political review remain a third stage of approval, beyond the two regulatory levels of the Office of the Superintendent of Financial Institutions and the Competition Bureau. "I'm not sure why they went to all that trouble to say nothing," I told the *Globe and Mail* from Washington, where our committee was doing the rounds on the issue of corporate governance. "I just don't think they added to the debate … We took a stand. You can disagree with what we said, but at least we started a debate." The House Finance Committee report was so wishy-washy that the committee vice-chair, Nick Discepola, told me he was on the verge of not signing it.

By then, the Senate committee had received the lion's share of coverage and credit, and it was our report that was taken seriously by both the government and the media.

But first I had to persuade the Conservatives on the committee that it was a serious and substantive process, not a sham designed to cover the government and buy it time. It didn't help to make the case that, on the very first day of the hearings, both Manley and Maurizio Bevilacqua, the junior minister for financial institutions, as well as Deputy Minister Kevin Lynch, stiffed the committee. Here they were, kicking the problem to us, and then refusing to come before the committee. They clearly wanted to avoid opposition questioning on the tick-tock of who killed the proposed BMO-Scotia deal and when. Was it Manley who nixed it, or the Prime Minister's Office, or even the PM himself?

To make matters worse, they sent several mid-level bureaucrats in their place. The Tories were furious, and so was I. "Kevin, you can't do this to me," I fumed at Lynch, to no avail. The CEOs of four big banks found time to fly in from Toronto on the same day, in the middle of earnings season, but the finance minister and his deputy couldn't be bothered to drive four blocks. The Conservative deputy chair, David Tkachuk, was so annoyed that he made an angry opening statement and put out a press release denouncing the "Ministers' Dis-Appearance" and dismissing Manley's letter asking us to look into the issue of larger bank mergers as "nothing more than a smokescreen to cover a failed government policy."

The Conservatives immediately took it out on Scotiabank president Peter Godsoe, one of four CEOs to appear before us on November 25, the first day of hearings. Godsoe had been the one left without a dance partner in the 1998 merger round, and he was apparently determined that it wouldn't happen again. Godsoe was also known as a big Grit, with Liberal friends in high places. Onex Corporation's Gerry Schwartz, chief fundraiser for Paul Martin's leadership campaign, was on the Scotiabank board, not that it would do him much good with Chrétien or his PMO, or with Manley, Martin's main rival in the party leadership race. I also had it on pretty good authority that Manley was prepared to recommend the BMO-Scotia deal to the PMO, but Godsoe evidently preferred to take it forward himself. At the committee, the Tories tried to get him on the tick-tock, but Godsoe amiably refused to play.

"Didn't have a deal," he insisted.

"The consensus on this side," suggested Conservative senator Jim Kelleher in a loud stage whisper, "is that he's lying through his fucking teeth."

Then it was David Tkachuk's turn as he tried to draw Godsoe out with a simple country boy routine. "Mr Godsoe," he began, "I do not know how old you are, but it is like, when we were young, going to a dance where all the guys would stand at the back and the girls would be on the side, and we would be afraid to ask them to dance. We would mull around and then the girls would get tired and they would start dancing with each other. It was a strange thing from small-town Saskatchewan. Later on you would walk out, have a few beers, and then maybe you got the nerve to ask one girl to dance."

While the room dissolved in laughter, Tkachuk turned serious and got to his point: "Since you say you did not make a proposal, and no one has made a proposal, how do we know there is a problem?"

Clearly, building trust and achieving unanimity was going to be a bit of a challenge around the table of our committee's permanent hearing room on the fifth floor of the Senate Victoria Building and away from the hearings as well. But I thought that if I could foster a mood of cooperation and collegiality, then we had a good chance. For starters, on the

first evening of our five days of hearings, I invited the whole committee
to a private dinner on Parliament Hill with RBC Financial Group president Gordon Nixon. I could very easily have invited him to dinner
alone or included just a few Liberals. But I wanted the entire committee
to take ownership of the issue and the process, and the team dinner
with Nixon did wonders, at the end of a very long day, to establish a
bond of trust.

Except that the day wasn't over. After dinner, we all boarded a Parliament Hill bus and trooped back to our hearing room across Wellington
Street for a presentation by Ed Clark, president of TD-Canada Trust.
After killing the BMO-Royal and TD-CIBC mergers in 1998, Martin
later permitted the TD Bank to merge with Canada Trust in 2000, on
the grounds that CT was a trust company rather than a bank. This was
a fiction carefully cultivated by Imasco, the Montreal-based consumer
products and services conglomerate that owned CT. Having carefully
positioned CT as the sixth-largest bank in the country, with the best asset portfolio in the industry – home mortgages – Imasco shamelessly re-
positioned CT as a trust when it decided to sell it off in the breakup of
the holding company engineered by its parent, British Tobacco. Ed
Clark had clearly come a long way from his bureaucratic origins as the
author of the hated National Energy Program in 1981. "He's a solid citizen now," Imasco chairman Purdy Crawford once said with a chuckle.
He was also a solid presenter, and along with the Royal Bank's Gord
Nixon, made the strongest pro-merger case of the Big Six CEOs, who all
appeared before our committee within the space of three days.

On the first day of the hearings, we sat from nine in the morning until
nine at night in a room heated by noisy steam radiators from another
era, under the hot glare of television lights. The next day we picked up
in the morning and in the afternoon resumed in the Summit Room of
the East Block, where Pierre Trudeau had chaired the G7 summit in
1981 and where we had a witness, HSBC Canada president Martin
Glynn, appear by satellite uplink from Vancouver. And so it went for
five hectic days – so much for the reputation of the Senate as a bunch of
doddering old men.

As I looked around the table of the Senate Banking Committee, there
was some pretty impressive talent, more of it, to be perfectly honest, on
the Conservative side. The deputy chair, David Tkachuk, was a very
bright light, though our relationship continued to be a work in progress.

He had a partisan's flare for the political game that he had acquired while working for Grant Devine in the Premier's Office in Saskatchewan. We had got off on the wrong foot back in 1999, when I foolishly confided to John Lynch-Staunton, the Tory leader in the Senate, that I wished he would have given me a vice-chair who knew something about banking. We were attending a black-tie reception at the governor-general's at the opening of a parliamentary session, and I assumed we were having a private conversation. Lynch-Staunton, later claiming I had maligned a colleague, shared my indiscreet comment with Tkachuk. I took him to dinner in a private room at Café Henry Burger in Hull, the best table in the national capital region, and tried to repair the damage.

"I know what you said," he said, "and it is your perfect right to say it."

"David, I'm sorry," I said. "But we have to work together, if you want to work together."

"Absolutely," he said.

"I would like an understanding with you," I went on. "On any matter of substance, you can be as partisan as you like, you can fight me tooth and nail. But if you start nitpicking with me on process, with stupid motions and delaying tactics, I'll outvote you every time, and it will be a complete waste of time for both of us. I want to accomplish something in this committee, and I hope you do, too."

And we shook hands on it. Then about six months later, while the committee was sitting, a couple of Liberal senators decided they had to go back to their offices. Before I knew it, Tkachuk was motioning to his executive assistant, two more Conservatives suddenly showed up, he proposed a procedural motion, and we were defeated.

"Now you have declared war on me," I shouted at him.

"It's not personal," Tkachuk insisted, "it's business."

"That's what the Mafia say," I replied. "Why are you giving me this crap?"

I have to say it was the first and last time he ever pulled such a stunt. Since then, we developed a protocol that he was in charge of allocating Conservative speaking time on the committee. Then, before we started the hearings on mergers, I knew we needed to bring in a communications consultant to make sure we got properly covered in the media. I spoke to Tkachuk, and he said he knew of someone named Michael Krauss, principal of the Hartwell Group in Toronto, who had worked in the communications branch of the Privy Council Office during the Mulroney years. Since Krauss came recommended by the Tories, they happily authorized the money to hire him.

It's remarkable, when you think of it, that the committee didn't have its own director of communications on staff, but the Senate is notoriously understaffed for the very real work it is supposed to do. I once met a guy named Steven Solarz, a member of Congress in the U.S. and vice-chairman of the House Foreign Relations Committee. I was sitting next to him at the wedding of Geraldine Ferraro's daughter, who was a close friend of Jonathan's from Salomon Brothers on Wall Street. "What sort of staff do you have?" I asked at one point. "Forty-six in Washington," he said, "and twenty-three in my constituency office in Brooklyn." To say nothing of committee staff, including majority and minority staff directors overseeing the work of dozens of full-time employees. Our committee had one part-time clerk, whom we shared with another committee, two part-time researchers, and no legal counsel. That was it.

The other regular Conservative members of the committee, Jim Kelleher, Michael Meighen, and David Angus, were all extremely well versed in financial services because of their own banking and business affiliations. Don Oliver, who sometimes sat for the Tories, was the most articulate of the bunch, an outstanding representative of Nova Scotia and the Atlantic Canada region. Occasionally, Lynch-Staunton would grace us with his presence.

The question arises as to whether banking affiliations placed members of the banking committee in a conflict of interest. Kelleher is non-executive chairman of the Italian Bank of Canada, Meighen is a director of Deutsch Bank Canada, both small Schedule 11 banks. David Angus is a lawyer at Stikeman Elliott, which has been CIBC's outside counsel for decades.

So when CIBC chairman John Hunkin came before our hearings on the first day, Angus welcomed him and congratulated him "on the clarity and candour of your comments. It is very refreshing."

At which point, knowing of Stikeman's legal brief with CIBC, two of Angus's Tory colleagues jumped in with a couple of digs at him.

"Watch the next one," Jim Kelleher warned.

"Something's coming," Don Oliver agreed.

"I think he is giving us the straight goods here," Angus maintained. "Mr Hunkin, I clearly understand from your comments that there is no merger in the works, or even under consideration with the other five banks, is that fair?"

"Are there rumours?" Hunkin replied. "I left Toronto two hours ago, and look what happens. I am not aware of any, Senator."

That was the kind of good-humoured give-and-take I was looking for, and my reading of it was that, after a rough start, the Tories were going to stay the course in the committee.

For more than twenty years, Angus and I were senior bagmen for the Tory and Liberal parties, in which capacity we talked to the Big Five CEOs all the time. And of course, I had been a director of the TD Bank for twenty-eight years. When I went off the TD board, around the time I became chairman of Senate Banking, I had this discussion in a media scrum at a committee hearing.

"I want you to know," I said, "that I am no longer on the TD board, so that removes any question of a conflict. Does it change what I know about banking issues? Does it change my views? Not one bit." The reporters insisted it was a question of appearance. Yet my association with the bank was well known, and in my view real conflicts occur only when affiliations are concealed. On any discussion of Schedule II banks, for example, Kelleher and Meighen would be the first to recuse themselves. But it is a legitimate debate. These affiliations can be seen as conflicts of interest on the one hand and experience of the real world on the other.

On the Liberal side, Winnipeg businessman Richard Kroft had a strong appreciation of banking issues, but that's about as deep as our talent went. Raymond Setlakwe from Thetford Mines in Quebec had a penchant for asking bank presidents about their branch in his hometown. Well, at least he looked out for the interests of his region, one of the things we are supposed to do in the Senate.

For myself as committee chair, I preferred to play a low-key role during the merger hearings. It wasn't my job to grandstand in the committee, but to nurture a consensus that would get us to where I wanted to go.

In all, over thirty witnesses testified before the committee, including several academic authorities. I had personally tracked one of them, James McIntosh, down at his office in the economics department at Concordia University. My secretary got him on the line for me.

"Professor McIntosh," I began, "my name is Leo Kolber, and I am the chairman of the Senate Banking Committee. I've heard about your paper on banking and I understand your view is that unless Canadian banks are allowed to merge, our industry will not be competitive within ten years."

"Actually, five years," he replied.

"Well, I want to invite you to appear before our committee. Naturally, we will reimburse your expenses."

As for the banks, they weren't lobbying for mergers so much as asking for transparency in the process and for removal of uncertainty at the political level. The headline in the *Globe and Mail* on the morning after four CEOs all appeared on the same day perfectly captured the banks' agenda: "Bank executives want merger rules clarified." As RBC's Gordon Nixon later put it in *Policy Options* magazine, "Canada needs a bank merger review process that properly addresses the public interest, advances the country's prosperity, and ensures our nation's future political sovereignty."

We got twice the bang for our media buck when someone leaked our recommendations to the *Globe and Mail* on December 12, the day of the report's scheduled release. The *Globe* ran it at the top of the front page under the headline "Canada needs only three banks, Ottawa told." Reporter Simon Tuck characterized our report as "a huge win for the five big banks' long-held aspirations to bulk up." And on the front page of the same day's *Report on Business* in the *Globe,* Andrew Willis observed in his *Streetwise* column, "Quite sensible, these senators," for our telling the politicians "to butt out of the bank merger debate."

We were back on the front pages the next day with the official release of our report at the National Press Theatre in Ottawa. I was happy to share the media coverage with David Tkachuk, and had him sit in the centre of three seats, flanked by Raymond Setlakwe and me. To all appearances, Tkachuk was the chairman. Fine with me. "In a news conference," the *Globe* reported, "the committee's two key players went a step further" than recommending mergers "by suggesting that the highly regulated industry be completely opened to foreign investment." The story added that "Mr Tkachuk urged the federal government to move quickly. 'They've got to get working on it.'"

I decided to take the debate to the next level in a speech to the Toronto Board of Trade in February 2003, when I suggested that the government lift its prohibition of cross-pillar mergers between banks and insurance companies. The Mulroney government had knocked down the pillars separating banks, trusts, and brokerages in financial services while keeping insurers outside the reform. In the summer of 2002, when the Canadian Imperial Bank of Commerce wanted to merge with Manulife Financial, Manley told them to forget it. I was simply stating the obvious when I told reporters after my speech that it would have been "a marriage made in heaven, because it eliminates a lot of objections that some people have to large bank mergers."

As it happened, Manley was in Toronto the same day to promote his budget, and both of us visited the *Globe.* "If the chairman of the Senate banking committee asks us to look at it, we'll look at it," Manley told the newspaper's editorial board, quickly adding the qualifier that he would "want to know what the policy rationale was and give some thought to the impact of it." One bank spokesperson wryly observed: "Unfortunately, these types of marriages are made in Ottawa, not heaven." Yet as the *Globe* reported on my speech, I had made the point that "the lack of overlap between banks and insurers makes them ideal corporate partners because they could avoid many of the public interest concerns surrounding the issue of regular bank mergers."

Among other things, it is a question of creating a level playing field. Citigroup, the world's second-largest financial services company, with assets of U.S.$1 trillion at the end of 2001, owns Travelers Insurance in addition to an investment bank, Salomon Brothers Smith Barney. Canada's largest bank, the Royal, was only forty-eighth in the world in terms of assets, at $350 billion, or about U.S.$225 billion. The Royal also owns an investment bank and brokerage, RBC Dominion Securities, but is not permitted in the insurance business. How can Canadian banks be world-competitive if they are not allowed to play on the same terms as the U.S. and international banks? The simple answer is that they can't. And if the rules aren't changed, Canadian banks will fall further and further behind. In my view, if Canadian banks are not able to grow and compete in the international market, they will quickly become unable to serve Canadian corporations in their global transactions and will become irrelevant within the next ten years. In order to protect the Canadian financial services sector, we must allow Canadian banks to grow.

Furthermore, as BMO Financial Group chairman Tony Comper observed at our committee hearings, "It is critically important to the Canadian economy to have world-class Canadian-headquartered banks." And who is to say Canadian companies can't cut the competition in financial services? Throughout my own business career, I was associated with two Canadian companies, Seagram and Cadillac Fairview, that were world champions. I am convinced that similar success awaits Canadian financial services in North American and world markets.

At the end of March and beginning of April 2003, in the middle of the Second Gulf War, the Senate Banking Committee travelled to New York and Washington on a fact-finding mission on the issue of corporate governance. The two cities, victims of the September 11 terror attacks at the symbolic heart of U.S. financial and military might, were understandably both on a high state of alert. Getting around the financial district of Lower Manhattan and the office buildings of Congress and government in Washington proved to be a major logistical challenge, especially for me, given my obsession for everything running on time.

We had been holding hearings on and off over the previous year, in the wake of the governance scandals that had engulfed corporate America, vaporizing billions of dollars of market valuations and leaving investor confidence badly shaken in Canada as well as the United States. The U.S. Congress had since adopted the Sarbanes-Oxley Bill on accounting standards and corporate governance, and my strong sense was that Canada had to take steps in the same direction. For one thing, many Canadian stocks were inter-listed on the NYSE and the NASDAQ, and as such would be required to be in compliance with Sarbanes-Oxley. For another, as I told the *Financial Post* in an interview from Washington, "Some form of legislation is a complete necessity in this climate. We have to hold Canada out as a safe place and a haven for investors. They can compare us to the United States. We have to do some of the same."

The committee had been getting decidedly mixed signals from stakeholders in Canada about whether we needed to adopt tough legislative remedies such as Sarbanes-Oxley. Tom d'Aquino, president of the Canadian Council of Chief Executives, the big business lobby, insisted business could enforce its own ethical standards. "If the business community is so good at looking after themselves," I retorted, "how come we have all these scandals?"

Barbara Stymiest, president of the Toronto Stock Exchange, Canada's national stock market, came before us with a similar view, saying legislation was not needed to prevent insider trading, conflicts of interests, and other scams common on Bay Street during the bubble era. But David Brown, head of the Ontario Securities Commission, the regulator of the TSE, thought we should be emulating Sarbanes-Oxley. So we went to see Sarbanes and Oxley in Washington.

But first, eight senators went to New York, where Robert Baitz, the president and chief operating officer of the New York Stock Exchange, had us to breakfast. We also had a good meeting with Eliot Spitzer, the state attorney general who has been the biggest scourge of Wall Street since Rudy Giuliani was prosecuting corporate greed as New York district attorney in the 1980s. Like Giuliani before him, Spitzer is clearly poised to use his fame as a springboard to higher office, but in the meantime he has put the fear of the law back into Wall Street, with investment banks agreeing to billion-dollar fines and one-time star analysts such as Henry Blodget accepting lifetime trading bans in addition to steep financial penalties. A Park Avenue lawyer and a compelling presenter, Spitzer is clearly marked for higher things in life than reading Henry Blodget's e-mails.

In Washington, we had a working lunch at the Canadian Embassy with several think-tanks, including the Brookings and the Cato. The view of the U.S. Capitol from the chancery's sixth-floor dining room was magnificent. No wonder so many senators and congressmen take in the Fourth of July fireworks from the Canadian embassy's top-floor terrace, though they generally like to avoid pictures of the occasion that might turn up in the press in their home states and districts.

Then we met with Senator Paul Sarbanes and Congressman Michael Oxley, co-authors of the Sarbanes-Oxley Bill. Oxley was chair of the huge House Committee on Financial Services, and Sarbanes, ranking Democratic member of the Senate Banking Committee, had been chairman when Sarbanes-Oxley was adopted in 2002 in the political fallout from the Enron, WorldCom, and other corporate governance scandals. Chatting about our meeting with Eliot Spitzer in New York, Oxley told one of our members: "There is not enough mustard in the United States to cover that hot dog." We were so tightly scheduled in Washington that we had to split the committee up to make all our meetings; while some met with Oxley, others were meeting with Bill Donaldson, chairman of the Securities and Exchange Commission, who was very supportive of a legislative framework on corporate governance.

And we met with Federal Reserve Chairman Alan Greenspan at the Fed's office on Constitution Avenue. The seven other senators were escorted right up to his boardroom, but I had to wait nearly half an hour because my name wasn't on the guest list. I thought, this is pretty ironic – I've arranged the meeting, I'm the chairman of the committee, and I can't get in. Eventually, Greenspan's assistant came down to the front door, offered a tearful apology, and brought me up to the meeting with the Fed chairman. "Apparently, we have something called security here," Greenspan deadpanned in his trademark Fedspeak.

He gave us a half-hour dissertation on corporate governance and the economy, and lived up to his reputation for brilliance. Greenspan's view was that Sarbanes-Oxley wasn't needed in the new era of corporate reform and governance; still he was very glad it had been passed. "In ten or fifteen years," he said, "we're going to have the same irrational exuberance all over again. And then you want Sarbanes-Oxley in your pocket." So that was Greenspan's read on it – he saw it as a good insurance policy.

Afterwards we had a chance for a bit of a social visit. I reminded Greenspan that we had met on several occasions in New York when he had been one of Seagram's advisers in 1981 – as we had sold off Texas Pacific Oil and were looking for the acquisition that eventually became DuPont.

Then Greenspan said he had noticed that there was a senator from Winnipeg on my committee, and he asked to meet him. So I introduced him to Richard Kroft. Greenspan explained that he had once been married to a girl named Mitchell from Winnipeg, and as it turned out, Dick knew the family.

"Is it just a coincidence," Richard asked, "that you were married to a Mitchell forty years ago and are married to a Mitchell again?"

"When I finally decide to get married, I always marry a Mitchell," Greenspan said of his wife, Andrea Mitchell, the diplomatic correspondent of NBC News.

In the banking committee report on corporate governance, entitled *Navigating through the Perfect Storm* and released in June 2003, we made fourteen recommendations, all from the school of common sense. For example, we proposed that a majority of board members be outside directors and that legislation be introduced to "obviate real or perceived conflicts of interests by financial analysts." The *Globe and Mail* agreed in an editorial entitled "Leo Kolber's Rules," concluding that "Federal legislation would play a valuable role in bringing strong and mandatory investor protections to all of Canada's major public companies."

I cannot leave the Senate, after twenty years of service, without some thoughts on the institution itself. Conceived by Sir John A. Macdonald as the chamber of "sober second thought" – an interesting way for him to put it – the appointed Senate has for decades been an object of discussion to those who would reform it, and of derision to those who would abolish it. It has been the constant object of scornful humour, with appointment to the Senate known as a "taskless thanks" to those, like me, who had performed "thankless tasks" such as fundraising.

My own experience of the Senate is somewhat different. Though I was among its most delinquent members during the initial period of my wife's long and confining illness, I later took the work quite seriously, especially during my four years as chairman of Senate Banking, which has long been regarded as one of the most influential committees on Parliament Hill.

The media don't always understand this, partly because they can't be in two places at once, and the action is usually in "the other place," as the Senate calls the House of Commons. Yet judging by the quantity and quality of briefs my committee received on bank mergers in the fall of 2002, as well as by the number of submissions we received at our corporate governance hearings, our work was regarded as important by stakeholders in banking, trade, and commerce. And those three segments cover the waterfront of the economy.

I have never been one for making speeches, either in the Liberal caucus or in the Senate chamber. But I was profoundly disturbed by the wave of anti-Americanism in Canada, and in our own Liberal ranks, before and during the American invasion of Iraq in March 2003. One of our MPs, Carolyn Parrish, made headlines when a microphone caught her in a stage whisper as she left caucus saying, "Damn Americans, I hate those bastards." Feelings ran so high in our caucus that two senior ministers, David Collenette and Don Boudria, later suggested in all seriousness that U.S. ambassador Paul Celluci be expelled for stating the obvious, that his government was "disappointed and upset" that Canada was not participating in or even supporting the U.S. "coalition of the willing."

The American anthem was lustily booed at a hockey game in Montreal, and the U.S. flag was burned at anti-war rallies in Canada. I decided, as other senators did, to make a statement in the Red Chamber. "We Canadians would be the first to be scandalized by the burning of our flag and the booing of our anthem in the United States," I said. "We should not be surprised, then, if some Americans vote with their wallets by deciding not to visit Canada or buy Canadian products."

Then I targeted Carolyn Parrish for her idiotic outburst. "It is one thing to disagree with the United States, as the government has done in the exercise of our sovereignty," I said, "but it is another for members of Parliament, including members of my own caucus, to state their position in language that would be deemed unparliamentary, either in this place or the other place."

I went on to address the issue of anti-Americanism, particularly in the larger context of hate mongering, which is a crime in Canada. "Suffice it to say that discrimination comes in many pernicious forms, whether against Jews, cultural communities, or Americans. Anti-Americanism is just as detestable and unacceptable as anti-Semitism or anti-Arabic sentiment or the dissemination of hatred against 'any identifiable group.' That is not just a matter of opinion, it is a matter of fact in the Criminal Code. It is also a matter of decency. Good neighbours do not spit across the back fence; they talk across it. Good neighbours also mend fences when need be rather than tearing them down."

Finally, I saw "no moral equivalency" between the United States and the Iraqi regime, or between the American president and Iraqi dictator Saddam Hussein, whose torture methods, as I pointed out, "include the rape of wives and daughters in front of their families." I noted as well that he "pays blood money to the families of suicide bombers to blow up innocent Israelis."

And I concluded: "I do not see a problem in choosing between Saddam Hussein and George W. Bush. Choosing war is difficult. Choosing sides isn't."

It was something that needed to be said, and being in the Senate gave me the opportunity to say it. Public opinion in Canada, which had been strongly opposed to the war before it began, quickly moved to become just as strongly in favour of the U.S. winning the war once it started. The Chrétien government, which understandably preferred a UN Security Council resolution authorizing force, was left scrambling to catch up to public opinion it had previously been reflecting rather than leading. Yet even as the Americans approached the gates of Baghdad, Chrétien still spoke out in the House of Commons against regime change. And he only declared his hope that the Americans would win the war after they had actually won it. George W. Bush subsequently cancelled an official visit to Ottawa that had been scheduled for May 2003. Just to make sure Canada got the message, Bush subsequently invited Australian prime minister John Howard to visit his Texas ranch for two days. Clearly, Baghdad wasn't the only capital where Bush wanted regime change.

I was due to leave the Senate on January 18, 2004, my seventy-fifth birthday. But I decided to relinquish the banking committee chairmanship at the end of the spring session in June 2003 and to leave the Senate a month early at the end of the year, exactly twenty years after being appointed by Pierre Trudeau. I felt that we had done work of enduring value on the issues of large bank mergers and corporate governance. I'd also played a role in the 50 per cent reduction of the capital gains tax, most of which is reinvested to create new jobs for Canadians.

I've always been able to move on from other things. Now it was time to move on from the committee and the Senate, time to get on with the rest of my life.

Afterword

I'm one of those people who have always been lucky in life. And I'm a firm believer that luck and happenstance, being in the right place at the right time, have a lot to do with success. The rest of it is about what you do with the opportunities presented to you.

Well, I've been exceptionally lucky in every part of my life. I had the good fortune to attend McGill University and to switch from science to arts, which allowed me to transfer to the main campus in downtown Montreal from a suburban one south of the city. Otherwise, I would never have met Charles Bronfman and become his best friend. But for my friendship with Charles, I would never have become close to his brother, Edgar. Without my friendship with the brothers, I would never have been hired by their father to run Cemp Investments. Without Sam Bronfman as my mentor, and without his name and the Seagram brand behind all our projects at Fairview Corporation, we could never have built anything on the scale of the Toronto-Dominion Centre and the Eaton Centre.

Without Mr Sam asking me to go to Florida with Sam Sair, I would never have heard of Sandra Maizel, who became my partner and closest friend throughout forty-four years of marriage. And without her, of course, there would have been no Lynne or Jonathan. I'm sure I would have married someone else eventually and had other children, but I'm very grateful for the ones that I have. And that is the result of sitting out on a hot summer's night in Daytona Beach and being told by a man from Winnipeg about this girl from Montreal he'd met in Israel, whom I absolutely had to look up. It was luck, that's all. Or fate.

It was pure luck that shopping centres were the next big thing in the late 1950s, just as we were looking to spread our wings at Cemp and branch out into real estate. But then, we also made our own luck, building a reputation for being the best in the business. And when we had pretty much built our way across Canada, from Halifax to the Pacific Centre in Vancouver, we made our own luck in the United States, building one of the biggest real estate firms in North America. Then we had the extraordinarily good luck to sell the company at the very top of the market in 1987. In all the years since, it has never come back to those levels.

It was my association with the Bronfmans and Cadillac Fairview that opened all kinds of doors for me as a political fundraiser for the Liberal party. But I also made my own luck, or saw to it that luck intervened on my behalf, in my appointment to the Senate by Pierre Trudeau and my appointment as chairman of the Senate Banking Committee by Jean Chrétien. Where I come from, if you don't ask, you don't get.

My twenty years in the Senate have been among the most interesting of my life, a continuous learning experience about politics and public policy. There might be some things about the Senate I'll miss – the title, for one. It's nice being called "Senator." It has a certain cachet, not so much with the political class as in business circles. And in the U.S., when you check into a hotel as a senator, it really makes a difference in terms of the service. I'll miss some of my colleagues, on both sides of the floor, who have become good friends over the years. But I won't miss the haggling in committee and the posturing in the Senate chamber.

Besides, I'm not one who looks back very much. Every day on the way to my office, I drive by the Seagram castle on Peel Street in Montreal. I don't think of it as the abandoned seat of a once great business empire. I think of it as part of the past, where it belongs. As much as Cadillac Fairview and Cemp represented thirty years of my life, I moved on very quickly from both. I expect to move on just as quickly from the Senate after my retirement at the end of 2003. A few months before that, in June 2003, I voluntarily stepped down as chair of Senate Banking, after releasing our report on corporate governance. During my four years as chairman, we did important work on issues such as business ethics and bank mergers. I guess the most important work I did was on the capital gains tax. When I became chairman, I had the prerogative, if the legislative pipeline was bare, of doing a special study. I chose to do one on capital gains in Canada, which were totally uncompetitive with the United States. I also made an intervention in caucus about the matter, and to my great surprise, I was roundly applauded. I convinced both the prime minister and the finance minister to cut the capital gains tax in half, which puts us on a level playing field with the Americans, and I consider this a significant achievement.

But the work was done, and it was time to step aside. If I can serve the incoming prime minister, Paul Martin, in some modest way, I'll be delighted.

But mostly, I'm going to try to learn how to relax. And that may be one of the big challenges of my life. My son keeps telling me that I go too hard and do too much. It's true that from so many years of being tightly scheduled, I still tend to be overscheduled. But now that I won't have to spend three days a week in Ottawa when the Senate is in session, that's going to free up a big chunk of time. It's going to allow me ten days a month in Palm Beach during the winter. I'm going to get reacquainted with the game of golf. There's a pile of books on my night table waiting to be read. I've got continuing business interests in real estate and a lot of charitable and voluntary work to do.

And there's a new lady, a new love, in my life. It was one more stroke of good luck that I met Mona Golfman in the summer of 2002. She's bright and beautiful. We travel a lot together. We entertain quite frequently, and she is a brilliant hostess. She golfs, and she skies as badly as I do. She has her own work as a librarian in art and architecture at McGill, and she has grown children of her own. We have a wonderful relationship, and she is a very significant part of my future. No one is happier for me than my own children, and that alone brings me great joy.

When we started work on this book, I wasn't sure how it was going to come out. I wasn't even sure it would be worth doing, but I can see now that it has been. At the beginning, I wondered if there would be enough material; by the end, I wondered if we were leaving too much out. Doing it has taken me back through all the chapters of my life and reminded me what an eventful journey it has been. I was flattered in the beginning that my co-author, L. Ian MacDonald, thought I had a book in me. It has been an entirely agreeable partnership and much more work than I could have ever imagined, much less undertaken alone.

For my part, there are many people to be thanked, starting with my assistants Maria Scandella and Peggy Gaon, who have for many years endured my obsessive-compulsive nature, including my obsession that every appointment start on time. In my Ottawa office, Shirley Strean has been a devoted assistant for many years. On my personal staff, Yves Poirier has been my driver for more than twenty-five years. At my home, I'm fortunate that Felipe and Sonia Gago and Helena Oliveira have taken such good care of me, and my late wife, for so many years.

It would be very difficult to thank all the friends and colleagues of a lifetime – like Rick Doyle, who steered me throughout the vagaries of the tax laws – but I would like to say that aside from all the work that I've done, I also love to relax with a game of golf and a round of pinochle. To this end, I must thank Peter Burnett, who really goes the extra mile in helping to arrange many golf games, and my good friends George Rosengarten, Richard Reben, and "Louis the Jeweller" Goldberg for putting up with my lousy pinochle play. I would also like to thank Nicki and Ira Harris, friends of forty years, for their many acts of kindness to me and my family.

As a confirmed hypochondriac, I've been fortunate to receive good medical advice. I want particularly to thank Michael Malus, our family physician for many years; my medical guru Sheldon Elman and his wife, Meryl, good friends who showed special kindness to my wife during the last difficult years of her life; and Henri Elbaz, executive director of the Jewish General Hospital, who guided me through the two years of my presidency there.

Michael Vineberg, my valued legal advisor, has been a friend for all the years. My friend and neighbour Jonathan Dietcher has for years offered good advice as my stockbroker.

In the last question of the last interview for this book, I was asked how I would like to be remembered. I would say, as a good husband, a good father and grandfather, as a builder of enterprise in Canada, and as a good senator.

But I'm not planning on disappearing any time soon. I'll be around, in my new job, doting on my grandchildren.

Co-author's Acknowledgments

This book began with a conversation over lunch at the Montefiore Club in Montreal. Leo Kolber was telling stories about the Bronfmans – his mentor, Mr Sam, and his lifelong friends Charles and Edgar. Leo spoke of his travels with Pierre Trudeau, his friendship with Danny Kaye, and the night Frank Sinatra came to his house.

"You know," I suggested, "this is fascinating stuff. You really ought to write a book."

"How would I do that?" he asked.

"Well, you would get a collaborator, who would interview you, and use the transcripts as the basis of the book."

"Nobody would read it," Leo said.

"You'd be surprised," I said, letting it go at that.

About six months later, in October 2001, Leo gave a small dinner for his friend Richard Kroft, a Manitoba senator and member of the Senate Banking Committee, and his wife, Hillaine. It was the first time Leo had invited people to his home since the death of his wife, Sandra, after a long illness, and it was good to see that he was trying to move on. Over drinks and dinner, Leo began telling more stories of his remarkable life, the life of a man of influence at several centres of power. In business, in politics, even in Hollywood.

"Leo," Kroft said, "you really should write a book."

"That's what I've been telling him," I chimed in.

Another six months passed before Leo called in the spring of 2002 and invited me to his house to discuss working with him on his autobiography. I was about five minutes late for our appointment when I rang the doorbell.

"If we are going to work together," he said as he answered the door, "you are going to have to learn to be on time."

That was when I learned of Leo Kolber's obsession for punctuality. On another occasion, during the Senate Banking Committee hearings on large bank mergers in November 2002, Leo was clearly annoyed as he pointed to his watch. It had been a long afternoon, and no fewer than three bank CEOs had appeared before his committee, which was scheduled to have a private dinner with one of the bank presidents across the street on Parliament Hill before resuming with a fourth bank president in an evening session.

"We are late," Leo said impatiently. "Ten minutes late."

"Trust me, Leo," I replied, "there is no such thing as being ten minutes late on Parliament Hill."

Over the course of a year, from May 2002 to May 2003, Leo sat for nearly fifty hours of personal interviews, most of which were recorded in the study of his home in Montreal, while some took place in his office at Claridge Inc. After a late-afternoon interview of two hours at his home, he would usually invite me to stay for dinner, where he would unwind with more stories and background for the book.

From the beginning, I made it clear to Leo that there was no point in doing a vanity biography, that it would have to be the real deal, particularly in terms of his thirty years as *consigliere* to the Bronfmans and his twenty years as a top fundraiser for the Liberal Party of Canada. From the first, he agreed, and never flinched, finagled, or fudged on any question.

This is very much Leo's book, as well as his story, told in his own words and very much in his own voice. He is blessed with near total recall and is a gifted storyteller in the best Jewish sense of the word. On rare occasions when memory would fail him as to a date, he would offer other clues to track it down.

"The night Trudeau came here for dinner with Jean Chrétien about the Liberal leadership," he said, "was a Friday night in the summer of 1989. I remember it as the night of a lunar eclipse, and walking Pierre out to his car."

"I can find the date," I said.

"You can look it up in my diaries," he said, pointing to a shelf lined with yearly *Economist* agendas handsomely bound in red leather. "It'll be in there."

Sure enough, there it was, pencilled in as "dinner, Trudeau and Chrétien," on the night of August 16, 1989, a Friday. Lunch with John Turner at Stornoway, about ten days before the call of the 1988 election on free trade? There it was, "Stornoway" at one o'clock on September

19. Did Frank Sinatra come for a late-night dinner and reception after his Montreal concert of May 1975 or in October 1976? There it was again, under October 15, 1976: "Sinatra" along with most of a guest list that included Paul and Jackie Desmarais, as well as Brian and Mila Mulroney. Leo had kept his agendas going all the way back to 1970, and they proved to be invaluable in tracking his movements over the years.

Other sources can be found in the bibliography, but several works in particular have been extremely useful points of reference. Michael R. Marrus's *Mr Sam* was particularly helpful, as were two of Edgar Bronfman's books, *Good Spirits* and *The Making of a Jew.* Rod McQueen's history of another family, *The Eatons,* details the decline and fall of another Canadian business empire. Peter C. Newman has made Canadian business interesting to read about over the last three decades with his series that began with *The Canadian Establishment.* Anthony Bianco's *The Reichmanns* is invaluable on the rise and fall of another Canadian Jewish family in the North American and global real estate industry. John Rothchild's *Going for Broke* captures the frenzy and froth of the 1980s, the era of junk bonds and leveraged buyouts, which another Canadian real estate mogul, Bob Campeau, brought to a screeching halt with his $11-billion LBO of Allied and Federated department stores. Dennis McDougall's *The Last Mogul* tells the story of Lew Wasserman and MCA, including the suckering and sinking of Garth Drabinsky and Cineplex Odeon Theatres in the 1980s, as well as the sale of MCA by Matsushita Electric to Seagram in 1995, which foretold the fall of the Seagram empire itself. Even Drabinsky's autobiography, *Garth Drabinsky,* written with Marq de Villiers, is unconsciously revealing about the recklessly acquisitive growth of his film exhibition business, when he took on more debt than he could manage in an honest accounting of his books. Michael Eisner's *Work in Progress* details the making and unmaking of Edgar Bronfman Jr's deal with super-agent Michael Ovitz to run MCA for an unheard of $250 million up front, a deal that Leo played a role in killing.

There is a new research tool in this new century – the Internet, particularly remarkable search engines such as Google, which can find virtually anything about anyone in a microsecond. Online sources are also acknowledged in the bibliography. But there is still no substitute for a good library, and the Westmount Municipal Library in Montreal is one of the best, with a wonderful staff under the direction of Ann Moffat. The *Gazette* library in Montreal is not only an outstanding news archive and online source, but it is run by terrific people, notably Michael Porritt and Pat Duggan. Thanks, as well, to the paper's publisher, Larry Smith, and editor-in-chief, Peter Stockland, for their continuing support.

There are many other people to be thanked, beginning with Leo's own children, Lynne Halliday and Jonathan Kolber, who were very helpful on their parents and their family life. In Montreal, Leo's assistants Peggy Gaon and Maria Scandella were of great help, not only for handling the logistics of scheduling him for interviews, but also for drawing on their own extensive recollections of Leo's career and turning up many of the thirty-two pages of photographs in the book. In Ottawa, his executive assistant, Steve Campbell, provided transcripts of the Senate Banking Committee hearings on large bank mergers, as well as other transcripts of Leo's media interviews on this important issue. Leo's research assistant, Kelly J. Bourassa, was extremely helpful in providing articles and speeches she had worked on with the senator on the issue of bank mergers. His secretary in Ottawa, Shirley Strean, was also most helpful.

At McGill-Queen's University Press, executive director Philip Cercone was immediately enthusiastic about *Leo: A Life,* and from the beginning saw it for what it is – much more than the story of one man's remarkable life, but equally the story of the times in which he has lived and the interesting people he has known. Not many people can say that they hired Mies van der Rohe as their architect and built the Toronto-Dominion Centre. Leo can, because he did.

Thanks also to our coordinating editor, Joan McGilvray, and our editor, Judith Turnbull, for the care with which they have handled the book. At Mosaic Design in Montreal, our thanks to Maggie Alongi for the cover of the book, as well as for the layout of the photo section. At J.M. Transcriptions, June O'Connell got all the tapes transcribed and turned around in remarkably good time, providing the material at the heart of the story. The transcripts are the proof that this story is told in Leo's own words. My role has been primarily one of organizing and shaping the material, as well as moving the furniture of the story around.

For myself, deepest thanks and love to my family, Natalie Zenga, and our daughters, Grace and Natacha, who have once again endured my disappearances and distractions for another year of weekends. I thank them all for their love and forbearance.

Thanks, as well, to friends and colleagues for their enthusiastic encouragement, and particularly to Bill Fox, now a senior vice-president of Bombardier Inc., who was the first to see the potential of a book on Leo's life and the many levels on which it was a fascinating story. Thanks also to Anthony Wilson-Smith, editor of *Maclean's* in Toronto, another early enthusiast of this project.

Most of all, thanks to Leo himself, who worked as hard as I did on the manuscript. "My great fear," he said on more than one occasion, "is that when we are finished, I will have left something out."

I don't think so. Above all, Leo has been good at taking advice, and has always been as good as his word. Many times in the last year, I've been asked what kind of book Leo was going to write.

My answer has always been the same: "an honest one."

L. Ian MacDonald
Montreal, August 2003

Selected Bibliography

PRINTED SOURCES

Abella, Irving, *A Coat of Many Colours: Two Centuries of Jewish Life in Canada*. Toronto: Lester and Orpen Dennys, 1990.

–, and Harold Troper. *None Is Too Many: Canada and the Jews of Europe, 1933–1948*. Toronto: Lester & Orpen Dennys, 1982.

Adams, James. "Seagram artworks in New York to be sold." *Globe and Mail* (Toronto), December 13, 2002.

Ambrose, Stephen E. *Eisenhower: Soldier and President*. New York: Simon & Schuster, 1990.

Babad, Michael, and Catherine Mulroney. *Campeau: The Rise and Fall*. Toronto: Seal Books, 1990.

Bedell Smith, Sally. *In All His Glory: The Life of William S. Paley – The Legendary Tycoon and His Brilliant Circle*. New York: Simon & Schuster, 1990.

Bercuson, David. *Canada and the Birth of Israel*. Toronto: University of Toronto Press, 1985.

Bianco, Anthony. *The Reichmanns: Faith, Family, Fortune, and the Empire of Olympia & York*. New York and Toronto: Random House, 1997.

Black, Conrad. *Duplessis*. Toronto: McClelland and Stewart, 1976.

– *A Life in Progress*. Toronto: KeyPorter Books, 1993.

Blake, Peter. *The Master Builders: Le Corbusier/Mies van der Rohe/Frank Lloyd Wright*. New York: W.W. Norton & Company, 1960, 1996.

Bliss, Michael. *Northern Enterprise: Five Centuries of Canadian Business*. Toronto: McClelland and Stewart, 1987.

Bronfman, Edgar M. *The Making of a Jew*. New York: G.P. Putnam's Sons, 1996.

– *Good Spirits: The Making of a Businessman*. New York: G.P. Putnam's Sons, 1998.

–, with Catherine Whitney. *The Third Act: Reinventing Yourself after Retirement*. New York: G.P. Putnam's Sons, 2002.

Bronfman, Samuel. *From Little Acorns: The Story of Distillers Corporation–Seagrams Limited*. Montreal: Distillers Corporation–Seagrams Limited, 1970.

Brooker, Kevin. "The Velvet Underground." *En Route*, December 2002.

Brownlow, Kevin. *David Lean: A Biography*. New York: St Martin's Press, 1996.

Brunt, Stephen. "Garth Drabinsky will NEVER go away." *Globe and Mail* (Toronto), *Report on Business Magazine*, 29 November 2002.

Burns, Patricia. *They Were So Young: Montrealers Remember World War II*. Montreal: Vehicule Press, 2002.

Buzzetti, Helene. "10,000$ pour avoir acces à Chrétien." *Le Devoir* (Montreal), May 24, 2002.

Cahn, Sammy. *I Should Care: The Sammy Cahn Story*. New York: Arbor House, 1974.

Cannon, Lou. *President Reagan: The Role of a Lifetime*. New York: Simon & Schuster, 1991.

Caplan, Gerald, Michael Kirby, and Hugh Segal. *Election: the Issues, the Strategies, the Aftermath*. Scarborough, Ont.: Prentice Hall Canada, 1989.

Carter, Jimmy. *Keeping Faith: Memoirs of a President*. Toronto and New York: Bantam Books, 1982.

Chrétien, Jean. *Straight from the Heart*. Toronto: McClelland and Stewart, 1985.

—"Our journey is not over." Text of Prime Minister Jean Chrétien's retirement statement at Saguenay, Quebec, August 21, 2002. *Ottawa Citizen*, August 22, 2002.

Christie, Carl A. *Ocean Bridge: The History of RAF Ferry Command*. Toronto: University of Toronto Press, 1995.

Clark, Edmund. *Statement to the Standing Committee on Banking, Trade and Commerce*. Toronto: TD Bank Financial Group, November 25, 2002.

Clarkson, Stephen, and McCall, Christina. *Trudeau and Our Times*. Vol. 1: *The Magnificent Obsession*. Toronto: McClelland and Stewart, 1990.

Clement, Wallace. *The Canadian Corporate Elite: An Analysis of Economic Power*. Toronto: McClelland and Stewart, 1975.

Cohen, Andrew. *A Deal Undone: The Making and Breaking of the Meech Lake Accord*. Vancouver-Toronto: Douglas and McIntyre, 1990.

Collenette, Penny. "What the Banks Must Do." *Maclean's*, January 20, 2003.

Comeau, Sylvain. "Bank mergers are beneficial: economist McIntosh to Senate." *Concordia's Thursday Report* (Montreal), January 30, 2003.

Cosgrove, Gillian. "Feeding the troops, and the kitty." *National Post* (Toronto), May 19, 2002.

Courchene, Thomas J. "Half-Way Home: Canada's Remarkable Fiscal Turnaround and the Paul Martin Legacy." *Policy Matters* (Institute for Research on Public Policy, Montreal), July 2002.

Cruise, David, and Allison Griffiths. *Lords of the Line: The Men Who Built the CPR.* Markham, Ont.: Viking Publishers, Penguin Books, 1988.

DeCloet, Derek. "Peter Godsoe: The Artful Dodger." *National Post* (Toronto), November 26, 2002.

– TD sorry for 'screwy' comment. *National Post* (Toronto), January 31, 2003.

Dennison, Merrill. *Canada's First Bank: A History of the Bank of Montreal.* Vols 1 and 2. Toronto: McClelland and Stewart, 1967.

Den Tandt, Michael. "Bold Senate outshines Commons." *Globe and Mail* (Toronto), December 13, 2002.

– "Mergers will have to wait for Martin." *Globe and Mail* (Toronto), February 21, 2003.

Desbarats, Peter. *René: A Canadian in Search of a Country.* Toronto: McClelland and Stewart, 1976.

Drabinsky, Garth, with Marq de Villiers. *Closer to the Sun: An Autobiography.* Toronto: McClelland and Stewart, 1995.

Duffy, John. *Fights of Our Lives: Elections, Leadership and the Making of Canada.* Toronto: HarperCollins, 2002.

Eban, Abba. *My Country: The Story of Modern Israel.* New York, Random House, 1972.

– *Abba Eban: An Autobiography.* New York: Random House, 1977.

Eisner, Michael, with Tony Schwartz. *Work in Progress.* New York: Random House, 1998.

English, John. *The Worldly Years: The Life of Lester B. Pearson.* Vol. 2: 1949–1972. Toronto: Alfred A. Knopf Canada, 1992.

Fafard, Joe. *The Bronze Years.* Montreal: Museum of Fine Arts, 1996.

Fife, Robert. "Secret Liberal fundraiser sells access to Chrétien, oppostion charges." *National Post* (Toronto), May 23, 2002.

– "PM assailed for using 24 Sussex Dr. to fundraise." *National Post* (Toronto), June 12, 2002.

Fleming, James. *Circles of Power: The Most Influential People in Canada.* Toronto: Doubleday Canada, 1991.

Fraser, Graham. *Playing for Keeps: The Making of the Prime Minister, 1988.* Toronto: McClelland and Stewart, 1989.

– *René Lévesque & the Parti Québécois in Power,* 2nd ed. Montreal and Kingston: McGill-Queen's University Press, 2001.

Fraser, Matthew. *Quebec Inc: French Canadian Entrepreneurs and the New Business Elite.* Toronto: Key Porter Books, 1987.

Friedland, Michael. *The Secret Life of Danny Kaye.* New York: St Martin's Press, 1996.

Friscolanti, Michael. "Anti-Semitism endures in Canada: Mulroney." *National Post* (Toronto), February 10, 2003.

Frost, Stanley Brice. *McGill University: For the Advancement of Learning.* 2 vols. Montreal: McGill University Press, 1971.

– "Who Runs This Place Anyway?" In *McGill: A Celebration.* Montreal and Kingston: McGill-Queen's University Press, 1991.

Frum, David. *The Right Man: The Surprise Presidency of George W. Bush.* New York: Random House, 2003.

Gabler, Neal. *An Empire of Their Own: How the Jews Invented Hollywood.* New York: Crown Publishers, 1988.

Gagnon, Alain, and Montcalm, Mary Beth. *Quebec: Beyond the Quiet Revolution.* Scarborough: Nelson Canada, 1989.

Gerstner, Louis V., Jr. *Who Says Elephants Can't Dance: Inside IBM's Historic Turnaround.* New York: Harper Business, HarperCollins, 2002.

Gilbert, Martin. *Israel: A History.* New York: William Morrow and Company, 1998.

Glanz, James, and Eric Lipton. "The Height of Ambition: In the epic story of how the World Trade Towers rose, their fall was foretold." *New York Times Magazine,* September 8, 2002.

Godsoe, Peter. *Address to the Standing Senate Committee on Banking, Trade and Commerce.* Toronto: Bank of Nova Scotia, November 25, 2002.

Gotlieb, Allan. "Remarks to the Woodrow Wilson Award Dinner." Toronto, May 7, 2002.

Gottfried, Martin. *Nobody's Fool: The Lives of Danny Kaye.* New York: Simon & Schuster, 1994.

Graham, Ron. *One-Eyed Kings: Promise and Illusion in Canadian Politics.* Don Mills, Ont.: Collins Publishers, 1986.

Gray, Brian, and Garth Whyte. *Bank Mergers: In Whose Interest?* Ottawa: Canadian Federation of Independent Businesses, November 25, 2002

Greenspon, Edward, and Anthony Wilson-Smith. *Double Vision: The Inside Story of the Liberals in Power.* Toronto: Doubleday Canada, 1996.

Gwyn, Richard. *Trudeau: The Northern Magus.* Toronto: McClelland and Stewart, 1980.

Haas, Richard, and Melissa Williams. *Reykjavik Summit: Watershed or Washout?* Cambridge, Mass: John F. Kennedy School of Government, Harvard University, 1988.

Hadekel, Peter. "Senators open a can of worms." *Gazette* (Montreal), December 16, 2002.

Hamilton, Graeme. "Chrétien a no-show for political dinner." *National Post* (Toronto), May 27, 2002.

Hanson, Elizabeth Ida. *A Jewel in a Park: Westmount Public Library, 1897–1918.* Montreal: Vehicule Press, 1997.

Henderson, Maxwell. *Plain Talk! Memoirs of an Auditor General.* Toronto: McClelland and Stewart, 1984.

Hoy, Claire. *Nice Work: The Continuing Scandal of the Canadian Senate.* Toronto: McClelland and Stewart, 1999.

Hunkin, John S. Submission to the Standing Committee on Banking, Trade and Commerce. Toronto: Canadian Imperial Bank of Commerce, November 25, 2002.

Hunter, Douglas. *Molson: The Birth of a Business Empire.* Toronto: Viking Press, Penguin Group, 2001.

Hutchison, Bruce. *The Incredible Canadian: A Candid Portrait of Mackenzie King: His Works, His Times, His Nation.* New York, Toronto, London: Longmans, Green and Company, 1953.

Ibbitson, John. "Waiting for the final act." *Globe and Mail* (Toronto), August 21, 2002.

Jack, Ian. "Senate banking chair favours mergers." *National Post* (Toronto), November 7, 2002.

– "Strict corporate governance needed: Kolber." *National Post* (Toronto), April 3, 2003.

– and Keith Kalawsky. "Committee sanctions bank deals." *National Post* (Toronto), December 13, 2002.

Johnston, Ann Dowsett. "The University Crunch, Special 2002 Edition Rankings." *Maclean's,* November 18, 2002.

Kaplan, William. *Presumed Guilty: Brian Mulroney, the Airbus Affair and the Government of Canada.* Toronto: McClelland and Stewart, 1998.

Kalawsky, Keith. "Bank chiefs demand clarity." *National Post* (Toronto), November 26, 2002.

– "Lift veil on bank deals, urges Nixon." *National Post* (Toronto), November 26, 2002.

– "CIBC, Manulife merger 'made in heaven.'" *National Post* (Toronto), February 21, 2003.

Kelley, Kitty. *His Way: The Unauthorized Biography of Frank Sinatra.* Toronto and New York: Bantam Books, 1986.

Kolber, E. Leo, Chair. *Competition in the Public Interest: Large Bank Mergers in Canada, Report of the Standing Senate Committee on Banking, Trade and Commerce.* Ottawa: The Senate of Canada, December 2002.

– Address to the Toronto Board of Trade, February 20, 2003.

– "Insurer-bank mergers: let them join, we'd all be richer." *Globe and Mail* (Toronto), February 27, 2003.

– "Canada–United States relations: War with Iraq." In *Hansard, Debates of the Senate*, March 25, 2003.

–, Chair. *Navigating through "The Perfect Storm": Safeguards to Restore Investor Confidence, Report of the Standing Senate Committee on Banking, Trade and Commerce.* Ottawa: The Senate of Canada, June 2003.

–, and Kelly J. Bourassa. "Large Bank Mergers in Canada." *Policy Options* (Institute for Research on Public Policy Montreal), March 2003.

Kolber, Sandra. *Bitter Sweet Lemons and Love.* Toronto: McClelland and Stewart, 1967.

– *All There Is of Love.* Toronto: McClelland and Stewart, 1969.

Kollek, Teddy. *For Jerusalem: A Life.* New York: Random House, 1979

Krinsky, Carol Hersell. *Gordon Bunshaft of Skidmore, Owings & Merrill.* New York: Architectural History Foundation, 1988.

Kurzman, Dan. *Ben-Gurion: Prophet of Fire.* New York: Simon & Schuster, 1983.

Lacroix, Laurier. *Suzor-Coté: Light and Matter.* Montreal: Les Éditions de l'Homme, 2002.

Lamey, Mary, Catherine Solyom, and Jane Davenport. "It's a Montreal original: historic Place Ville Marie a beacon to Montrealers." *Gazette* (Montreal), September 26, 2002.

Lambert, Phyllis, ed. *Mies in America.* New York: Harry N. Abrams, 2001.

Leacock, Stephen. *Canada: The Foundations of Its Future.* Montreal: The House of Seagram, 1941.

LeDrew, Stephen. "Covering the Liberal Waterfront." *Policy Options* (Institute for Research on Public Policy, Montreal) March 2003.

Lee, Robert Mason. *One Hundred Monkeys: The Triumph of Popular Wisdom in Canadian Politics.* Toronto: Macfarlane Walter & Ross, 1989.

Legate, David M. *Stephen Leacock: A Biography.* Toronto and Garden City, N.Y.: Doubleday, 1970.

Leonard, Devin. "The Bronfman saga: From rags to riches to …" *Fortune,* November 25, 2002.

Lévesque, René. *An Option for Quebec.* Toronto: McClelland and Stewart, 1968.

–. *Memoirs.* Toronto: McClelland and Stewart, 1986.

Longman, Jere. "For Packers fans, the tundra is always frozen." *New York Times,* January 4, 2003.

Lorimer, James. *The Developers.* Toronto: James Lorimer and Company, 1978.

Lyman, Rick. "A big fat increase at the box office." *New York Times,* December 30, 2002.

Lynch-Staunton, John. Letter to the Editor. *Globe and Mail* (Toronto), March 8, 1997.

– Letter to the Editor. *Financial Post* (Toronto), May 5, 1998.

McCall-Newman, Christina. *Grits: An Intimate Portrait of the Liberal Party.* Toronto: Macmillan of Canada, 1982.

McCallum, John. "Two Cheers for Free Trade." *Econoscope* (Royal Bank of Canada, Toronto), June 1999.

McCallum, John S. "Corporate Governance Policy and the Case for Caution." *Policy Options* (Institute for Research on Public Policy Montreal), October 2002.

MacDonald, Gayle. "The World According to Garth." *Globe and Mail* (Toronto), October 23, 2002.

MacDonald, L. Ian. *Mulroney: The Making of the Prime Minister.* Toronto: McClelland and Stewart, 1984.

–, ed. *Free Trade: Risks and Rewards.* Montreal and Kingston: McGill-Queen's University Press, 2000.

– *From Bourassa to Bourassa: Wilderness to Restoration.* Montreal and Kingston: McGill-Queen's University Press, 2002.

McDougall, Dennis. *The Last Mogul: Lew Wasserman, MCA and the Hidden History of Hollywood.* New York: Crown Publishers, 1998.

McDowall, Duncan. *Quick to the Frontier: Canada's Royal Bank.* Toronto: McClelland and Stewart, 1994.

MacFarquhar, Neil. "Hezbollah becomes potent anti-U.S. force." *New York Times,* December 24, 2002.

McKenna, Brian, and Susan Purcell. *Drapeau.* Toronto: Clarke Irwin, 1980.

McLean Eric, and R.D. Wilson (illustrator). *The Living Past of Montreal.* Montreal and Kingston: McGill-Queen's University Press, 1993.

MacMillan, Margaret. *Paris 1919: Six Months That Changed the World.* New York: Random House, 2001.

McQueen, Rod. *The Money Spinners.* Toronto: Macmillan of Canada, 1983.

– *The Eatons: The Rise and Fall of Canada's Royal Family.* Toronto: Stoddart, 1998.

Marrus, Michael R. *Mr Sam: The Life and Times of Samuel Bronfman.* New York: Viking Press; Toronto: the Penguin Group, 1991.

Martin, Lawrence. *Chrétien: The Will to Win.* Toronto: Lester Publishing, 1995.

Martin, Paul. Economic statement and budget update. Ottawa: Department of Finance, October 19, 2000.

Medres, Israel. *Jewish Life in Montreal, 1900–1920.* Translated from the Yiddish by Vivian Felsen. Montreal: Vehicule Press, 2002.

Meir, Golda. *My Life.* Jerusalem, Tel Aviv: Steimatzky's Agency, 1975.

Milner, Brian. "Edgar's Blues: How Junior Sank the Family Fortune." *Globe and Mail, Report on Business Magazine,* September 2002.

– "Unmaking of a Dynasty." *Cigar Aficiando* (New York), April 2003.

Mulroney, Brian. *Where I Stand*. Toronto: McClelland and Stewart, 1983.

– Address to the Israel Bonds Dinner, Montreal, May 15, 1985. Ottawa: Prime Minister's Office, 1985.

– Address to the United Nations Association of Canada, Toronto, October 30, 2001.

– Address to the International Conference on Anti-Semitism, Munk Centre, University of Toronto, Toronto, February 9, 2003.

Neave, Edwin H. "Financial System Mergers." Presentation to the Senate Banking, Trade and Commerce Committee, Queen's University, Kingston, November 25, 2002.

Newman, Peter C. *The Canadian Establishment*, Vol. 1. Toronto: McClelland and Stewart, 1975.

– *Bronfman Dynasty: The Rothschilds of the New World*. Toronto: McClelland and Stewart, 1978.

– *The Canadian Establishment. Vol. 2: The Acquisitors*. Toronto: McClelland and Stewart, 1981.

– *The Establishment Man: A Portrait of Power*. Toronto: McClelland and Stewart, 1982.

– *Titans: How the New Canadian Establishment Seized Power*. Toronto: Viking Press, Penguin Group, 1998.

Nixon, Gordon M. "Building Canada's Prosperity in a New Century." Address to the Canadian Club of Montreal, May 6, 2002. Toronto: RBC Financial Group, 2002.

– Remarks to the Senate Committee on Banking, Trade and Commerce. Toronto: RBC Financial Group, November 25, 2002.

Owen, Gerald. "When does the duck become truly lame?" *National Post* (Toronto), August 22, 2002.

Pearson, Lester B. *Mike: The Memoirs of the Right Honourable Lester B. Pearson*. Vol. 1: *1897–1948*. Toronto: University of Toronto Press, 1972.

–, with John A. Munro and Alex Inglis, eds. *Mike: The Memoirs of the Right Honourable Lester B. Pearson*. Vol. 2: *1948–1957*. Toronto: University of Toronto Press, 1972.

– *Mike: The Memoirs of the Right Honourable Lester B. Pearson*. Vol. 3: *1957–1968*. Toronto: University of Toronto Press, 1975.

Peres, Shimon. *David's Sling*. New York: Random House, 1970.

–, with Ayre Naor. *The New Middle East*. New York: Henry Holt and Company, 1993.

Perley Warren. "The passion, the glory and the business story of the Orchestre symphonique de Montréal." *Gazette* (Montreal), December 18, 2002.

Peters, Thomas J., and Robert H. Waterman Jr. *In Search of Excellence: Lessons from America's Best-Run Companies*. New York: Harper & Row, 1982.

Phenix, Patricia. *Eatonians: The Story of the Family behind the Family.* Toronto: McClelland and Stewart, 2002.

Porter, John A. *The Vertical Mosaic: An Analysis of Social Class and Power in Canada.* Toronto: University of Toronto Press, 1965.

Quinn, Greg. "Canada's Kolber wants to mimic US accounting rules." *Bloomberg News* (New York), March 31, 2003.

– "Canada's Kolber says bank mergers unlikely for now." *Bloomberg News* (New York), March 31, 2003.

Rabinovitch, Jack. "Mordecai My Pal." *Maclean's,* June 24, 2002.

Radwanski, George. *Trudeau.* Toronto: Macmillan of Canada, 1978.

Reagan, Ronald. *An American Life.* New York: Simon & Schuster, 1990.

Rebick, Judy. "Victims must speak out first." *Globe and Mail* (Toronto), December 21, 2002.

Reguly, Eric. "Godsoe's epiphany on mergers." *Globe and Mail* (Toronto), November 23, 2002.

– "Banks try direct path in merger strategy." *Globe and Mail* (Toronto), November 26, 2002.

– "Bank merger denial has a price." *Globe and Mail* (Toronto), February 22, 2003.

Richler, Mordecai. *St. Urbain's Horseman.* Toronto: McClelland and Stewart, 1971.

– *Solomon Gursky Was Here.* Markham, Ont.: Viking of Canada, 1989.

– *Barney's Version.* Toronto: Alfred A. Knopf Canada, 1997.

Rock, Allan. Letter to the Editor. *Globe and Mail,* March 5, 1997.

Rockefeller, David. *Memoirs.* New York: Random House, 2002.

Rosten, Leo. *The Joys of Yiddish.* New York: McGraw Hill, 1968.

Rothchild, John. *Going for Broke: How Robert Campeau Bankrupted the Retail Industry, Jolted the Junk Bond Market, and Brought the Booming 80s to a Crashing Halt.* New York: Simon & Schuster, 1991.

Safdie, Michal Ronnen. *The Western Wall.* Introduction by Yehuda Amichai. Jerusalem: Hugh Lauter Levin Associates, 1997.

Sawatsky, John. *Mulroney: The Politics of Ambition.* Toronto: Macfarlane Walter & Ross, 1991.

Schuchat, Rabbi Wilfred. *The Gate of Heaven: The Story of Congregation Shaar Hashomayim of Montreal, 1946–1996.* Montreal and Kingston: McGill-Queen's University Press, 1996.

Schull, Joseph. *100 Years of Banking in Canada: The Toronto-Dominion Bank.* Toronto, Montreal: Copp Clark Publishing, 1958.

– *Laurier: The First Canadian.* Toronto: Macmillan of Canada, 1966.

Scrivener, Leslie. "Ex-PM blasts anti-Semitism." *Toronto Star,* February 10, 2003.

Segal, Hugh. *No Surrender: Reflections of a Happy Warrior in the Tory Crusade.* Toronto: HarperCollins, 1996.

Silverman, Stephen M. *The Films of David Lean.* Introduction by Katharine Hepburn. New York: Harry N. Abrams, 1989.

Sheppard, Robert, and Valpy, Michael. *The National Deal: The Fight for a Canadian Constitution.* Toronto: Fleet, 1982.

Simpson, Jeffrey. *The Friendly Dictatorship.* Toronto: McClelland and Stewart, 2001.

Slater, Robert. *Warrior Statesman: The Life of Moshe Dayan.* New York: St Martin's Press, 1991.

Smith, Graeme. "Canada asked to drop Hezbollah ban." *Globe and Mail* (Toronto), December 26, 2003.

Smith, Philip. *The Trust Builders: The Remarkable Rise of Canada Trust.* Toronto: Macmillan of Canada, 1989.

Snead, Robert E. *Himalayas.* Encarta 97 Encyclopedia, Microsoft Corporation, 1997.

Spector, Norman. "What took them so long?" *Gazette* (Montreal), December 16, 2002.

– *Chronicles of a War: How Mideast Became America's Fight.* Vancouver, Toronto, New York: Douglas and McIntyre, 2003.

St John, Robert. *Ben-Gurion: The Biography of an Extraordinary Man.* New York: Doubleday & Company, 1959.

Stewart, Sinclair, and John Partridge. "Bank-insurer mergers extolled: Senate committee head sees perfect fit." *Globe and Mail* (Toronto), February 21, 2003.

Stewart, Walter. *Towers of Gold, Feet of Clay: The Canadian Banks.* Toronto: Collins, 1982.

Stikeman, H. Heward. *The Mount Royal Club, 1899–1999.* Montreal: Price-Patterson, 1999.

Tagliabue, John. "Vivendi posts $25 billion loss; will explore shedding assets." *New York Times,* March 7, 2003.

Taraborrelli, Randy J. *Sinatra: Behind the Legend.* Toronto and Secaucus, N.J.: Birch Lane Press, 1997.

Taylor, Leslie. *Herbal Secrets of the Rainforest.* Rocklin, Calif.: Prima Publishers, 1998.

Thorsell, William. "The banker who insisted Toronto be remembered with respect." *Globe and Mail* (Toronto), November 4, 2002.

Togerson, Dial. *Kirk Kerkorian: An American Success Story.* New York: Dial Press, 1974.

Tomkins, Calvin. *Living Well Is the Best Revenge.* New York: Viking Press, 1971.

Torczyner, Jim L., Shari L. Brotman, and Kathy Virag. *Demographic Challenges Facing Canadian Jewry: Initial Findings from the 1991 Census.* Montreal: Council of Jewish Federations of Canada and McGill Consortium for Ethnicity and Strategic Social Planning, 1993.

Trudeau, Pierre Elliott. *Federalism and the French Canadians*. Toronto: Macmillan of Canada, 1968.

– *Memoirs*. Toronto: McClelland and Stewart, 1993.

– " 'Say goodby to the dream' of one Canada." *Toronto Star*, May 27, 1987.

– Testimony before the Senate Committee of the Whole. *Hansard, Debates of the Senate*, March 30, 1988.

Tuck, Simon. "Bank executives want merger rules clarified." *Globe and Mail* (Toronto), November 26, 2002.

– "Foreign banks back mergers." *Globe and Mail* (Toronto), November 27, 2002.

– "Canada needs only 3 big banks, Ottawa told." *Globe and Mail,* (Toronto), December 12, 2002.

– "Senator dismisses Commons merger report." *Globe and Mail* (Toronto), April 3, 2003.

–, Paul Waldie, and Jacquie McNish. "More competition in banking urged." *Globe and Mail* (Toronto), December 13, 2002.

Waldie, Paul. "Drabinsky, Gottlieb charged by RCMP." *Globe and Mail* (Toronto), October 23, 2002.

Wansell, Jeffrey. *Haunted Idol: The Real Story of Cary Grant*. New York: Collins, 1987.

Ward, Vicky. "Enemies in the Boardroom." *Vanity Fair* (New York), October 2002.

Weinfeld, Morton. *Like Everyone Else ... but Different: The Paradoxical Success of Canadian Jews*. Toronto: McClelland and Stewart, 2001.

Weintraub, William. *City Unique: Montreal Days and Nights in the 1940s and 1950s*. Toronto: McClelland and Stewart, 1996.

Welch, Jack, with John A. Byrne. *Jack: Straight from the Gut*. New York: Warner Books, 2001.

Wells, David, and Adrian Michaels. "Citigroup bears brunt of Wall St research censure." *Financial Times* (London), April 28, 2003.

Weston, Greg. *Reign of Error: The Inside Story of John Turner's Troubled Leadership*. Toronto: McGraw-Hill Ryerson, 1988.

Willis, Andrew. "Banks must win hearts, minds of MPs." *Globe and Mail* (Toronto), December 12, 2002.

Wilson, Earl. *Sinatra: An Unauthorized Biography*. New York: Macmillan Publishing Company, Inc, 1976.

Wiseman, Carter. *I.M. Pei: A Profile in American Architecture*. New York: Harry N. Abrams, 2001.

Yanosky, Joel. "Me & Mordecai." *Maisonneuve* (Montreal), autumn 2002.

Zeckendorf, William, with Edward McCreary. *The Autobiography of William Zeckendorf.* New York: Holt, Reinhart and Winston, 1970.

ONLINE SOURCES

Ben-David, Calev. "Charles in charge." *Jerusalem Post,* June 29, 1999. www.jpost.com

"Charles Bronfman's journey." *Jewish Times,* November 12, 1999. www.atljewishtimes.com

"China: Damned, but dammed again." *Asia Times Online* (Bangkok), July 4, 2001. www.asiatimes.com

"DeGunzburg Family Increases Support for Center for European Studies." *Harvard Gazette Online* (Cambridge, Mass.) www.news.harvard.edu/gazette

DuPont Overview: 200 Years of History. Wilmington, Del.: DuPont Corporation, 2002. www.dupont.com

Evans, K.J. "Kirk Kerkorian: The Quiet Lion." *Las Vegas Review-Journal* ("The First 100 Persons Who Shaped Southern Nevada"), Donrey Media Group, 1999. www.1st100.com

Francis, David, and Ben Arnoldy. "Q&A: The WorldCom debacle." *Christian Science Monitor* (Boston), June 27, 2002. *www.cs.monitor.com*

"Forbes 400: The World's Richest People." *Forbes* (New York), March 10, 2003. www.forbes.com

Glossary of Israeli Parties and Personalities, 1948–1981. Jerusalem Center for Public Affairs. www.jcpa.org

History of the Expos. 2002. www.montrealexpos.com

History of the Jewish General Hospital. 2002. www.jgh.ca

Howe, Jeffery. *Top Ten Buildings in America 1885–1995.* Boston College. www.bc.edu

Lenzer, Robert, and Christopher Helman. *"Edgar's Encore."* *Forbes* (New York), September 30, 2002. www.forbes.com

Major Debates of the Knesset, 1948–1981. Jerusalem Center for Public Affairs. www.jcpa.org

Manley, John. *Canada's Fiscal Progress.* Ottawa: Department of Finance, Canada, 2002. www.fin.gc.ca

Martin, Paul. *Canada's Debt Challenge.* Ottawa: Department of Finance, Canada, 1997. www.fin.gc.ca

– *Budget in Brief.* Ottawa: Department of Finance, Canada, 1998. www.fin.gc.ca

The Midtown Book: The Seagram Building. www.thecityreview.com

Mock, Karen. *Perspectives on Racism: Anti-Semitism in Canada.*
  www.nizkor.org

1999 Seagram Annual Report. Montreal: The Seagram Company Limited,
  2000. www.reportgallery.com

"Prince of Wales Terrace." *Virtual McGill* (Montreal). www.mcgill.ca

Rothman, Robert. *The Galapagos Islands.* Galapagos Pages/About Galapa-
  gos.html.www.*google*.ca, 2002

"Samuel Bronfman Building." *Virtual McGill* (Montreal). www.mcgill.ca

Shannon, Victoria. "Vivendi shows that Europe means business." *International
  Herald Tribune* (Paris), June 21, 2000. www.iht.com

Spencer, Charles S. *The Israel National Museum.*
  www.studio-international.co.uk

"Tyco Inquiry Finds No Major Fraud." BBC News, London, December 31,
  2002. www.bbc.co.uk/i/hi/business

Index